NETWORK INFORMATION PROCESSING SYSTEMS

IFIP TC6/TC8 Open Symposium on
Network Information Processing Systems
Sofia, Bulgaria, 9–13 May, 1988

sponsored by
IFIP Technical Committee 6
Data Communication
IFIP Technical Commitee 8
Information Systems
International Federation for Information Processing (IFIP)

organized by
The Bulgarian Academy of Sciences
Electronics Association
Software Products and Systems Corporation
Microprocessor Systems Corporation

NORTH-HOLLAND
AMSTERDAM · NEW YORK · OXFORD · TOKYO

NETWORK INFORMATION PROCESSING SYSTEMS

Proceedings of the IFIP TC6/TC8 Open Symposium on
Network Information Processing Systems
Sofia, Bulgaria, 9–13 May, 1988

edited by

Kiril BOYANOV
Bulgarian Academy of Sciences
Sofia, Bulgaria

Rasko ANGELINOV
Software Products and Systems Corporation
Sofia, Bulgaria

1989

NORTH-HOLLAND
AMSTERDAM · NEW YORK · OXFORD · TOKYO

ISBN: 0 444 87330 9

Published by:

ELSEVIER SCIENCE PUBLISHERS B.V.
P.O. Box 103
1000 AC Amsterdam
The Netherlands

Sole distributors for the USA and Canada:

ELSEVIER SCIENCE PUBLISHING COMPANY, INC.
655 Avenue of the Americas
New York, N.Y. 10010
U.S.A.

Library of Congress Cataloging-in-Publication Data

IFIP TC6/TC8 Open Symposium on Network Information Processing Systems (1988 : Sofia, Bulgaria)
Network information processing systems : proceedings of the IFIP TC6/TC8 Open Symposium on Network Information Processing Systems, Sofia, Bulgaria, 9-13 May, 1988 / edited by Kiril Boyanov, Rasko Angelinov.
p. cm.
"Sponsored by IFIP Technical Committee 6, Data Communication, IFIP Technical Committee 8, Information Systems, [and] International Federation for Information Processing (IFIP); organized by the Bulgarian Academy of Sciences ..."
Includes index.
ISBN 0-444-87330-9
1. Computer networks--Congresses. 2. Electronic data processing--Distributed processing--Congresses. I. Boi͡anov, Kiril L. II. Angelinov, Rasko. III. International Federation for Information Processing. Technical Committee 6. IV. International Federation for Information Processing. Technical Committee for Information Systems. V. International Federation for Information Processing. VI. Bŭlgarska akademii͡a na naukite. VII. Title.
TK5105.5.I3425 1988
004.6--dc19 89-2925
CIP

PRINTED IN THE NETHERLANDS

PREFACE

Modern society needs an improved quality of information services. This determines the development of new software and hardware tools to supply the required types of service. Therefore, considerable importance is paid to the development of the distributed systems which provide individual users with different information sources at their work site.

This makes the different types of local and global networks particularly suitable for the building of distributed systems. In a number of cases, however, the installation of additional network services to meet concrete requirements is needed. Since they change continuously, a new approach is necessary for the setting up of methods and standards for their implementation.

The computer networks are also a most appropriate environment for the development of information systems. They make possible the data communication among different data processing, allowing at the same time an easy introduction of new functions and services. The evident relation between the contemporary information services and the computer networks urges the experts to search for a complex solution of the problem.

Other key issues on which intensive research is being done, should also be mentioned. Planning of network systems forms a task preceding the development of an information network service. The network analysis including development of modelling, evaluation, testing and verification proves to be particularly important in the design. The problems arising in office automation should be complexly solved. At the moment intensive work is being carried out on the development of electronic mail systems, the main trend being the introduction of artificial intelligence.

The above mentioned scientific trends have formed the subject of the International Symposium on Network Information Processing Systems, held in Sofia and sponsored by IFIP's TC6/TC8. The papers for this Symposium, mentioned below, are grouped around different topics. Those on Network Analysis, Network Protocols, Special

Purpose LANs, Distributed Computing Systems, Computer Messaging Systems, Applications, and others, aroused particular interest.

Some other interesting problems were discussed at the Symposium. I shall mention two of them. The first one was about the trends of development and application of ISDN, in view of the alternative the local networks provide. The second was the setting up of standards and opportunities for their all-round introduction.

Some of the presented articles were of theoretical value, and a number of practical results of considerable interest were also reported.

I hope the Sofia Symposium has formed the next step towards the solution of at least part of the problems, and that the papers will help the researchers in their work and will provide good ground for new ideas and studies.

Not all presentations that were read are included in the volume of proceedings. It contains selected papers which follow the Symposium's programme.

Thanks are due to all authors and to my colleagues for their kind and selfless assistance in preparing this volume.

Prof. Kiril Boyanov

EDITOR'S NOTE

Part of the articles included in this issue, are not completed with the necessary references despite the presence of publications on the considered problems. Further, the references of the articles do not cover all publications in the respective research field.

The Editor considers this a serious setback which, for reasons beyond his control, he is not in a position to eliminate, and presents his apologies to the readers.

COMMITTEES

SYMPOSIUM CHAIRMEN

Blagovest Sendov
President of the Bulgarian Academy of Sciences
President of IFIP

Ivan Tenev
President of Electronics Association

Rascho Angelinov
President of Software Products and Systems Corporation

Plamen Vatchkov
President of Microprocessor Systems Corporation

PROGRAM COMMITTEE

Chairmen

K. Boyanov (BG)
R. Angelinov (BG)

Members

D. Biran (IL)
B. Borovsky (BG)
B. Boutmy (NL)
G. Bracchi (I)
C. Brookes (AUS)
A. Cerveira (P)
A. Danthine (B)
G. Davis (USA)
D. Khakhar (S)
F. Koenigshofer (USA)
P. Kovac (H)
G. Le Moli (I)
P. Lockemann (FRG)
H. Meier (GDR)

G. Mueller (FRG)
T. Olle (UK)
J. Puzman (CS)
P. Ravasio (I)
P. Schicker (CH)
A. Solberg (N)
T. Szentinvany (H)
A. Verrijn-Stuart (NL)
B. Naumov (SU)
L. Pouzin (F)
P. Radford (UK)
J. Roukens (B)
W. Sobczak (PL)
O. Spaniol (FRG)
R. Uhlig (USA)
E. Yakubaitis (SU)

ACKNOWLEDGEMENTS

The Programme Committee would like to thank the following people, who kindly acted as referees for the submitted papers.

B. Boutmy	Philips International B.V., NL
G. Bracchi	Dept. of Electronics, Politechnic of Milano, Italy
A. Danthine	University of Liege, Belgium
G. Gargov	Bulgarian Academy of Sciences
V. Getov	Bulgarian Academy of Sciences
D. Khakhar	DEPE International, Sweden
F. Koenigshofer	The World Bank, U.S.A.
W. Lamersdorf	IBM Scientific Center, F.R.G.
G. Le Moli	Politechnic of Milano, Italy
S. Moshe	Electrical Eng. Dept., Israel
G. Mueller	IBM Scientific Center, F.R.G.
T. Olle	Consulting Services in ISPA&D, U.K.
A. Petkov	Institute of Mathematics–BAS, Bulgaria
L. Pouzin	CNET – PAA, France
J. Puzman	SCSTI, Czechoslovakia
P. Radford	Logica, London, U.K.
P. Schicker	TH Zurich, Switzerland
A. Solvberg	Dept. of Comp. Science, T. University of Norway
O. Spaniol	RWTH Aachen, Dept. of Informatics IV, F.R.G.
T. Szentivanyi	SZAMALM, Hungary
A. Terziev	Bulgarian Academy of Sciences
A. Verrijn-Stuart	Astro, Netherlands
R. Uhlig	Northern Telecom. Inc., U.S.A.
E. Yakubaitis	IECS, Latvian Acad. of Sciences, Riga, SU

The editors are greatly indebted to prof. André Danthine for his kind and unremitting help with the final selection of the papers included in this volume.

TABLE OF CONTENTS

NETWORK PROTOCOLS

SPECIAL PURPOSE LANs AND NETWORK INTERCONNECTIONS

NETWORK ANALYSIS

Network Information Processing Systems
K. Boyanov, R. Angelinov (Editors)
Elsevier Science Publishers B.V. (North-Holland)

PLANNING AN OSI-BASED NETWORK FOR A MULTI-SITE POLYTECHNIC

E SUTHERLAND, D G ROBERTS, C J MASLEN and B V ANREP

Polytechnic of Central London, 115 New Cavendish Street,
London, W1M 8JS, United Kingdom
☎+44 1 486 5811 *Telex 25964 pcl g Telefax +44 15804319*

Abstract: The problems encountered in running the existing data network and computer facilities in the Polytechnic of Central London (PCL) are described. A number of critical areas are examined to determine where future developments should be given priorities. Consideration is given to potential solutions with existing and impending technologies. The method to be used for developing the OSI-based network and the migration strategy to that network are described.

1 INTRODUCTION

This paper arises from our writing a successful proposal to the Department of Trade and Industry (DTI) for support for an Open Systems Interconnection (OSI) Opportunity Study. Such studies are intended to examine practical applications of OSI in different sectors of the UK economy (e.g., software house, health authority). The execution of the proposal will take approximately 210 man-days over six calendar months beginning on 2 November 1987. The results will be publicly available.

Management of the existing computer system and data communications network is difficult and much of the day-to-day effort is spent on "fire fighting". Given the continuing changes in the use of IT within the Polytechnic, medium-term planning was increasingly felt to be necessary. The combination of the wish for a longer term view and the availability of external funding encouraged the planning of this work.

We describe the background to the proposed study and indicate the problems on which the study will focus and the framework within which the solutions will be considered.

2 THE POLYTECHNIC OF CENTRAL LONDON

The Polytechnic of Central London (PCL) is one of several polytechnics in London, where there are also a large number of universities and colleges of higher education. PCL is currently funded through by the Inner London

Education Authority (ILEA) but is expected to be transferred to a new body, the Polytechnics and Colleges Funding Committee (PCFC) in the near future. [1]

PCL provides courses for approximately 30,000 students each year, comprising about 18,000 short course students, 8,000 part-time students and 4,000 full-time students.

The Polytechnic is located on seventeen sites extending over a large part of the West End of London, this is mainly the result of the merger into PCL of a number of smaller institutions. Being in central London has both advantages and disadvantages. The large number of businesses, government departments and other organisations in London create a potentially large market for short and part-time courses. The high cost of property places limits on PCL as well as on staff and students.

The organisational structure consists of the Rectorate (senior academic management) and seven faculties (Communication; Engineering and Science; Environment; Languages; Law; Management Studies; and Social Sciences and Business Studies) within each of which there are several schools. Each faculty has a Dean who reports to one of the Deputy Rectors. There are also a a number of specialist units such, e.g., the Centre for Communication and Information Studies (CCIS) and the Library and Information Technology Centre.

In addition there are two units providing services to the Polytechnic; Computer Services and Library Services. The Head of Computer Services reports to the Rector. Overall computer policy is determined by the Academic Council.

The use and teaching of IT has grown steadily in PCL over many years. Information Technology Year (IT'82), sponsored by the government, accelerated this growth. All courses now contain at least familiarisation with the use of IT.

One of the considerations in purchasing systems is that it is usually necessary to buy in "chunks", that is in units sufficiently large to service whole modules and courses. For example, on the BA Business Studies course, the compulsory first year module Computers in Business has 144 students, divided into nine groups of sixteen who have each to receive two hours of "hands on" computer classes per week. This represents a total of sixteen timetabled hours which requires to be supplemented with additional unscheduled hours for students' private study and assigned work. Effectively, that is half the hours for which a laboratory is available.

The multiplicity of educational applications of IT which PCL has are not, in general, functionally interconnected. That is, one activity is usually for a group of students and is unrelated to other activities by those students and other classes. This distinguishes PCL from commercial organisations, where transaction processing and databases are linked to decision support systems and office information systems. However, administrative applications are subject to the pressures for integration found in other organisations.

March and Olson have likened decision making in universities to a "garbage can", that is a vessel into which solutions and problems are put and which are sometimes matched by decision makers [2]. In many ways this sort of ill-structured decision making process also applies to PCL, problems may never be solved, potential solutions may never be taken up.

3 COMPUTER SERVICES

Computer Services is an autonomous department providing computer services and technical support to staff and students for administration, research and teaching. It is located at New Cavendish Street (NCS) where it has a machine room of computers connected to some of the other PCL sites by a wide area network based on Case DCX statistical multiplexors and switches and lines leased from British Telecom (BT). It also has links to other networks. (See Figure 1)

The following time-sharing computer systems are available for general use. (All computers have been given the names of animals.)

- a DEC VAX 8600 mini-computer running VMS 4.5 (Mole)
- a DEC VAX 11/785 running VMS 4.5 supporting the Polytechnic's library system (Yak)
- two DEC Micro-VAXes running VMS 4.5 (Otter and Stoat)
- a DEC-10 mainframe computer running TOPS-10 (Fox)
- ten Sun workstations running Sun 3.2 Unix 4.2 BSD (Badger, Deer, Elk, Lynx, Mink, Moose, Rat, Serval, Shrew, Vole)

FIGURE 1 DATA COMMUNICATIONS NETWORK

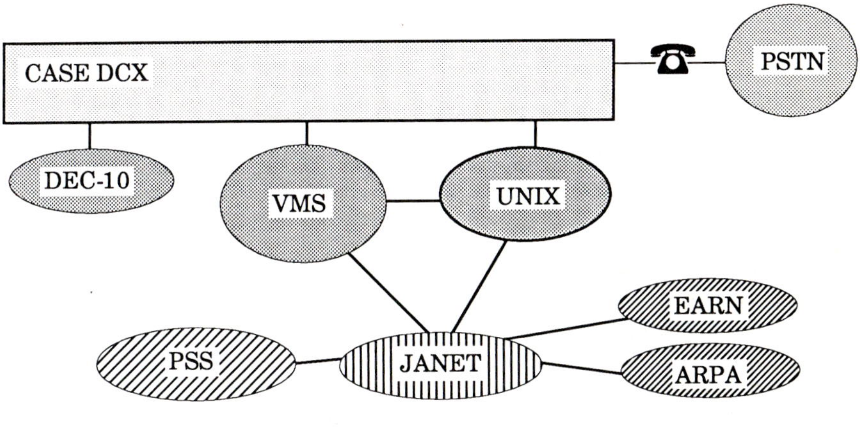

These machines support a variety of applications including

- program compilation and interpretation (Ada, Algol, Basic, C, Cobol, Fortran, Lisp, Modula 2, Occam, Pascal, Prolog, Simula, Smalltalk)
- computer aided design and graphics (Boxer, Dogs, GKS, GIMMS, GINO, NAG, Pafec, PIGS, Simpleplot)
- databases (Datatrieve, DBMS, FMS, Famulus, Oracle, Pascal/R, RDB)
- modelling (EPS, QNAP2, Spice2)
- statistics (Minitab, SPSS, TSA)
- text processing (NROFF, TEX, Word-11)

Two machines are used for administration, these are at 309 Regent Street where the main administrative offices are located

- a DEC VAX 11/750 running VMS 4.5 supporting general administration (Hare)
- a DEC VAX 11/750 running VMS 4.5 supporting financial applications (Rabbit)

In addition to a number of line printers at NCS there is a laser printer. Printers for Mole and Fox are available provided for local printing at Regent Street, Marylebone Road and Wells Street. There are plotters at NCS and Marylebone Road.

There is a single physical Ethernet in two logical parts, firstly four DEC VAX systems and DECservers using DECnet and secondly the Sun workstations and Spider terminal servers using TCP/IP. Mole will shortly be upgraded to run TCP/IP to act as protocol bridge between the two logical Ethernets. (See Figure 2.)

A Camtec PAD is used to connect Stoat, Lynx and the Case network to JANET and Yak to PSS.

FIGURE 2 NEW CAVENDISH STREET ETHERNET

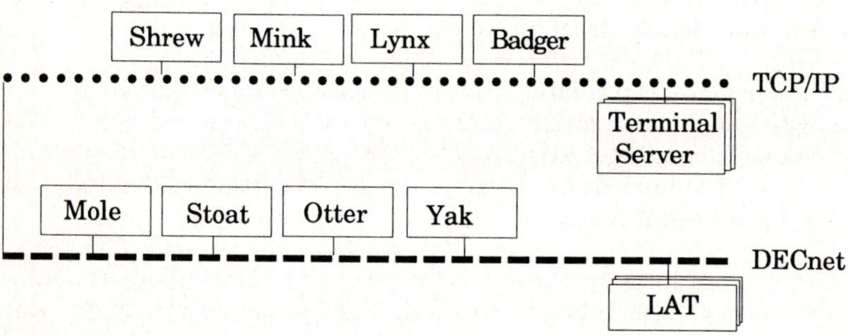

In addition to the facilities at the Computer Centre, all faculties and schools have local equipment bought from central or faculty funds. (See Appendix 1)

3.1 The DEC-10 World

The single DEC-10 runs the TOPS-10 operating system and supports a number of application packages, mainly program compilation, graphics and statistics. It has no connection to any other computer in the Polytechnic other than PC's using the Case network. The DEC-10 is due for replacement in the immediate future.

3.2 The VMS World

Six machines run the DEC VMS operating system. Of these Mole, Otter, Stoat and Yak are connected together using DECnet, allowing the transfer of files and mail, remote login and common access to JANET through Stoat. There are three DECservers on the DECnet supporting twenty-four terminals. Hare and Rabbit, at Regent Street, are also interconnected by DECnet.

Mole is a general purpose machine. Otter and Stoat are mainly used for CAD-CAM. Yak is used exclusively for Libertas, the library system including the online public access catalogue.

3.3 The Unix World

There are six Sun discless workstations (3/50's) supported by four fileservers (two 3/160's and two 3/280's). These are all connected using TCP/IP on Ethernet allowing remote login, file-transfer and a common mail system. There are seven Spider terminal concentrators supporting seventy terminals. Badger is connected to JANET using Sun X.25 software.

3.4 The CASE Network

The Case Data Concentration eXchange (DCX) consists of five routing nodes, three at NCS, one at each of Marylebone Road and Regent Street. There are ten end nodes; Euston Centre, Marylebone Road (two), Mortimer Street, High Holborn, Red Lion Square, 16 Riding House Street, 18-22 Riding House Street, 37-49 Riding House Street and Wells Street. (See Figure 3)

The Case network is primarilly a peripheral switch for terminals, printers, etc. It allows users with a dumb terminal (either VT100 or an older TVI910) or micro-computer to login to the machines at NCS. It permits restrictions to be made about the lines from which it is possible to login to the administrative machines at Regent Street.

Access is provided to the Case Network in most buildings for both offices and laboratories. Connections to the public switched telephone network are provided from the Case network allowing staff and students to login from home.

FIGURE 3 CASE DCX NETWORK

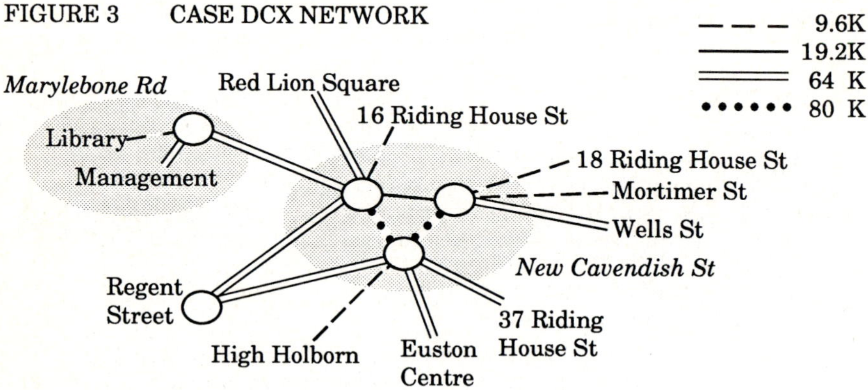

The network is difficult to manage in several respects

- it provides very limited management information
- it is difficult and time consuming to re-configure and expand
- it is "brand specific" and can only be expanded using Case equipment
- it has a poor operator interface, with severe consequences for relatively trivial mistakes

3.5 JANET and the Outside World

The Polytechnic is connected to the Joint Academic Network (JANET) through Lynx and Stoat by a BT leased line to the University of London Computer Centre. The connections to JANET use the Coloured Book Protocols [3,4,5] and imply support for and, ultimately, compliance with the Joint Network Team's Migration Strategy to OSI. [6]

JANET is used to send mail between machines in the Polytechnic not using the same operating system. It also allows mail to be sent to universities and other polytechnics in the UK. JANET has a number of gateways permitting mail to be sent to academic sites in most parts of the world. It also has a gateway to BT's *Gold 400* commercial X.400 service. The Government's Inter-Departmental Mail system (IDEM) is connected to JANET. (See Figure 4)

JANET is used for file transfers within the UK, e.g., from the Economic and Social Research Council's Data Archive at the Univeristy of Surrey, and by special arrangement overseas.

Access to BT's Packet SwitchStream (PSS) is made through JANET gateways, which allows PCL to economise through the bulk purchase of units. Library Services have their own dedicated line to PSS for their connection to SWALCAP (South West Area Libraries Catalogue Automation Project).

FIGURE 4 MAIL NETWORK

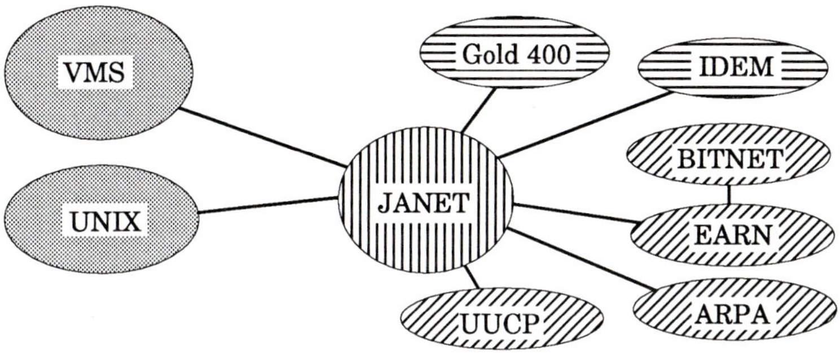

JANET provides terminal access to systems at other polytechnics and universities and *vice versa.*

4 TELEPHONES

The main part of the telephone system is a star network centred on Marylebone road, consisting of analogue leased lines and analogue private automatic branch exchange (PABX) systems and is due for replacement. The Regent Street site has recently had a new digital PABX installed as a temporary measure to overcome serious problems. Several sites are not connected to the central system, requiring BT calls to be made. (See Figure 5)

FIGURE 5 TELEPHONE NETWORK

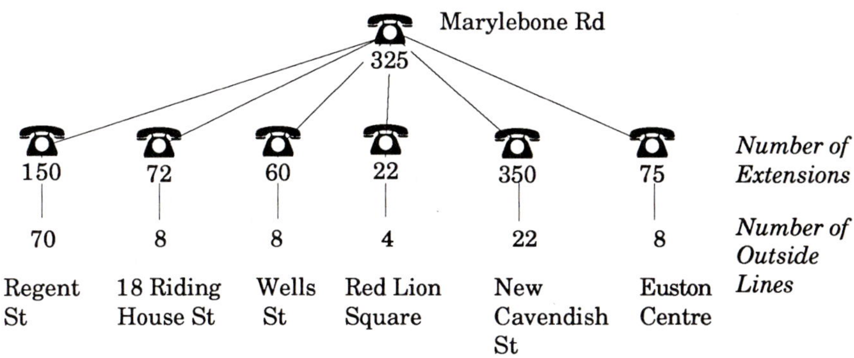

5 OPEN SYSTEMS INTERCONNECTION

The Open Systems Interconnection reference model is now well established and many standards and protocols have been developed based on it. Increasingly, there are products which conform to those standards and protocols or undertakings by suppliers to do so in the short term. [7]

OSI is a potential solution to the problems of running a diversity of systems at PCL. In order to meet the demands of the administration and of teaching staff it is necessary to purchase a very wide range of systems. Moreover, to do so economically often requires buying from the cheapest supplier. For example, in buying "Unix boxes" and micro-computers it is usually the processing power per pound sterling that is preferred, given a reasonable degree of conformance to *de facto* standards.

A functional profile from the OSI reference model should help in achieving a degree of commonality amongst systems which would ease interconnection, given an enforcing mechanism. The existing functional profiles Manufacturers' Automation Protocol (MAP) [8], Technical and Office Protocol (TOP) [9] and Government Open Systems Interconnection Profile (GOSIP) [10] are of interest to the study, both because they conform to OSI and because there will be commercial products complying with those profiles. It is not clear that any of these will meet PCL's requirements.

It is also important to consider the positions of British Telecom [11] and Mercury with regard to public telecommunication services.

6 APPLICATIONS AND USES

The major applications are currently terminal access and electronic mail. It is expected there will be a growing demand for File Transfer, Access and Management (FTAM). There is no significant demand for Job Transfer and Manipulation (JTM) and this is not expected to change.

6.1 Terminal Access

Most terminals are VT100 or compatible with that type, which has proved quite satisfactory for most purposes. VT100 is a recognisable type for VMS, Unix and the DEC-10. DEC Rainbow's and DECmates are suplied with VT100 emulation. A chip has been produced by PCL for BBC micro-computers to emulate the VT100. Other computers use Kermit for terminal emulation.

The growth of graphics applications, office automation and of windowing environments raises the question of the requirement for a higher level of functionality in terminal performance.

The virtual terminal protocol (VTP) seems to be one of less developed OSI standards and it is not clear when products based on this can be expected.

6.2 Electronic Mail

Three electronic mail systems are used (i) VMSmail, partially integrated with JANET, (ii) Unix, fully integrated with JANET, and (iii) JANET Mail known as "Grey Book". There has been a considerable, but unquantified, growth in the use of electronic mail amongst computer users, especially in VMSmail, and it is expected that this will continue. It is possible that there is a large untapped demand for what can be termed "mail only" users, that is for staff and students who would not use other computer facilities.

Without prior knowledge, there is no way of knowing to which machine mail should be sent for an individual or, indeed, what the username of an individual will be. The option of moving all mail to a single system named UK.AC.PCL has been considered but was rejected because of the resulting problems of heavy loading.

In selecting a standard for electronic mail it is clear that CCITT X.400 is already well-established. However, it exists in two versions 1984 (Red Book) and 1988 (Blue Book). For connection to JANET, X.400(84) is not being encouraged, though it will be tolerated with certain extensions. Therefore, PCL would be looking for products where suppliers comply with or have indicated an intention to migrate to X.400(88).

Moving to X.400 implies the use of faculties and schools for addressing. It is therefore necessary to consider how to agree on X.400 naming scheme and how to map this onto the existing addressing system, which is simply username and machine (or machines).

Currently there is only a very rudimentary username directory provided on Mole, this would require considerable enhancement or replacement.

Transfer to X.400(84) poses problems of poor support for group communications, e.g., distribution lists and electronic conferencing [12,13]. Currently, PCL is experimenting with wider use of a bulletin board facility, but has no electronic conferencing software. These sorts of activities also pose problems of high levels of traffic and of large amounts of associated disc space.

There is a Telex machine in Library Services, and available for staff use. Group III facsimile machines are located at NCS and Regent Street.

6.3 File Transfer

At present there is relatively little, but growing, demand for file transfer facilities. Micro-computer to mini-computer transfers are usually performed with Kermit.

It is possible that with the growth of larger storage capacity in PC's and the use of file servers on local area networks there will be a demand for central back-up facilities. In general it is expected that this could be handled at off-peak times.

7 CONSTRAINTS AND SOLUTIONS

The major restriction on any new network will be financial. It would be impossible to replace too much of the existing equipment at any one time. Therefore, it will be necessary to "migrate" to the new network over a number of years, probably two or three. A conventional phased migration would be difficult to plan, given the lack of knowledge about future budgets. Implicit in this is dual operation of the old and new networks. However, this poses serious problems of divided resources, both human and technical, and possibility of having to build gateways between the old and new.

Although the geographical separation of PCL's sites is not great, the height and density of intervening buildings rules out most forms of physical interconnections. The cost of digging up streets to lay cables specifically for PCL's use would be exhorbitant as would be subsequent maintenance. PCL does not have a legal "way leave" to lay such cables which would also present a major barrier. An alternative would be to obtain permission to use some of the tunnels under London.

Therefore, it may be necessary to continue to rely on the public telecommunications operators (PTO's) British Telecommunications and Mercury. They could provide leased optical fibre cables, digital and analogue lines. The installation and running costs of such lines are sufficiently high to make it a significant constraint on the network design. Therefore, it is important to determine current traffic volumes and to predict future volumes in order to determine inter-site traffic patterns and so select the most economical links.

One of the critical issues is the possibility of the incorporation of voice and data into a single network. At present the two networks are quite separate and link the various sites in different ways over different lines. The options for integration are as follows (i) continue separate networks, (ii) share inter-site links and (iii) fully integrate voice and data.

The first option is probably too expensive to continue with for any length of time. The second option would allow some economising, but without the ability to optimise the use of the inter-site links to the fullest possible extent. The third option would allow full optimisation. However, it would also increase the risks, since it would be much less tolerable for an integrated voice and data network to fail than for the data network alone to fail.

7.1 Baseband Network

Baseband networks (token passing ring, token passing bus and ethernet) have many attractions, not least their established record of performance. However, it would be necessary to build a complex series of bridges between sites. A single baseband network would almost certainly be vulnerable to breaks and over-loading. It would also be difficult to integrate voice with a baseband network [14].

7.2 Broadband Network

Each frequency segment in a broadband network would have to be connected between sites and although this need not apply to all segments it would be difficult and expensive unless a fibre optic Wide Area Network (WAN) were in use. If one site required large bandwidth it might be a locally acceptable solution.

7.3 Packet Switched Network

Packet switched networks are well established in the UK, for example JANET and BT's Packet Switched Service (PSS). Most universities use packet switched exchanges (PSE's) to provide access to services. It is an increasinlgy common commercial solution to data communications problems. The equipment, including high speed switches is readily available and is well tried and tested. It would therefore be a relatively easy option to adopt. However, it is not clear how X.25 and voice could be integrated.

In order to conform to standards for JANET and the OSI Network Service, an X.25(84) service or gateway would be required. [15,16]

7.4 Integrated Services Digital Network (ISDN)

ISDN has received a considerable amount of publicity and offers a wide range of services and interfaces [17]. However, there are very few, if any, working sites. The decision by BT to use Digital Private Network Signalling System (DPNSS) could result in the UK having a different standard from the rest of Europe, which would restrict available equipment.

ISDN would undoubtedly give PCL a technological edge, but it might not be sufficiently reliable in the early stages.

8 METHODOLOGY

In order to gather information about patterns of use and projected changes, representative users from each faculty, the Rectorate and the various other units will be interviewed. It will also be important to make use of the administration information systems. Traffic monitoring will be undertaken to determine patterns of use. However, it is recognised this will give only a small part of the picture, given the limited data the Case network yields and the variations in use over the academic year. Predictions will be made about expected future use of the system.

It is intended to visit other academic institutions and commercial organisations to determine what lessons can be learned.

The project will be conducted in three phases

> *Phase 1 - Specification of the Framework*
> Review and analysis of the existing system, analysis of requirements and definition of options.
>
> *Phase 2 - Design of the Network*
> Gathering data and traffic requirement analysis, derivation of criteria for the network, development of network design, liaison with suppliers and planning the network.
>
> *Phase 3 - Design of the Electronic Mail System*
> Identification of user communities and review of current use, specification of X.400 profile, product identification, selection of an addressing scheme, specification of administrative and operational procedures for implementation.

Reports will be produced after each phase.

9 CONCLUSION

What is to be attempted is the specification of the solution to a difficult problem - even consultants were surprised at its complexity. It is a moving target and the solution will require to be updated relatively quickly. However, when a new architecture and OSI profile have been identified, it will provide a clear target for planning. As and when money becomes available it will be possible to match it against parts of the architecture.

Given a favourable outcome to the study, it is intended to seek further funding from the Department of Trade and Industry for a Demonstrator Study which would implement the proposals.

Even in the formulation of this plan, it has been necessary to clarify our understanding of the issues and problems involved. We hope that in executing it we will gain a better understanding both the problems and of how OSI can be used to solve or mitigate them.

ACKNOWLEDGEMENTS

To the staff of the Computer Centre and to the various consultants who helped us to focus on the problems. To the DTI for funds to carry forward this study.

TRADEMARKS

DEC, DECmate, DECserver, DECnet, VAX, VMS, Micro-VAX, VT100 are trademarks of the Digital Equipment Corporation. Unix is a trademark of American Telephone and Telegraph Inc. IBM PC, IBM PC AT, PS/2 are trademarks of International Business Machines.

REFERENCES

[1] "Higher Education - meeting the Challenge" (HMSO, London, 1987, Cm 114, ISBN 0101011423)
[2] Michael D Cohen, James G March and Johan P Olsen "A Garbage Can Model of Organisational Choice" *Administrative Science Quarterley* **17** (1972) pp 1-25.
[3] Data Communications Protocols Unit "A Network Independent File Transfer Protocol" (National Physical Laboratory, Teddington, 1981).
[4] Steve Kille (editor) "The JNT Mail Protocol" (Joint Network Team, Didcot, 1984).
[5] Data Communications Protocols Unit "A Network Independent Transport Protocol" (Joint Network Team, Didcot, 1981).
[6] Joint Network Team "Transition to OSI Standards - Final Report of the Academic Community OSI Transition Group" (Joint Network Team, Rutherford, July 1987).
[7] Central Computer and Telecommunications Agency "Open Systems Interconnection - CCTA's Expectations and Suppliers' Implementations" *IT in the Civil Service* **15** (HMSO, London, 1986. ISBN 0113300123).
[8] General Motors "MAP: Manufacturing Automation Protocol Specification: Version 3.0" 1987.
[9] Boeing Corporation "TOP: Technical and Office Protocol Specification: Version 3.0" 1987.
[10] CCTA "Government Open Systems Interconnection Protocol" Central Computers and Commnication Agency, London, 1988.
[11] British Telecom "Open Network Architecture" (BT, Ipswich, 1987).
[12] W F Racke and T E Schütt "Integration of Group Communication into CCITT X.400 Message Handling Systems" in: Günter Müller and Robert P Blake (eds.) *Networking in Open systems - International Seminar, Oberlach, Austria, August 1986* (Springer-Verlag, Berlin, 1986, ISBN 0387177078) pp 117-127.
[13] Jacob Palme "X.400 and Group Communications" *Computer Networks and ISDN Systems* **14** (1988).
[14] D C Swinehart, L C Stewart & S M Ornstein "Adding Voice to an Office Computer Network" Research Report CSL-83-8 (Xerox PARC, Palo Alto, California, USA, February, 1984).
[15] CCITT "X.25" CCITT, Geneva, 1985. (Red Book)
[16] ISO/IEC "Specification of the Protocols to Provide and Support the OSI Network Service" DIS 8880 (ISO, Geneva, 1987).

[17] P J Kuehn "ISDN - Technology, Networking Concepts and Applications" in: Günter Müller and Robert P Blake (eds.) *Networking in Open systems - International Seminar, Oberlach, Austria, August 1986.* (Springer-Verlag, Berlin, 1986, ISBN 0387177078) pp 73-93.

The Final Report of this study (four volumes) is available for £50 from Computer Services at PCL.

APPENDIX 1

Euston Centre - One laboratory of twelve IBM PC's connected to the Case.

Marylebone Road - One laboratory of twenty terminals on the Case network. One laboratory of seven terminals on the Case network. One laboratory of eleven BBC micro-computers. One laboratory of sixteen IBM PC's or Olivetti compatibles.

New Cavendish Street - One laboratory of twenty TVI910 on DECnet. One laboratory of mixed terminals on the patchboard. Three laboratories of twenty terminals, one the on Case network and two on the Sun systems. One laboratory of fourteen BBC micro-computers. One laboratory of thirty Apollo workstations running Aegis on a token passing ring. One laboratory of IBM PC clones on a Novell token passing ring. Three Sun workstations on the Computer Services Ethernet. A number of mini-computers including; DG Nova, PDP11's and HP3000.

Red Lion Square - One laboratory of twelve BBC micro-computers - connected to the Case network. One laboratory of eight DEC Rainbows and 16 IBM PC's.

Regent Street - One laboratory of eighteen TVI910's on the Case network.

18-22 Riding House Street - One laboratory containing a network of sixteen Apple Macintoshes with hard disc servers and laser printer. One laboratory of twelve BBC micro-computers - connected to the Case network.

37-49 Riding House Street - Two laboratories of sixteen DEC Rainbows. One laboratory is connected to the Case network.

Wells Street - One lab of fourteen VT100's on the Case network. One laboratory of sixteen Amstrad PCW 8256's (word processors). One laboratories of sixteen Amstrad IBM PC clones with 20 Mbyte hard discs. One laboratory of sixteen IBM PC AT clones. One resource room containing two DEC Rainbow's, three Amstrad 8256's, two Plessey Ibis's, one Compaq 286 (portable). Some Apple IIe's and BBC micro-computers. One Apple Macintosh Plus and Laserwriter.

Network Information Processing Systems
K. Boyanov, R. Angelinov (Editors)
Elsevier Science Publishers B.V. (North-Holland)

A MODEL FOR SINGLE SERVER DATA SHARING IN A LOCAL AREA NETWORK

Vladimir LILOV, Bojan DIMITROV, Petko RUSKOV, Valentin KISIMOV

Center of Informatics and Computer Tehnology
acad.Bontchev str.,bl 8,1113 Sofia,BULGARIA

An analytical model of a user request,which works with a shared database in a local area network is considered in the paper.The structure of the request and the execution times of its parts are determined.The request is executed from the microcomputers connected to the network and works with a shared data element in the shared network disk with multiuser access to the data. A queueing theory model and Markov chains are used for the mathematical representation of the system.The basic elements of the queue system - input requests flow,service mechanism and queue discipline are described.The state transitions of the system are examined and a system of equations for calculating the probabilities of the possible transitions are derived. Some basic characteristics of the model are determined and the mathematical expressions for their evaluation are presented.
Keywords: local area networks,queueing theory,data sharing,data processing

1. INTRODUCTION

Local area networks are widely used to connect micro-computers and to allow their users to work with shared disk managed by the network server.All or a part of the users of many information systems work with shared database in the shared disk of the local network with multiuser access to the data.In such information systems every user works with one and the same element of the shared database - file, record or field.He occupies the element until the processing of the data in the element is finished and after that he releases the element for another user.In this way,all users perform the multiuser access to shared data elements. Synchronization among the users is nessessary to avoid information destruction in the shared database,when the access is concurrent.When this synchronization takes place the following events are observed: user software work time increase ,information traffic growth on the local network,decrease of the speed and the efficiency of the system,incorrect operator actions when the system response time is considerably increased.To study the system work in a multiuser access regime,development of a model and determination of the model characteristics is neccessary. There are different models analysing the hardware and software of the local networks [3,4,5,6], but they analyse different aspects of the local networks and can not be directly used.

The goal of the paper is to present a model for multiuser access to shared data in local area networks as a queueing system with repeated requests.The model is developed on the basis of a multiuser request structure to the network server.The characteristics for evaluation of the access to shared data are defined and the mathematical expressions for the characteristics are derived.

2. DESCRIPTION OF THE MULTIUSER ACCESS SYSTEM

2.1. Work of the System

In case of multiuser access to shared database,the user program occupies(locks) the shared element to avoid another user access to it.He works with the data of the element and after the end of the work releases(unlocks) the element. During the time when given element is locked if other users wish to hold it,they wait until its release and after that they compete to occupy the element.

The described working mechanism is implemented by the user request,which is a part of the user program and by the hardware and software of the local network.The request locks, processes and unlocks element of the shared database - file, record,field if the user has correct access rights.

2.2. Structure of the Request

The structure of the request is shown on fig.1. It consists of two main parts:

- lock operations.In the request,these operations may be commands to perform the lock procedure(LOCK) and the wait procedure if the wait procedure is included in the request.The time needed for execution of these operations is t_l.
- processing operations and unlock operations.These are read/write operations(R/W),close operations(if the element is a file) and unlock operations(UNLOCK).The time needed for execution of these operations is t_2.

3. DESCRIPTION OF THE MODEL

The queue system is described by its three basic elements: input request flow,service mechanism,queue discipline.

3.1. Input Requests Flow

The input requests flow to the local network server consists of two flows(fig.2):
a)primary requests input flow.It is a sum of all primary requests flows from the microcomputers working with shared database in the local network and generating requests to the server.We assume these flows to be random with Poisson distribution and intensities $\lambda_1', \lambda_2', \ldots\ldots\ldots \lambda_n'$,where n is the number of the shared database users.The combined primary requests input flow also has Poisson distribution with intensity $\lambda_1 = \sum_{i=1}^{n} \lambda_i'$.
b)repeated requests input flow.These are the requests that have not been immediately served because of a locked shared element,occupied by another user.We assume this flow to be with random hyper-poisson distribution and intensity k where k is the number of the repeated requests.

3.3. Service Mechanism

The requests service mechanism consists of two separate service units - SU1 and SU2 (fig.3).The mechanism performs two types requests service without priority:
- service,corresponding to the time for locking of the shared element (t_l).This service is done by SU1 and has exponential distribution with intensity $\mu_l > 0$.
- service,corresponding to the process time and unlock time of the shared element (t_2).This service is done by SU2 and also has exponential distribution with intensity

3.4. Queue Discipline

In the system is used random requests service.If the shared element is locked,the request becomes secondary and is put in the repeated requests queue.If a secondary request successfully locks the shared element (occupies SU1),the number of the repeated requests in the queue decreases by 1. If the shared element is locked by a primary request,the number k remains constant.If the shared element is occupied at the moment when a primary request arrives,it becomes secondary and k increases by 1.If during a given interval of time no other requests arrive and the service of the last request is completed,the system is free and is found in its initial free state.

3.4. States of the System

The states of the service system are determined by the SU1 state,SU2 state and the states k of the repeated requests source ,where k is the number of the repeated requests in the source k=0,1,2..... (fig.4).
The system is in the following states at the moment t:
- state k,0,0,when SU1 and SU2 are free,
- state k,1,0,when SU1 is being occupied,but the operations for data processing in SU2 have not started.
- state k,1,1,when SU1 and SU2 are occupied.

In state k,0,0,at the moment ($t+\Delta t$) the system can pass from state k,0,0 and k,1,1 at moment t.
In state k,1,0 at the moment ($t+\Delta t$) the system can pass from states k+1,0,0; k,1,0; k,0,0 and k-1,1,0 at moment t.
In state k,1,1 at the moment ($t+\Delta t$) the system can pass from states k,1,1; k,1,0; and k-1,1,1 at moment t.

4. EQUATIONS FOR THE PROBABILITIES OF THE STATES

The probability,a request to be absent at the moment Δt is $1-\lambda(\Delta t) + o(\Delta t)$,the probability to come only one request is $\lambda(\Delta t) + o(\Delta t)$.The probability to come two or more requsts at moment Δt is $o(\Delta t)$.The probability to release the system at moment ($t+\Delta t$),if SU2 was occupied,is $\mu(\Delta t) + o(\Delta t)$, and the probability the system to be occupied at the moment (t+ t), if it has been occupied at the moment t is $1- \mu(\Delta t) + o(\Delta t)$;
λ and μ are the intensity of the requests that enter the system and the intensity of the service.The probability SU1 to be released if it has been occupied is $\mu_l(\Delta t)$.
The equations for the transitional probabilities of the possible transitions at the interval ($t,t+\Delta t$) of the system are:

$$P_{k,0,0}(t+\Delta t) = [1-(\lambda_1(\Delta t) + k\lambda_2(\Delta t) + o(\Delta t))]P_{k,0,0}(t) + \\ + \mu_2(\Delta t)P_{k,1,1}(t)$$

$$P_{k,1,0}(t+\Delta t) = (k+1)\lambda_2(\Delta t)P_{k+1,0,0}(t) + [1-(\lambda_1(\Delta t) + \mu_l(\Delta t) + \\ + o(\Delta t))]P_{k,1,0}(t) + \lambda_1(\Delta t)P_{k,0,0}(t) + \lambda_1(\Delta t)P_{k-1,1,0}(t)$$

$$P_{k,1,1}(t+\Delta t) = [1-(\lambda_1(\Delta t) + \mu_2(\Delta t) + o(\Delta t))]P_{k,1,1}(t) + \\ + \mu_l(\Delta t)P_{k,1,0}(t) + \lambda_1(\Delta t)P_{k-1,1,1}(t)$$

We ignore the members $o(\Delta t)$ as infinite small and after transfering the members with indices k,i,j to the left of the equations we divide by t.When t-->0 we get the following system of differential equations:

$$P'_{k,0,0}(t) = -(\lambda_1 + \lambda_2)P_{k,0,0}(t) + \mu_2 P_{k,1,1}(t)$$

$$P'_{k,1,0}(t) = (k+1)\lambda_2 P_{k+1,0,0}(t) - (\lambda_1 + \mu_2) P_{k,1,0}(t) + \lambda_1 P_{k,0,0}(t) + \\ + \lambda_1 P_{k-1,1,0}(t)$$

$$P'_{k,1,1}(t) = -(\lambda_1 + \mu_2) P_{k,1,1}(t) + \mu_2 P_{k,1,0}(t) + \lambda_1 P_{k-1,1,1}(t)$$

We find the result of these equations when the system is in equilibrium and with the following additional conditions:

$$P_{k,i,j}(t) \geq 0$$

$$\sum_{k=0}^{\infty} \sum_{i=0}^{1} \sum_{j=0}^{1} P_{k,i,j}(t) = 1$$

Equilibrium exists when λ / μ <1.Then is fulfilled:

$$P_{k,i,j} = \lim_{t \to \infty} P_{k,i,j}(t) > 0 \; ; \quad \lim_{t \to \infty} P_{k,i,j}(t) = 0$$

$$k = 0;1;2\ldots\ldots ; \quad i = 0;1 \; ; \quad j = 0;1$$

To find Pk,i,j the left side of the system differential e equations is put equal to 0,and Pk,i,j are replaced by their limit values.The differential equations system turns into linear equations system:

$$0 = -(\lambda_1 + k.\lambda_2).P_{k,0,0} + \mu_2 . P_{k,1,1}$$

$$0 = (k+1)\lambda_2 . P_{k+1,0,0} - (\lambda_1 + \mu_2).P_{k,1,0} + \lambda_1 . P_{k,0,0} + \lambda . P_{k-1,1,0}$$

$$0 = -(\lambda_1 + \mu_2) P_{k,1,1} + \mu_2 . P_{k,1,0} + \lambda_1 P_{k-1,1,1}$$

$$k = 0,1,2\ldots\ldots ; \quad i = 0;1 \; ; \quad j = 0;1$$

5. CHARACTERISTICS OF THE SYSTEM

After solving the linear equations we obtain the probabilities Pk,i,j for the possible states of the system at the moment t.Knowing these probabilities we can calculate the following characteristics of the system:

System utilization coefficient.It represents the ratio between the time when the system is busy and the total operating time of the system.It is identified with the sum of the probabilities of the system to serve a request and is defined by the expression:

$$a = \sum_{k=0}^{\infty} (P_{k,1,0} + P_{k,1,1})$$

The average number of repeated requests for a time interval t.Define the length of the repeated requests queue:

$$\bar{k} = \sum_{i=0}^{1} \sum_{j=0}^{1} \sum_{k=0}^{\infty} k . P_{k,i,j}$$

Probability for noncollision service

a) probability for noncollision service of a primary request.It is determined by the ratio between the number of the successful attempts to occupy the system by primary requests and the total number of attempts to occupy the system.It is represented with the expression:

$$B_1 = \sum_{k=0}^{\infty} \frac{\lambda}{\lambda_1 + k.\lambda_2} P_{k,0,0}$$

b) probability for noncollision service of a secondary request.It is determined by the ratio between the number of the successful attempts to occupy the system by secondary requests and the total number of attempts to occupy the system.It is represented with the expression:

$$B_2 = \sum_{k=0}^{\infty} \frac{k.\lambda_2}{\lambda_1 + k.\lambda_2} P_{k,0,0}$$

Coefficient for successful system occupation
a) coefficient for successful occupation by a primary request.It is defined by the ratio between the probabiility of the system to be occupied by a primary request and the intensity of the primary requests input flow:

$$\alpha_1 = \frac{B_1}{\lambda_1} = \sum_{k=0}^{\infty} \frac{1}{\lambda_1 + k.\lambda_2} . P_{k,0,0}$$

b) coefficient for successful occupation by a secondary request:

$$\alpha_2 = \frac{B_2}{\bar{k}.\lambda_2} = \frac{1}{\bar{k}} \sum_{k=0}^{\infty} \frac{k}{\lambda_1 + k.\lambda_2} . P_{k,0,0}$$

$\bar{k}$ - average number of secondary requests

Average number of unsuccessful attempts for a request to occupy the system :

$$\tau = \sum_{j=0}^{1} \sum_{k=0}^{\infty} (\lambda_1 + k.\lambda_2).P_{k,1,j} \quad ; \quad j = 0,1$$

Request delay time.This is the time when the request tries to occupy the system:

$$\bar{w} = \bar{k}/\lambda_1$$

Total request delay time.This is the sum of the request delay time,the time to lock SU1 and the service time in SU2:

$$\bar{V} = \bar{W} + \frac{1}{\mu_\ell} + \frac{1}{\mu_2}$$

Coefficient for effective work of the system.It is defined by the ratio between the pure request service time (the service time in SU1 and SU2) and the total request delay time:

$$\bar{e} = \left(\frac{1}{\mu_\ell} + \frac{1}{\mu_2}\right) \cdot \frac{1}{\bar{V}}$$

6. CONCLUSION

The presented model and its characteristics examine the multiuser access to shared data in a local network and define request delay time,total request delay time,average number of secondary requests,coefficient for effective work of the multiuser system.The model is used as a basis to design multiuser distributed applications for microcomputers in a local network.The proposed concepts can be used to develop new models for multiuser work in a local network with more than one server and for study a system with distributed data and distributed applications.

REFERENCES:

[1] Distributed computing systems, Elsevier Science Publishers,Amsterdam,1985.

[2] Kleinrock,L., Queueing Systems, vol. 1 and 2, Wiley International Publishers, 1975,1976.

[3] Molva,R.,Novali,J.M.,Juanole,G., Observer: A traffic analisys tool for local area networks, Local Communication Systems: LAN and PBX, IFIP, 1987.

[4] Jones,R.,Distributing data in a networking environment Data Processing, vol. 28, no 1, 1986.

[5] Suppan - Borowka,J., Analyses of communication requirements and requested capacity of LAN and PBX systems in a program development environment, Local Communication Systems: LAN and PBX, IFIP, 1987.

[6] Tsuchiya,M., Shannon,D., Simulation of distributed processing networks, Computer Networks and ISDN Systems no 11, 1986.

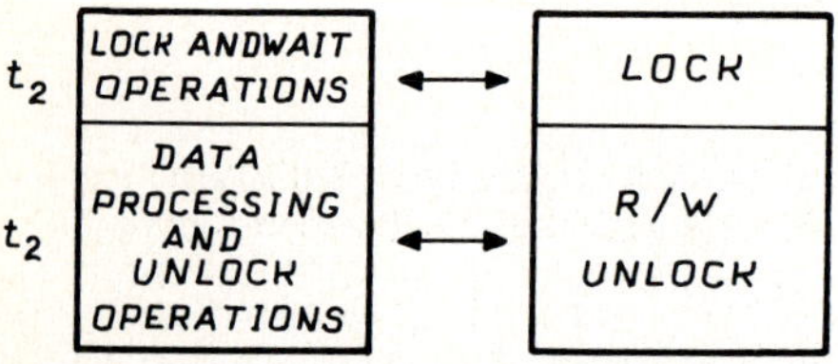

fig.1

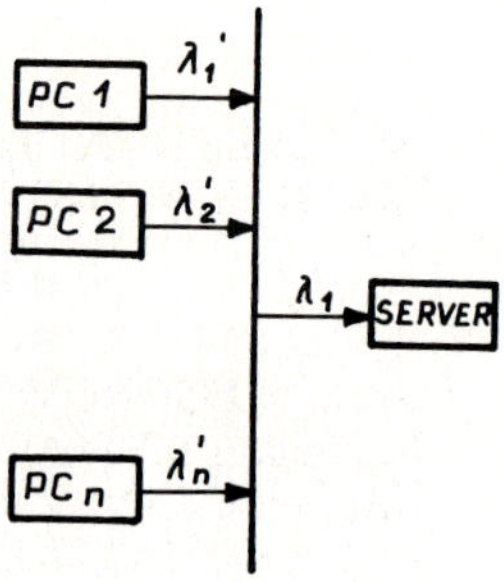

fig. 2

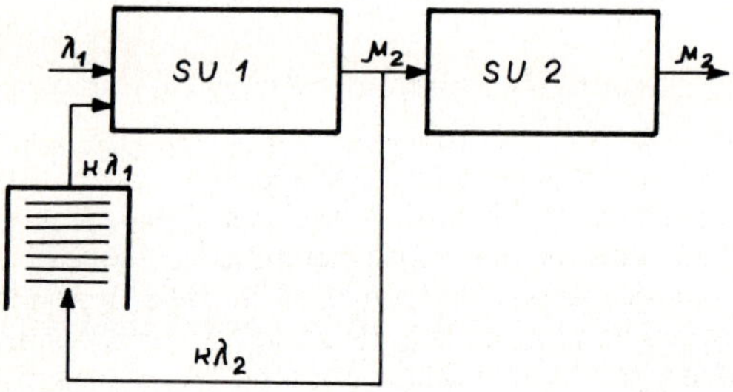

fig. 3

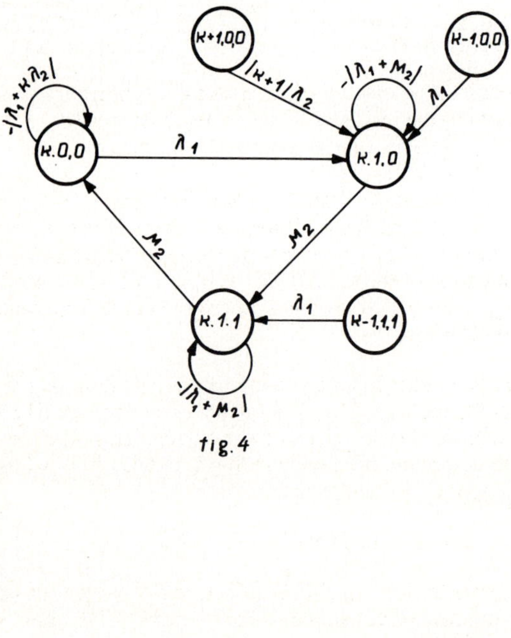

fig.4

Network Information Processing Systems
K. Boyanov, R. Angelinov (Editors)
Elsevier Science Publishers B.V. (North-Holland)

AN INVESTIGATION OF THE INFORMATION TRAFFIC IN A LOCAL AREA NETWORK BY SIMULATION MODELLING

Alexej E.EGOROV
Radmila A.STOYANOVA
Krasimir C.JANEV
Radi P.ROMANSKY

Bulgarian Academy of Sciences,
Center of Informatics and Computer Technology

The paper describes some of the basic results obtained by a simulation investigation of the information traffic in a local net of professional computers with a common channel. A brief description of the program module for the realization of the local net basic functions is included together with considerations for defining of the preliminary information for the model. On this basis a simulation model is proposed as assuring the estimation of the main system characteristics of the discussed class of local nets.

1. Introduction

Bus network topology has some advantages as full connection between all stations, simple organization of the information processes, easy functional and space extension, etc. Performance parameters of a local area network (LAN) with a single phisical channel to a considerable degree depend on the protocol of the channel distribution between the users, because the channel occupation frequency, the coefficient of its utilization, idle times etc. change for different values of the length of the transmiting information blocks [1,4,5]. The paper considers some basic results obtained from simulation investigation of the information traffic in a LAN of proffesional computers with bus topology under the control of a program module for maintaining local net basic functions (PMBF) [6].

Bus topology characteristics hampen analytical investigation that force applying of simulation modelling methods [2,3]. The model is realized on GPSS and supposes the presence of three basic objects - channel, server and users. The aim of the simulation investigation is to determine usability, loading and delay for the basic objects in different cases.

2. Functional description of the PMBF

The program module for maintaining local net basic functions ensures the access to the common system resourses (common shared disk - CSD) from user and/or server

stations of LAN using the functional possibilities of the net adapter (NA) and its monitor routine [1,2], which realizes the basic process IS.
The local net process IS divides the common shared disk into volumes with a capacity of 64KB to 32MB which are used analogously to a diskette. For each user station up to 4 fictitious diskettes can be declared by a registration in IS.

The declared volumes are classified into one of three types according to their mode of access. A private volume can be accessed for reading or writing only by its owner. The access to a shared volume is permitted for a group of users. A common volume can be accessed by all the users only for reading, writing being allowed only to its owner. When a volume is created it is defined as private by default. After saving files in it its type may be redefined. Volumes with restricted access may be simultaneously used by a multitude of clients using a mechanism of semaphores for prohibiting a combined change in it which may lead to errors in the local net functioning.

The resident part of PMBF is designed to distribute the requests from the user stations in the LAN, to control the access to the shared disk and to attend to the LAN in file interchange. The non-resident part of PMBF ensures the access to the shared disk for an user by a set of commands available for all the users.

3. Simulation modelling organization

The functional structure of the model is shown on Fig.1 and includes the three basic objects, connected in a queueing system. It presumes the existence of 'n' users USR_j ($j=1,...,n$) taking part in distribution of the input information stream μ. These users are presented as equivalent service objects with complex structure, that consists of an information buffer with limited capacity, input queue of requests and a server. The guidance of the requests to the users is realized on random access and an even distribution of the hit density. The input request enters the user for analysis and depending on the current state of the information buffer can be accepted for processing or lost. An accepted request can engender a new one, that could be oriented to the server SRV through the CHAN channel or could finish the current information process, correspoding to the basic network process for file exchange management.

So the workloading of our model, representing a multitude of successively generated transactions with definite frequency, can be divided in three transaction classes:

class/1/: orientated to the server
$\{ USR_i \dashrightarrow SRV \}, i \quad \{1,...,n\}$
class/2/: orientated to an user
$\{ SRV \dashrightarrow USR_j \}, j \quad \{1,...,n\}$
class/3/: transactions "user-user"
$\{ USR_i \dashrightarrow SRV \dashrightarrow USR_{j1},..., USR_{jk} \}$
$i, j1, ..., jk \quad \{1,...,n\}$

It is presumed that transactions of classes /1/ and /2/ finish spreading after reaching the respective receiver. Transactions of class /3/ require:

$j_1 = j_2 = ... = j_k$, $USR_i = USR_{jr}$ being allowed if j_r is an element of the multitude $J = \{j_1, j_2, ..., j_k\}$.

On the stage of simulation model organization these three classes of transactions realize the workloading model in the LAN. For that purpose service parameters are defined that determine the belonging of a current transaction to a definite class,the number of the user - a transaction source, the number of the user - a transaction receiver, and besides the multiplication of the transactions from class /3/ and their guidance to several receivers is ensured. Probability principle of generation is accepted. At every moment of the modelling time the presence of transactions of the three classes is possible, that compete to occupy the channel and orient to different directions. The channel is included in the model with a server and a queue for input transactions that contribute to the performance parameters defining.

The main characteristics of the simulation model can be summarized as follows:

a) three groups of investigation objects are differentiated - channel, server and users; the inter-dependence of different performance parameters,connected with these objects at change of user numbers is investigated;

b) the influence of input request stream intensity (its generation is with an even distribution) on performance parameters is investigated;

c) probability principle is accepted for the transactions generation and also for multiplication (if necessary) of the transactions from class /3/;

d) the circulating transactions in the model can finish their spreading in the server (class /1/) or in some of the users (class /2/ and /3/) using always the channel resource that leads to appearance of conflicts.

4. Results from the simulation investigation

The simulation investigation was carried out for different values for some input work parameters: model time (T_M), input stream intensity (μ), number of active users in the network (n). In connection with this it is possible to isolate two groups of results for the investigation parameters - depending on μ and on n.

Fig.2 (a,b,c) shows the graphical dependences of some parameters as functions of the input stream intensity μ, where = 1/60 is accepted for an intensity unit. The parameters are: utilization of the network elements (U), average length of the channel waiting queue (L) and average delay for processing a transaction (TZ) by the corresponding elements. The dependences regard to a network model with n=4.

Considering Fig.2a we can make a conclusion that the utilization of the server is to a considerable degree higher than that of the users (for n=4) as the dependence $U(\mu)$ for the users is significantly steeper for increasing values of μ. As for SERVER and CHANNEL a saturation of $U(\mu)$ is obtained for $\mu>2$

The dependences on Fig.2b concern different values of the model time T_M. Trends toward increase are similar for the two graphics, but the gradient for the model "A" is greater because of its longer work time. Thus the conclusion for the saturation of the channel utilization for increasing values of μ is confirmed that result in significant growing of the channel waiting queue for $\mu > 2$. This explains the saturation of the dependence U(μ) for a SERVER (Fig. 2a), because of the fact that the traffic passes through the channel.

The growth of the transaction number increases the server delay - Fig.2c, so the most powerful influence is over $TZ_{CHANNEL}$ and the weakest - over TZ_{SERVER}. In this connection, it is necessary to account that a channel delay consumes a part of the server delays.

The results for the parameters average queue length (L) and percentage of the direct service (Z) at variation of μ and n values are generalized on Table 1. It is possible to draw a conclusion that the trend to change (as function of n) stabilizes at bigger values of the input stream intensity, so an obvious dependence can be defined for the USERS parameters. For the channel and the server the current state of the workload in the model is significant.

Fig.3(a,b,c,d) presents generalized results for some parameters as functions of n: server utilization (U_{SRV}), channel utilization (U_{CHAN}), average user utilization (U_{USR}) and average server delay (TZ) for SERVER and USERS. The tendency of increasing the dependences ($U_{SRV}(n)$ and $U_{CHAN}(n)$) with the growth of n is obvious, with $U_{CHAN}(n)$ inclining to the lower bound. It is remarkable that for lower intensities a certain drop of U_{SRV} is obtained for $n>6$. About the family dependences $U_{USR}(n)$ (in Fig.3c) there exists a stability for variation of n for different μ - values.

On this basis we can make several conclusions:

1) The increazing of the user utilization with the growth of intensity μ (Fig.2a) is significant, but this complicates the channel work because of the increase of the transaction access (queue length - Fig. 2b) and leads to saturation of the U_{SRV} and U_{CHAN} dependences at $\mu > 2$ (Fig.2a).

2) There exists an interdependence between U_{CHAN} saturation (Fig. 2a), L_{CHAN} increasing (Fig. 2b) and TZ_{CHAN} delay with μ-change. This tendency is demonstrated on Table 1 as well.

3) Usually the users utilization increases with μ-increasing, but when n grows, it decreases, however the $U_{USR}(n)$ decreasing is stronger than $U_{USR}(\mu)$ increasing (Fig.3c). Analogous inferences can be drawn for L_{USR} and Z_{USR} (from table 1).

4) Generally the channel utilization increases when n grows (Fig.3b) and the dependences family thicken forward the upper bound. At higher values of the n, the parameters connected with conflict and service time-out, increase unconstantly (Table 1).

5. Conclusion

The simulation investigation was carried out not only in regard of the change of the input stream intensity but also with variation of the model time. The model experiments, that were carried out at μ,n=const retain apparent trends between the parameters and at the maximum model time the dependences stabilize. In this connection, the results shown above, are obtained at the maximum model time.

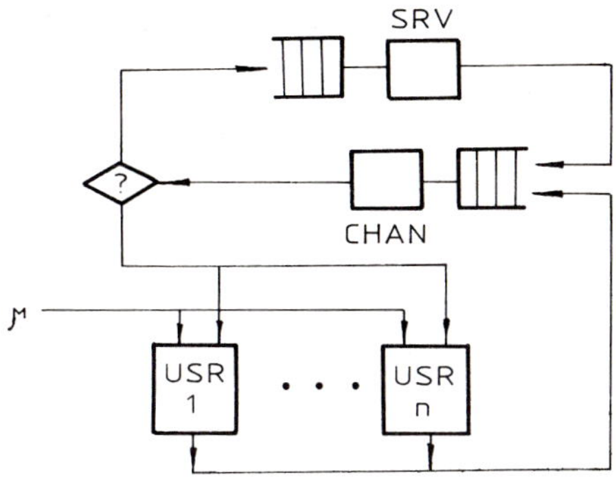

fig. 1

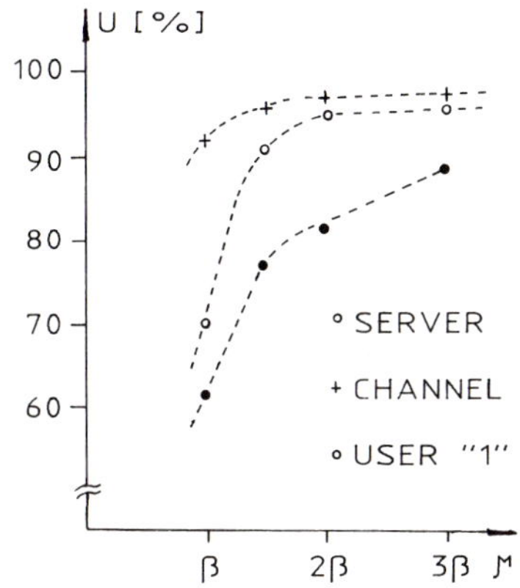

fig. 2a

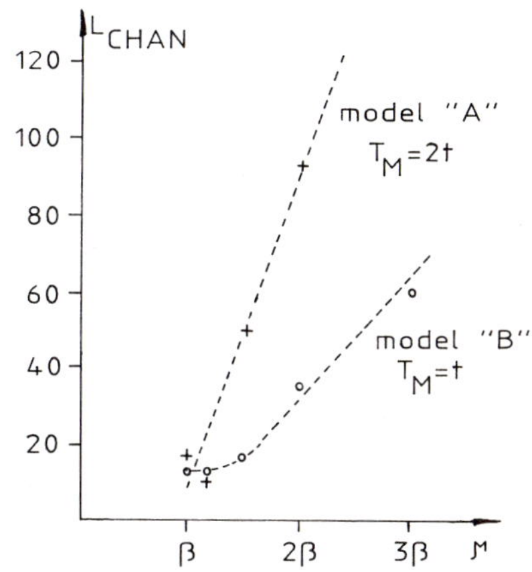

fig. 2b

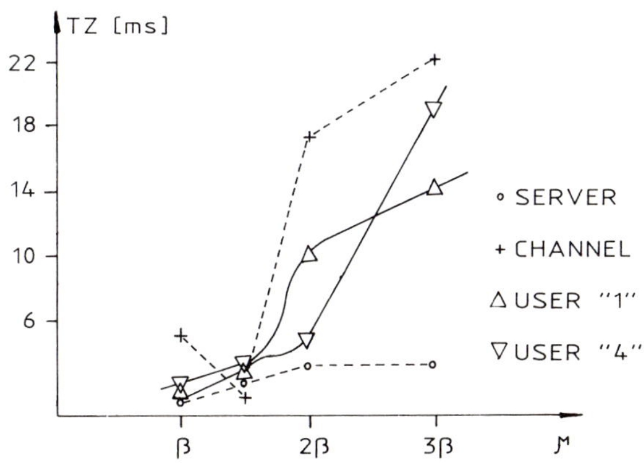

fig. 2c

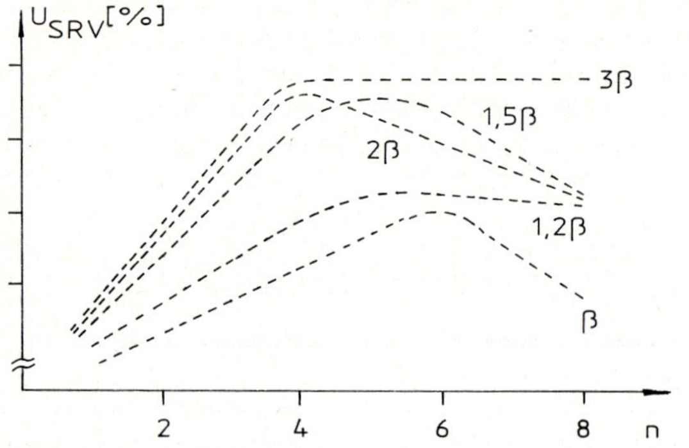

fig. 3a

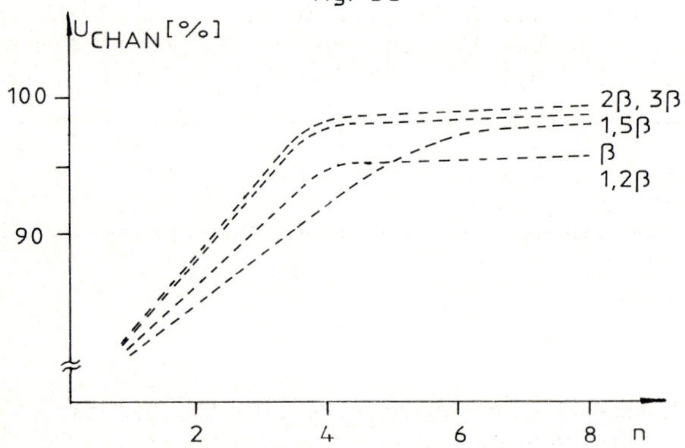

fig. 3b

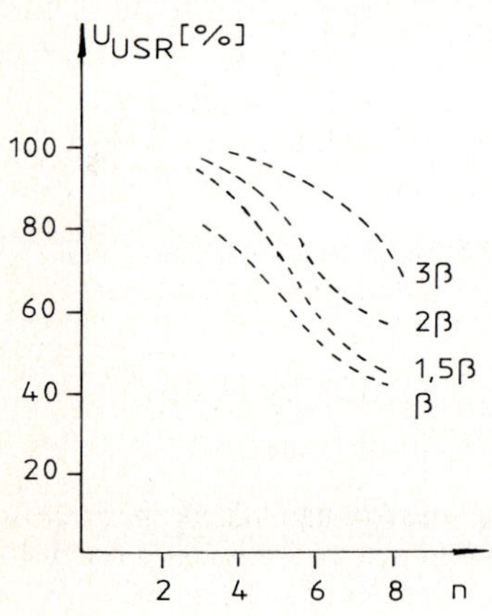

fig. 3c

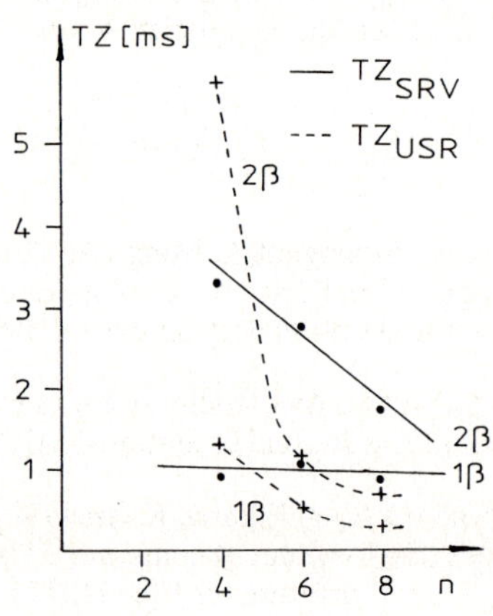

fig. 3d

The results obtained at the different model experiments allow to determine optimal values for an input stream intensity and for the icrease of the users number in the network in view of preserving the performance parameters and the efficiency in acceptable limits. From the model results it is possible to point recommendable intensity μ about 2 , and as for the investigated values for the number of the users the optimal results for the complete group of investigation parameters are obtained at n=6.

Table 1

Parameter	μ=1/60=β			μ= 1,5β			μ = 2β			μ = 3β		
	n=4	n=6	n=8	n=4	n=6	n=8	n=4	n=6	n=8	n=4	n=6	n=8
LSRV	0,7	1	0,7	2,3	4,3	1,5	4	3	1,7	3,8	5,9	9
LCHAN	18	10	56	51	77	96	94	118	146	135	438	247
LUSR	1	2	0,1	3	0,5	0,2	7,5	1	0,4	26	6,5	0,7
ZSRV %	31	17	27	8	4,3	17	6	12	15	4	0,2	1,5
ZCHA %	4	3	1,4	2	0,5	0,5	1	0,7	0,3	0,6	2,3	0,1
ZUSR %	28	51	61	15	41	58	4,5	31	48	1,5	12	33

References

[1] Ettinger, B., Z. Rozenberg , An Investigation of the Abonent System Carrying Capacity in a Local Area Network. Automatics and Computer Art, 1986, 5

[2] Gorbatkov, M.A., Simulation Model for Analysis and Optimization of the Local Area Networks Characteristics. Automatics and Computer Art, 1986, 3

[3] Hac A., Modeling Parallel Access to Shared Resources in a Distributed File System Using Queueing Networks. The Journal of Systems and Software, 1986, 1/2 (v.6)

[4] Shet A., A. Singhal, L. Ming , An Analysis of the Effect of Network Load and Topology on the Performance of a Concurency Control Algorithm in Distributed Database Systems. Proc. Computer Network Symp., 1985

[5] Tsuchiya M. , Availability Analysis for the Design of Distributed Processing Networks. The Journal of Systems and Software, 1985, 5

[6] Stoyanova R., A.Egorov, K.Janev, A program module for maintaining the basic functions of a local net of computers, Proceedings of the scientific session #The 7-th May#, Higher Institute for Electrical and Mecanical Engineering, Sofia,1987

Network Information Processing Systems
K. Boyanov, R. Angelinov (Editors)
Elsevier Science Publishers B.V. (North-Holland)

SOME ASPECTS OF THE JITTER PERFORMANCE OF LOCAL NETWORKS

J.TRENOVSKA

Institute for Communication Industry,
Dept.Digital Transm. Syst.
1309 Sofia, Bulgaria

V.PULKOV

Higher Inst. Mechanical & Electrical Engineering
Dept. Telecommunications
1156 Sofia, Bulgaria

ABSTRACT

With the development of digital networks· attention is given to the jitter performance of new and existing digital equipments and networks. This problem is known with PCM transmission for a long time. Our aim is to address this matter in the aspects of local networks, especially local area ring networks. The results are valid also for other types of local networks, when in the repeat mode the stations can be regarded, from a transmission point of view, as regenerative repeaters.

1. INTRODUCTION

The term jitter refers to "short term variations of the significant instants of a digital signal from their ideal positions in time". The following degradations can arise in a local network due to jitter phenomena:

a/ increase in the probability of introducing errors at points of signal regeneration;

b/ introduction of slips into digital signals, resulting from the overflow or underflow of storage devices or the overload of phase comparators;

c/ excessive jitter can eventually lead to intermittent synchronization failures, causing burst transmission errors.

One of the main factors influencing jitter generation and accumulation is the choice of synchronization method of the local network. The most frequently used method in local ring networks is when all stations are synchronized to a single master clock, which is provided by the ring adapter with the active monitor function. From a transmission point of view such a ring consists of a chain of regenerative repeaters, with the effects of timing jitter throughout the whole repeater chain /fig.1/. In this case jitter phenomena will determine the probability of introducing errors and slips, electrical stability of the ring and the maximum number of stations which can be interconnected.

2. JITTER PARAMETERS

Jitter performance can be described by the following basic terms - systematic, random, accumulated and alignment jitter.

A. Systematic and random jitter

The generated jitter at the output of each station in the local ring network contains both systematic and random /non-systematic/ components. Systematic jitter refers to jitter produced in the equipment which is strongly dependent on the pattern content of the input signal [1,2], i.e. refers to the fact that the same data passes each repeater serially and the generated jitter is identical or correlated.

The remaining components of generated jitter are random.

B. Accumulated and alignment jitter

Accumulated is the amount of jitter produced at the end of the repeater chain. This type of jitter increases pricipally due to the coherent summation of systematic jitter. At the end of a long chain the amplitude statistics of accumulated jitter are well aproximated by a filtered Gaussian random variable with a power spectral density related to the characteristics of the repeaters' timing recovery circuits.

For a timing recovery circuit based on a single tuned LC tank, the jitter transfer function is equivalent to a single pole lowpass filter [1] with cutoff frequency equal to the half bandwith of the tuned circuit,

$$H[W] = \frac{1}{1+2Qw/w_0}$$

where W_0 is the resonant frequency and Q is the quality factor of the tuned circuit. This transfer function has also been found to be a good approximation for timing recovery circuits based on crystal tuned circuits and PLL [3,4]. From this it is obvious that the low-frequency content of the generated jitter in the repeater chain determines the amount of accumulated jitter. For a sufficiently large number of repeaters in cascade, accumulated jitter resembles a bandpass process whose variance increases with their numbers.

The accumulated jitter at the end of the chain determines the elastic buffer size in the active monitor. The elastic buffer lenght must be chosen such that the probability of overflow is very small in order to be negligible compared to errors caused by noise.

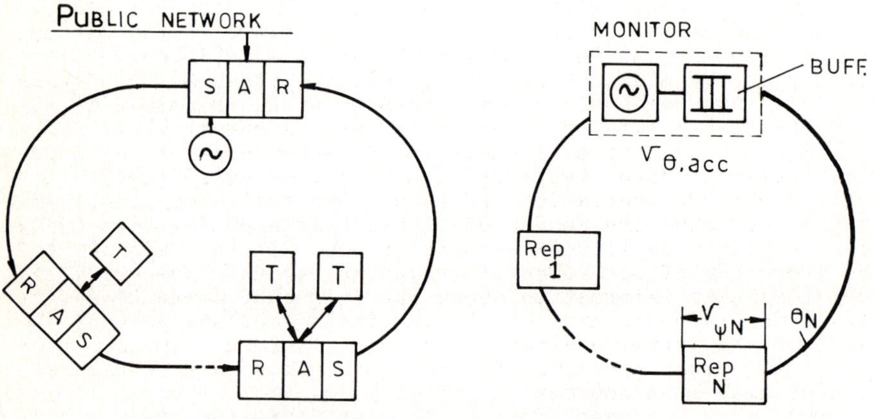

Fig.1 Block diagram of a ring system /S-sender, R-receiver, A-access, T-terminal/

The alignment jitter is defined as the dynamic phase difference between the phase of the incoming signal and the phase of the recovered clock. Another way of expressing alignment jitter is as the difference between the output and input jitter of a repeater. The spectrum of the alignment jitter is:

$$\theta_{Al} = [\theta out(jw) - \theta in(jw)]$$

where $\theta out(jw)$ is the input jitter and $\theta in(jw)$ the output jitter of the repeater. The output jitter spectrum is:

$$\theta out(jw) = \theta in(jw) . H(jw)$$

and hence

$$\theta_{Al}(jw) = \theta in(jw) . [1 - H(jw)]$$

As H(jw) corresponds to a low-pass filter characteristics, the function [1 - H(jw)] is equivalent to a high-pass filter. This implies that it is the high-frequency components of the input jitter that determine the amount of alignment jitter.

The alignment jitter is responsible for errors and potential synchronization failures in the repeater. If the difference in the phase between the signal appearing on the input of the repeater and the timing signal is sufficient an error or cycle slip in the process of decision is probable. Cycle slips represent statistically occuring synchronization failures of short duration. Each slip introduces a burst of errors degrading ring performance.

In most digital tranmission systems the amount of alignment jitter and its rate of growth is small, so that it does not impose a practical limit on the number of cascaded repeaters. However some peaking of the transfer function of the tuned circuit may lead to a very high rate of accumulation of the alignment jitter and bad performance of the whole network. Alignment jitter includes both the systematic and random components of the input high-frequency jitter.

As it was shown the low frequency components are these which accumulate along the chain significantly, while the higher-frequency content of the input jitter determines the alignment jitter. With low-frequency jitter the phase deviations present in the input signal coincide with these of the timing signal and no errors or slips are introduced. On the other side, the amount of high-frequency jitter and the grade of its attenuation in the timing path of the repeater determine the probability of occurence of errors and slips.

In order to determine the overall performance of a local ring network both types of jitter must be considered, with their amplitude statistics and power spectrum. The amplitude statistics give the amount of jitter /rms and effective peak-to-peak jitter amplitude/ present in the digital signal and the frequency of occurence of large amplitudes. However, they do not contain information about the frequency content of jitter, which is necessary for distinguishing and analysis of the two types of jitter - accumulated and alignment. In this case the jitter power spectrum must be known. This is also necessary when analysing sources of jitter in digital networks, main or local. It has been shown [2,7] that different sources produce jitter with a different power spectrum and hence influence the alignment and accumulated jitter differently.

3.SOURCES OF JITTER

A. Intersymbol interference.

Application of a mis-equalized pulse sequence to the timing recovery circuit causes a positional displacement of each pulse and as a result phase variation in the extracted timing signal. The jitter generated due to intersymbol interference is pattern dependent and hence systematic. It spreads over a wide frquency spectrum.

B. Finite pulse-width effect

Nonzero pulse-width of the pulses which exite the tuned circuit is one significant source of jitter. The amount of jitter generated from this source is strongly dependent on the pulse shape of the signal applied at the input of the nonlinear device of the timing circuit. This type of jitter is mainly high-frequency and is strongly pattern dependent. Certain statistics of the input pulse sequence in correlation with different types of pulse shapes, generate jitter which varies as in amplitude and power spectrum, thus in some cases significant low-frequency components of jitter can occur.

C. Amplitude to phase conversion

As a result of voltage offsets in practical limiting amplifiers, the output phase and pulse-width are affected by the amplitude of the input signal at the timing circuit, which varies according the pulse density of the input digital signal. Fluctuations of the level of decision in the limiting amplifiers and logical circuits also result in this type of jitter, which is pattern dependent and of low-frequency content.

D. Tuned circuit mistuning

When the transmitted pulse squence is random, the rms value of this jitter produced at each repeater is proportional to the product of the square root of the quality factor and the degree of mistuning of LC circuit or voltage offset of PLL used for timing extraction. Since the probability of all tuned circuits in the repeater chain to be mistuned alike is very low, the jitter generated from this source is considered to be random. Nevertheless this is an inportant source of jitter, because of the generation of significant amplitudes of high-frequency jitter. Thus if due to mistuning of the timing circuit in the repeater, jitter is generated, the latter will cause an increase of the alignment jitter in the next repeater in the chain and hence deteriorate its performance.

E. Other sources

Other sources of jitter are channel noise, intrinsic phase noise of electronic components, etc., but they are of minor importance because of their lower amplitudes in comparison with the other sources and random character.

4. JITTER ACCUMULATION

Based on the model of fig.1 the growth of systematic and random accumulated and alignment jitter can be computed. This has been investigated by many authors before [2,3,4,5,6] and the main results will be outlined here. The jitter growth characteristics are shown in fig.2. These characteristics are derived for a second order PLL but they are also applicable for other types of timing circuits. In [4] was shown, that jitter accumulation in a secind order PLL repeater chain is almost equivalent to that of a single-tuned filter repeater chain if

$$2y^2(\sqrt[N]{2-1}) >> 1,$$

where y is the PLL's damping factor and N the number of repeaters in the chain. The transfer function of the first order PLL is the same as that of a single tuned filter and thus jitter accumulation laws are the same. In fig.2a and 2b is shown the growth of accumulated jitter with the number of repeaters in the chain. It is obvious that is possible to reduce accumulated jitter growth, both random and systematic by making the damping factor - y of the PLL as large as possible. But in practice a joint optimisation of the damping factor and the natural frequency of the PLL is necessary so that the accumulated jitter and the transient response time after N repeaters in the ring are under the specified limits or system requirements.

As mentioned previously, the accumulated jitter determines the elastic buffer size in the active monitor. To keep overwriting or underwriting errors within a desirable limit, the number of the store's memory cells - E must be at least as large as the peak-to-peak jitter difference between the recovered and the independent clocks in the active monitor. This difference is a function of the equivalent bandwith of the PLL - B_A , and the rms accumulated jitter $\sqrt{a_N}$ in rad. In estimating the number of the memory's cells, the probability that this difference doesn't exceed E more than a given number of times for a given period must be taken into consideration. Usually this is called the average interarrival time between overflow and underflow events - t_E . Normally, some extra margin must be included to account for the propagation chracteristics of the memory's cells, their read and write characteristics. Usually it is assumed that two cells are enough. A formulae has been derived in [6] which gives the number of cells in the elastic buffer store. A good approximation is

$$M = \frac{\sqrt{\theta N}}{2}(\ln B_A \cdot \sqrt{\theta N} \cdot t_E + 1)^{1/2} + 2$$

The systematic and random alignment jitter performance along a chain of repeaters with second order PLL timing extraction is shown in fig.2c and 2d. After an initial decrease the alignment jitter tends to grow with the number of repeaters. Here also proper choice of PLL parameters leads to favorable alignment jitter accumulation. Peaking of the transfer function is to be avoided, as it results in jitter accumulation exponentially proprotional of the number of repeaters for both systematic and alignment jitter.

As mentioned, large amounts of alignment jitter causes statistically intermittent synchronizatin failures, usually refered as cycle slips [5]. The synchronization failure rate depends mainly on the number of cascaded repeaters - N , the PLL's damping factor - y , and the systematic jitter variance - $r_{\psi 1}^2$, dependent on the interpulse interference at the input of the timing circuit and PLL's bandwith. Normalized synchronization rate as a function of $V_{\psi 1}^2$ and N is shown in fig.3-5. The strong dependence of the synchronization failure rate on these three key parameters is illustrated. Having a bond value for h_0 /from the requirements of the ring/ and the number of repeaters connected in cascade the maximum permissible amount of alignment jitter can be estimated.

5. JITTER REDUCTION

There are two basic methods of jitter reduction:

a/. By reduction of the amount to which the jitter has grown along the chain.

b/. By ensuring minimun jitter generated from the main jitter sources.

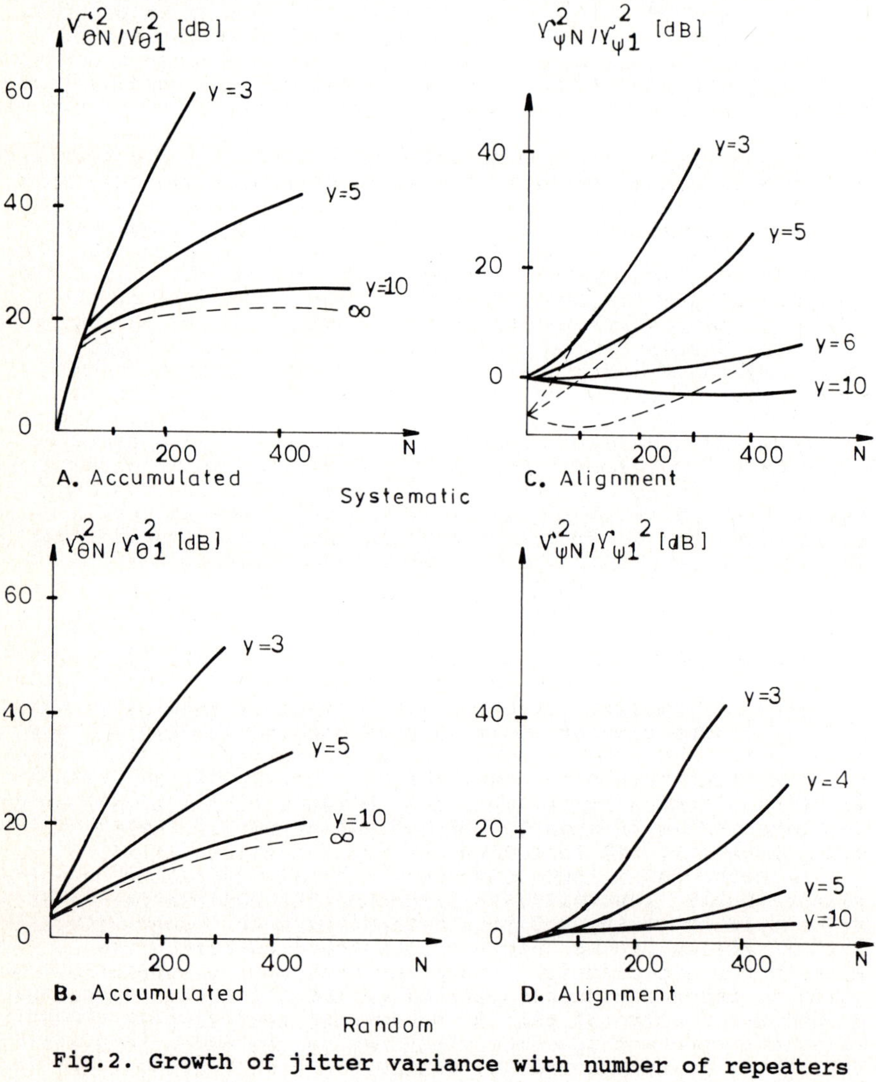

Fig.2. Growth of jitter variance with number of repeaters

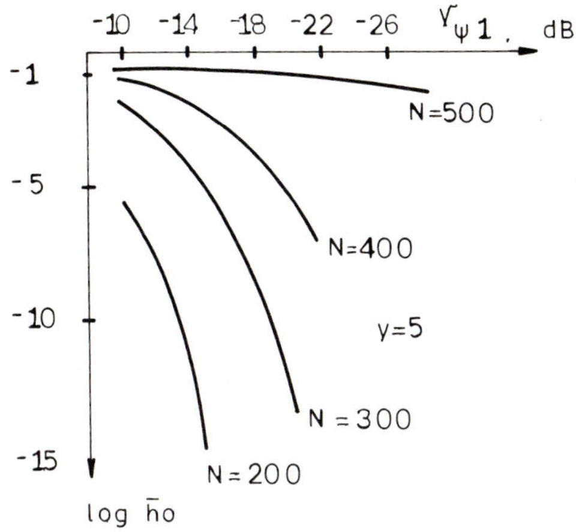

Fig.3. Normalized synchronization failure rate as function of $\Gamma^2_{\psi 1}$

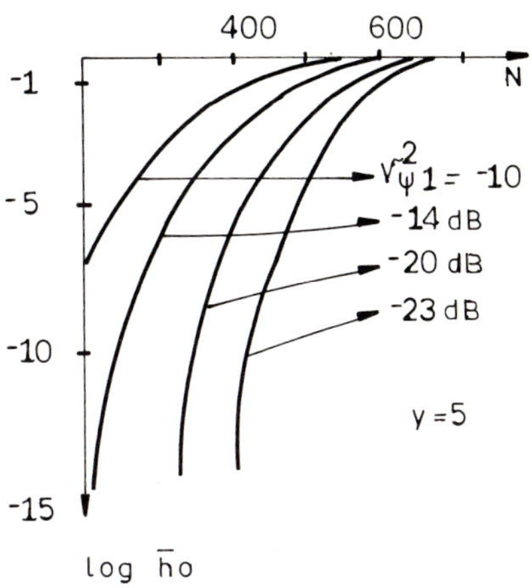

Fig.4 Normalized synchronization failure rate as function of N /parameter $\Gamma^2_{\psi 1}$/

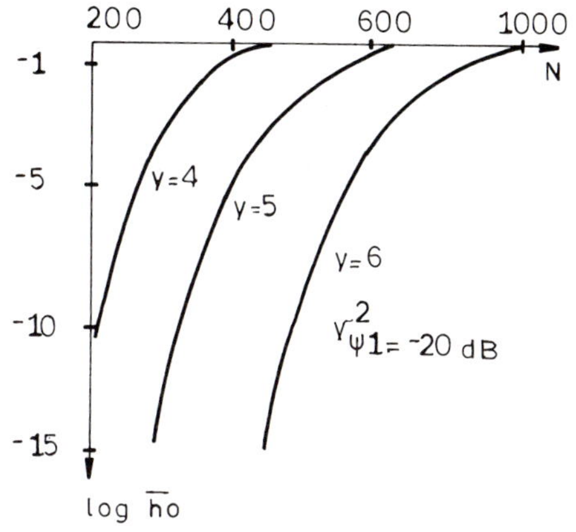

Fig.5. Normalized synchronization failure rate as a function of N /parameter damping factor - y /

The first method involves the use of a jitter reducer, which is basically a retiming circuit with a small jitter passband. This is usually achieved with the help of FIFO buffers timed by PLL locked to the input digital signal. These jitter reducers are put along the chain of repeaters in the places where the jitter has reached the maximum permissible values. Shortcomings of this method are that lower-frequency jitter /below 20 Hz/ can not be attenuated effectively, and also to achieve practical reduction and good performance regarding both accumulated and alignment jitter such a reducer should be an integral part of every repeater /ring station/.

The second method concerns proper system design and choice for realizing timing recovery circuits in such a way that the generated jitter is minimal. This means influence on each of the major jitter sources. For example, concerning intersymbol interference, in [9] a method incorporating a predistortion technique is proposed for simultaneous minimization of intersymbol interference and timing jitter. In [10] a method for eliminating jitter caused by finite pulse-width effect and mistuning is reported. Mistuning relates generally, concerning jitter generation and accumulation, all the different types of tunning circuit realizations with their corresponding parameters. Regarding timing recovery with PLL which is widely used in local networks it was shown that accumulated and alignment jitter performance depends strongly on the parmeters of the PLL's damping factor, transfer function, etc.

As mentioned previously the major jitter sources are pattern dependent. Randomization of the transmitted digital signal using scramblers is expected to reduce jitter. Experimental results reported in [8] verify this, showing that effective randomization of the digital signal ensures minimal jitter generation and accumulation due to the predominant pattern-dependent mechanisms within a repeater. This is one of the major reasons for recommending use of scramblers in local networks, where in most cases transmitted signals are highly correlated.

6. CONCLUSION

This article gives an outline of the nature of jitter and its influence on local network design and performance. The study of jitter is a complex subject and more experience is required for its precise investigation. Although jitter is one of the major impairments in digital networks one advantage is that by proper system design jitter could be reduced to a desirable level to ensure satisfactory system performance.

REFERENCES:

[1] Byrne C.J. et al. Systematic Jitter in a Chain of Digital regenerators. BSTJ, 1963, 42(6), pp. 2679-2714.

[2] Manley J.M. The Generation and Accumulation of Timing Noise in PCM Systems. BSTJ, 1969, 48(3), pp.541-613.

[3] Duttweiller D.L. The Jitter Performance of PLL Extracting Timing from Baseband Data Waveforms. BSTJ, 1969, 55(1).

[4] Shimamura T.Analysis of Jitter Accumulation in a Chain of PLL Timing Recovery Circuits. IEEE Trans. Comm. 1977, No.9.

[5] Meyr H., Popken L. Synchronization Failures in a Chain of Repeaters. Conf. rec. Globecom, 1982, vol.2, pp. 859-869.

[6] Keller H., Meyr H. Transmission Design Criteria for a Synchronous Token Ring. IEEE J.Selected Areas Comm. 1983,No.5.

[7] Cariolaro J., Todero F. A General Spectral Analysis of Time Jitter Produced in a Repeater. IEEE Trans.Comm.1977,No.5.

[8] Kasai H., Senmoto S. Jitter Suppression by Scrambling. IEEE Trans. Comm., 1974, COM-22(8), pp. 1114-22.

[9] Takasaki Y. Optimizing Pulse Shaping for Baseband Digital Transmmission with Self Bit Synchronization. IEEE Trans. Comm. 1980, No.8.

[10] Franks L., Bubrouski J. Statistical Properties of Timing Jitter in a PAM Timing Recovery Scheme. IEEE Trans. Comm. 1974, No.7.

Network Information Processing Systems
K. Boyanov, R. Angelinov (Editors)
Elsevier Science Publishers B.V. (North-Holland)

CONFORMANCE AND INTEROPERABILITY TESTING OF COMPUTER COMMUNICATION PROTOCOLS

Volker HEYMER

Academy of Sciences of the GDR
Institute of Informatics and Computing Technique
Rudower Chaussee 5
DDR - Berlin, 1199

A project on conformance and interoperability testing of computer communication protocols is being carried out on the background of network development and implementation. This paper deals with our experience in testing communication software for the computer network DELTA and describes some basic ideas of a new project. Our main effort is focussed on a test system for upper layer protocols of the OSI reference model, based on the distributed test method. It is our intention to find out principles for a generalized architecture. So that it may be applied to different upper layer protocols.

1. INTRODUCTION

The Institute of Informatics and Computing Technique has specialized in computer communication, in connection with the elaboration of the computer network DELTA for research and development /CAR 81/.
Conformance testing to the protocol specifications and interoperability testing was done with ad hoc methods based on general software technology experience. Some of the lessons learned through this work are shown in the first part of this paper.

In the process of developing further OSI standards, of gathering experience with the implementation, and operating computer networks it was found necessary to assess the conformance of implementation to specification /RAYN 86, ISN 1525/.
To meet the user's requirements it is not only the correct implementation of the protocols that is of importance, but also the provision of the services in the quality needed for the various forms of application.

The assessment of the conformance of a real system includes
- the proof of the conformance of the implementation to the standard's mandatory demands,
- the reviewing of the range of options and of parameter values supported,

- the measurement of the performance (e.g. throughput, response time, quality of service parameters) of the implementation,
- the evaluation of the robustness (error behavior, recovery) of the implementation.

In the literature the range of tasks concerning conformance assessment differs. But in most cases the term conformance test covers the first two points. So will it be done here. Furthermore interoperability tests are required to meet the user demands /MAP 86/.

In the second part of the paper the basic ideas are discussed of the conformance testing project started last year, with the intention in mind to find principles for a generalized architecture, which fits for different upper layer protocols. The favored method for the experimental implementation is the distributed test method.

2. TESTING COMPUTER NETWORK DELTA COMPONENTS

The computer network DELTA was developed in the late 70's. The communication architecture is similar to that of the OSI reference model, but the protocols used are nonstandard, partly in accordance with former IFIP work in this field.
The special requirements in testing communication software were fully understood only at the end of the first phase of the development, when the complex debugging and the interoperability tests were to be provided.

The test environment for the components of the communication software was characterized by
- a state machine oriented specification of the protocols and services, based on a graphic representation and state tables,
- the implementation of the end system software at two highly different (hardware and operating system) host systems of EC and BESM6 type,
- different implementation teams at different locations of the host systems,
- the absence of a well developed test method for distributed systems.

For statistics and measurement purposes, at the very beginning of the project, any program module was instrumented with observation points. The information obtained from these points was designed to be for conformance and performance assessment, too. It represented one part of the logging information about the behavior of the system while carrying out the tests.

The test of the implementation under test (IUT) was made on the basis of a distributed test method (Fig. 1). One BESM 6 computer became the test system which provided its function on the basis of a reference implementation with an exeption generator. The implementation team at this site supervised the external tests with the IUTs at the other sites.

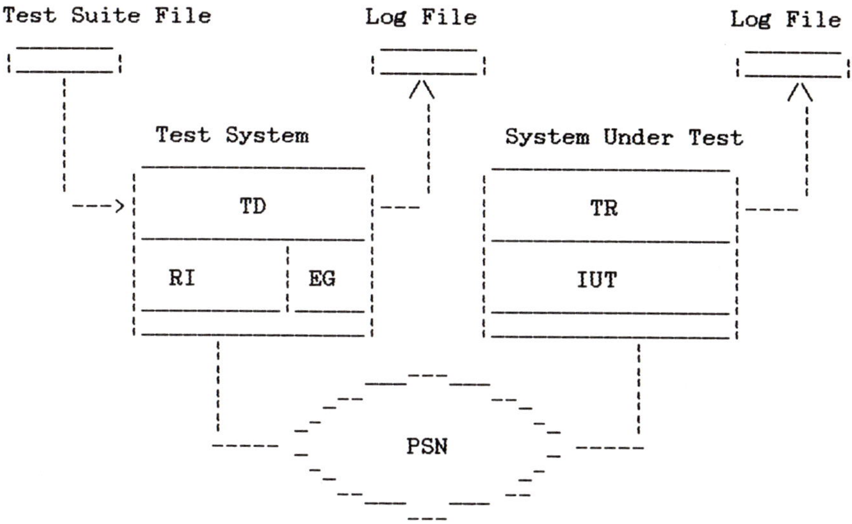

TD - Test Driver
RI - Reference Implementation
IUT - Implementation Under Test
TR - Test Responder
EG - Exeption Generator

Fig. 1: Test architecture for the computer network DELTA

Testing was done in three steps with two types of tests /HEYM 84b/. The first step was a normal software test in both simulated and native system environment at the local hosts.
In the second step, the service used at the lower interface and that provided at the upper interface were tested. This is a kind of static conformance review.
In the third step, the cooperation among the peer entities within the same system and with those of remote systems was tested, especially a multi-layer test was provided for basic interconnection testing.

Single test and long term tests were performed.
Single tests were carried out partly with a simulated system environment and with test suites for conformance resolution tests and for the assessment of performance limits.
Long term tests were carried out in the native system environment with test suites for behavior tests and for the assessment of the average performance of the implementation. With these tests also the interoperability problems were solved.

In a first phase all the testing was done by the implementors of the communication software. After getting a ready to run software the operation of the network went over to an operating group, who used the basic interconnection test suites and the behavior test suites to manage the tests after a restart of the entire network, after connection further computers, and in cases of error or undefined situations.

3. TEST SYSTEM PROJECT FOR STANDARD PROTOCOLS

Since the situation is changing in so far as we have networking in many industrial and management areas now, with local area and wide area networks, which are in need of interconnection, and last but not least owing to the international standards in the field of computer communication widely accepted now, we considered it useful to launch a project on conformance assessment in accordance with the ISO work. But unlike ISO it contains, in addition to the conformance testing, the problems of performance and robustness assessment and interoperability testing. This range of tasks is in the interest of both the standard body and network service providers and is therefore supported by them.

These demands necessitate a flexible control of the testing procedure.There must be test suites for these goals. They will be taken from ISO/CCITT documents, e.g. /MHS 87/, if available or manually made.Research is under way to derive test suites from formal specifications written in ESTELLE.

The testing of a real implementation with a special purpose is carried out under the control of a test program. The test program is the concrete test course. It is a selection of executable test cases taken from the test suites and chosen for the special purpose. These test cases are connected by control statements which above all contain actions for all nonregular events.

Beginning with the static composition of the test program research is done to come to adaptive stragegies for the dynamic compiling of these programmes.
To further improve this process an attempt is made to use the results obtained by other groups in the application of knowledge based systems.

The test system is being implemented on an minicomputer.

The basic considerations for the architecture of the test system are:

- The IUT is considered to be a black box, i.e. the upper and lower interface should be controllable and observable by the test system.

- The control and observation points are distributed to two test facilities, the upper tester (UT) and lower tester (LT).

- External test methods are used to ensure the independence of the test system from the system under test (SUT).
- The responder at the SUT has to be portable and small in order to ensure the implementation at the SUT with little effort and also for systems with limited resources.
- The LT is to be based on an encoder/decoder device with a test driver to control the test procedure.

The first version of the test system will be used for conformance testing on its own but the system was to be designed in a way to allow the integration of elements for performance and robustness assessment.

The work being done for the session layer is aimed at finding a generalized architecture of the test system for the upper layers of the OSI reference model.
The structure chosen is similar to that described in /RAFI 86/ as "astride technique" or in /ZENG 86/ as "ferry concept". Figures 2 and 3 illustrate this solution.

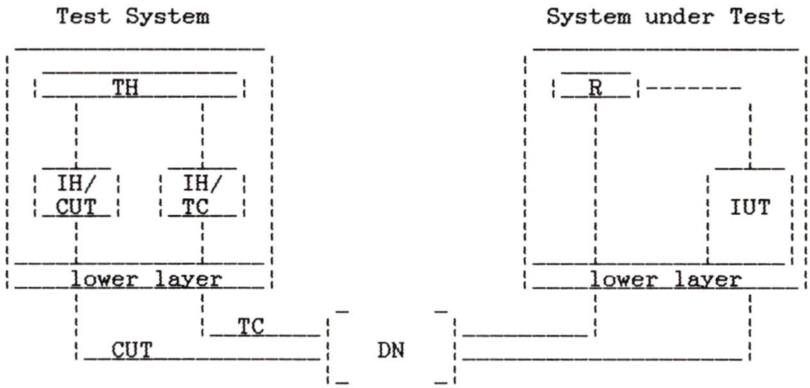

TH - Test Handler
R - Responder
IH - Interface Handler
TC - Test Connection
DN - Data Network
IUT - Implementation Under Test
CUT - Connection Under Test

Fig. 2: Test architecture for upper layer protocols

The UT and LT are both implemented at one host system, the test centre, allowing one
- to minimize the effort of the implementation of a responder at the SUT, which only passes the service primitives between IUT and UT,
- to omit a test management protocol or an implicit synchronization, in favor of the direct communication of LT and UT inside the test centre,

- to bring together the test results at the upper and lower observation points in an easy way, a good prerequisite for an adaptive test strategy.

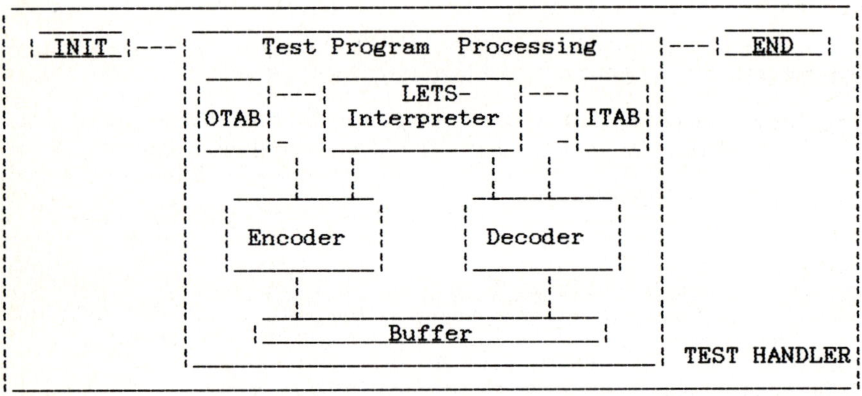

ITAB/OTAB - parameter tabels for incoming/outgoing messages
LETS - test description language

Fig. 3: Structure of the test handler

The decision to have "both sides" of the test system implemented at one host system has great influence on the test strategy. There are no restrictions from the point of view of the complexity of the coordination between UT and LT, such as high demands on the test management protocols or how to synchronize UT and LT actions in distributed systems. Therefore it is possible to have a test control which is determined only by the behavior of the protocol to be tested and the constraints on the permitted sequences of service primitives.

The test connection will be a transport connection providing a more powerful service than needed for this purpose.

4. CONCLUSION

To ensure the reliable work of heterogeneous computer systems of different vendors in computer networks conformance testing, performance and robustness assessment is required. The tools needed for this purpose should be developed and given to certification centres to fulfil this task.

Moreover, interoperability tests for the real networks must be provided to guarantee the interworking of the certificated systems. To manage this task with reasonable efforts the testing facilities should be of generalized functionality to be tuneable to different protocols and test goals.

The orientation to ISO activities on conformance testing and the collaboration of teams working in this field might be a way to solve these problems.

REFERENCES

/CAR 81/ Carl, D. at all
The Architecture of the Communication Services Hierarchy of the Computer Network DELTA and Experiences in its Implementation
Proc. COMNET'81, North-Holland, Amsterdam 1981

/RAYN 86/ Rayner, D.
Towards Standardized OSI Conformance Tests
Protocol Specification, Testing and Verification V. M. Diaz (ed.), North-Holland, Amsterdam 1986

/ISN 1525/ Proposed Draft Proposal for OSI Conformance Testing methodology and framework
ISO/TC97/SC21/WG1 E58, Sept. 1986

/MAP 86/ MAP/TOP User Group Summary, 1(1986)3
MAP/TOP User Group of SME, Dearborn, Michigan, USA

/HEYM 84/ Heymer, V.
Verkopplung von Rechnersystemen zu Rechnernetzen
ZfR-Informationen, ZfR 84.13, 1984

/RAFI 86/ Rafiq, D.; Castanet, R.; Chraibi, C.
Towards an Environment for Testing OSI Protocols
Protocol Specification, Testing and Verification V. M. Diaz (ed.), North-Holland, Amsterdam 1986

/ZENG 86/ Zeng, H.; Rayner, D.
The Impact of the Ferry Concept on Protocol Testing
Protocol Specification, Testing and Verification V. M. Diaz (ed.), North-Holland, Amsterdam 1986

/MHS 87/ Message Handling: Conformance Testing
CCITT, Q.33/VII, COM VII-176 - COM VII-170, April 1987

Network Information Processing Systems
K. Boyanov, R. Angelinov (Editors)
Elsevier Science Publishers B.V. (North-Holland)

GROUP ACTIONS IN FAULT-TOLERANT NETWORKS

Konstantin G.SAMOFALOV, Oleg V.VICTOROV and Peter T. POPOV

Computer engineering dept.
Kiev Politechnic Institute
Kiev, USSR

The method based on the diagnostics of the faulty nodes of the network is proposed. It permits to achieve the agreement, performing group actions in the network consisted of 2k+2 nodes with no more that k faulty nodes without authentication of the messages. The method proposed is much more effective than the "Byzantine agreement" achievable in the network with the number of faulty nodes not exeeding I/3 of the total number.
The correctness of algorithms realizing the given method is proved. The effectiveness of the diagnostic procedures is illustrated by examples. The hierarchical sequence of the diagnostic procedures is offered. It permits to vary the complexity of the diagnostic means depending on the required effectiveness of the measures providing fault-tolerance. The realization of the algorithms offered will considerably increase the reliability of networks where the components can fail.

1. INTRODUCTION

To provide the consistent actions in the networks with faulty nodes "the Byzantine agreements" methods are widely used. In case of not using the authentication of the exchanged messages one can come to an agreement if the number of faulty nodes doesn't exceed I/3 of the total number[2]. To our mind it's possible to overcome this limitation in the case we carry out the diagnostics of the faulty nodes of the network and in order to achieve agreement we ignore them.
The essence of a class of well-known procedures [3,4,5,6] for the computer networks diagnostics comes to the control computing by various nodes and to the results comparison. The results obtained by correct nodes are supposed to be different from the results of the faulty nodes. The merit of diagnostics procedures of this class is their distributed character. Each node processes the incoming data independently and takes a decision about the faulty nodes.
The class of procedures of the centralized diagnostics is known. They are carried out by a coordinator performing the diagnostic procedure and being elected among the interacted

components in a decentralized manner.
The method based on the network diagnostics is proposed. It enables to achieve the agreement performing group actions in the network which consists of 2k+2 nodes and not more than k field nodes.

2. SYSTEM MODEL

Assumption 1: The links between the nodes inside the distributed system may be presented by a complete undirected graph, i.e. each pair of nodes can exchange the messages.(Message sender is defined unambiguously).
Assumption 2: The system is synchronous, i.e. there is a mechanism, permitting all the system nodes to come to the diagnostics phase simultaneously.
Assumption 3: The nodes exchange the messages from the set $V = \{a, \bar{a}, \emptyset\}$ where a is a message, the semantics of which depends on a concrete case; $\bar{a}$ is a message opposite to a.$\emptyset$ - empty message, i.e. a message, when during the certain time interval a or $\bar{a}$ wasn't received along the communication channel.
Assumption 4: Each node by means of self-diagnostics defines its own state S(i).
The state can assume 2 values: OK (correct) and FAIL (failed).
Assumption 5: The following inequality is taken place:

$$DELAY_i = k*DELAY\_MESSAGE(i,j)$$

where $DELAY_i$ - the time the node i spent to send the message a or $\bar{a}$; DELAY_MESSAGE(i,j) - the time spent by node i to receive the message from the node j.

3. INFORMAL DISCUSSION OF THE PROBLEM

Let us consider the system consisted of 2k+2 nodes, where there is not more than k faults. Let the node i be the "general" 2 . Node i is to pass the message to each of the nodes. In such a case the nodes which do not meet the loyalty conditions 2 are to be defined, i.e. the contradictory message are sent to various "lieutenants".
Then, the loyal nodes having been defined, the agreement on "general's" "order" - "to attack" or "to retreat" should be achieved. If the diagnostics of the distributed system performed by each of the loyal nodes leads to the only solution concerning the "trators" (not to several variants of the solution), the agreement between the loyal "lieutenants" and the loyal "general" (if any) will be achieved, if each "lieutenant" considers the opinion of loyal "lieutenants" only (in the sense of the diagnostics results).
Suppose that a = I, $\bar{a}$ = 0, such that the unique number i (I, 2k+2) is applied to each node in the system. This number is known to all nodes of the system.

The algorithms proposed are completely distributed, i.e. they are performed by each of the nodes.

ALGORITHM 1.

Step 1: "general" sends the messages to all the rest nodes from the set $V = \{I, 0, \emptyset\}$.
Step 2: Each of the "lieutenants" sends the message received from the "general" at the step 1, to all of the rest "lieutenants". The "traitor" can send the contradictory messages to various "lieutenants". "Lieutenant" i forms from the messages received, a vector m_i, each component of which contains the message obtained from lieutenant at the step 2, with corresponding number, including in $m_i(i)$ its own message. For the convenience let us consider that after the arbitrary choice of "general" the renumbering of the nodes is performed in such a way that "general" takes the number 2k+2. Hence, now the vector m_i contains 2k+1 components from the messages received from all "lieutenants" at step 2.
Step 3: Each "lieutenant" i sends m_i to all "lieutenants" (and itself). From the vectors obtained at this step, each "lieutenant" forms the matrix M_j. Here the vectors m_i, received from "lieutenants" (i=1, 2k+1), are arranged as the matrix rows in increasing order of numbers of "lieutenants"-senders (according to assumption I, they may be defined unambiguously).
Step 4: Using the function majority to the matrix columns, we obtain one meaning of this function for each column. The vector maj_i=majority(M_i) is formed from these meanings.
Step 5: Mark the corresponding elements $M_i(j,l)$ of M_i matrix with the asterisks ( ) if the following specifications are performed:

$$maj_i(j) \neq M_i(j,l)$$

where $l = 1, 2k+1$; $j = 1, 2k+1$.

Step 6: Set up the expression:

$$\text{COND\_SUB\_M}_i = \bigwedge_{K=1}^{p} (i_k j_k) \qquad (1)$$

where p is the total number of the marked elements of the matrix M_i; i_k and j_k corresponding to the row and column number of the k-th marked element of M_i.

Step 7: Form from COND_SUB_M_i a set of conjunction SUB_M_i, containing not more than k-elements.
Step 8: Define variable ALGI_RESULT$_i$ such that:

a) ALGI_RESULT$_i$ = 0, if the set SUB_M_i contains one element; i.e. SUB_M_i = 1.

b) ALGI_RESULT$_i$ = 1, if SUB_M_i 1.

Step 9: The end of the algorithm.
The function majority may be defined in different ways. We'll

follow the function definition in [2]. Let the vector $e = \{e_i\}$ $(i=1,n)$ is given and let its digits are formed with the correspondance to meaning equality in groups M_1, M_2, ..., M_k not crossing each other. It's obvious that $(k \leqslant n)$. Let $|M_1| < |M_2| < \ldots < |M_k|$, where by $|E|$ the power of the set E is defined, i.e. the number of elements including.
If the digits $\{e_i\}$, being included into the group M_k have the meaning V, then the majority function is defined by the equality:

$$maj\ \{e_i\} = v$$

The Algorithm 1 is illustrated by an example. The system consisted of 8 nodes (k=3, 2k+2=8) is regarded in both cases. The faulty nodes are the "general" and the "lieutenants" with the number 4 and 7.
Example : The system under investigation is shown as graph (Fig. 1), where the "traitors" are marked by cross-hatching. For simplicity, only the links with the "traitors" and the meanings they send are shown in Fig.1.
One of the possible matrix, for instance M^1, is shown in Table 1a. Vector maj_1 is shown in Table 1b. In Table 1a according to step 5 of Algorithm 1 the elements of matrix are marked. They differ from the corresponding digits of maj_1 vector.

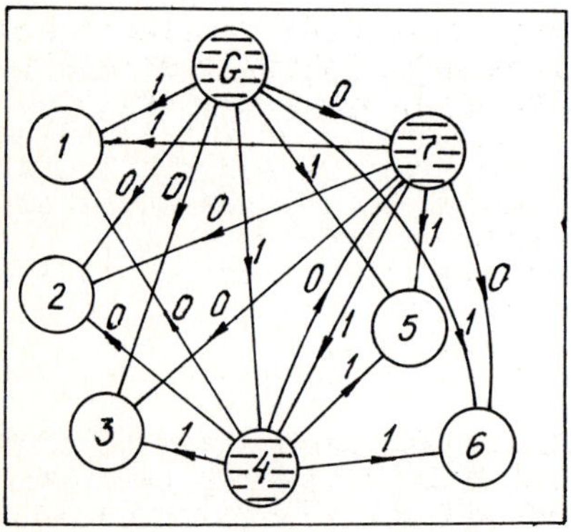

Fig.1

1	0	0	0	1	1	1
1	0	0	0	1	1	0*
1	0	0	1*	1	1	0*
1	0	0	0	1	1	1
1	0	0	1*	1	1	1
1	0	0	1*	1	1	0*
1	0	0	0	1	1	1

1	0	0	0	1	1	1

Table 1

According to step 6 of Algorithm 1 we have:

$$COND\_SUB\_M_1 = (2^v7)\ (3^v7)\ (5^v4)\ (4^v6)\ (6^v7) =$$
$$= 4.7 \text{ v } 2.3.4.6 \text{ v } 3.5.6.7 \text{ v } 2.3.5.6$$

Thus, there are 4 solutions for SUB_M_1. Now, take account of the fact that not more than k=3 faults are assumed by the system. We consider solutions presupposing the greater number of the "traitors" to be illegal. In such a case, the only legal solution for our SUB_M_1 is the matrix, where the

rows and columns with the numbers 4 and 7 are excluded.Let's refer to the remaining nodes - 1,2,3,5 and 6. It's clear that they received various messages from the "general" (unmarked digits of maj_1). Thus we come to the conclusion that the "general"'s behaviour was not loyal.
It may be shown that there exist cases with not only possible legal solution.

THEOREM 1: The right solution is always present among the solutions given by $COND\_SUB\_M_1$.
Proof: Let S = $s_1, s_2, \ldots, s_k$ is the set of "traitors". They send faulse messages either at step 2 or at step 3 of Algorithm 1. Thus marked elements of matrix M_p may appear either in row i S or in column j S. In both cases the marked elements can be presented as:

$$COND\_SUB\_M_p = \bigwedge_{j=1}^{k} (s_j \vee LOG\_MULT_j) \qquad (3)$$

where LOG_MULT_j is the logical multiplication of all row and columns that contain the marked elements in M_p at the crossing with row or column s_j. After the brackets having been removed in (3), the element $\bigwedge_{j=1}^{k} s_j$ is appeared, q.e.d.
Corollary: If $COND\_SUB\_M_i$ contains the only legal solution, this solution is correct. Note that the node i is a "traitor" if it sends various messages to loyal nodes at steps 2 or 3.

Now we must consider assumption 5. Absolutely reliable and strictly synchronous tests will be used below. Absolutely reliable are the tests containing no program faults, i.e. the tests of similar behavior irrespective of initial data to which they applied. Strictly synchronous are the tests the performing time of which is known to all the nodes of the distributed system at each node of the system.
The algorithm following to algorithm 1 is given below. Node i comes to performing the new algorithm only in the case when Algorithm 1 leads to AlGI RESULT = 1.

ALGORITHM 2:

Algorithm 2 consists of several stages. Each stage includes several phases. The mechanism assigning the node performing the diagnostics each stage is supposed to be present. Later such node will be refered as "tester". The stages differ from each other according to "tester". The "tester" isn't changed in the course of the stage. At each stage the algorithm assigns the "tester" operations and the nodes operation of being not the "testers" of the stage.
A. Node i is the "tester" of the stage.
Every phase of the stage includes the following steps:
Step 1: "Tester" sends the messages to other nodes. The messages may be as follows:
1a - "I'VE DEFINED THE TRAITORS". The message is sent in the case when "tester" having performed Algorithm 1 and the previous stages of the stage given, defined the faulty nodes unambiguously.

1b. "TO PERFORM THE TEST$_i^r$". The following test to be performed in phase r is announced. The tests assigned by node i are supposed to be available to each of the remaining nodes. Here node i knows the required time of each of the nodes j to process the following test (strictly synchronous tests). Define this time as DELAY_T$_i^r$(j).
In the course of time t = DELAY_T$_i^r$(j) node i sends "TO PERFORM THE TEST$_i^{r+1}$" to the node j , etc.

Step 2. "Tester processes the received messages.
2a. If in the course of time

$$t = \text{DELAY\_T}_i^r(j) + (n-1) * \text{DELAY\_MESSAGE}(i,j)$$

no message is received from j then the node i considers the node j to be faulty.

2b. If in the course of t (from 2a) a message:

RESULT$_i^r$(j); (messages from other nodes)

is obtained (result$_i^r$(j) is the result of the test processing by node j, assigned in the phase r by the "tester" i of the current diagnostics stage; the expression in the brackets is the message, obtained by node j from other nodes in phase r) the following facts are checked:

- the correctness of the test result;
- the time of receiving the answer. The strict time limits take place here.

They are defined by strictly fixed time periods for processing the tests and the time used to process the every message received. If one of these conditions is not met, the node is considered to be faulty and is excluded from the further consideration.

Step 3: The previously defined number of phases of current stage having been completed, node i after a small waiting (necessary in the case of different duration of test processing at different nodes) sends the mesage: "I'VE COMPLETED MY STAGE".
Note, that node i can complete its stage even earlier without expecting the completion of all the presupposed phases at this stage, if i comes to the unambiguous solution of the diagnostics problem of the distributed system. In such a case the stage completion is initiated by the message: "I'VE DEFINED THE TRAITORS".

B. The node is not a "tester".

Step 1: Having received the current task, the node sends information about the message it received to all the rest nodes. If there is one task in the system, "tester" is considered to be loyal; otherwise the given stage is missed.
Step 2: The node j processes the test$_i^r$(j) and, after the result being received the node j sends it to the "tester" and to other nodes. At the same time j receives messages from other nodes and they are also given to the "tester". The number of nodes, from which the messages have been received, are transmitted to the other nodes.
Each node composes "the history of the stages", where the

time for processing the stage phases is fixed. The conducting of this "history" is going on up to the beginning of its own stage, before the processing of which the "history" of previous stages is processed.
After the completion of its own stage, the "history" is being led again and is being processed after the completion of all the stages, i.e. all the diagnostics.

Step 3: The node processes "the history of the stages".
3a. It checks up the correctness of the test results, received from the nodes.
3b. It checks up if the actually spent time to receive the next message doesn't exceed the previously known time limit. If one of these conditions is not met, the node sending the message is considered to be faulty. If node j doesn't send any message concerning the result of certain phase of some diagnostics stage, the solution on given "silent" node is postponed up to the completion of all the stages. If even after the completion of the last stage there is no solution concerning j (silent all the time), the node j is considered to be faulty.
Let's prove the correctness of Algorithm 2.
We can single out the 3 following cases:
1. If the node i is a traitor, it sends the contradictory information at least once during all the stages of diagnostics Otherwise, the transtent fault is considered to take place during the performing Algorithm 1. If the illoyalty of i took place, then according to assumption 5, processing the following test it will delay by DELAY(i,j) and the "tester" will detect this. The transmission of the second message in current phase will be fixed in "the history of stages" of those nodes, to which the message was addressed. Beginning from the following phase the node, once being late, is not able "to make up" (for lost time) and it will be displayed as illoyal.
There is another possibility - the sending of a fault result of the tests. Then, according to failure of coincidence the node transmitted the fault result is declared to be illoyal [4] and [6] .
The illoyalty of behaviour is displayed also in such a way: the illoyal node "will conceal" its receiving the message from the loyal one, thus it "casts a shadow" on loyal node. In such a case there will be discrepancy between the time used to obtain the result of the $test_i^r(j)$, the processing of messages declared to "tester" and the limit, assigned to this purpose. Thus the illoyal node will be late again and this will make it possible for all the nodes to find out its illoyalty.
3. Special interest is provoked by the case when the node is "silent", i.e. it sends an empty message (Ø). It doesn't cause to the waste of time, on which the detecting power of Algorithm 2 is based and makes it different from Algorithm 1 and other appropriaches [4] and [6]. If during all the stage node i didn't receive any message from the node j, then after the last performing, i declare j to be illoyal. In such a case if j is really illoyal, it became clear to all whom he sent its messages (according to assum ption 5, it will be

late with the answer if it conceils its message receiving from i; ot its illoyalty will be disposed at any attempt to send the contradictory message).
If j is loyal but the communication path between two nodes is broken, the situation, when each of the loyal nodes will consider its neighbour along the failed communication path to be faulty, will tale place. The situation can be solved by suitable mechanism of the lower levels of data processing.

THEOREM 2: If the illoyalty of node j is firstly exposed during the test$_i^r$ performing, all the loyal nodes of the system will known of it not later than in phase (r+1) of the stage.

5. CONCLUSION

The algorithms, permitting to design the multileveled diagnostics system of the distributed computing system, are given: The idea of it lies in the adaptive increasing of diagnostics procedures power being dependent on the character of the faults arrised.
The 1-st stage of the diagnostics will be the Algorithm 1 performance. The usage of it seems to be effective in the case technical faults. If the class of faults is more extend, that is to be the illoyal behaviour including the deliberate operations in order to mislead the diagnostics, the more vital feature of Algorithm 2 - forcing the nodes to work at an extreme rate (without pauses between the tests), is to be used.

REFERENCES

1. Anderson T., Lee P.A. Fault-tolerance: Principles and practice, Englewood Cliffs N.J.: Prentice Hall Intern., 1981, 396.
2. Lamport L.,Shostak R.,Pease M. The Byzantine Generals Problem, ACM Trans.Program.Lang.a.Syst.,1982,vol.4,No3.
3. Hosseini S.H.,Kuhl J.G.,Reddy S.M. An integrated Approach to Recovery in Distributed Computing Systems, FTCS 13th Annu. Int.Symp.Fault-Tolerant Computing, Milano,28-30 June,1983, pp.56.63.
4. Dal Cin M. Distributed Diagnosis for Computing networks. Microprocess.and Microprogramm. - 14,1984, pp.139-144.
5. Reddy S.M.,Kuhl J.G. Distributed Fault-Tolerance in Computing Networks. - IEEE int.Symp.Circuits and Syst.,Proc. Montreal, 7-10 May,1984,Vol.1, pp.24-27,N.Y. 1984.
6. Amman E.,Brause R.,Dal Cin M.,Dilger E.,Luts J.,Risse T. ATTEMPTO: A Fault-Tolerant Multiprocessor working station; Design and Concepts, FTCS 13th Annu. Int.Symp. Fault-Tolerant Comput.,Milano, 28-30 June, 1983, pp.10-13, Silver Spring, Md,1983.
7. Garcia-Molina H. Electrons in a Distributed System.,IEEE Trans.Computers,Vol.C-31, pp.48-59
8. Schneider F.B. Fail-Stop processors, COMPCON Spring 83: 26 IEEE Comput.Soc.Int.Conf., San Francisco, Calif., Febr.28 - March 3, 1983, Dig.Pap.,New York, 1983, pp.66-70.

NETWORK PROTOCOLS

Network Information Processing Systems
K. Boyanov, R. Angelinov (Editors)
Elsevier Science Publishers B.V. (North-Holland)

OSI TRANSPORT LAYER: OVERVIEW AND ANALYSIS OF ISO STANDARDS

Dmitrij KUTZEVALOV and Sergej ROTANOV

The Institute of Electronics and Computer Science,
Academy of Sciences Latvian SSSR
14, Akademijas st., Riga USSR

This paper gives an overview of the status of International Sanddards on transport layer services and protocols. Consideration is given to the documents of International Standard Organization (ISO) that governs the services and protocols of the two types: 'connectionless' and 'connection-oriented'. Indicated are the peculiarities of each type and some problems arising during their use. Besides, the authors present the analysis of the ISO documents that governs an extended use of network service and the operation of class four transport protocol over the 'connectionless' network service. Some recommendations on the use of standards in question are given.

1. INTRODUCTION

In accordance with the ISO Reference Model of Open Systems Interconnection [1], the transport layer includes all the procedures, needed for providing a reliable and efficient data transfer among end systems. The existance of various data transmission network applied in practice as well as user requirements has led to the appearence of a number of standard protocols for transport layer with different functionality. The paper gives an analysis of currently existing standards for transport layer protocols and services:

- transport service definition for connectionless-mode transmission [2],
- transport service definition for connection-oriented transmission [3],
- transport protocol specification for connectionless-mode transmission [4],
- transport protocol specification for connection-oriented transmission [5],
- transport protocol specification for connection-oriented transmission, class four operation over connectionless network service [6],
- network connection management subprotocol [7].

The relationship among the enumerated ISO documents is conditionally shown in Fig. 1.

2. THE PECULARITIES OF TRANSPORT SERVICE

The connectionless transport service provides the transmission of Transport Service Data Units (TSDU) of limited length from a data source to a data sink by a single access of transport service without a preliminary establishment and subsequent release of a transport connection.

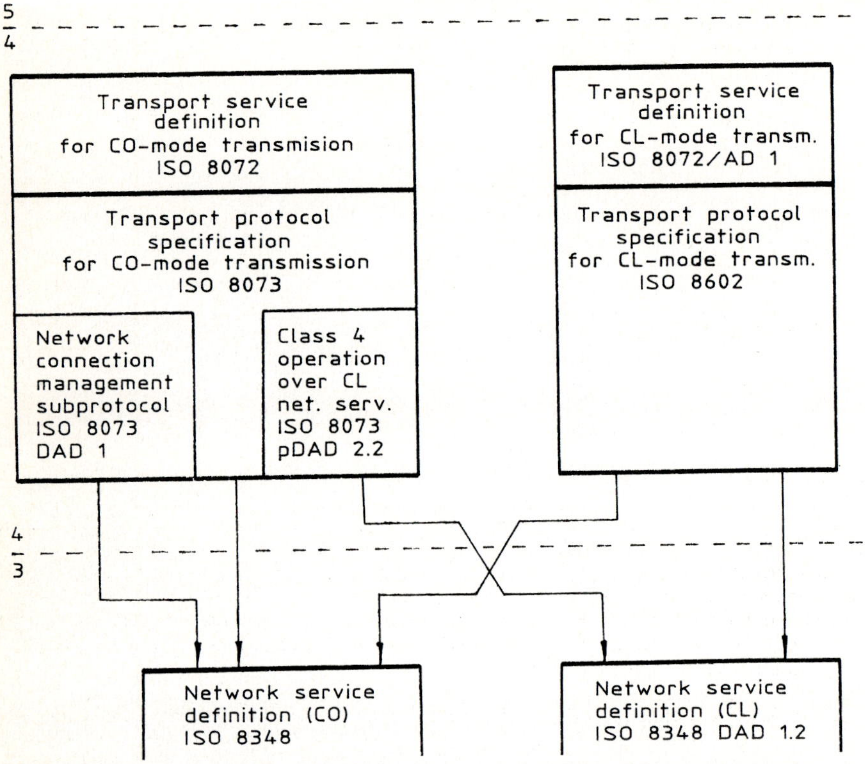

The service provider must have facilities for TSDU delimiting and transmitting while preserved their boundaries and contents.

The service includes two primitives: T_UNITDATA_request and T_UNITDATA_indication, which contain adresses, quality of service parameters and user data.

The connectionless transport service has the following peculiarities.

a) The guaranty that the initial sequence of TSDU's will be preserved does not exist. In the case of loss, distortion, or reordering of TSDU's neither the sending nor receiving user get informed about it (the appropriate service primitives are not used).

Such a solution can not be called an efficient one, since there are possibilities of indicating an unsuccessful attempt both in the transport protocol and in the network service used. For example, when using the connectionless network service, there is an additional facility (the N_REPORT_indication primitive) which allows to indicate unsuccessful transmission of a service data unit. Using the connection-oriented network service the transfer after which the release or reset of the network connection takes place within timer interval (see [4]) could be judged as unsuccessful. It is desirable that such kind of indication be introduced locally.

b) TSDU are transferred only between two service users. It means that neither multiadress nor broadcast transmission is provided when a unit is sent from one source to several destinations with the single invocation of transport service.

c) Document [2] determines the following QOS parameters, provided for the user, 1) transit delay; 2) protection from unauthorized access; 3) TSDU priority; 4) residual error rate.

It is essential that document [2] does not require that QOS parameters in the indication primitive be identical to that in the request primitive. The relation between these values depends on the specific application and the preliminary agreement about the use of the QOS parameters. Thus, for instance, the parameter "transit delay" in the indication primitive is allowed to indicate the delay which has been provided for the given specific TSDU. Since there is no dynamic negotiation about QOS parameters, the sender in effect does not know what are the real QOS parameters, but the receiver does not know to what degree the QOS has deteriorated in comparison with requested one.

Connectionless transport protocol contains no specific procedures to provide such QOS parameters as transit delay, protection and priority. To support these services the transport layer uses the appropirate services of the network layer. Thus, the real quality of transport services will be determined by the quality of the network services. The exeption is the residual error rate parameter, whose value indicates whether the chechsum must be used in the transport layer. Note that in this case a priory (i.e. before TPDU transmission) knowledge of the error level in the network connection is required.

Apart from the connectionless service, connection-oriented transport service contains a very large list of QOS parameters. These parameters are in good agreement with network service parameters. The mapping of QOS parameters between layers 4 and 3 for the transport connection request primitive (T_CONNECT_request), the network connection request primitive (N_CONNECT_request) and the transport connection organization TPDU (CONNECT_REQUEST) is shown in talbe 1. Thus the majority of QOS parameters are provided by the network services, while the role of the transport layer is reduced basically to the selection of a single or several network connections with the required QOS.

3. CONNECTIONLESS TRANSPORT PROTOCOL

The draft standart [4] describes two transmission modes for connectionless protocol: the connectionless transmission mode - with the use of connectionless network service (CLN), and the connection-oriented transmission mode - with the use of connection-oriented network service (CON).

The protocol with CLN can be characterized as the minimum functionality protocol: a single function provided by the protocol is the TPDU protection from distortions using the checksum. It must be remembered that use of such a protection is determined by the user for each TPDU, then, in principle, a situation is possible when the transport layer adds nothing to the network service, while requiring some overheads associated with the processing TPDU headers and TPDU transmission.

Table 1

Parameters mapping between transport and network service primitives

T_CONNECT_request primitive parameter	CONNECT REQUEST TPDU parameter	N_CONNECT_request primitive parameter
Connection establ. delay	-	Connection establ. delay
Connection establ. failure probability	-	Connection establ. failure probability
Throughput	Throughput	Throughput
Transit delay	Transit delay	Transit delay
Residual error rate	Residual error rate	Residual error rate
Resilence of conn.	-	Resilence of conn.
Transfer failure probability	-	Transfer failure probability
Connection release delay	-	Connection release delay
Connec. release failure probability	-	Connec. release failure probability
Protection	Protection	Protection
Priority	Priority	Priority

An essential similation for the users in this case is the limitation on the length of data transmitted. Since the segmenting function is not provided, the TSDU is always pucked into a single TPDU, which is transmitted in a single NSDU. Since the length of the latter is limited by the characteristics of data transmission network (the maximum permissible value is 64512 octets), TSDU length can not exceed this value minus the length of transport layer header (which has a minimum length of 8 octets). This is in agreement with the maximum TSDU length specified in the service definition [2], which equals to 63488 octets. In contrast to described above connection-oriented protocol, in this case the length of TPDU is not limited by any range of values and can be arbitrary chosen within the range of 1 octet up to the maximum length of NSDU.

The protocol with CON features higher functionality that the protocol with CLN. With the transmission of each TSDU the following actions are carried out - the establishment of network connection (or allocation of already establishment or free connection, if any), the transmission of a single TPDU which includes the entire TSDU, and the release of network connection (if needed).

After the network connection has been established both partners get equal rights for data units transmission and subsequent connection clearing. The latter is performed on condition that no data transmission request was issued during some prolonged period of time (the procedure is optional and may be substituted by a more suitable for a specific implementation).

It should be born in mind that the use of the network connection by both partners on the basis of equal rights can have undesirable consequences. Thus, under certain conditions, this can result in the loss of data of one of the partners. Fig. 2 shows one of the possible situations when the data unit sent by partner B does not reach partner A due to the fact that the latter has initiated the network connection release. Similarly, the situation is possible when the data unit sent by connection initiator does not reach its destination due to release initiated by the receptor (see fig. 3). It is easy to see that the mentioned loss takes place only due to the equal rights of the partners for the release of the network connection even in good network operation. To eliminate such situations it is desirable to introduce the following natural limitation: the network connection can be released only by the partner who has initiated its establishment.

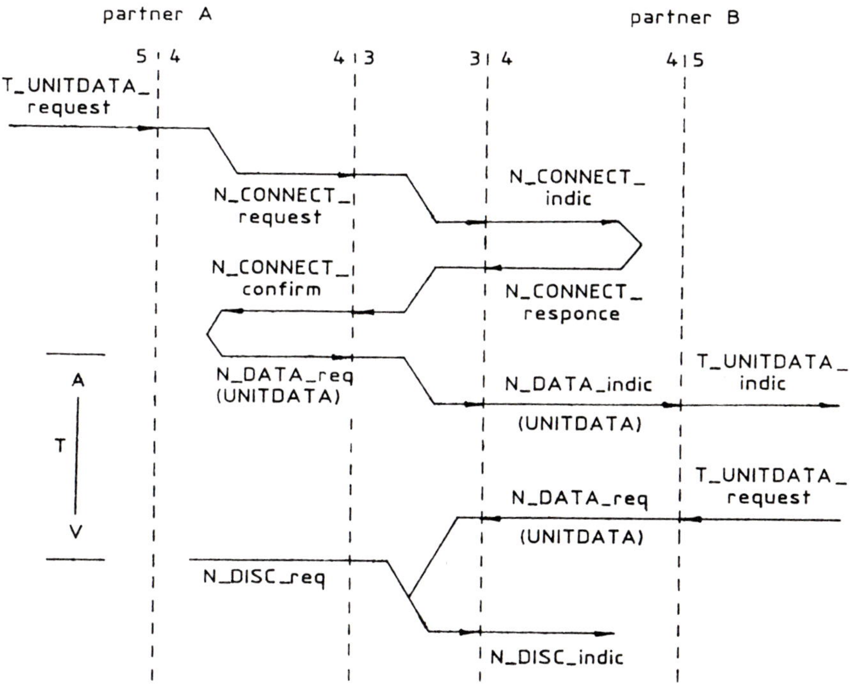

Fig. 2. Loss of data send by partner B

We should note that to satisfy the conditions of standard conformance it suffices to implement only protocol with CLN. The protocol with CON is optional and its implementation is up to the designer.

4. CONNECTION-ORIENTED TRANSPORT PROTOCOL

Standard [5] which specifies the connection-oriented transport protocol has received the fairly detailed analysis in literature. Less known is specific of the use of documents associated with standard [5] or developped on its basis.

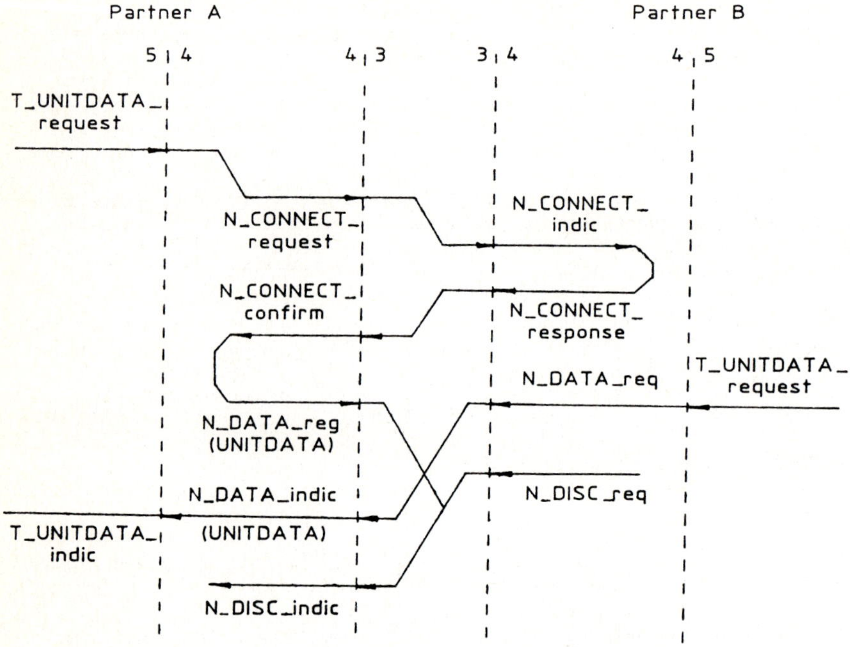

Fig. 3. Loss of data send by partner A

4.1. Connection-oriented transport protocol using connectionless network service

The draft addendum to the standard [6] allows to use the modified procedures of ISO transport protocol class 4 over the connectionless network service. The modification involves the following.

The connectionless network service includes only two service primitives (N_UNITDATA_request and N_UNITDATA_indication), which contain sender and receiver addresses, QOS parameters and user data. The TPDU being transmitted are placed into the "user data" parameter. Thus the single operations of iteraction between transport and network layers are transmission of N_UNITDATA_request primitive and reception of N_UNITDATA_indication primitive. Due to this fact in the modified class 4 protocol the following procedures are not present: - establishment and release of network connection; - the attachment and reattachment of transport connection to the network connection; - the multiplexing of transport connections into the network connection; - the splitting of transport connection over several network connections; - the reaction caused by the reset of the network connection.

The facilities used for association the accepted TPDU's with one of the transport connections are the references. However, in contrast to the standard protocol [5] in the assocaition procedure the references are not compared to the network connections.

Since no protocol of any other class can be used over the connectionless network service, there is no negotiation of classes in the modified transport connection establishment procedure.

The negotiation of maximum TPDU length is based on the same set of values, as in the [5], however, in this case it is allowed that this set be limited by the maximum size of the NSDU.

The reaction to incorrect TPDU's and protocol errors is reduced to the ignoring of them. ERROR TPDU is not used.

4.2. Network connections management

In order to improve the use of network connections the ISO has developped addendum [7] to the transport protocol [5], which allows,

1) both the initiator and the receptor to attach (or to reattach) the transport connection to the network connection;

2) to provide a transmission of more detailed information of the causes of disconnection of network connections in order to optimize their reestablishment;

3) to provide the identification of protocols (both standard and non-standard ones), which are used over the given network connection.

This task is solved using a special network management subprotocol. This protocol operates with the following data units:

- UN (Use of Network connection);
- NCM (Network Connection Management);
- DIAG (DIAGnostic);
- NCMC (Network Connection Management Confirmation).

The UN indicates in what way network connection will be used - either by single of by several transport protocols, and what exactly protocols are (i.e. standard ones, with connections or without connections, non-standard ones and so on). The UN unit is transmitted in the "user data" parameter of the N_CONNECT_request primitive.

The NCM unit is also transmitted in the "user data" parameter of the N_CONNECT_request primitive (this is necessary for recovery), to specify the method of recovery and the owner of connection. The owner can be both the receiving and the transmitting entity. Besides, the NCM unit may indicate that the right for connection have both entities. Then each of them has the right to multiplex transport connections into the network connections.

The DIAG unit is transmitted in the "user data" parameter of N_DISCONNECT_ request primitive and serves for specifying more precisely the reason of network disconnection (for example, the network connection is not needed any more, receptor congestion and so on).

The NCMC unit is transmitted in the "user data" parameter of the N_CONNECT_ response primitive. It contains only the code of the unit and is the response to the NCM unit.

The procedure which governs the use of units involves the following. Then the network connection is established the initiator sends UN, or NCM or both of them. If the partner agrees to use the network connection management subprotocol (Fig. 4), it responds with NCMC unit. The partner may reject the use of the subprotocol, i.e. to ignore the UN and NCM units. In this case the network connection will be used according to protocol [5].

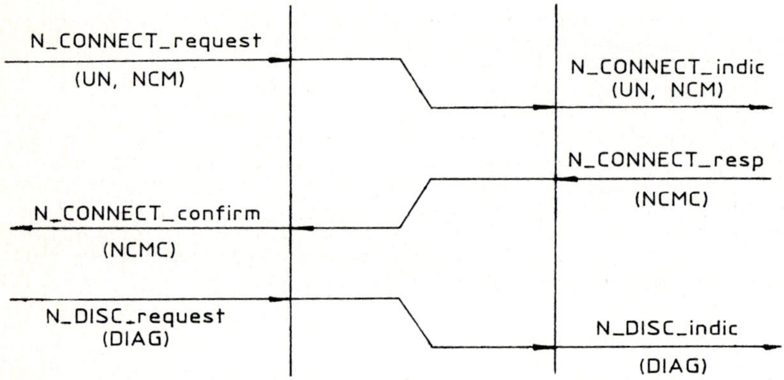

Fig. 4. Use of protocol data units for network connection management

The DIAG unit is sent only when the partner does not agree to establishment the network connection, or disconnects it (Fig. 4).

The protocol in question has also the facilities for detecting and eliminating the dublication of network connections (the situation of the collision of connection requests between the partners for which a single network connection is sufficient). Such a situation can be a consequence of the equal rights for the network connection, when each of the users attempts to reestablish the released connection, or can be a consequence of colision of requests for different network connections. In both situations one of the connections will ne eliminated.

Identification of protocol using the UN unit has the following percularities. According to [7], a transport entity must make use of one of the following procedures:

a) to transmit no data in the "user data" parameter of N_CONNECT_request primitive;

b) or to transmit UN TPDU in the "user data" parameter of N_CONNECT_ request primitive.

In the case a) the absence of user data is interpreted as an indication of the fact that connection-oriented transport protocol is used. This gives some possibility of interacting with the systems which implement only standard [5], since such systems transmit no information in the "user data" parameter and ingore such data in the primitives which they accept.

For the case b) the standard [7] presupposes the following identifiers:

- the identifier for connection-oriented transport protocol [5];
- the identifier for connectionless transport protocol [4];
- the identifiers reserved for specific applications.

The use of these identifiers involves the following. The network connection initiator puts the identifier of the protocol used into the appropriate field of the UN TPDU and transmits the TPDU in the "user data" parameter of the N_CONNECT_request primitive.

The network connection receipient indicates to its transport layer entity the N_CONNECT_indication primitive with the appropriate "user data" parameter. The transport entity decodes the UN TPDU, analyses the protocol identifier, and in the case of agreement responds with the N_CONNECT_ response primitive, but in the case of rejection - with N_DISCONNECT_ request. Unfortunately, the thus defined procedure does not safeguard against the erroneous negotiation, when the receipient which implements only standard [5] agrees to the proposal of use of protocol [4]. In this case the error will be detected only during the exchange of subsequent TPDU's.

5. FURTHER DIRECTIONS OF INVESTIGATIONS

The given overview has not covered the problems of use of CCITT Recommendations similar to the ones considered in the ISO standards (in particular, T.70 Recommendation), as well as the analysis of the formalized descriptions of transport protocols contained in the addendums to the ISO standards. Here we should note that in the whole the T.70 protocol is compatible with the standard ISO class protocol. However, the coding of the protocol identifier does not conform to the ISO coding, therefore in attempting to negotiate a protocol, the recipient which uses ISO procedures detects the error and releases the connection. Such a discrepancy must be eliminated.

Formalized descriptions of procedures in ISO standards are far from the perfection and require refinement and checking. In particular, there are no procedures which would allow to analyse the correctness of the received units and the response to the protocol violation by the partner.

Incompletness of description leads to the necessity of further definition of protocol. However, in doing this there is no garanty that protocol versions will be compatible between themselves (an example of such incompatibility is shown in [9]. Thus, the problem of development of the adequately complete standard formal specification of ISO transport protocols at the present moment is an open one and requires its solution.

REFERENCES

1. ISO/IS 7498. Inform. proc. syst. - Open syst. intercon. - Basic reference model.
2. ISO/IS 8072/ADDENDUM 1. Inform. proc. syst. - Open syst. intercon. - Transport service definition. Connectionless-mode transmission.
3. ISO/IS 8072. Inform. proc. syst. - Open syst. intercon. - Transport service definition.

4. ISO/DIS 8602. Inform. proc. syst. - Open syst. intercon. - Protocol for providing connectionless-mode transport service.
5. ISO/DIS 8073. Inform. proc. syst. - Open syst. intercon. - Connection oriented transport protocol specification.
6. ISO/DIS 8073/pDAD 2.2. Inform. proc. syst. - Open syst. intercon. - Connection oriented transport protocol specification. Class four operation over connectionless network service.
7. ISO/DIS 8073/AD 1. Inform. proc. syst. - Open syst. intercon. - Connection oriented transport protocol specification.
8. Ротанов С.В., Куцевалов Д.В. Формальная спецификация процедур транспортного уровня. В сб. Локальные вычислительные сети. Рига, ИЭВТ, 1986, с. 276-280.

Network Information Processing Systems
K. Boyanov, R. Angelinov (Editors)
Elsevier Science Publishers B.V. (North-Holland)

CONCURRENCY CONTROL IN OSI TRANSACTIONAL ENVIRONMENTS

Andrea Bondavalli and Enrico Gregori

C.N.R.- CNUCE, Via S. Maria 36, 56100 Pisa-Italy. tel. +39 50 593111

OSIRIDE [1] is the Italian Research Council heterogeneous, OSI-compatible network. The OSIRIDE project started at the beginning of 1982 and now OSI layers 1-5 are operational on computers of several manufacturers. Implementation of FTAM, the OSI file transfer, is underway. Within the OSIRIDE project team we are now analyzing possible further enhancement of the network services. One direction is that of providing a distributed transactional environment using OSI protocols. The OSI support available at the moment is a certain configuration of layers 1 to 6 according to CCR requirements plus CCR itself.

This paper contains a feasibility study and solutions to Concurrency Control in transactional environments based upon OSI-CCR. First the characteristics of some transactional models are briefly discussed. Our attention has been focused on three models that in our opinion are the most interesting and that in this paper will be referred as Serializability approach [Bernstein 81], Optimistic approach [Kung 81] and Spector Semantic approach on shared abstract data types [Spector 84]. Secondly OSI-CCR is introduced and its characteristics are pointed out, while in the last sections the feasibility of the support provided by CCR for each of these three Transaction Management approaches is discussed and solutions are proposed.

1. TRANSACTION CONCEPTS

Among the various definitions of transaction processing we assume Gray's definition [2]. A transaction is therefore defined as a sequence of operations on data with the following properties:

- atomicity: either all or none of the operations of any transaction are performed;
- durability: the effects of the operations of a transaction successfully completed will never subsequently be lost ;
- consistency: the effects of each transaction executed alone must be correct ;

It is important to point out that this definition is not intended to be a mathematically complete definition. We consider the above defined points as the major highlights of the transaction paradigm [3]. We shall denote a transaction T as a sequence (T, ai, ei)i=1,..,n of n steps, where T is an identifier for the transaction, ai is the action, at step i, of the transaction T on data ei.

Schedule: any sequence obtained by collating the actions of transactions T1,...,Tn is called a schedule for T1,...,Tn.

Dependency Relation: the dependency relation induced by schedule S, DEP(S), is a ternary relation on TxExT, where T is the set of transaction identifiers and E is the set of all the data, defined by (T1,e, T2) $\in$ DEP(S) iff for some i<j S = (..., (T1, ai, e),..., (T2, aj, e),...) and there is no k such that i<k<j and ek = e.

Equivalence: two schedules S1 and S2, are equivalent iff DEP(S1) = DEP(S2).

Serial schedule: a schedule S for T1,...,Tn is serial iff for some permutation π, S = Tπ(1),..,Tπ(n).

Consistency: any schedule S is consistent iff it is equivalent to some serial schedule. Of course, any serial schedule is assumed correct because every (complete execution of a) transaction must not violate any consistency constraint on data.

From the above definition of consistency it follows that a consistent (nonserial) schedule differs from a purely serial one only because some of the operations of different transactions which operate on different data can be executed in a different order. In [4] sufficient conditions for consistency are also given.

1.1. Serializability

As we can see, from the definition of consistency, the level of concurrency allowed is lower than the one we could intuitively expect. For example a schedule, which differs from a serial one only by the order in which two "read" operations on the same data are executed, is considered not consistent. In order to overcome such a limitation, the concept of serializability was introduced [5]. It refers to the effect of the schedule execution, more than to the structure of the schedule itself.

Serializability: a schedule is serializable iff it produces the same output and has the same effect on the database as some serial execution.

Bernstein gave sufficient conditions on the structure of schedules to assure serializability [5]. The key point of such approach stems from the fact that update operations are to be considered differently from other ones (read). Serializability always meets any consistency requirement because it is only based on syntactic information; it assures that each transaction cannot observe any (partial) inconsistency produced by other transactions concurrently executed. On the other hand systems which perform serializable execution never reach a satisfying amount of concurrency. In addition, as Spector points out, problems exist whose solutions don't require serializability. Such solutions can admit a higher amount of concurrency than that allowed by serializability. While becoming conscious of the drawbacks of serializability, people in the research community observed that the possibility of achieving satisfactory solutions to the problem of concurrency control was strongly related to the degree of knowledge on the semantics of data, as well as applications, available to the system. As a result several proposals exist that try to include as much semantic knowledge as possible into their models [6], [7] and [8] .

1.2. Synchronization On Shared Abstract Data Types

An interesting approach to the problem of defining models for concurrency control, is the one in which instead of considering a database as an unstructured collection of records the database itself is considered as set of instances of abstract data types, shared among applications [8]. The methodology arising from such approach consists in two steps:the first consists in giving suitable definitions of the operations of each data type and of dependencies between such operations (or classes of operations). The second step consists in characterizing the way in which the various dependencies affect the correctness of data using the semantic knowledge available from such definitions.

Dependency: Given a schedule S, a transaction Tj depends on a transaction Ti with respect to operations ak, al and data e iff Ti performs operation ak on data e and after Tj performs operation al on the same data e. Therefore a dependency D is an element of TxOp2xExT, where Op is the set of operations on the elements of E; such dependency will be denoted by Ti : ak $\rightarrow$ e Tj : al. We shall also say that Ti precedes Tj.

Dependency Relation: Given a couple of operations x y, the set {<Ti,Tj> for which exists e such that Ti : x $\rightarrow$ e Tj : y } forms a relation on transactions denoted by <xy.

Orderability: A schedule S is orderable with respect to a dependency relation <xy iff the transitive closure of <xy , tc<xy, is a partial order.

Generally we say that a schedule S is orderable with respect to a set of dependency relations <a1a2,<a3a4,..,<an-1an iff the transitive closure of the union of such relations is a partial order. It is worth noting that orderability is a rather general and powerful concept; it is very easy to prove that both consistency [4] and serializability [5] can simply be expressed as orderability with respect to particular sets of dependencies relations.

1.3. Optimistic approach

The approaches discussed before are both conservative; i. e., actions are verified, by performing checks or by assuring correctness, before being performed. This style is completely changed within the optimistic approach. This approach is characterized by the fact that checks on correctness of actions are performed after the end of the transactions which the actions belong to. Considerations to point out disadvantages of locking techniques (conservative approaches) and to support this approach are [9]:

1) lock maintenance represents an overhead not present in sequential case
2) there is no general-purpose deadlock-free locking protocol that provides high concurrency
3) locks cannot be released until the end of transactions
4) locking may be necessary only in the worst case.

Ideas behind Optimistic approach are :

a) reads are completely unrestricted
b) writes are severely restricted
c) any transaction consists of three phases
    1) read phase
    2) validation phase
    3) write phase

If in conservative approaches lock is necessary only in the worst case (conflicts between transactions) than in optimistic approach validation fails in the same worst case. The criterion used by Kung for verifying the correctness of concurrent execution of transactions has been serial equivalence; i.e., serialization. Given two transactions Ti and Tj with Timestamps T(i) and T(j) and $T(i) < T(j)$ conditions for serial equivalence are:

1] Ti completes w-phase before Tj begins r-phase
2] w-set of Ti does not intersect r-set of Tj and Ti completes w-phase before Tj starts w-phase

3] w-set of Ti does not intersect r-set or w-set of Tj and Ti completes r-phase before Tj completes r-phase.

2. CCR OVERVIEW

The International Standard for CCR (Commitment Concurrency and Recovery) is described by two Standards [10] and [11]. The aim of this standard is to enhance the services provided by the Presentation Layer in order to meet some of the requirements of the so-called "Transactional Applications" . The basic brick provided by CCR is the possibility of having a distributed computation with the Atomicity property. Within OSI a distributed application is modelled by a cooperation of application entities [12] and this means that generally more than one Open System will be involved.

The only structural limitation on the distribution is that the cooperating application entities must organize their activity into a tree structure. This tree may be built statically or dynamically with the inclusion of new branches as the Atomic distributed computation evolves.Distributed computation, coordinated by CCR, can be considered as a sequence of Atomic Action (AA) where each AA has the following properties (see [10]):

- it is directly or indirectly controlled by a unique application-entity
- it progresses without interference from external "actions"
- the parts of the atomic action performed by different application entities either

(i) all complete successfully; or

(ii) all terminate with no change to unvolatile/secure "AA bound" data and with the controlling application entity having available one or more diagnostic messages supplied by the other application entities involved in this AA.

A detailed analysis of the CCR documents also reveals other AA properties not contained in the official definition. The following is a more detailed list of the CCR AA properties:

- it is based on a two phase commitment protocol- a distributed two phase commitment protocol is used to coordinate the evolution of the AA

- it is distributed- pieces of elaboration take place in different Systems connected through an OSI network

- it is dynamically built - this means that the tree describing the AA distribution may be built dynamically according to the evolution of the AA

- it is centralized controlled- there is a unique application entity that directly or indirectly controls the AA

- it can be nested - The AA tree may be considered subdivided in subtrees; that is, the AA can be considered as subdivided in subAAs; a rollback (abort, backout are synonyms often found in the literature instead of rollback) of a single subAA doesn't necessarily imply a rollback of the entire AA.

- it is isolated - The AA defines a clear boundary. AA temporary data are invisible to the external environment until commitment. Concurrency control hides the effects of an AA from other concurrent AAs therefore guaranteeing isolation. The standard doesn't explicitly define a concurrency control strategy.

3. COMMENTS ON THE STANDARD

The comparison between the CCR standards and transactions management systems immediately shows an extremely important point: the concurrency control strategy is not specified in the OSI documents.CCR when addresses the problem of concurrency, only states that any strategy compatible with the AA properties can be applied. Note that the *concurrency control strategy* is a core characteristic of any transactional environment. It is also very important to point out the strict correlations between concurrency and the performance of the local Operating System. In fact concurrency control is only a particular aspect of resource management.

Among the CCR features, *isolation,* is the one directly correlated to the concurrency control. In OSI-CCR standard it is stated (par 5.4) that "Each application entity accesses resources within its own open system and makes changes to these resources as part of the operation of an atomic action. Local mechanisms, such as locking, are used to provide concurrency control".

The design of a distributed transaction management system requires the definition of the global strategy for concurrency control, such as serializability, orderability, serializability without cascading aborts, etc. Each system is then "free" to chose a local mechanism to provide concurrency control provided that this mechanism correctly supports the global strategy chosen. In fact, it is extremely difficult to imagine general strategies (non ad hoc) for concurrency control that can be managed in a completely local way and based on completely independent mechanisms on the various systems. Furthermore, even if mechanisms are local to each open system, there must be an agreement on these mechanisms because all of them must guarantee the correct local application of the selected distributed strategy. In fact, compatibility among the mechanisms locally used must be guaranteed. For example, serializability may be obtained by means of locking or timestamps, but global correctness is hard to achieve if some systems use locking and others use timestamps.

In appendix B 8.2 of the standard it is said " Concurrency control ensures that if bound data is changed other than by an action, commitment doesn't occur." This sentence seems to enforce the isolation characteristic that it is said CCR/AA must have; if this indication is exactly followed, the possible criteria (which derive as logic consequence) are serial execution of transactions or at best (from the amount of concurrency admitted) the serializability criterion while correctness criteria weaker than serializability seem to be forbidden.

Another sentence to be commented is: "Concurrency control assures that if an atomic action uses (as bound data) data which is subject to rollback by some other action, then the action is not committed until (unless) the earlier action commits". This sentence clarifies the position of OSI/CCR about cascading aborts: it states that the possibility of having cascading aborts must be given or better yet that in the strategy for concurrency control nothing should be done to prevent them. We may agree with this position, we just want to recall that in many proposals one of the requirements for transaction management systems is to prevent cascading aborts.

4. INTEGRATION BETWEEN CCR AND CONCURRENCY CONTROL

In order to solve the problem of concurrency control we first have to decide which global strategy we want to adopt and than the possible local mechanisms. In the following we analyze three case studies hypothesizing an a priori agreement on the global strategy and the local mechanism between the entities involved in the distributed transaction. In all these case studies the correctness criterion is serializability.

4.1. Serializability with locking

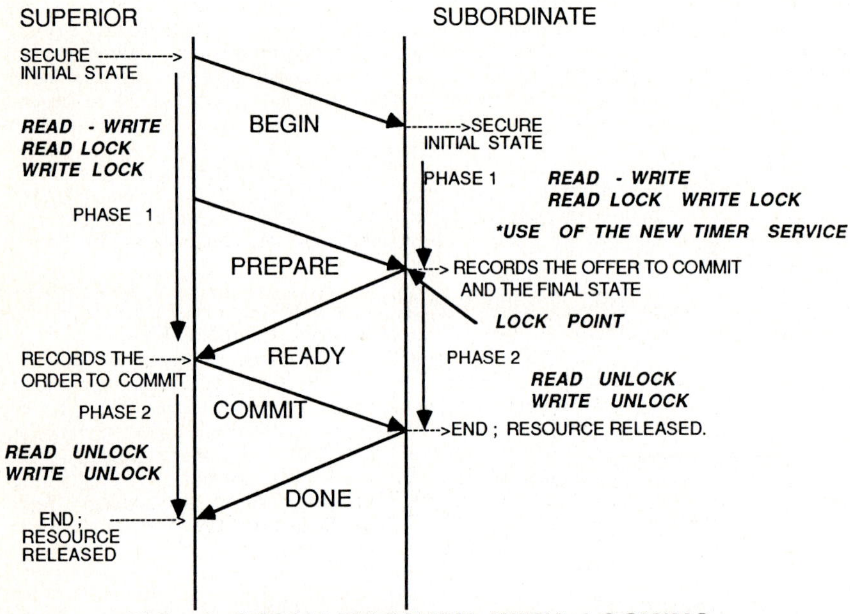

FIG. 1 SERIALIZABILITY WITH LOCKING.

The concurrency control related features required in this case are pointed out in bold letters in figure 1. Each transaction component (both CCR Superiors and CCR Subordinates) in Phase 1 use mechanisms such as readlock and writelock to control resource access. Note that read/write locks may cause an a priori unpredictable processing time and therefore the introduction of a service to enable a subordinate to ask the superior an increment of the waiting time without ordering rollback has been envisaged as extremely important. This service is referenced in figures 1,2,3 as *new timer service*. The end of phase 1 is often called in the literature LOCK POINT . If a subordinate completes its work up to the lock point than its answer to a Prepare indication can only be a Ready request. During phase 2 read/write lock are released. Note that this policy may generate deadlocks, therefore a dealock resolution distributed manager is always required in this class of distributed transactional systems. Different deadlock resolution strategies can be used [13] often requiring the abort of one or more transactions; so a service to ask the master to abort the transaction is required.

4.2. Serializability with timestamps

The additional features required in this case are pointed out in bold letters in figure 2. The transaction master must define a timestamp. For instance it can be composed of master's name, master's time and a predefined precedence rule between masters' title. In any case, any collection of information enabling a total unambiguous ordering of the transaction is applicable. The timestamp must be transported in the C-Begin. The User Data or the Atomic Action Identifier parameters can be used . The timestamp is used to manage the conflicts between transactions. It is meaningless to talk about release of resources in this case because there isn't any resource acquisition. Therefore the phrase, found in figure 5 -at the end of phase 2 - in ISO CCR service document, "RESOURCE RELEASED" is wrong. But this figure belongs to an Appendix and not to the standard. The standard doesn't explicitly forbid this policy. Sometimes the only way to solve conflicts between transactions is by aborting one or more of them. Therefore a service to request a transaction master to abort is essential for the conflict resolution.

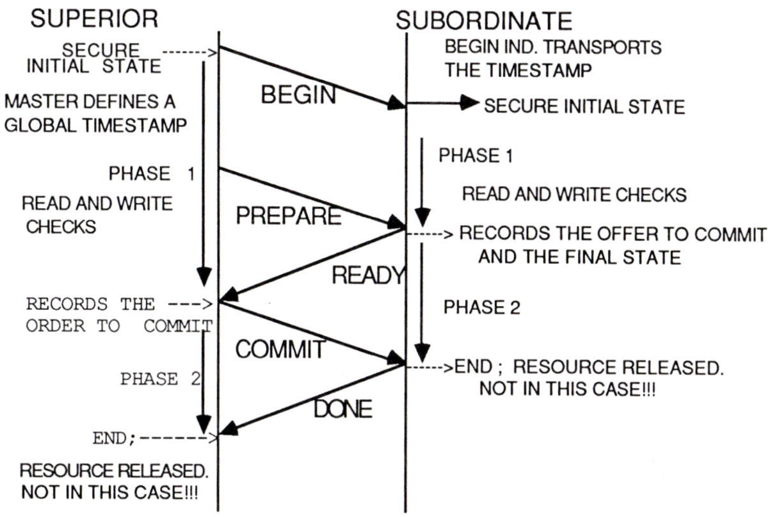

FIG. 2 SERIALIZABILITY WITH TIMESTAMPS.

4.3. Optimistic Approach

The additional features required in this case are pointed out in bold letters in figure 3. The core phase of this method is the validation. This action must be carried out by a local validator (the concurrency manager). In order to do its job this manager must apply the three conditions defined in section 1.3 to every transaction. Therefore, up to date information on each transaction must be provided. A transaction descriptor contains at least read/write working sets and timestamps. It is created and initialized upon reception of the Begin indication and dynamically updated in the read phase. To process the Prepare indication means that the validation phase is going to start and therefore the read and write sets are completely defined. When validation ends up, an answer to the Prepare is sent; Ready request, if positive validation, Refuse request otherwise. At the end of the second phase the transaction descriptor is frozen for a certain time; it cannot be immediately destroyed because this information may be required by the validation of some younger transaction; i.e., those ones started before the termination of the transaction (see condition 1 in section 1.3).

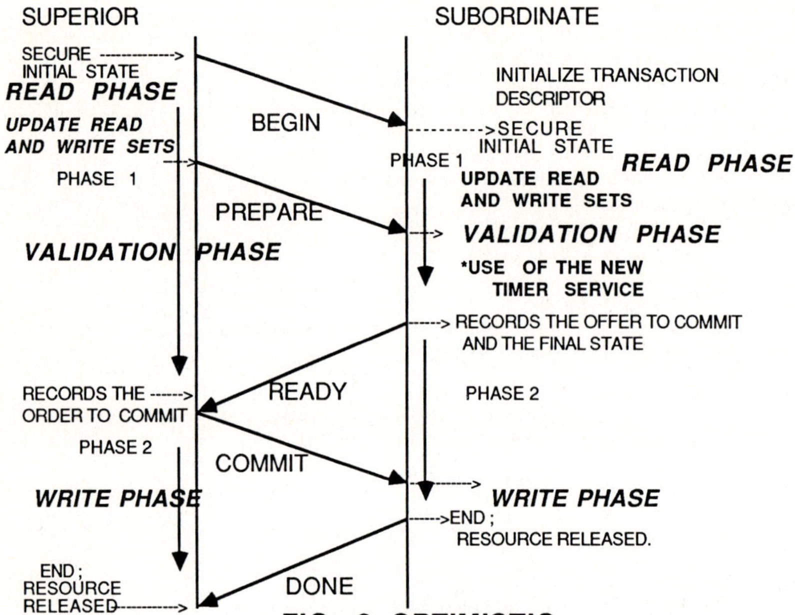

FIG. 3 OPTIMISTIC.

5. CONCLUSIONS

CCR has to be extended to fulfill the requirements of a transactional environment. Some recent correctness criteria for concurrency control (see sect. 1.2) don't completely fit with the atomic action characteristic. Others, well established, such as serializability and optimistic approach fit but a lot of work, namely the global concurrency control management, has to be done. Concurrency control management means:

- definition of global concurrency control strategy
- definition of local mechanisms applicable (each system shall adopt one of those possible)
- final correctness analysis i.e. the proof of a deadlock-free environment. Deadlock can be prevented or eliminated. In the latter case distributed tools to eliminate deadlock have to be defined.

From the above it can be seen that it is extremely difficult to build a standard transactional environment mainly because of a lack of standardization on a fundamental feature: the concurrency control. The ISO transactional standards defined so far [10], [11] don't solve the global problem of transaction processing. They can only be considered as a basic brick of the future standard transactional environment.

REFERENCES

[1] F. Caneschi, E. Gregori, L. Lenzini,
"OSIRIDE: State of the Art and Future Developments", Proceeding of the Eigth Int. Conference on Computer Communication", Munich, F.R.G., 15-19 September 1986, pp. 84-88.

[2] Jim Gray
"The Transaction concept: Virtues and Limitation"; IEEE Proc. of 7th International Conf. on very large Databases; Sept 1981.

[3] T. Haerder, A. Reuter
"Principles of Transaction-oriented Database Recovery"; ACM Computing surveys, Vol. 15, No. 4, Dec 1983.

[4] K.P. Eswaran, J.N. Gray, et al.
"The notion of Consistency and Predicate Locks in a Database System"; ACM Communications Vol. 19, No. 11, Nov 1976.

[5] P.A. Bernstein, N. Goodman
"Concurrency Control in Distributed Database Systems"; ACM Computing Surveys Vol. 13, No. 2, June 1981.

[6] H.F. Korth
"Locking Primitives in a Database System"; Journal of the ACM, Vol. 30, No. 1, Jan 1983.

[7] H. Garcia-Molina
"Using Semantic Knowledge for Transaction Processing in a Distributed Database"; ACM Transactions on Database Sys., Vol. 8, No. 2, June 1983.

[8] P.M. Schwarz, A.Z. Spector
"Synchronizing shared abstract types" ACM Transactions on Computer systems, Vol. 2, No. 3, Aug1984.

[9] H.T. Kung, J.T. Robinson
"On Optimistic Methods for Concurrency Control"; ACM Trans. on Database Systems, Vol 6, No. 2, June 1981, pp 213-226.

[10] ISO/TC 97
" Information processing Systems - Open Systems Interconnection - Definition of Application Service Elements - Commitment, Concurrency and Recovery";

[11] ISO/TC 97
"Information processing Systems - Open Systems Interconnection - Specification of Protocols for Application Service Elements - Commitment, Concurrency and Recovery";

[12] ISO/TC 97
" Information processing Systems - Open Systems Interconnection - Basic Reference Model";

[13] D.J. Rosenkrantz, R.E. Stearns, P.M. Lewis II
"System level Concurrency Control for distributed database systems", ACM Transactions on Database Systems, Vol 3, No. 2, June 1978, pp 178-198.

Network Information Processing Systems
K. Boyanov, R. Angelinov (Editors)
Elsevier Science Publishers B.V. (North-Holland)

BEHAVIOR OF A NEW MIXED SELF-ADAPTIVE MULTIPLE ACCESS PROTOCOL AND COMPARISON WITH THE CSMA/CD PROTOCOL

R.Z. HALIABALIAS and S.A. KOUBIAS

Computer Technology Institute of Patras
Technological and Educational Institute of Patras
Patras, Greece

In this paper we present a new protocol which combine the operation of a random access protocol and the behavior of a fixed access protocol using a new network topology. The new protocol employs an adaptive scheme that switches between the random access state and the fixed access state according to the channel's load. we give some simulation results for this new protocol that are compared with the corresponding results of the non-persistent CSMA/CD protocol.

1.INTRODUCTION

Local Area Networks are characterized in terms of their topology and the distributed algorithms (multiple access protocols) used by the stations to share the channels that are avai lable for the network users communication. Two dominane archi tectures are used for the users' connection, the broadcast bus (bidirectional or unidirectional) and the ring (single and double) systems.

There are several categories of maltiple access protocols for the bus LANs like the random access protocols and the fixed access protocols. The random access protocols offer good performance at low values of channel traffic, while the fixed access protocols offer good channel utilization at high channel loads.(1), (2),(3) and (4). In the broadcast systems where there is a bidirectional transmission medium, random access schemes like the Carrier Sense Multiple Access (CSMA) schemes are used. The most popular multiple access protocol is the Carrier Sense Multiple Access with collision detection (CSMA/CD) which is obtained by introducing the collision detection capability in the original CSMA protocols proposed by Kleinrick and Tobagi (5). The performance of CSMA type protocols degrades as the ratio $\tau * W/B$ increases (where τ: is the end to end propagation delay of the channel, W : is the channel bandwidth and B : is the packet length in bits). So these schemmes exhibit performance limitations when the channel bandwidth is high or the geographical area to be spaned is large (6).

The broadcast bus systems that use unidirectional transmission medium as Expressnet (7) and Fasnet (8) attempt to overcome these limitations. Another type of Networks that try to achieve the same goal is the Multichannel Local Area Networks. In this kind of networks a set of M separate bidirectional channels is used eachone with W bandwidth and equal length l instead of one bidirectional channel with bandwidth Wt=M*W and length l. Several schemes that belong to this category and use CSMA/CD protocols are proposed by Marsan and Roffinella(9)

The trend, today, is to combine the advantages of robust random access protocols (principally of the CSMA/CD) with the operation of a deterministic protocol in order to create a mixed protocol with small packet delay for low channel traffic and deterministic behavior for heavy channel traffic. A mixed protocol can be used in a bursty type communication as well as in applications where bounded delay is needed (voice and video signal transmission). Another point of interest is to reduce the influence of increasing a parameter in the CSMA type protocols.

In this paper a new mixed self-adaptive multiple access protocol is presented. Also a new network topology is proposed in which the users are connected via one buffet in two bidirectional communication channels.

The paper is organized as follows. In section II we give an analytical description of the rules for the new protocol. Section III contains simulation results relating throughput and packet delay to system and traffic parameters of the new protocol and comparison of the results with the corresponding results of the non-persistent CSMA/CD protocol. Also in this section a discussion is made about the simulation curves and the behavior of the new protocol.

II. SYSTEM DESCRIPTION

In the proposed system the users are connected via one buffet (with capacity one) with two bidirectional channels so that every user can sense or transmit only in one channel.

The concept of using more than one bidirectional communication channels for CSMA/CD type networks has adopted by Marsan and Roffinella (9) but it is quite different from the idea of the scheme proposed in this paper. The basic difference is that in (9) the users are connected in M channels via M interfaces-buffers, while in the proposed topology the users are connected with two bidirectional communication channels via one buffer. Some other differences that exist deal with the operation of the protocols.

Eachone of the channels has W bits/sec bandwidth so that the total available bandwidth is 2*W. Time axis is assumed to be minislotted with duration of each minislota=(r*W)/B. It is assumed that the length of transmitted packets is constant and the format of the packets is similar to the format described in the standards IEEE 802.3 and IEEE 802.4. The header of the packet that contains the preamble, the sourse and the destination addresses fields is equal with the 1/20 of the whole packet length. Also it is assumed that the packet arrival process is a Poisson process and there is a finite number, N, of users.

The symbolism sl, dl (S2,d2) denotes the sourse and the destination addresses of the packet transmitted in channel-1 (channel-2) when there is no transmission in chanel-2 the users that"are" in channel-1 operate like in the 1-persistent CSMA/CD protocol (10), with $\gamma=2$ and retransmission probability equal to 0.1 (where γ is the time - in minislots needed to sense the occurence of a collision all the users in the network) with the following variations: When a packet is transmitted successfully in channel-1 (in fig. 1 user #2 sends a packet to user #7) all the users (except Sl and dl), after the sensing of the source and the destination of the packet "switch" the channel-2 (this is shown with dash lines in fig. 1).

If there is a packet transmission in channel-2 these users wait until the end of this transmission if there is any)they act as following: if a user wants to transmit a packet in channel-2 (in fig. 1 user #6) transmitts a short control signal and he senses the channel after a seconds. After this there are two cases:

i) the control signal is transmitted successfully so that the transmitter of that signal can send his packet from the begining of the next minislot

ii) the control signal is collided (this means that more than one users attempted to transmit like user #5 and user #1 in fig.1) so a resolution period follows the collision. This resolution period consists of a number of minislots each of them corresponds in one user that operate in channel-2 with the following characteristics:

a) it begins with the minislot that corresponds to the user with address next to sl

b)it holds until the corresponding minislot of the first user that wants to transmit when he starts his transmission (11)

c)it doesn't contain corresponding minislots to sl, dl

d)contains corresponding minislots to the previous S2,d2 but these minoslots can not be used because the users s2, d2 (previous) don't know always the current sl, dl.

The users of channel-2 (except s2, d2) after the sensing of the header of the transmitted packet, "switch" in channel-1. After the end of the existing transmission -if there is any- they participate in a resolution period that was described for channel-2 with the following defferences from that:

a) the users (like users #0, #7 and #8 in fig. 1) that want to transmit a packet with destination s2 or d2 can reserve for that by transmission of a "1" in the corresponding minislot

b)this period can be finished with none of users have been transmitted (like the resolution period that consists of minislots corresponding to the users #8,#9,#0,#1,#2,#3,#4 and#6)

when a similar with CSMA/CD like period (as it is described above) begins
c)it begins a seconds after the transmission that exists in channel-1
d)no control signal is transmitted
with respect to (a) we must say that if the users that reserve for a transmission in channel-2 are more than one and their addresses are not equal with dl then the user with the smaller address predominates and the way of the operation of the users that will "switch" in channel-2 (after the sensing of sl, dl) will be full deterministic. This will be happen because the user that made the reservation can transmit in channel-2 after a seconds of the transmission that probably takes place there.

In the example that is shown in the fig. 1 there is one resolution period in channel-1 that consists from minislots corresponding to the users #6,#7,#8,#9,#0 and #1. If three of these users (#0,#7 and #8) reserve for transmission in channel-2 by transmitting of an "1" in the corresponding minislot then the user that would be the transmitter in channel-2 (according to their addresses) is the user #0 but after the transmission of the header of the packet the user which acquire the rights of transmission in channel-2 is the user #7. We can conclude from the above that in heavy traffic conditions, when reservations are made in channel-1 for transmissions in channel2, then the performance of the protocol approach the 99 % utilization of the channel-2. This utilization is the maximum possible that can be obtained in a bidirectional communication channel since a seconds must follow after one successful transmission in order to sense all the users the end of the transmission. The users that "are" in channel-2 (exept the users #5 and #7) after the sense of the header of the packet that is transmitted in channel-2 "switch" in channel-1 where they participate in a resolution period. This period finishes with none of the users have attempted transmission in channel-1 so a CSMA/CD type period starts (similar to that which is refered in the begining of this section) while the reservations that probably made for transmissions in channel-2 are not valid any more. This is another indication of self adaptation of the protocol since in light channel loads approaches the CSMA/CD protocol.

III. RESULTS - DISCUSSION

The new protocol is compared with the non-persistent CSMA/CD (with $\gamma = 2$ and retrasmission probability equal to 0.1).It is noted here that for the CSMA/CD there is a communication channel with bandwidth 2*W, length l,length of transmitted packets B and a0=(2*r*W)/B. In the new protocol there are two buses, eachone of them has bandwidth W, length l, length of transitted packets B and a1=a2=(r*W)/B. It is evident that a1=a2=a0/2. Also, the normalization of the delay is assumed with respect to the transmission time T0=B/(2*W) of one packet for the single channel.

In fig. 2.7 the relation throughput vs delay is described for the two compared protocols. The parameters that are changed in these curves are the value of a, the number N of users and the duration of jamming period. For the curves of the fig.2-4 is taken N=10 while in fig. 5-7 is taken N=20.

From the simulation results we can say that CSMA/CD behaves a little better in light traffic conditions but in heavy loa-ds the new protocol predominates. The superiority of the new protocol is obvious:

i) when the a increases
ii)when the jamming period becomes equal to 1

The i) happens because the performance of the two compared protocols is affected from the value of a (because both use bidirectional communication channels) but an increasing of a has different results in the performances of the two pro-tocols since a1=a2=a0/2. The ii) is due in the conflict free operation that the new protocol presents in the heavy traffic conditions where the jamming period doesn't affect the performance of the new protocol opposite with the CSMA/CD. The last observation explains the reason why the curve of the new protocol for given a,N and jamming period equal to 0 concides with the curve (for the same protocol) with the same a,N and jamming period equal to 1 under heavy traffic condi-tions.

In every pair of curves that is refered in given a,N and Jam-ming period there is an intersection point that devides the scheme in two regions: the region of light load and the re-gion of heavy load in every one of them dominates defferent protocol. The worse behavior of the new protocol in light traffic conditions is due to the insufficient utilization of the channel-2 because under these conditions of traffic the larger number of transmissions occurs in the channel-1(accor-ding to the rules of the CSMA/CD type protocol) in addition the available bandwidth of channel-2 is the half of the band-width that has the channel that operates with the rules of the non-persistent CSMA/CD protocol so the normalization of the delay with respect to the duration of a packet transmis-sion in the later channel has as consequence the reduced performance of the new protocol. In the heavy traffic condi-tions begins the sufficient utilization of the channel-2. This happens because the resolution periods become small and reservations are made in the channel-1 for transmissions in the channel-2.

The intersection point that is refered above transposes to the start of axes for N=20 in relation with the corresponding curves that exists for N=10. This is due in the efficient utilization of the channel-2 under light traffic conditions because the number of users is now larger.

IV. CONCLUSIONS

In this paper a new mixed self adaptive protocol was presented which combines the operation of a CSMA/CD-like protocol and the behavior of a deterministic protocol using a new network topology. According to this topology users are connected with two bidirectional communication channels via one buffer. The simmulation results show the high performance of the new protocol in light loads and the optium performance in heavy traffic.

V. REFERENCES

1. F.A. Tobagi, "multiaccess protocols in packet communication systems, " IEEE Trans. Commun., vol.COM-24,pp.208-216,April 1980.
2. J.F. Kurose, M. Schwartz and Y. Yemeni, "Multiple Access protocols and Time-constrained Communication, "ACM Computing Surveys, Vol. 16,pp.43-70,March 1984.
3. S.A.Koubias and G.D. Papadopoulos, "Analysis of an adaptive multiple access protocol (ATP-1) with mixed structure," IEE Proceedings Vol. 134, pt.E,No.1,pp. 54-60,Jan. 1987.
4. S.A.Koubias and G.D. Papadopoulos, "Further results of the performance of the adaptive MAP ATP-2 for bus Local Area Networks", to appear in the IEEE Transactions on Computers.
5. L. Kleinrock and F. Tobagi, "Packet switching in radio channels: Part I, Carrier Sense Maltiple Access modes and their troughput delay characteristics, " IEEE Trans. Commun. pp. 1400-1416, vol. COM. 23, Dec. 1975.
6. F.A. Tobagi and M. Fine, "Performance of unidirectional broadcast local area networks Expressnet and Fasnet, "IEEE select. Areas Commun., Vol. SAC-1,pp. 913-926,Nov.1983.
7. F. Tobagi, F. Borgonovo and L. Fratta, "Expressnet : A high performance intergrated-services local area network, "IEEE Select Areas Commun., Vol. SAC-1, pp. 898-913,Nov.1983.
8. J.O.Limb and C. Flores, "Description of Fasnet- A unidirectional local area communications network, "Bell Syst. Tech. J., Vol. 61,pp. 1413-1440, sept. 1982.
9. M. Ajmone Marsan and D. Roffinella, " Multichannel Local Area Network Protocols, "IEEE Select. Areas Commun., Vol. SAC-1, pp. 885-897, Nov. 1983.
10. F.A. Tobagi and V.B.Hunt, "Performance analysis of carrier sense multiple access with collision detection, "Comput. Networks, Vol.4, pp. 245-259, October 1980.
11. L. Kleinrock and M. Scholl. "Packet switching in radio channels: New conflict free multiple access schemes, "IEEE Trans. Commun., Vol. COM-28, pp. 1015-1029, July 1980.-

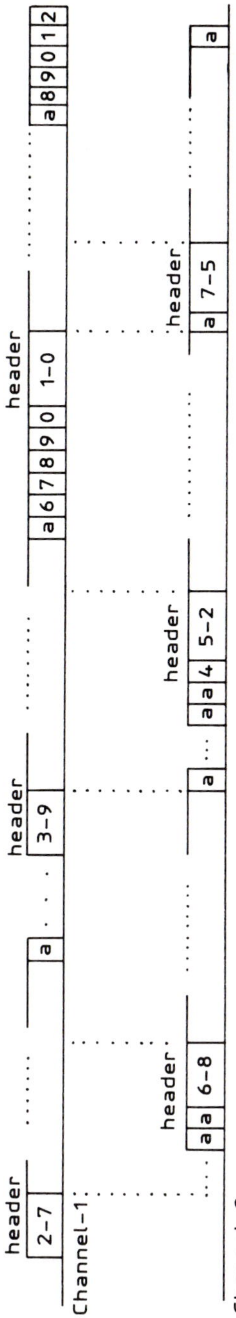
header
2-7
Channel-1
header
a
3-9
header
a 6 7 8 9 0 1-0
a 8 9 0 1 2
header
a a 6-8
Channel-2
a
header
a a 4 5-2
header
a 7-5
a

Fig. 1

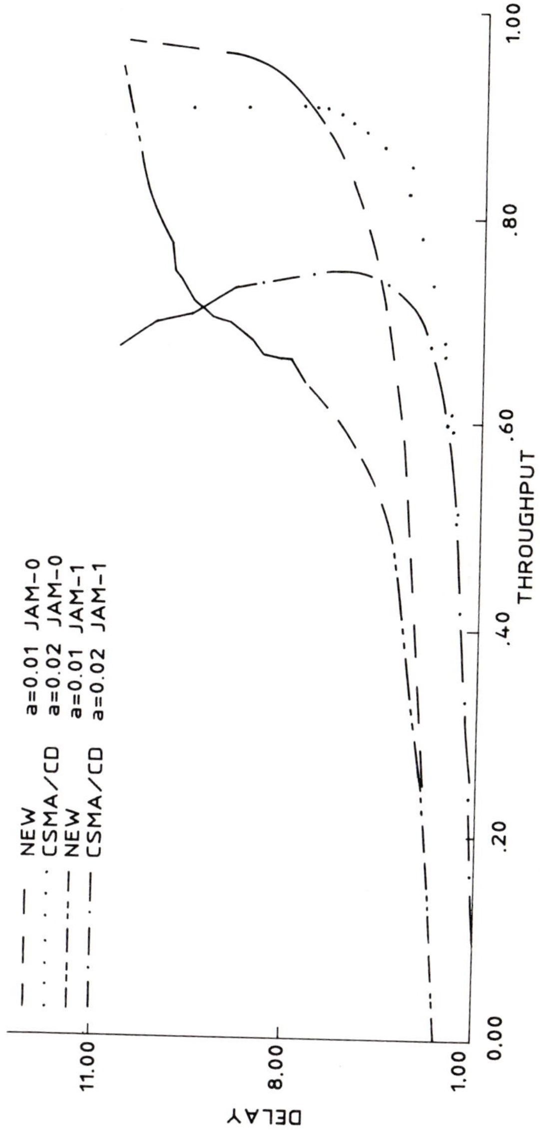
NEW a=0.01 JAM-0
CSMA/CD a=0.02 JAM-0
NEW a=0.01 JAM-1
CSMA/CD a=0.02 JAM-1
DELAY
11.00
8.00
1.00
0.00
.20
.40
.60
.80
1.00
THROUGHPUT

Fig. 2

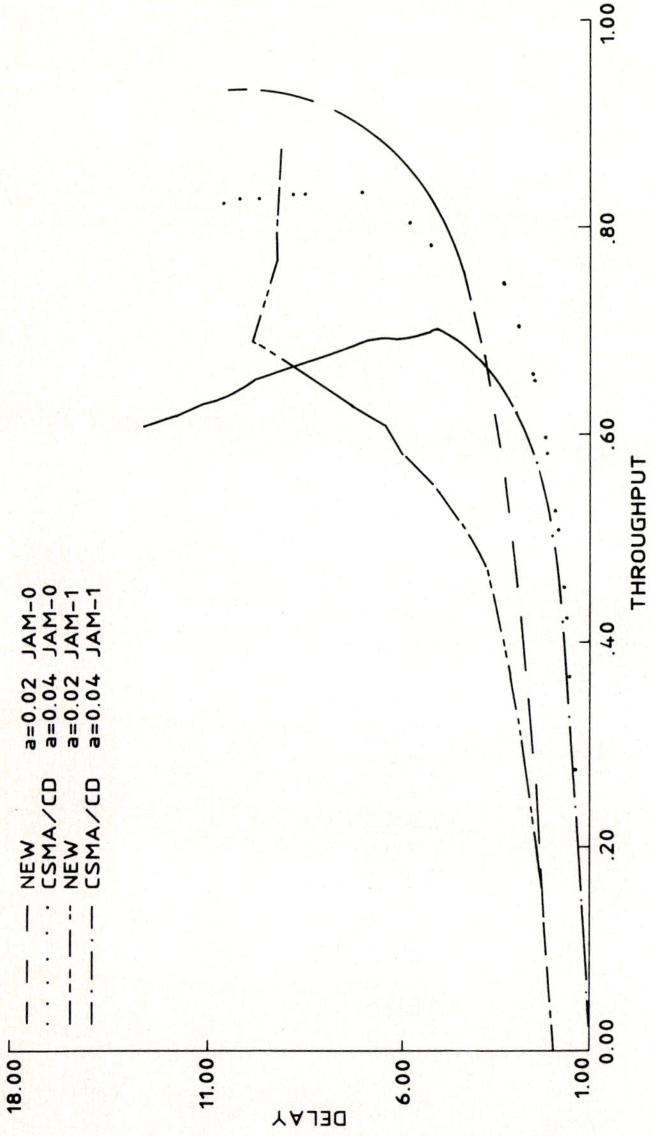

NEW a=0.02 JAM-0
CSMA/CD a=0.04 JAM-0
NEW a=0.02 JAM-1
CSMA/CD a=0.04 JAM-1
DELAY
18.00
11.00
6.00
1.00
0.00
.20
.40
.60
.80
1.00
THROUGHPUT

Fig. 3

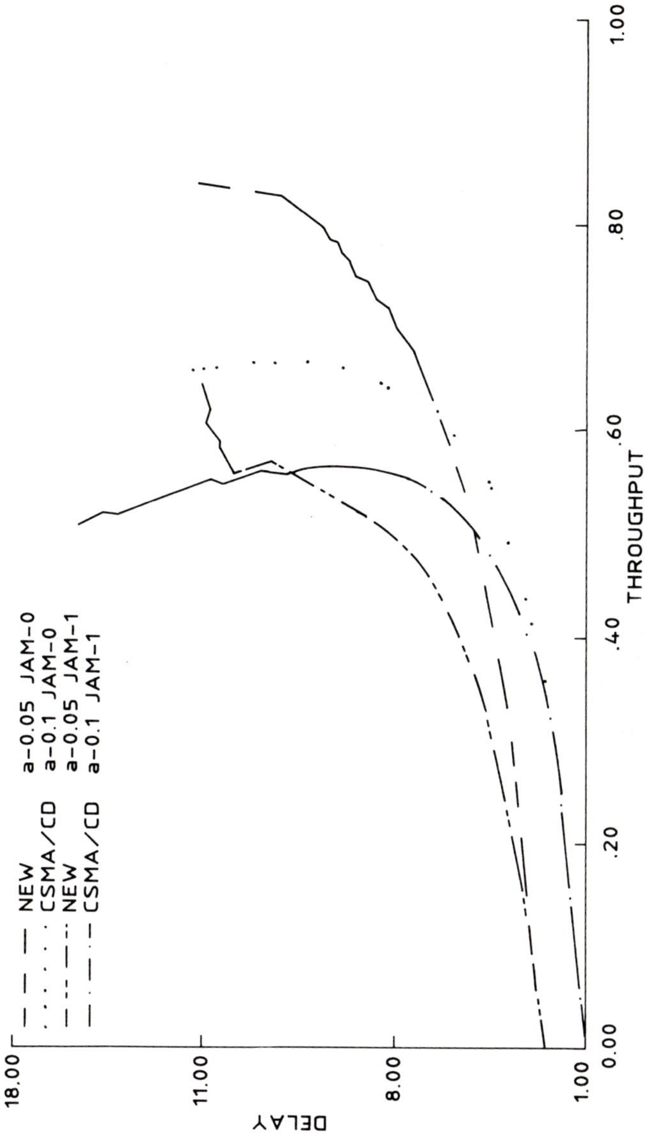
NEW a-0.05 JAM-0
CSMA/CD a-0.1 JAM-0
NEW a-0.05 JAM-1
CSMA/CD a-0.1 JAM-1
DELAY
18.00
11.00
8.00
1.00
0.00
.20
.40
.60
.80
1.00
THROUGHPUT

Fig. 4

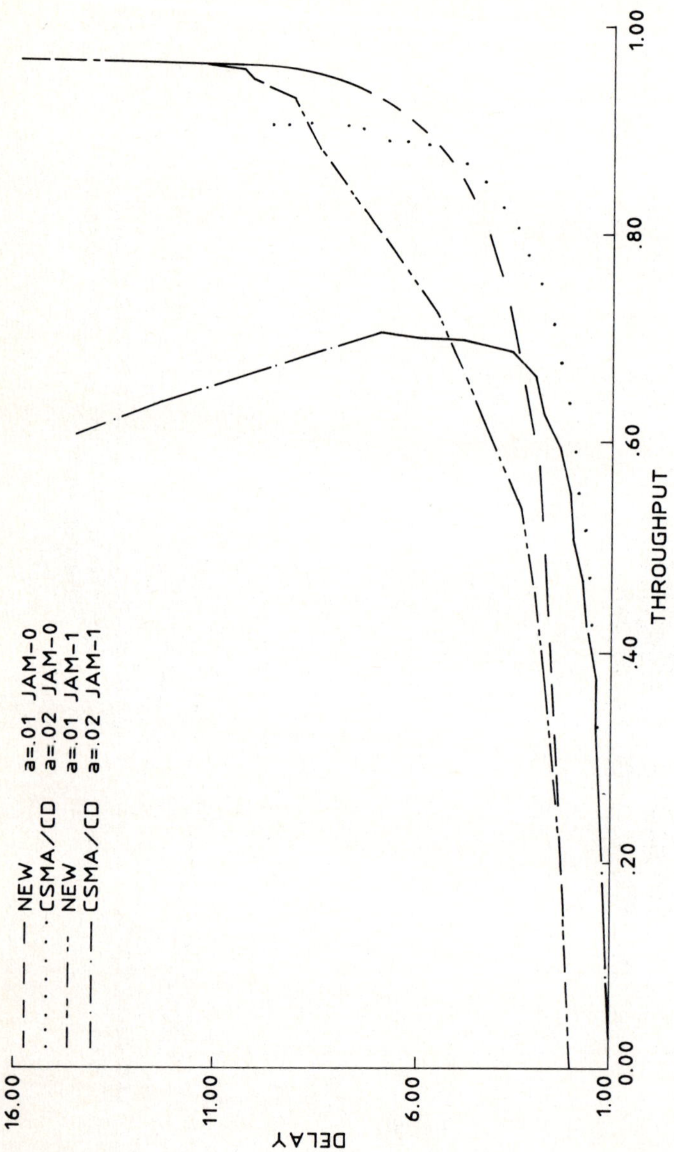
NEW a=.01 JAM-0
CSMA/CD a=.02 JAM-0
NEW a=.01 JAM-1
CSMA/CD a=.02 JAM-1
DELAY
16.00
11.00
6.00
1.00
0.00
.20
.40
.60
.80
1.00
THROUGHPUT

Fig. 5

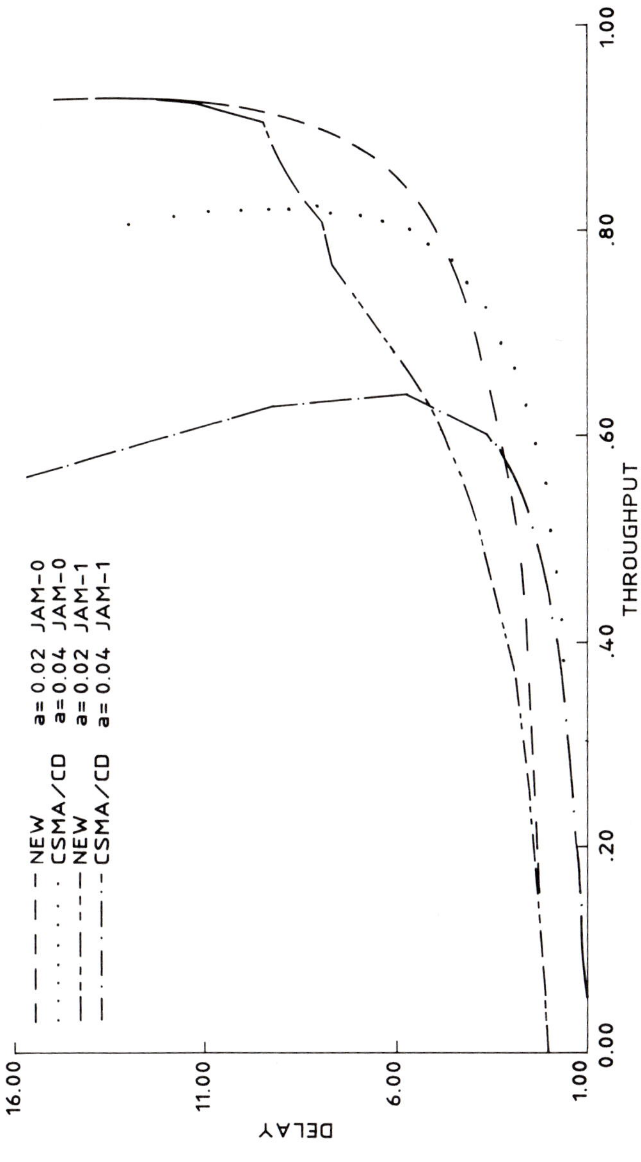
NEW a= 0.02 JAM-0
CSMA/CD a= 0.04 JAM-0
NEW a= 0.02 JAM-1
CSMA/CD a= 0.04 JAM-1
DELAY
16.00
11.00
6.00
1.00
THROUGHPUT
0.00
.20
.40
.60
.80
1.00

Fig. 6

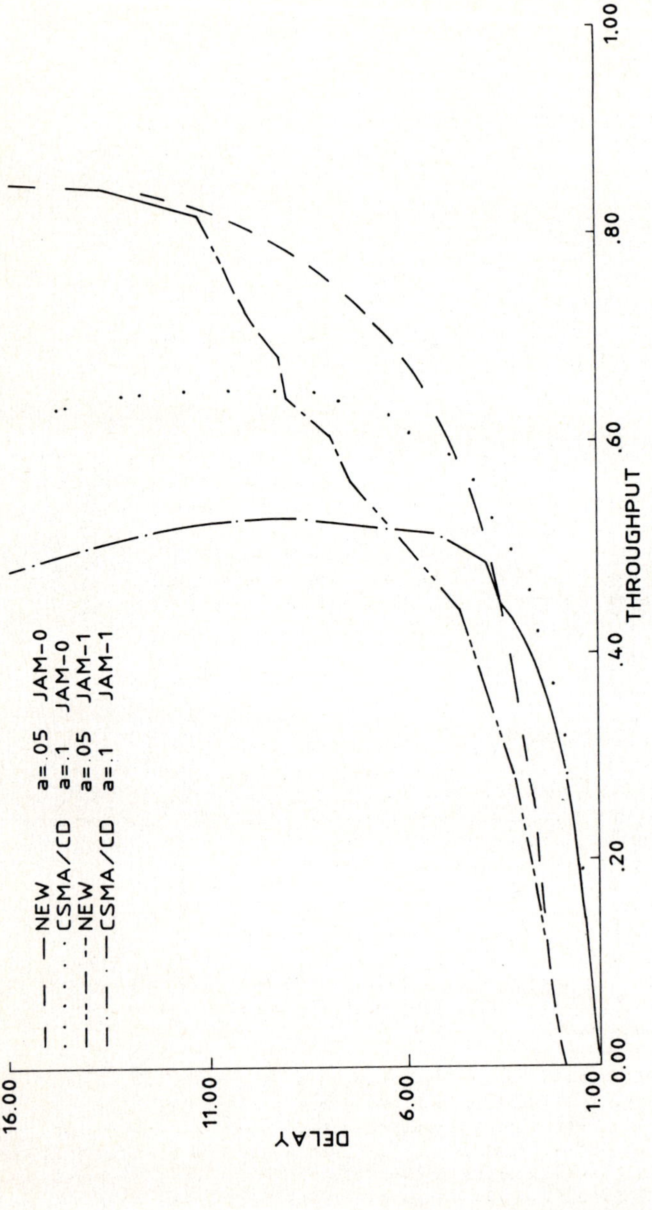
DELAY
16.00
11.00
6.00
1.00
THROUGHPUT
0.00
.20
.40
.60
.80
1.00
NEW a=.05 JAM-0
CSMA/CD a=.1 JAM-0
NEW a=.05 JAM-1
CSMA/CD a=.1 JAM-1

Fig. 7

Network Information Processing Systems
K. Boyanov, R. Angelinov (Editors)
Elsevier Science Publishers B.V. (North-Holland)

EXPERIENCE WITH PETRI NET BASED VERIFICATION OF COMMUNICATION PROTOCOLS SPECIFIED BY LANGUAGE MEANS

Monika HEINER

Academy of Sciences of the GDR
Institute of Informatics and Computing Technique
Rudower Chaussee 5, DDR-1199 Berlin

This paper continues a short survey published at COMNET '85 and is closely related to the paper by Koenig/Tarnay in this volume. According to our design goal, much attention has been paid on supporting an engineer in his task of software quality assurance. Recent results are especially presented to two topics: discussion of time-invariant Petri net structures and Petri net reduction in a manner preserving synchronization structure.

1. INTRODUCTION

Communication protocols like any form of distributed systems are inherently concurrent and asynchronous. Their behaviour often critically depends on the possibly unpredictable timing of its components. The large numbers of subtle interactions that can take place among the components of even a moderately-sized distributed system make it extremely difficult to evaluate properties of the system's behaviour.

Powerful techniques are needed, therefore, for rigorously analyzing the possible kinds of behaviour of distributed software systems to assure that they exhibit all and only the properties intended. Because of the complexity of the arguments involved, developers of distributed systems would greatly benefit from automated tools to aid in the analysis of the system they create.

Ideally, these tools should be integrated in an environment providing tools to support all the activities required for developing and maintaining large, distributed software systems. Such an environment realized by a powerful workstation should provide a diverse array of tools. In particular, it should offer tools supporting a wide variety of analysis techniques (compare fig. 1), since different techniques have complementary strength and weaknesses /Groz 85/.

This paper deals with one of the approaches of desirable analyzing tools (double surrounded in fig. 1). The implementation is part of a general workstation of protocol development supporting also other validation tools /Koenig 87/.

2. A CLASSIFICATION OF VALIDATION TECHNIQUES

Perhaps the most distinguishing and significant feature of verification as a static analysis is that it is capable of assuring the absence of certain kinds of errors in a program. Testing and simulating approaches, on the other hand, are best at detecting the presence of errors, by noting their occurrence in the course of (an usually heavily monitored) execution of the program with carefully selected test data.

Moreover, in /Gait 86/ the experience is reported that some synchronization failures could not be detected by debugging. This phenomenon of error masking called probe effect and well known in the theory of Petri nets (refer section 8) emphasizes the need of an other way than testing to get assurance of the impossibility of certain system states.

In this paper, verification comprises all techniques stating something of a given program system without executing it. In this connection, two types of verification can be distinguished: special and general verification. The *special verification* approach tries to show equivalence by proving that the program text is in accordance with an external description of the special program semantics intended. *General verification*, however, proves general properties which must be valid in any system independent of its special semantics. A context examination of program text yields general aspects of the so-called static semantics.

```
                              |--------------|
                              |  Validation  |
                              |--------------|
                                     |
           |----------------|--------------|--------------|
           V                V              V              V
  |--------------|  |------------|  |---------|  |---------------|
  | Verification |  | Simulation |  | Testing |  | Certification |
  |--------------|  |------------|  |---------|  |---------------|
   |                      |                                      |
   |                |---------------|                            |
   |                V               V                            |
   |     |---------------|    |-------------|                    |
   |     |  Prediction   |    | Prediction  |                    |
   |     | of functional |    |     of      |                    |
   |     |   Behaviour   |    | Performance |                    |
   |     |---------------|    |-------------|                    |
   |                                                             |
   |   |--------------|                |-----------------|       |
   |-->|   Special    |                | Conformance Test|<--|
   |   | Verification |                |-----------------|       |
   |   |--------------|                                          |
   |                                   |-----------------|       |
   |   ||============||                | Performance Test|<--|
   |-->|| General    ||                |-----------------|       |
       ||Verification||                                          |
       ||============||                |-----------------|       |
                                       | Robustness Test |<--|
                                       |-----------------|
```

Fig. 1: Survey on validation techniques - not competing, but complementing each other.

3. ABOUT THE PROS AND CONS OF PETRI NET BASED GENERAL VERIFICATION

It is a common opinion, that behavioural properties such as mutual exclusion, deadlocks/liveness, livelock, and self-synchronization, which involve interactions among the parts of a distributed system, are most naturally analyzed in terms of the order (and number) of event occurrences. Especially for these problems, the Petri nets offer a suitable theory under development.

Our approach tries to combine the advantages of high-level languages with those of theory of Petri nets. The Petri net based subcomponents of the PDL System /Koenig 85, 87/ are connected together in the so-called Petri net framework (refer section 4). An important property of the Petri net framework is its extreme generality. It aids developers in a general way in reasoning about the behaviour of distributed systems.

Because of its generality, the Petri net framework can be used with distributed systems expressed in a wide variety of specification or programming languages. The semantics of a particular language are captured by the procedure for deriving Petri net representations for distributed systems expressed in any high-level language (refer the Petri net generator in section 4 and 5).

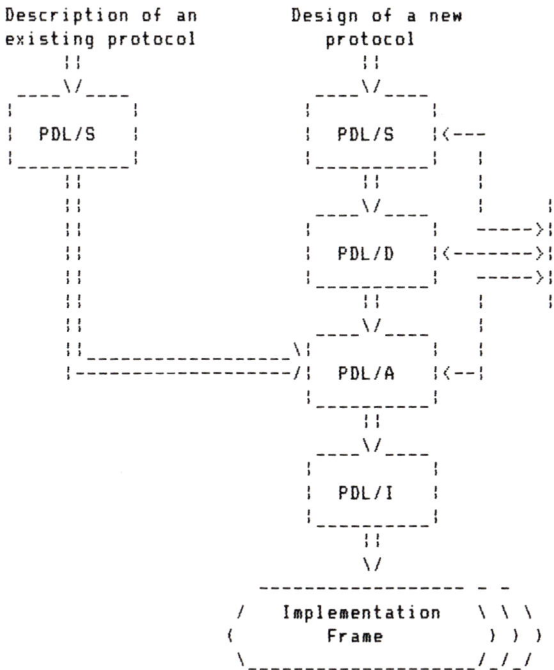

Fig. 2: The language hierarchy in the PDL System

Aiding tools for analyzing and reduction extract information about events and their orderings directly from this intermediate representation of the system. Therefore, they don't rely on any assumptions, but regard general features of distributed systems and can be applied to any system once a Petri net representation for the system was obtained.

Furthermore, due to the generality of the Petri net framework, tools based on Petri nets could be extended to provide common analysis methods across a number of phases in the software development process, including specification and implementation. This could be a source of valuable commonality and integration in a software development environment. Following this idea, an important feature of our workstation can be seen in the concept of different language levels, each refining the former one. Our Petri net framework supports different specification/programming levels (compare fig. 2).

The most important shortcomings of a Petri net based general verification can be traced back to the following fact. Since all program paths are assumed to be executable, also superfluous reports are generated. While it can effectively be used to assure that specific phenomena do not occur, additional techniques would be desirable to determine which reports are spurious and which correspond to actual errors in the software.

4. THE PETRI NET FRAMEWORK

The Petri net framework has four components: the Petri net generator, linker, analyzer, and the error reporting and interpretation system. All parts are influenced by the available possibilities of reduction of Petri nets. We briefly describe below the approach to modelling and analyzing used in the Petri net framework (compare fig. 3).

```
                      ||=================||
        /------\      || error reporting ||  -  /------\  +
        | SDP- |<---- ||       and       ||<----| CSN! |--------->
start   \------/      || interpretation  ||     \------/  exit
-------|   |          ||=================||        A
       V   V                  /\                   |
      |----------|            ||           ||===========||
      |   HLL    |         Petri Net ---\  || Petri Net ||
      |  Editor  |         Reduction ---/  || Analyzer  ||
      |----------|            ||           ||===========||
           |                  \/                   A
           V            ||===========||            |
        /------\        || Petri Net ||         /------\
        | SDP? |------->|| Generator ||-------->| CSN? |
        \------/        ||===========||         \------/
                               |                   A
                               V                   |
                              -----\\\     ||===========||
                           /------\ |||    || Petri Net ||
                           | CSNi | // ----->||  Linker   ||
                           \------/        ||===========||
```

Fig. 3: The Petri net based subcomponents of the PDL System

The starting point for this cyclic technology in software development is an *editor*, which assists in creating a system of distributed processes (SDP). To get some answers to interesting static properties of the programmed system, it must be compiled and translated into Petri nets. This will be done by the help of the Petri net *generator*. In the case of separate compilation of system parts, the corresponding Petri nets parts must be put together by the *linker*, too.

The result of the former steps is a so-called control structure net with some *unknown* properties (CSN?). This is the input into the Petri net analyzer. The *analyzer* /Starke 87a/ is a generic name for a collection of tools implementing specific analysis techniques applicable to Petri nets. Among the tools composing the analyzer, the available procedures for checking structural properties are of special importance. The analyzer proves the existence (or nonexistence) of some special properties of the Petri net under investigation. (The character "!" in "CSN!" stands for *known* properties.)

In the case of error reporting by the analyzer, now the difficult task of *error interpretation* has to be started. The difficulties result on the one hand from the need of retranslation of the failure hints in terms of Petri nets into terms of the programming source we were coming from, and on the other hand from the need of decision about the sincerity and gravity of the failure situation for the actual behaviour of the real system.
While the former task is obviously automatable (but not yet implemented in the PDL system), the later one is still an open question and remains the intelligence-expensive duty of the programming team and software quality assurance team, respectively.

5. MODELLING WITH PETRI NETS

The following design considerations are realized in the Petri net generators of the PDL system. A set of communication protocols located in some layer and described in PDL/D or PDL/A (refer fig. 2) is modelled as a Petri net as follows.

(1) At first, the common frame of the layer is constructed by generating a place for each synchronization item (objects of the types messages, service asked, service responded). For the purpose of better identification, these places are called synchronization places.

(2) Secondly, for each process, i.e. for each protocol part, a Petri net is constructed by using transitions to represent statements and places to represent control points. More precisely, a sequence of general statements not including synchronization operations (e.g. send/receive statements) is represented by a single transition. The Petri net representation of statements of the control structure including synchronization operations is refined in such a way that it reflects all structurally possible threads of control. Each process (state machine) has the remarkable property that it contains a token in only one of its places. This token can be interpreted as program counter.

(3) The processes are loosely connected via synchronization places. These places can have a certain capacity; then they are a priori bounded. Otherwise, it is an interesting question, if an upper bound of the token numbers can be found by analyzing the net behaviour.

In this model, the termination of any synchronization-free statement sequence is assumed, perhaps proved by special verification. The corresponding model assumption is the finite firing duration of any transition.

Please note, until now only the control flow is modelled by abstraction from all actual values of any data. This means, that generally more threads of control are discussed than possible in reality. This fact has to be taken into consideration in the event of error interpretation requirement. These disadvantages can be reduced by enhancing the modelling power related to discrete data types. It is a result of our experience with general verification of the transport protocol (class 0) that we are now incorporating Petri net components for Boolean data and all related operations into the model to be analyzed following the proposal presented in /Arendt 87/.

The behaviour of a communication protocol is stimulated by the service primitives provided in the upper layer. For this reason, some appropriate basic assumptions about the environment must be made to verify a protocol within one layer. All known assumptions about the behaviour of the upper layer are described in the service specification written in PDL/S. Therefore, the modelling of environment behaviour needed for protocol verification can be extracted from the generated Petri net representation of service specification by a suitable reduction.

6. ANALYZING WITH PETRI NETS

Having the model of the distributed system, let's now ask: What kind of programming errors are detectable by means of Petri nets?

Additionally to the desired buffer size already mentioned above, the most important properties concerning transitions are given here in an hierarchical manner supporting the engineer in his difficult task of interpretation of a general mathematical theory with the context of a special application.

(1) *Dead code*
Statements which may never be executed are called dead code. It may be caused by simple programming errors. But after linking individual processes to make a greater network it is not always easy to detect them by simple observation. The detection of such dead code is useful since programmers may by mistake expect that they are executed; this is especially true in the case of extensive exception programming.
Dead code of Petri net can be detected easily as transitions which do not appear in the reachability graph.

(2) *Total deadlock*
This is a property of the arrival in some system state or set of states from which there is no exit.
In terms of Petri nets, this property corresponds to the fact that the system can reach at least one state from which no other state is reachable. In the reachability graph, these states of a total deadlock of a system are reflected as final nodes (sheets).

(3) *Partial deadlock*
Freedom of total deadlock only guarantees a permanent progress of the system without stating that something "good" will actually be achieved. Going further, freedom of partial deadlock is the property stating that for all times all parts of the system are available for the common goal.
In terms of Petri nets, this property means that from each reachable

state an other state is reachable, but not all strongly connected components in the reachability graph contain all transitions.

(4) *Livelock*
If some processes cannot run for ever due to the scheduler's strategy (or something else not contained in the model), they are said to be in livelock (individual starvation, potential deadlock).
In terms of the reachability graph this property looks like one without sheets, but not all circles contain all transitions. This analysis delivers hints about possible locations of livelocks. But in general, the decision between the actual existence or nonexistence of livelocks in a real distributed system is a difficult matter .

(5) *Fault tolerance and self-synchronization*
This means that after a failure or from any abnormal state the protocol will return to normal execution (recovery from failure) within finite time. This property can be transformed into safety property stating that if anything ever happens, it is not going to be "bad" (nothing bad will happen).
In the theory of Petri nets, these properties are reflected in the terms of home state, resetability (total reproduction demand), and reproducibility (partial reproduction demand). To analyze these properties the set of all failure states is needed. But it is an open question how we can get a complete one.

7. REDUCTION OF PETRI NETS

It is our experience that great attention has to be focussed on a continuous reduction of the size of resulting Petri nets in order to save computing resources (memory and time).

For this reason, we have accepted the expenditure of separate compilation with subsequent linking. Only the relevant parts of the protocol portion under investigation have to be linked. Open external references like synchronization connections are reported by the linker and must be resolved in a suitable way by the user. Furthermore, only the synchronization skeleton is produced by the Petri net generator (compare point (2) in section 5).

A drawback of automated Petri net generation lies in some inevitable inefficiencies resulting from context-free assembling of universal net-building components. To overcome this disadvantage we have to continue with a reduction of the automatically generated nets. For this purpose, the analyzer in use provides a set of local reduction rules preserving liveness and boundedness.

However, an uncontrolled application of these transformations destroys the synchronization structure, and an error interpretation, if necessary, on source text level is completely impossible. Therefore, a supplementing reduction set preserving the synchronization structure has been realized. The basic idea of a corresponding general implementation consists in the exception of nodes from reduction. This means, a reduction rule can be applied only, if no excepted node would be involved. Evidently, all synchronization places and all sending or receiving transitions have to be excepted. Our experience has proven that the value of the Petri net framework has been significantly enhanced by this supplement.

But, if the resulting total net cannot be mastered efficiently by available computing resources, then it is advisable to repeat this principle in slightly different manner. We have to concentrate on a protocol portion we want to analyze. All processes out of this portion are reduced consecutively whereby only their synchronization places are excepted. By this reduction, we get a consistent minimized description of the environment of the protocol portion under investigation.

Last not least, if in spite of all these precautions the computing resources are not sufficient for analyzing a given net, then we have reached the point where we have to reduce without any restrictions. However, the application of such a reduction should be kept as very last way out in due of the difficult error interpretation.

Some problems are still open. The collection of transformations could be extended. Moreover, a heuristics is needed to choose the sequence of transformations to be applied efficiently.

8. TIME-INVARIANT PETRI NETS

The method applied is characterized essentially by the conclusion from the properties of a Petri net representing the synchronization structure of given software with parallel processes to the properties of actual parallel processes in a real environment.

$$\mathrm{prop}(\ pn\ ) \;\Longrightarrow\; \mathrm{prop}(\ program\ )$$

This conclusion is similar to that from the properties of a given Petri net PN to the properties of any corresponding timed Petri net TPN (which has the same structure, but each transition possesses any time constant giving the duration of firing). Unfortunately, there is generally no justification for this deduction with respect to liveness, rather it applies:

$$\mathrm{LIV}(\ PN\ ) \;\not\Leftrightarrow\; \mathrm{LIV}(\ TPN\ )$$

because time constraints can restrict the reachability set:

$$R_{PN(m0)} \;\supseteq\; R_{TPN(m0)}$$

The problem of time consumption can thus be rephrased to: How applicable are the results of net analysis to real systems? We look for results for all possible time restrictions in order to gain independence from the "unprecise" time inscription of the net. In connection with the general verification intended two cases have to be distinguished.

(1) $\overline{\mathrm{LIV}}(\ PN\ ) \;\overset{?}{\longrightarrow}\; \mathrm{LIV}(\ TPN\ )$

A non-live Petri net becomes live by the influence of timing. This phenomenon of error masking is known as "probe effect" /Gait 86/ and can be observed during debugging (without hardware support) of distributed software .

(2) $\mathrm{LIV}(\ PN\ ) \;\overset{?}{\longrightarrow}\; \overline{\mathrm{LIV}}(\ TPN\ )$

A live Petri net becomes non-live by the influence of timing. In context with software interpreted Petri nets, this case is not as comprehensible as the former one. Instead of this, the static analysis is based on the (so far implicit) guess that there are interesting subsets of Petri net structures which are time-independently live (shortly time-invariant).

The influence of timing upon liveness of a net was firstly discussed in /Godberson 82/. He pointed out that there is no difference in the behaviour of timed Petri nets and an equivalent Petri net in the case of conflict-free nets. In the meantime, there are two further results available. In /Starke 87b/, it has been proven that Petri nets are time-independently live if they are live and (general) extended free choice (EFC). In /Starke 88/, this result is generalized to extended simple nets (ES).

The degree of conflict can be classified structurally in more detail by the language means available for communication. We have to regard two features: type of waiting and of addressing. The table below summarizes the relevant results. For a more detailed discussion see /Heiner 88/.

Waiting \ Addressing	direct/ semi-direct-by-sender	indirect/ semi-direct-by-receiver
deterministic (unconditional)	EFC => time-independent	ES => time-independent
non-deterministic (alternative)	ES => time-independent	possibly time-dependent

It has been shown:

- Without the possibility for alternative waiting there is no chance for time-dependency for all types of communication in due of the standardized conflict structures.
- The combination of alternative waiting together with indirect or semi-direct-by-receiver communication bears the danger of time-dependencies. This statement is proven by the following example.

Time-dependencies can occur if at least one alternative in an alternative waiting action of a process SM_j depends on a synchronization object s_k which another process SM_i is also waiting for. For this alternative, the danger of non-liveness has to be taken into account.

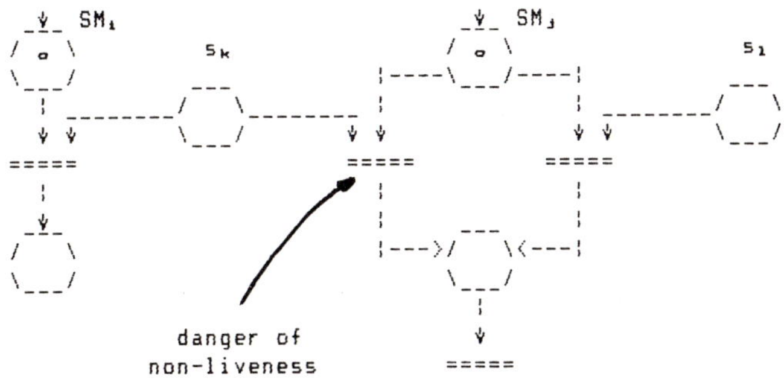

As a side-effect, we have obtained a new local structure whose appearance in a Petri net model should produce a warning to the programmer. At least as long as a more precise criterion to check the timing behaviour is not available. It is a common opinion in software development technology that the relative progress of processes to each other must not have any influence on the general behaviour of the whole system.

9. CONCLUDING REMARKS

Our investigations are greatly influenced by the goal to provide such a tool which can be applied by an engineer engaged more in software quality assurance then in Petri net theory. It is our opinion that the level of practicability of a method like this is greatly influenced by the level of an engineer-like preparation of the tool provided. To fill the gap between theory and application, a lot of work has still to be done to support engineers to handle the underlying model in an effective and easy way.

Until now, we have only considered protocol verification (horizontal verification within one layer). The second step consists in proving the conformity of the protocol with the service required (vertical verification going beyond adjoining layers).

The method proposed is applicable independently from the used programming language. Communication protocols play the role of a case study standing for a wide range of applications of distributed processing. The transfer of the technology presented to other languages is under development.

REFERENCES

/Arendt 87/ Arendt, F.; Heltzig, H.F.; Kluehe, B.: Modelling and Verification of Real-Time Software Using Petri Nets; MMPS 87, Eisenach 1987, proc. part II, pp. 72-83.

/Gait 86/ Gait, J.: A Probe Effect in Concurrent Programs; Software Pract. & Exp. 16(86)3, pp. 225-233.

/Godbersen 82/ Godbersen, H. P.: On the Problem of Time in Nets; IFB 52, 1982, pp.23-30.

/Groz 85/ Groz, R.; Jard, C.; Lassudrie, C.: Attacking a Complex Distributed Algorithm from Different Sides: An Experience with Complementary Validation Tools; Computer Networks and ISDN Systems 10(85)dec, pp. 245-257.

/Heiner 80/ Heiner, M.: Ein Beitrag zur Deadlockanalyse anhand einer sprachlich gefuehrten Programmiermethodik; Diss. A, TU Dresden, 1980.

/Heiner 88/ Heiner, M.: Some Remarks on Time-independently Live Petri Nets; Petri Net Newsletter 8/88, in print.

/Koenig 85/ Koenig, H.; Heiner, M.: The PDL System - An Unified Approach to the Specification, Verification, and Implementation of Protocols; in Csaba, L. et al. (eds.): COMPUTER NETWORK USAGE, North-Holland Comp., Amsterdam 1986, pp. 567-582.

/Koenig 87/ Koenig, H.: Kommunikationsprotokolle - Prinzip und Entwicklung; Diss. B, TU Dresden, 1987.

/Starke 87a/ Starke, P.: Petri Net Machine; LNCS 255, 1987, pp. 43-44.

/Starke 87b/ Starke, P.: Remarks on Timed Nets; Petri Net Newsletter 27/1987, pp. 37-48.

/Starke 88/ Starke, P.: Remarks on Timed Nets; 9. European Workshop on Application and Theory of Petri Nets, Venice June 1988.

Network Information Processing Systems
K. Boyanov, R. Angelinov (Editors)
Elsevier Science Publishers B.V. (North-Holland)

AUTOMATIC VERIFICATION OF ESTELLE SPECIFICATIONS OF COMMUNICATION PROTOCOLS USING PETRI NETS

Dr. Vladimir DIMITROV, Researcher
Dr. Anton PETKOV, Associate - Professor

Institute of Mathematics
Bulgarian Academy of Science
P. O. Box 373
Sofia 1090
Bulgaria

Ab approach for automatic verification of communication protocols specified in an Estelle subset is presented. The transformations from Estelle specifications into Petri nets, the connection among the characteristics of Estelle language units, the specifics of communication protocol specifications and the possibilities of using the analytical apparatus of Petri nets for verification purposes are investigated. The basic principles of implemented program system for automatic transformation of Estelle class of communication protocol specifications allowing automatic verification of their properties employing analytical methods of Petri nets are described.

1. INTRODUCTION

This paper presents the basic concepts used in the implemented system for verification of communication protocols. ISO's Estelle - a formal description based on an extended state transition model |1| is used for system input language. Its linearity permits a simple translator into Petri nets implementation employing compiler to compiler. A shortcoming of the language was detected on our experience in full specification of simple real transport protocols, because the extended state transition model is two times bigger than the Pascal implementation. On the other hand, the usage of the extended state transition model simplifies our approach for analytical analyzing of protocol properties. The correct interpretation of communication protocol terms with Estelle language constructs is essential. We assume that the concrete system of protocol objects is a set of processes communicating to each other by communication protocol rules. In Estelle we describe processes by parallel interacting modules, and we assume that one process is described by one module. It is necessary that the interacting mode of a process with the others to be fully described in the module transition part, and the message types interchanged between processes to be described in the channel type of its interconnecting interaction points. Taking the real case in account we assume that each concrete system can be described by a fixed number of processes, respectively fixed number of module variables in the main specification. By the same reason we assume that interaction point queues have limited capacity. In the specification of protocol system we assume that processes interchange is performed according to OSI model following the principles mentioned in |1|. At the end we assume that the system specification describes the real interchange with the outside world.

The main schema of the program implementation in terms of program component - translation, verification and retranslation, and of two language interfaces - Estelle and the internal Petri net based model, is given at fig. 1. The type of components functioning is different - translation and retranslation have intensive application of grammar production rules for syntactical/semantical analysis and transformations, but verification process manipulates and analyze Petri net objects. That is why we have used different approaches in the implementation of the schema from fig. 1, by implementing the second component in Ada |6|, and the first and third ones have been generated by LEX and YACC |7|. An prototype of verification subcomponent have been implemented, and investigation on effective algorithms for Petri net analyzing have been done for effective final version implementation of the component. This subsystem can be used independently for analyzing Petri nets. The component is given at fig. 2.

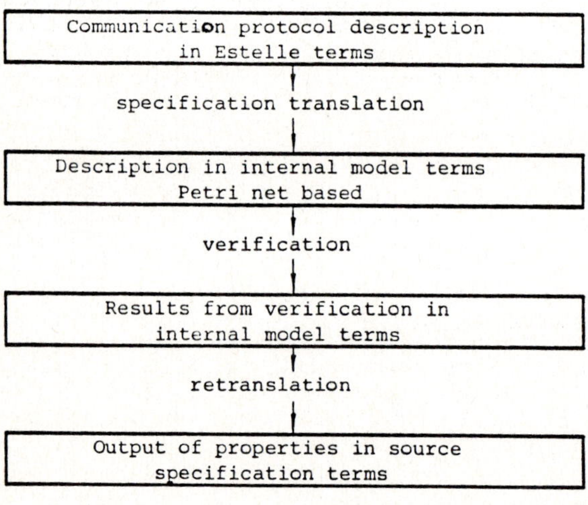

FIGURE 1
Main schema of the approach

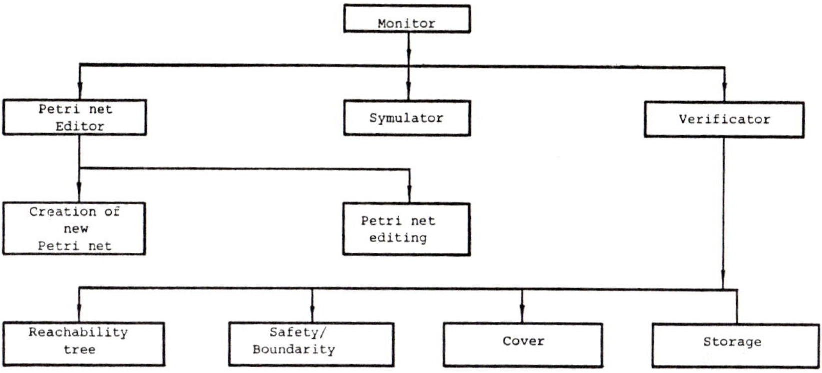

FIGURE 2
Main schema of simulator/verificator of Petri nets

2. VERIFICATION PROBLEMS

In the verification of the protocol system we look for the following two kinds of properties: a) system activity and b) main type errors. The main type errors in terms of processes and their interconnecting channels by |2| are deadlock errors, reception errors and overflows. We will interprete this properties in Estelle terms in the next sections. Deadlock in Estelle terms means that two module variables as result of system execution are in states, where each of them waits to receive an interaction underway in the interaction points that link them, but there are no such interactions at the heads of the corresponding queues. Reception error in Estelle terms means that a module variable at some state cannot accept an interaction generated during system execution, i.e. there is no transition from the given state which to input the interaction. Overflow in Estelle terms means overflow of channel capacity or overflow of work variable.

3. POSSIBILITIES FOR VERIFICATION OF ESTELLE SPECIFICATIONS

Estelle is based on extended finite state machine, which by |1| "is a simple finite state machine augmented with:
- memory (variables),
- predicates used in selecting transitions,
- priorities used in selecting transitions,
- actions or operations associated with a transition, which are specified in Pascal and may include output operations,

- interaction points for input and output,
- interactions with an environment."

With this augmentations finite state machine is extended to the power of Turing machine. So the extended finite state machine cannot be analyzed, since there is no such annalytical apparatus permitting analysing of models with such power. The only exit from this situation is to choose an Estelle subset with a model power less than Turing machine power, but which model has powerfull analytical apparatus. Taking in account that the full Estelle specification is a set of parallel modules communicating with each other, it is clear to use Petri nets, because they are an extension of finite state automatas for concurrency specification. Petri nets can be analyzed for the following problems: safety, boundness, cover and storage. Reachability, activity, equality and inclusion, which are equivalent to each other cannot be approved in the main case. For more details see |3|.

Now an Estelle subset transformable in fully verificationable Petri nets will be described. If a communication protocol can be specified using only finite state machine of Estelle, i.e. without augmentations, there are no problems for its analyzing. Such an assumption has no real cover and that is why we will investigate the influence of augmentations over the basic model in Estelle - finite state machine:

- memory (variables). The usage of variables for specification of module structure is sensible, but with module variables there are no problems. The others variables are divided in two classes - buffer variables, used for information storage, and control variables participating in the control flow. We have no good interpretation for the last one class, because their influence is connected with empty marking analyzing, which cannot be done by usual Petri nets |3|. Due to the above statements in our Estelle subset we include only module and buffer variables.

- predicates used in selecting transitions. Predicates are over control variables, and so we remove them from selecting transitions.

- priorities used in selecting transitions. Priorities usage means conflict removing, which extend finite state machine to Turing machine. That is why we will not use priorities.

- actions. Actions are used for module output specification. There are several kinds of control flow statements in actions. Their removing is connected with the transformation of Estelle specification in a canonical form, which will be discussed later. We will mention, that is must not use control statements with output statement, for the sake of transformatability into canonical form.

- interaction points for input and output. Interaction points and their interconnection specify interconnection of the system components, so they are of great importance. Due to our assumption for queue limited capacity the finite state automata is not extended to Turing machine.

- interaction with an environment. Because the above mentioned structural principles of specification such interaction points used for internal structure description are not used.

At the end of this informal description we will add some final remarks. In communication protocol specification we assume that processes hierarchy is described by one level module interconnection. From this assumption follow, that interconnections are defined at the higher system level. Because the static system structure once established, interconnections are not changed during system execution. The purpose of the higher system level, in a hierarchy of protocol system is to specify module interconnections and to coordinate relationships. A formal specification of the above settled Estelle subset and analysis of its computing power is given in |4|.

After the Estelle subset description we will introduce the meaning canonical form. Under specification in canonical form, described in above settled Estelle subset and following the structural principles, we understand, such specification which has no default clauses and options - they are specified explicitly, there are no state sets in the specification - they are expanded, and in which specification the additional statements simplifying the specification process, like 'forone', 'all' and so on, are expanded to equivalent Pascal sequences. The canonical form is functionally equivalent to the source specification. The program system automatically transforms specification into their canonical forms, and after that a transformation into Petri nets is done automatically.

4. TRANSFORMATION OF ESTELLE SPECIFICATIONS INTO PETRI NETS

According to the structural principles, the above settled protocol system has one main process and several subprocesses. First we shall describe the transformation of each module, independently of the others, into Petri net. The control flow of a module is described by its transition part. For each state, describing the finite state automata of the protocol machine, is generated a position, which is uniquelly named by the module name and the state machine mentioned in the specification. For every Estelle transition is created a Petri net transition with input arc from the position generated for the state mentioned in the from clause, and with output arc to the position generated for the state mentioned in the 'to' clause. In this Petri net only the position, which state name is mentioned in the clause 'initialize to' of the module, is marked. For every module variable a Petri net is generated in this way. Due to the choice of Estelle subset transitions have no clauses 'provided', 'any' and 'priority', and the clause 'with' is removed by the canonisation. The clause 'delay' we ignore, because we are interested in control flow, but not in time characteristics. For the same reason we are not interested in the other modules' structural elements like Pascal procedures, statements and so on. The generated Petri nets are automatic and can be fully verified |3|.

The next stage of transformation consists of interconnection of Petri nets received at the last stage, into a Petri net, modelling control flow of the source system. The system is composed of interaction points defined over channel types. The connection between interactive points and transitions is defined with 'when' clause. Every channel type has two roles, each role defines set of interactions. Interaction points are defined by a channel type and by one of its roles. An interaction point can have individual queue, common queue or no queue. In the next section will be described first the case when all module interaction points have one common queue.

The module receives through the interaction points interactions send to him, for an interaction point these are interactions from the other role of channel type. A position is generated for each interaction point and for each of its supplementary interactions. Positions of input interactions are connected with transitions by input arcs for the last one. Only transitions, which wait for input interactions of the type mentioned in their 'when' clause are connected. For so generated set of positions a full/empty position is generated in order to indicate whether the buffer is full or empty. The position is marked with a token, which indicate that initially the queue head is empty. Every transition connected with a position from the queue head we connect with an output arc from it to the full/empty position. In this situation when an interaction from the head is consumed, the head is marked as empty. On the other hand every transition, which stores interaction positions is connected with input arc to it from a full/empty position. In such a way store transitions are permitted only when the queue buffer is empty, only one store transition is executed and only one position marking interaction type receives a token. The initial state of the system is restored after interaction consuming.

Now we will look at the queue structure. Let a module has k interactions, then k+1 positions are generated. If the queue has interaction capacity s, then s-1 times head positions are duplicated. Every two positions marking the same interactions from neighbour places in the queue are connected with transition, which is connected with full/empty position in the above described style. The last position level of the queue receives its tokens from output arcs of transitions, which have statement output at actions part of contragent modules communicating by this interaction points. This kind of net do not model queue overflow. For such purpose can be used an internal buffer level of positions in the queue, which do not interconnect store transitions with a full/empty position. Analysis of this positions indicates queue overflow. An example of queue Petri net is given at fig. 3.

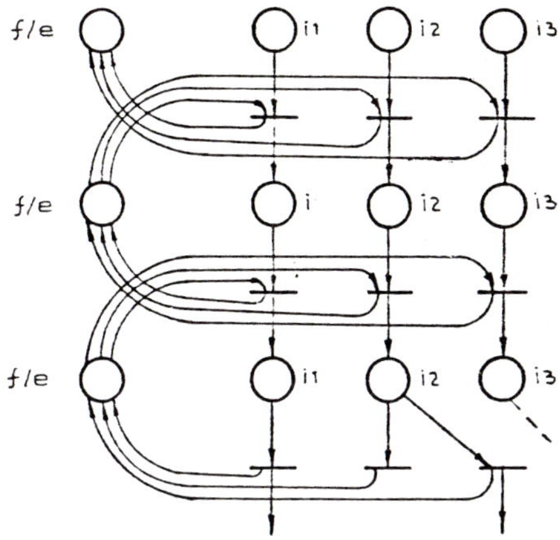

FIGURE 3
Queue Petri net with three interaction types

If an interaction point has no queue, only a queue head is enough. When there are individual queues, a structure of the above type is created for every individual queue, for positions generation only supplementary interactions of interaction point channel type are used.

In this way we receive a Petri net modelling the control flow of a source specification.

5. ANALYSIS OF GENERATED PETRI NETS

Now the verification and its Estelle interpretation will be discussed. The first problem is queue overflow errors. As it was mentioned for every queue under investigation an internal level of positions is created. For this net, reachability tree |3| is constructed, which analytically is analyzed for queue positions marking. If positions under question have marking greater than queue capacity this is an indication for queue overflow. If there are no overflow indication module investigation is continued. This stage is based on the fact that reachability tree for the net has no endless token, because the processes are working like finite state automata, which is formally approved in |5|. From this follows that such a net can be fully analyzed |3|. The existence of terminal lists in the reachability tree means that the system can be in a situation, where the next execution is impossible. This is a deadlock error, for which execution sequences must be analyzed. If a queue marking is invariant to some list, this is a reception error, and in this case execution sequences are analyzed too.

Since transformation of Estelle specifications into Petri nets is a homomorphic process, there are no problems for automatic retranslation of analyzed results back in Estelle terms.

6. CONCLUSION

By choosing the Estelle subset, we limited expressing power for the sake of increasing analytical characteristics. This approach is sensible for protocol verification, but not for simulation or effective implementation.

The limitations permit using of formal model with a well investigated analytical apparatus, such as Petri nets. On the other hand limitations permit creations of algorithms for transformation of source specifications in to the formal model and retranslation of received results. The system for automatic protocol verification can be used for every protocol, which is based on finite state machine.

At the end we shall note, that it is possible Petri nets with inhibitor arcs to be used for full transformation of any Estelle specification in this kind of nets, but since they have the Turing machine power they can be used only for simulation.

REFERENCES

|1| A Formal Description Technique Based on an Extended State Transition Model, ISO/TC 97/SC 21/WG 1 (Dec. 1984).
|2| West, C.H., General Technique for Communication Protocol Validation, IBM J. Res. Develop., v. 22, No. 4 (July 1978).
|3| Peterson, J.L., Petri Net Theory and the Modelling of Systems, Prentice - Hall, Inc., Englewood Cliffs, N. J. (1981).
|4| Dimitrov, V., Petkov, A., A Formal Specification of Estelle Subset, which Can Be Fully Verified, Inst. of Math., Sofia, Internal Report 34 (1986).
|5| Dimitrov, V., Petri Nets Subset Usefull for Verification, Inst. of Math., Sofia, Internal Report 30 (1986).
|6| Reference Manual for the Ada Programming Language, ANSI/MIL-STD 1815A (Jan. 1983).
|7| UNIPLUS+ SYSTEM V Support Tools Guide, Unisoft Systems (1984).

Network Information Processing Systems
K. Boyanov, R. Angelinov (Editors)
Elsevier Science Publishers B.V. (North-Holland)

A PROTOCOL FOR UNBALANCED LOAD LOCAL AREA NETWORKS: THE PROPOSAL PETITION PROTOCOL

by Josep FUERTES, Lawrence Berkeley Lab. (California, USA), and
Ramon PUIGJANER, Dept. Ciències Matemàtiques i Informàtica, Universitat de les Illes Balears (Spain)*

*This work was done when both authors were teaching at the Facultat d'Informàtica de Barcelona (Spain)

ABSTRACT

In this work we introduce a significant improvement on the Proposal-Petition Protocol, as it was stated in [4]. This improvement affects the search process by allowing a global three code alphabet system to be transmitted over the channel. Whenever a Petition message is being sent by more than one station simultaneously or no station is sending, the old search process is used, but if only one station is sending the Petition message, the global system knows wich station will need the token. Our results show that the overhead is drastically reduced if the system is lightly loaded and tends to be the same as the token-passing under a heavily loaded condition.

1. INTRODUCTION

Multiple access protocols provide an attractive way of sharing a common channel in a distributed system. Numerous static load sharing policies have been proposed, [7, 9], with the aim of allocating the channel to the stations, so that the delay in each message being sent be minimized. They are attractive because of their simplicity, but their potential is limited by the fact that they do not react to the current system state.

Adaptive load sharing policies have also received attention. The advantage in using such policies is taht they do respond to the system state, and, so, they are better able to attain the goal of minimum delay. However, adaptive policies must collect and process the system state information, and, so, they are more complex than static ones. There are some proposals for adaptive multiple access protocols based on random access techniques [2, 6, 8, 12, 13], and on deterministic access techniques [3, 4, 5].

The protocol will concentrate on token-passing like disciplines. The primary drawback of the token-passing technique is the overhead. Token-passing is inefficient for lightly loaded systems. Even when the system is lightly loaded it is necessary to select each of the stations. The delay suffered by a message in this situation is purely determined by overhead and not by contention caused by other messages. Although, it has very good response under heavy and symmetrical load conditions.

The main goal of this work is the reduction of the overhead which is the primary limitation in lightly loaded systems. In a recent paper [4], we have presented the Proposal-Petition Protocol. It is a modification of the token-passing technique with the motivation for adapting to the load by minimizing the overhead. In this paper we study a significant improvement to it, which improves response time even further, specially when the load is concentrated in a small number of stations, as it happens during short periods of time, for exemple, in control systems environments.

Section 2 exposes the initial and improved versions of the Proposal-Petition Protocol; Section 3 studies their performance by means of simulation and analytic-graphic approximate models; and finally Section 4 concludes on the advantages and the domain of use of the proposed protocol

2. PROTOCOL DESCRIPTION

We consider the operation of a system with **N** stations connected to a single multi-access channel The stations take control of the bus under the token-passing basic scheme At each moment only one station has the right to control the communication channel, the one that has the token. We call it the master station and it changes as the token is being acquired by the stations of the system. A logical ring is formed by the sequential and ordered addresses of all the stations, and, for simplicity, we assume that the stations are indexed and ordered lexicographically from 1 to **N**.

The ordered exploration of all the stations determines the cycle time. For any station, it is the time interval wasted between two successive opporunities to effectively use the channel, and it is, in general, dependent of the number of stations in the logical ring and of the service discipline of the stations

For our purposes, we define the virtual ring (for any station) as the sequence of stations which have been sent any data message during the preceding cycle

The standard token-passing bus scheme forces the token to explore all the stations of the logical ring although only few of them have data messages to transmit

The Proposal-Petition Protocol proposed scheme aims at taking advantage of the circulating information on the bus to approximate the proposals to the expected virtual ring

We can conceptualize the functions of the Proposal-Petition Protocol as two fold. 1 Determining which of the stations have waiting messages; 2.Scheduling the usage of the communication line for stations having waiting messages

The token will jump forward across the logical ring between stations not necessarily in consecutive order in the logical ring. Each station collaborates to the protocol by estimating, according to some established criteria, which is the next station to send the token (Proposal process) However, in order to insure that all stations can send their messages in the actual cycle, a process, by which erroneous estimation of the virtual ring could be corrected, must be provided (Petition and Search processes).

The virtual ring will only be known a priori if there is deterministic knowledge of load distribution among the stations in the logical ring. As this is not the case, we will use some probabilistic knowledge of the load distribution to estimate the virtual ring The virtual ring is estimated at each step by the master station before sending the token to a station

2.1. THE PROPOSAL PROCESS

In determining a method to estimate the virtual ring or, in other words, to choose the next station in the virtual ring to which the token will be sent, we consider the use of three criteria. They are based on the method used to select the length of the jump. The first one is not new but allows a direct comparison with the token-passing bus method. The second one uses the same basic criterion as in the adaptive Probing or centralized polling scheme of Hayes [5], and the last one is also an adaptive method suitable for systems with non symmetrical load distribution. If we denote by ***d*** the circular distance between the master (actual token holding) station address and the address of the estimated station following the master one in the virtual ring.

> Protocol pppl1. ***d*** : = 1. The proposal is sent to the next station in the logical ring in a round-robin fashion; the token will explore all the stations in sequential order It is a static scheme equivalent to the classical Token-Passing Bus scheme.

Protocol ppplm $d := \lfloor \mathbf{N}/\mathbf{m} \rfloor$, where **m** is the number of stations which have sent any data message during the preceding cycle and **N** is the number of stations in the logical ring. Such a scheme incorporates statistical knowledge about the number of active users per cycle and it conjectures the best strategy to follow is to jump the average number of active stations and to search for a new bus user in the next group of $\lfloor \mathbf{N}/\mathbf{m} \rfloor$ stations of the logical ring. When **m** is greater than the half the number of stations, it works like a pppl1 scheme.

Protocol pppla $d :=$ **apc**, where **apc** is the distance to the next station which, in the preceding cycle, has sent any data message. It is a jump to the first active station in the last cycle. Such a scheme incorporates distributed statistical knowledge about all the active stations of the network. The logical ring is divided into **m** variable-size groups and it is estimated that the best policy consist in considering that a station which has sent a data message in the preceding cycle will probably use the channel in the next one. On burst, biased or asymmetric load conditions, it seems to be a good policy. Furthermore, the pppla scheme tends to the pppl1 scheme under heavy and symmetric load conditions.

They may be other criteria for determining the proposal of estimated next station to which the token will be sent, but the ones presented are of very low cost. The first one needs nothing because it is pre-stablished. The second scheme needs only counting the number of active stations per cycle and perform an integer division. The last one must only memorize one address in each cycle. Obviously it is possible to devise other criteria that, with greater cost, realize some calculations about access time of each station in order to determine the estimated period of each of them.

2.2. THE PETITION AND SEARCH PROCESSES

This a way to correct a bad estimation of the virtual ring. The token jumps forward in the logical ring as long no station with data messages to transmit is by-passed. If so, that station must be located in order to preserve the cyclical sending of the stations.

In a previous paper [4] we have presented a search process that used an alphabet formed with two elements, "Noise" and "Silence": The first element was used to indicate the Petition of one or more stations to acquire the token, and "Silence" indicated that no stations with pending messages were waiting. It was a blind-like search process because the controlling token station (the master station) did not know anything about the petitioner stations.

In the present work we extend the alphabet to be formed with three elements, adding to the preceding ones a "Target" element. Each by-passed station, when it wants to get the token because it has pending messages, sends a Petition message and includes in it its own address. If there is no Petition message, the master station detects, as in the previous case, the "Silence" element. When there is only one Petition message, the master stations detects the "Target" element with the address of the closest station with pending messages. Finally, if there are two or more stations sending Petitons messages simultaneously, the channel acts performing the logical addition of signals sent by all the stations; the colliding information will be lost and, so, the global petition will appear as the "Noise" element. Furthermore, if any station that sends a Petition message detects that other ones are currently sent, it can reinforce the noise in the channel in a similar way the CSMA/CD reacts from a collision.

The result of such a scheme is that the master station,which was looking for the new estimation of the virtual ring after the "Noise" element, in the preceding version of the protocol, will acquire more information of the petitioner station if the Proposal only overlaps one station with pending messages ("Target" element). From here, the next proposal will be sent directly to that station. Alternatively, if it detects "Noise" in the channel, the next Proposal will be sent to a half distance of the last Proposal, as in the blind-like search process.

3. PERFORMANCE EVALUATION

In order to evaluate the performance of such a system, a simulation model has been built using QNAP2 language [14] and trying to represent as exactly as possible how the system runs in the different hypothesis. By this way, we can obtain better results than with approximate analytic analysis like in [11]. However, an approximate analytic-graphic model is built to estimate the cycle time. The performance is compared, like in [1], with conventional protocols (token-passing) and with its initial version with the blind-like search process.

3.1. SIMULATION MODEL CHARACTERISTICS

Each station is composed of two queues: the entry and the processing queues. The entry queue is passive and represents the data messages storage from their arrival to the system until the moment in which the processing queue of the same station has the token and the messages are sent to their destination through the bus. In consequence, it has no explicit service time. The interarrival time is simulated by an exponential distribution of constant mean, whose value depends on the studied case.

The processing queue is active and receives only one customer: the token, when it arrives from the preceding station through the bus. When the processing queue receives the token, its sends the data messages waiting in the associated entry queue and it estimates the new virtual ring, according to the different criteria, waht means to decide the next station to which the token must be sent. After sending the token, it looks for any Petition message (Target or Noise elements). In any of those cases, it takes again the token to start the search process that depends on the number of overlapped stations in the preceding Proposal jump of the token. Once the closest overlapped station is discovered (directly in Target case, and through the blind-like search process in Noise case), it sends the token to that station through the bus.

Finally there is a single queue server that links all the stations: the bus. It receives two classes of customers: token and data messages. The bus receives the token from a station processing queue and tries to send it to the next scheduled station in the estimated virtual ring. If there are no overlapped stations with data messages waiting (Silence), the token arrives to the proposed station. If only one of the overlapped stations has som data messages waiting in its entry queue (Target situation), the bus returns the token to the sending station with the identification (Target) of that station. If more than one of the overlapped stations have some data messages waiting in their entry queue (Noise situation), the bus returns the token to the sending station to begin the dichotomic search process. An auxiliary semaphore avoids the collision problems in the transmission of token and data messages.

The simulation values are parametrized by **a**, the normalized propagation delay [**a = Tp/Tm**], **b**, the normalized token transmission time [**b = Tr/Tm**], and **c**, the normalized petition window time [**c = Ts/Tm**]. In the case to have **a** = 0.1, **b** = 0.1 and **c** = 0.05, the may represent, for a 10 Mhz frequency channel, the case corresponding to 1000 bits message length (**Tm**), 100 bits proposal (token) length (**Tr**) and 50 bits petition window (**Ts**), in a 2 km (100 bits time) channel length (**Tp**). The considered network has **N** = 64 stations.

To estimate the confidence intervals of the results, the spectral method is used. The simulation time is chosen long enough to ensure confidence intervals less than 5 per cent for the main results.

3.2. SIMULATION RESULTS

The main results to obtain are the response and cycle times (normalized by the service time) under different load conditions, station service disciplines and virtual ring estimation criteria, and they are presented as follows:

Figure 3.1 shows the normalized response time (ratio between message response time and service time) versus the channel utilization (arrival frequency times the message service time) with balanced load and exhaustive service. For comparison, there is also represented the response time for the protocol with blind-like procedure [3].

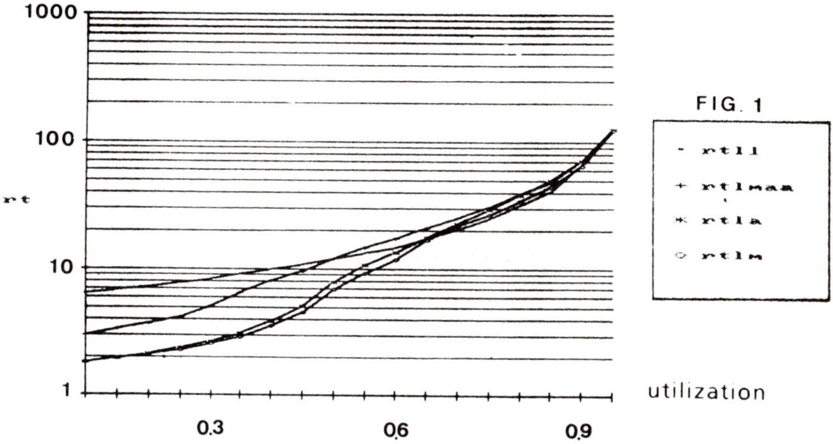

FIG. 1

Figure 3.2 shows the normalized response time versus the channel utilization with unbalanced load (30 and 50 per cent of the load arriving at a given station) and exhaustive service

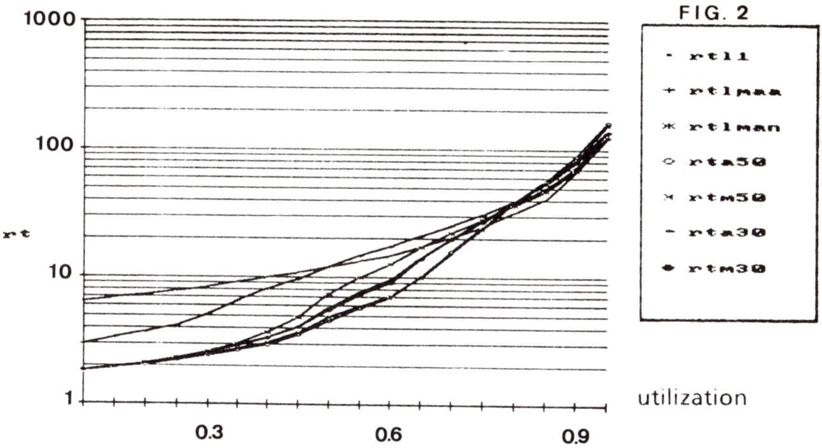

FIG. 2

Figure 3.3 shows the normalized response time versus the channel utilization with unbalanced load (concentrated in two and three consecutive stations) and exhaustive service

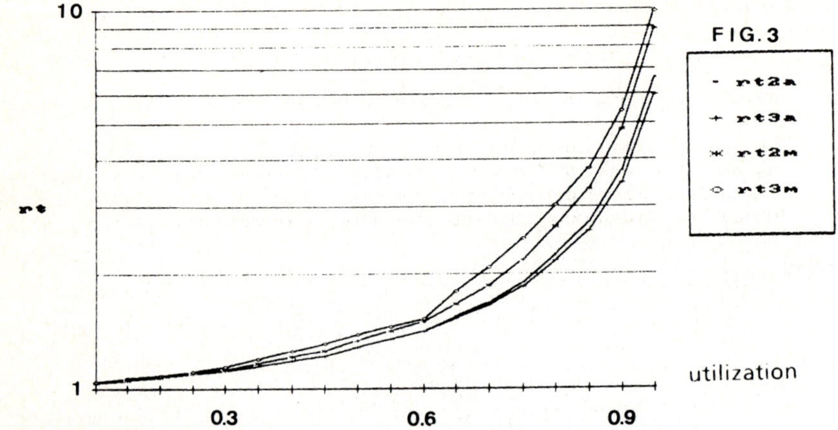

Figures 3.4 , 3.5 and 3.6. show the normalized cycle time (ratio between cycle time and service time) versus the channel utilization in the same conditions of figures 3.1 , 3.2. and 3.3., respectively

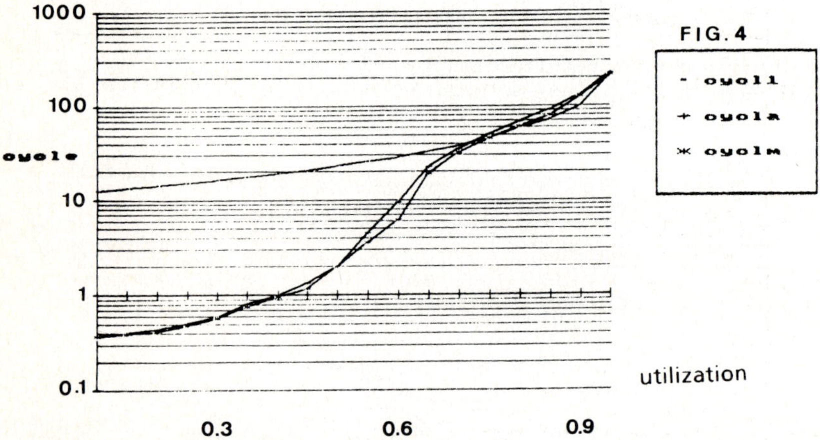

For most of the results, confidence intervals are around 1 per cent. In the worst cases, the confidence intervals are always under 5 per cent.

The legend for all the figures is

rt	Response time
cyc	Cycle time
l1	Token-passing protocol
lmaa	Proposal Petition protocol (ancient version)
la	Proposal-Petition protocol (pppla scheme)
lm	Proposal-Petition protocol (ppplm scheme)
lman	Proposal-Petition protocol (average of pppla and ppplm schemes)
a50	Proposal-Petition protocol (pppla scheme) with one station receiving 50 per cent of the load

m50	Proposal-Petition protocol (ppplm scheme) with one station receiving 50 per cent of the load
a30	Proposal-Petition protocol (pppla scheme) with one station receiving 30 per cent of the load
m30	Proposal-Petition protocol (ppplm scheme) with one station receiving 30 per cent of the load
2a	Proposal-Petition protocol (pppla scheme) with the load concentrated in two stations
2m	Proposal-Petition protocol (ppplm scheme) with the load concentrated in two stations
3a	Proposal-Petition protocol (pppla scheme) with the load concentrated in three stations
3m	Proposal-Petition protocol (ppplm scheme) with the load concentrated in three stations

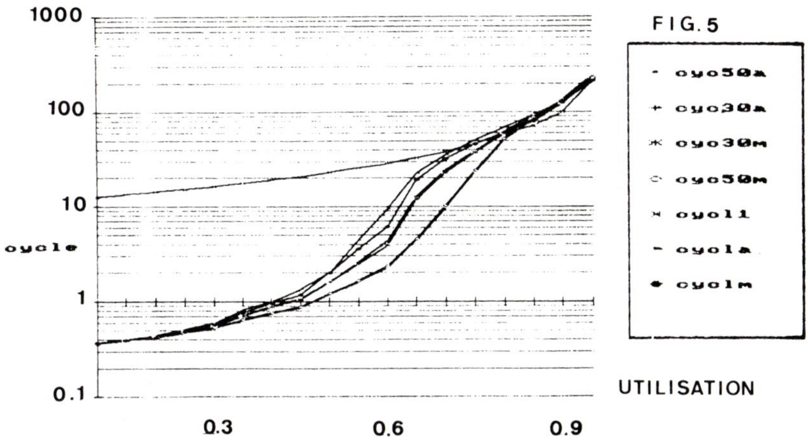

FIG. 5

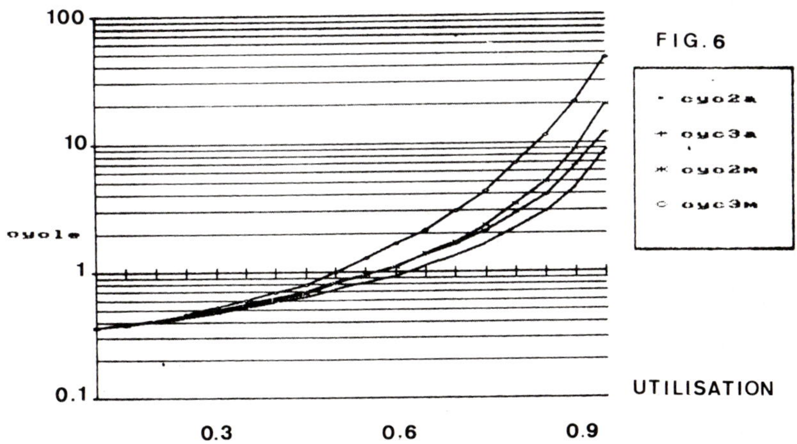

FIG. 6

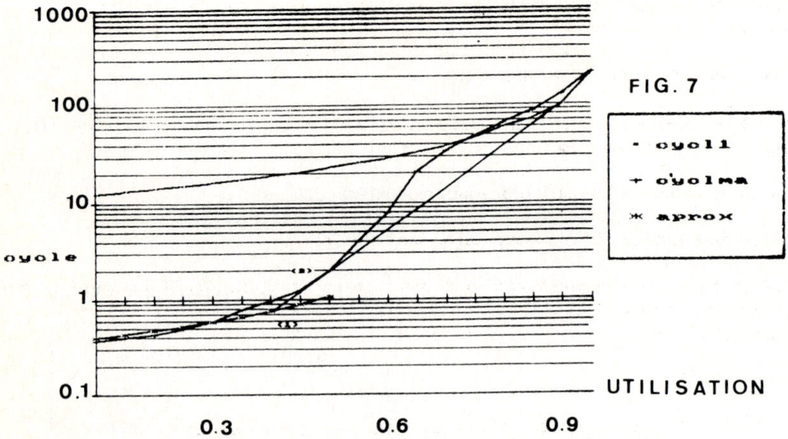

FIG. 7

3.3. COMMENTS

As we can see by inspection of figure 3 1 , the results corresponding to both policies in the definition of the virtual ring (pppla and ppplm schemes) are very close for balanced load and exhaustive service Also, the use of the improvements on the search process (three possible answers to a petition: Silence, Target and Noise) makes a reduction of about 50 per cent in the normalized response time over the Proposal-Petition Protocol with only two possible answers (Silence and Noise) at low load level (for utilizations between 0 and 0.45); this reduction can be explained by the better knowledge in the estimation of the virtual ring, due to the information sent with the petition message. This fact represents to reduce the number of trials to discover the station with data messages waiting from base two logarithm of the distance to one As the load increases over this level the reduction decreases and both response time curves (pppla and ppplm schemes) cut the token-passing protocol one at a utilization of about 0.7 From this point all the curves are almost confused. This similar behaviour for both criteria (pppla and ppplm) might be expected because, at low load level (zero or one active stations per cycle), the token is sent several times from master station to itself until a new arrival appears and a petition message is sent. The inspection of figure 3.4. shows the reason this better behaviour: the cycle time reduction with respect to token-passing protocol.

When load is unbalanced, we obtain a small advantage in response time at low load level (zero or one active stations per cycle), as we might expect due to the fact that the overloaded station has the greatest arrival probability. For the overloaded station the response time is still better.

When load is concentrated in a small number of consecutive stations (two or three), we obtain a still better behaviour at all load levels, due to the high number of hits in the definition of the virtual ring This is especially true for pppla search method, that avoids visits to non-active stations. In ppplm search method, the token visits a reduced number of non-active stations. As consequence, we obtain significant improvements in both response and cycle time.

3.4. APPROXIMATE ANALYTIC-GRAPHIC MODEL

At low load level (small number of arrivals per cycle), we can consider that the cycle time (**Tc**) will be approximately composed by:

- the proposal time (**Tr**) plus the propagation time (**Tp**)
- the petition window (**Ts**) plus the propagation time (**Tp**)
- the time spent in processing the arrivals (**Y** per time unit) in a cycle (**Tc**). This processing time is composed by a new proposal time (**Tr**) plus a new petition window (**Ts**) with their associated propagation times plus the message transmission time (**Tm**).

Thus,

$$Tc = Tr + Tp + Ts + Tp + Y\,Tc\,(Tr + Ts + 2\,Tp + Tm)$$

We can derive

$$Tc = (Tr + Ts + 2\,Tp)/[1 - Y\,(Tr + Ts + 2\,Tp + Tm)]$$

Using normalized variables **C** = **Tc/Tm** and **U** = **Y Tm**, we obtain

$$C = (2a + b + c)/[1 - U(1 + 2a + b + c)] \qquad (1)$$

When we are around one arrival per cycle time, the cycle time will be, following a similar reasoning as in the previous case,

$$Tc = 2(Tr + Ts + 2\,Tp) + Y\,Tc\,(Tr + Ts + 2\,Tp + Tm)$$

We can derive

$$C = 2(2a + b + c)/[1 - U(1 + 2a + b + c)]$$

For exactly one arrival per cycle, it will happen

$$Y\,Tc = 1 \qquad \text{or} \qquad U\,C = 1$$

From the last two expressions, we can derive

$$C = 1 + 3(2a + b + c) \qquad (2)$$

Finally, at high load level, our protocols will tend to work like the pppl1 protocol.

In a semi-logarithmical graphic, as we can see in figure 3.7., we can approximate the cycle time by the curve in eq. (1) at low load level, by the well known cycle time of the pppl1 (token-passing protocol) at high load level and, in the intermediate zone, by a straight line tangent to the pppl1 curve and passing by the point given by eq. (2).

4. CONCLUSIONS

In conclusion, we consider this new search process of the Proposal-Petition Protocol an easy and cheap improvement to incorporate to the initial version.

This protocol will be useful for a large number of stations with low load, as it happens in a L.A.N. to connect the components of a distirbuted control system.

The policy of sending the token to the last active station (pppla scheme) is better than the one of the average number of active stations per cycle (ppplm scheme), when we have a small number of overloaded stations or the load concentrated in them. Nevertheless, in case of balanced load, both schemes having similar performance, the ppplm scheme is cheaper in information to be stored.

5. BIBLIOGRAPHY

[1] BUX, W.: "Local Area Subnetworks: A Performance Comparison". IEEE Transctions on Communications. Vol. COM29 (10). pp. 1465-1473 (Oct. 1981).

[2] CAPETANAKIS, J. I.: "Tree Algorithms for Packet Broadcast Channels". IEEE Transctions on Information Theory. Col IT25 (5). pp. 505-515. (Sept. 1979).

[3] FUERTES, J. M.: "Protocol adaptatiu de nivell dos "proposta-Petició" per a l'accés múltiple a un canal de comunicació". Ph. D. Thesis. Universitat Politècnica de Catalunya. Barcelona (July 1986).

[4] FUERTES, J. M.: "The Proposal-Petiton Protocol: A Multiple Acces Dynamic Scheduling Scheme for Channel Communication": Inst. Symposium on LAN Communication Systems: LAN and PBX". Toulouse (Nov. 1986).

[5] HAYES, J. F.: "An Adaptive Technique for Local Distribution". IEEE Transactions on Communications. Vol. COM26 (8). pp. 1178-1186. (Aug. 1978).

[6] KLEINROCK, L.; YEMINI, Y.: "An Optimal Adaptive Scheme for Multiaccess Broadcast Communication". Proc. ICC Conference. pp. 7.2.1-7.2.5. Toronto (June 1978).

[7] KUROSE, J. F.; SCHWARTZ, M.; YEMINI, Y.: "Multiple-Access Protocols and Time-Constrained Communication". ACM Computing Surveys. Vol 16 (1). pp. 43-70 (Mar. 1984).

[8] MARKUS, G. D.; PAPANTONIS-KAZACOS, P.: "Dynamic Scheduling Protocols for a Multiple-Access Channel". IEEE Transactions on Communications. Vol COM31 (9). pp. 1046-1054 (Sept. 1983).

[9] SCHWARTZ, G. B.: "Polling in a Loop System". Journal of the ACM. Vol. 27 (1). pp. 42-59 (Jan. 1980).

[10] SLOMAN, M. S.; PRINCE, S.: "Local Network Architecture for Process Control". Proceedings IFIP-80. Zurich. (1980).

[11] STUCK, B. W.: "Calculating the Maximum Mean Data RAte in Local Area Networks" IEEE Computer. pp. 72-76 (May 1983).

[12] SYKAS, E. D.; PROTONOTARIOS, E. N.: "Adaptive CSMA and CSMA/CD Protocols". IEEE Melecon'83. Vol. 2. pp. 537-543.

[13] TOWSLEY, D.; WOLF, J. K.: "On Adaptive Tree Polling Algorithms". IEEE Transactions on Communications. Vol. COM32 (12). pp. 1294-1298. (Dec. 1984).

[14] QNAP2. Manuel de Réference. Simulog 1984.3

Network Information Processing Systems
K. Boyanov, R. Angelinov (Editors)
Elsevier Science Publishers B.V. (North-Holland)

A Toolkit for Specifying and Implementing Communication Protocols

A. Fleischmann, S. Pappe, K. Urbschat, T. Kunz

IBM European Networking Center
West-Germany, Heidelberg
September 1987

Abstract

This paper introduces a system of tools, based on a specification language called PASS (Parallel Activities Specification Scheme) for communication protocols. PASS allows the separate description of the main aspects of parallel processes: process communication/synchronization, process behavior and process data. Based on PASS a toolkit for specification, validation and implementation of communication protocols is presented. We conclude the paper with a discussion of experiences of applying the PASS tools to ISO/OSI protocols from layer 3 up to layer 7.

1. Introduction

For describing communication protocols, several specification languages have been developed (for an overview see [SPECS87]). In particular, the International Standard Organisation (ISO) and the International Telegraph and Telephone Consultative Committee (CCITT) are working on the standardization of formal description languages for protocols [ESTELLE], [LOTOS], [SDL]. All of these languages allow parallel processes. Processes are defined by programs. A program consisting of several processes which can run in parallel is called a parallel program. Programs containing only one process are called sequential programs.

The description of processes has the following main aspects:

- Communication and synchronization
  In general, processes must cooperate to meet their common task. For organizing their cooperation they have to exchange information (communication) and to synchronize. For communication, processes share variables or exchange messages. Related to this type of communication, certain methods of synchronization (see [Barr86]) are available.
- Process behavior
  A process operates on its variables, transfers information to other processes and receives information from other processes. The allowed sequences of such actions define the behavior of a process.
- Data
  A complete process specification contains the description of variables of processes and the corresponding operations.

In the currently suggested specification languages for protocols, these aspects are not separately described from each other. In particular, process behavior aspects and data aspects are mixed. This interleaving has impacts on tools. It is not possible to develop separate tools for the different aspects of process specifications.

In the following sections, a specification language is presented which allows the separate description of communication/synchronization aspects, process behavior aspects and data aspects. According to this separation, tools have been developed for the different parts of a process specification. These tools are described in chapter 3 of this paper. Finally, the experience gained with this specification language and the related tools are discussed.

2. *Main Concepts of the Specification Technique PASS*

PASS is a specification technique for describing systems of communicating processes. A system described in PASS consists of a number of processes exchanging messages. Processes are activities which send messages, receive messages and execute operations on local or shared variables. Each process is described in an extended state model.

In the following sections, only the main aspects are described (i.e. shared variables in PASS are not discussed). A complete description is contained in [Fleis87].

In PASS, the communication relation between processes is represented by the communication structure. It describes which processes belong to a process system and which messages are exchanged. Messages have names and parameters. Messages with the same name are of the same message type.
In the graphical representation of a communication structure, processes are represented by boxes marked with the name of the process. An arrow, marked with the name of the message, points from the sending to the receiving processes. In PASS, the description of a process consists of

- an input pool,
- a PASS graph, and
- the PASS graph refinements.

2.1. Input Pool Concept

In general, processes can exchange messages either synchronously or asynchronously. Synchronous message exchange means that the sending process waits until the addressee accepts a message and vice versa. If processes exchange messages asynchronously, a sending process is never blocked. The messages are deposited in an unbounded queue (usually a FIFO queue) and the sending process continues working. Both kinds of message exchange have several advantages and disadvantages. The main disadvantage of synchronous message exchange is, that communicating processes are coupled very tightly, whereas asynchronous message exchange has the disadvantage that a very fast sending process can fill up the queue of a slow receiver until it runs out of memory. In order to avoid these disadvantages in PASS a so called input pool concept is introduced. Each process has an input pool. In the input pool of a process the properties of the communication with that process are described.

Input pools have a designer-defined size. The **input pool size** specifies how many messages can be stored in an input pool. An input pool size of zero corresponds to synchronous message exchange. If a process sends messages to a process with an input pool size of zero, the sending process is blocked until the receiver accepts the message directly. If the input pool size is greater than zero, a sending process will be only blocked if the input pool of the receiver is full (input pool size = number of messages in the input pool).

Input pools of a size greater than zero can be structured. An **input pool structure** defines the maximum number of messages of a certain type or from a certain process which can be in the input pool at the same time. If a maximum number of zero is specified for certain messages, then these messages must be exchanged synchronously.

If an input pool is full and an additional message shall be deposited in that input pool the corresponding sending process is blocked. A different reaction can be specified in the attribute clause of an input pool specification. **Input pool attributes** specify the input pool behavior if it is full. Instead of the default behavior 'block the sending process' messages in the input pool can be replaced by the offered message using different policies (oldest one, youngest one etc.).

In the **reaction time** clause of an input pool, the time frame is specified in which a message will be accepted by the corresponding process. In this clause it is defined how long a message will be in the input pool at least and after which time it will be accepted by the corresponding process.

The input pool concept allows a flexible definition of the communication between processes without introducing support processes (e.g. buffer processes). The reaction time clause describes the time restrictions of the communication.

2.2. PASS Graph

PASS graphs describe the sequences in which a process sends messages, receives messages and does computations on variables. In this model, the transitions from one state to another can have four different reasons: A transition can be triggered by sending messages, receiving messages, results of internal operations and internal functions (internal operations change variables, internal functions check the values of variables). Corresponding to this four types in the description of PASS graphs, two types of communication nodes and two types of internal nodes are distinguished:

1. A **send node** corresponds to a main state where a process intends to send a message to another process. Depending on the input pool specification of the receiver, the sending is done synchronously or asynchronously. A sending process can be blocked if the message cannot be deposited in the input pool of the receiver (asynchronous) or if the message is not expected by the receiver (synchronous).

   If a process wants to send different messages alternatively then send nodes can have multiple outgoing edges. The outgoing edges are marked with the message type and the name of the process which shall receive this message. Depending on the message to be sent, the process performs the corresponding transition. If a send node has two or more outgoing edges, and two or more messages can be sent, one of the possible transitions has to be chosen. For this purpose, a priority list can be defined. The transition with the highest priority is then executed. If a process can not send any message and shall be blocked only for a certain time period a time-out edge can be provided. If a process cannot send any message the time-out transition is executed.

   The graphical representation of a send node (figure 1) is a box with double- or bold-line arrows for the transitions. A priority list can be entered in the lower left half of the box. A time-out transition is represented by an edge marked "time", and the timer value is entered in the lower right half of the box.

2. A **receive node** corresponds to a state where a process expects a message from another process. If a process has an input pool and the expected message is in the input pool, the transition to the next state is executed. If a process has no input pool but the expected message is offered by the corresponding process, the transition to the successor state can be performed. If the expected message is not in the input pool (input pool size greater than zero) or is not offered by the corresponding process (input pool size equal zero), the receiving process will be blocked. The receipt of different messages, possibly from different processes, is allowed in one receive state; a corresponding number of edges leave the state. The outgoing edges are marked with the message type and the name of the sending process from which the message is expected.

   If a receive node has two or more outgoing edges, and two or more messages can be received, one of the allowable transitions has to be chosen. For this purpose, a priority list can be defined. The transition with the highest priority is then executed.

   When none of the expected messages arrives, a receiving process is blocked. In order to avoid permanent blocking, a time-out mechanism is modeled in PASS. A time-out transition is specified with its own edge, similar to the time-out edge in the send state.

   The graphical representation of a receive node (figure 1) is a box with single-line arrows as the outgoing edges. The type of the expected message and the name of the sending process are marked on each edge. A priority list can be entered in the lower left half of the box. A time-out transition is represented by an edge marked "time", and the timer value is entered in the lower right half of the box.

3. An **internal function** corresponds to a main state where a process evaluates local variables. Since PASS is based on *extended* finite state machines, it must be possible to evaluate the status of local variables and make transitions based on their values. For example, process execution can depend on the contents of an arriving message. Since a receive node only distinguishes types of arriving messages, but not their contents, message contents are evaluated in a subsequent internal function node. Another example for an internal evaluation is a counter for the number of unacknowledged frames. Since the result of an internal evaluation is deterministic, exactly one transition will be executed. There are no priorities, and there is no time-out.

   The graphical representation of an internal function (figure 1) is an oval with single-line arrows for the transitions. The lower half of the oval contains the name of the internal function. The upper half contains the optional state name. Each outgoing edge is marked with the result of the variable evaluation, leading to this transition.

4. An **internal operation** corresponds to a state where a process assigns new values to local variables. Depending on the computed new value, different transitions to successor states can be made. As for internal functions, the internal operation is deterministic; therefore, there are no priorities and no time-out.

   The graphical representation of an internal operation (figure 1) is an oval with double-line arrows for the transitions. The lower half of the oval contains the name of the internal operation. The upper half contains an optional state name. Each outgoing edge is marked with the outcome of the internal operation, leading to this transition. A common case for an internal operation is to provide for an error exit.

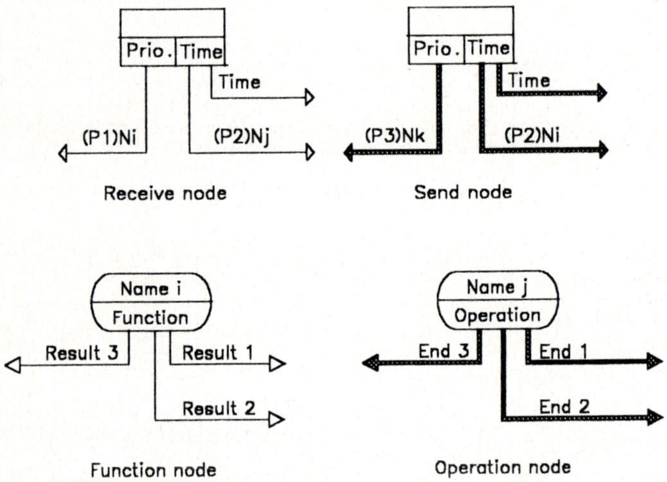

Figure 1. The four node types of PASS

2.3. PASS Graph Refinements

The PASS graph refinements contain the local variables of a process and the operations and functions defined on the local variables (operations change the values of local variables, functions leave them unchanged). Corresponding to the node types in PASS graphs, there are four different types of operations and functions. For each message type which can be received by a process, a *receive message specification* exists. The receive message specification describes the message parameters and the effect of a received message on the values of the local variables. For each message type which is sent by a process, a *send message specification* exists. The send message specification describes the message parameters and how the values of the message parameters are derived from the values of the local variables. The *internal operation specification* describes how an internal operation changes the values of the local variables. Besides the changes of the values of the local variables, an internal operation can yield different results (for example a PUSH operation on a stack of limited depth can have the result 'done' or 'stack full'). The internal operation specification also contains the possible results. The *internal function specification* defines the possible results of the internal functions independent of the values of the internal variables.

Between the PASS graph and the PASS graph refinements there is only a textual relationship (names of internal operations, internal functions and messages), therefore, for describing PASS graph refinements, any specification technique can be used (natural language, algebraic specification etc). The choice of the specification language depends on the problem given and the taste of the designer.

3. Tools

The tools for PASS are classified into tools for constructing PASS specifications, tools for the validation of PASS specifications and tools for deriving code from a PASS specification.

3.1. Specification Tool: PASS Transition Editor

PATE (PASS Transition Editor) is a special editor which was developed to support users in editing PASS graphs. PATE is a menu-driven program which is operating on a line-oriented notation of a PASS graph. In contrast to the graphical notation (see chapter 2.2.), a line-oriented notation is much easier to implement. Each single-line entry in a PASS table corresponds to a transition in the PASS graph and consists of the four items:

1. current-state
2. event type
3. event
4. successor

In addition, each PASS entry may have an info-line. An info-line can be used for example to document the history of changes in a PASS table.

The procedures supplied by PATE for manipulating and managing PASS tables are accessible via menu and can be divided into five groups:

- INPUT/OUTPUT: The input/output procedures are used to store, load and print a PASS table according to the user's requirements. It is also possible to unload a PASS table in such a way, that it can be processed as input for the code generating program.
- EDITING: There are special functions to edit a PASS table and its corresponding state and event names. PASS entries and info-lines can be added and deleted and manipulated in several other ways.
- ERROR CHECKING: Sinks, sources, islands and unreachable states in a PASS graph can be detected via special check-procedures.
- OPTIMIZATION: States and transitions in a PASS graph can be removed in such a way that the original and the optimized PASS graph are equivalent with respect to the sequence of events in the PASS graph.
- SUBSETTING: Not needed events and their following paths can be discarded.

In the following, the last three items are discussed in more details:

Error checking

PATE provides two kinds of error checking mechanisms: implicit or local error checking and explicit or global error checking.

Implicit error checking relates to a subset of transitions which are affected by the specification of new transitions. In order to avoid invalid transitions in a PASS graph new PASS entries which do not match certain consistency conditions are rejected. The consistency conditions are taking into account that a PASS graph has to be a deterministic graph. For example, it is not possible to specify a transition twice or to enter PASS entries which are distinct only with respect to their successors. This kind of local error checking is always and automatically done, if a new PASS entry is added to a PASS graph.
Explicit error checking can also be regarded as global error checking, as the whole PASS graph is searched for specification errors.
A special menu supplies a set of procedures, which are able to detect errors of the following kind:

- Sinks and sources
  A PASS graph can be checked up for states which have no direct successors (sinks) or predecessors (sources).
- Unreachable states
  Every PASS graph has an entry point which is also called starting state. All other states in a PASS graph must be reachable from this entry point, i.e. there must be a path between the starting state and every other state. States which are not reachable from the starting state are marked by a special procedure.
- Islands

An island denotes a set of states which are not reachable by the remaining states in the PASS graph.

In large PASS graphs these errors are not obvious and usually hard to detect during the specification process.

Optimization

The possibility of optimizing a PASS table is based on the fact, that only the sequence of events and the relations between them is relevant for the PASS graph specification. As every event in a PASS graph corresponds to special program code produced by the generator, the deletion of an event not only results in a smaller PASS table but also will reduce the size of program code produced for the specific application. There is a special optimization procedure which compresses a PASS table in such a way that the original and the optimized PASS graph are equivalent in the sense that both graphs have the same sequences of events. In many cases, a PASS graph contains transition sequences with identical parallel transition events. This means that starting from different PASS graph states identical sequences of events can be found, leading into the same successor state.

In extensive protocol specifications as in the PASS specification of the full ISO-Session-layer [ISO8326], [ISO8327], [FlChEf87], the above optimization step leads to a reduction of the number of transitions from 5540 to 5081 (8%) and of states from 1462 to 1183 (19%).

Subsetting

An application using a communication protocol could be runable with only a part of the functionality of the communication protocol. For decreasing the number of possible service primitives and protocol data units those being unnecessary for the involved user could be removed. Some standards ([ISO8326], [ISO8327] and [ISO8822]) have introduced the possibility to realize only the needed parts of a protocol in case of limited user requirements. The common technique is to define **functional units** representing a certain functionality. Functional units are defined by a set of service primitives respectively protocol data units. Functional units themselves are combined in so-called **subsets** which are negotiated by the peer entities at connection time.

The PATE provides a function to remove service primitives represented by messages if a complete protocol specification is not requested. This leads to a flexible adaptation of the protocol to the user requirements.

3.2. Validation Tools

To validate a specification means to check whether a system is correct. Two aspects of correctness can be distinguished:

- independent from a special application a system must hold certain properties (e.g. live lock free, deadlock free etc.)
- a specified system must do what a designer has intended.

Both aspects of correctness can be supported by tools. For PASS these tools are based on the formal description of the PASS semantics in Prolog [NMMF87] and a graph replacement system [Feder86].

Prolog based tools

For communication structures, input pools, PASS graphs and some parts of PASS graph refinements (variables) the transformation from PASS into Prolog can be done automatically. For this automatic transformation a program is available. The Prolog program automatically derived from a PASS specification contains all information about system behavior. This information about a system and the rules about PASS semantics built an expert system for a certain system originally described in PASS. Basically, this expert system knows all about possible execution paths initiating at a state x ending at a state y, and producing or accepting the sequence S of messages. The expert system can answer questions about [NMMF87]:

- paths of length I (Prolog goal step (X,Y,S)),
- paths of maximal length N (Prolog goal steps (X,Y,S,N)),
- and paths of arbitrary length (Prolog goal reach (X,Y,S)).

The different Prolog goals represent the allowed types of questions to such an expert system. In these questions, parameters are the initial and the final state and the according sequence of events.

This expert system allows to analyse the behavior of a process system. A designer is supported to find out whether a system does what he/she has intended.

PASS Graph Replacement System

Instead of Prolog rules the semantics of PASS are contained in graph replacement rules which interpret a PASS specification. The graph necessary for a graph replacement system is derived automatically from a PASS specification. The graph replacement rules are also implemented in PASCAL (3.200 lines). In this PASS simulation, the behavior of a PASS system can be observed [Feder86]. Special tools based on that interpreter have been developed, especially for performance evaluations.

3.3. Implementation Tools

According to the structure of a PASS specification, code can be generated for input pools, PASS graphs and PASS graph refinements.

The structure of an input pool can be very complex. So far, we have developed a tool to produce automatically produce code for input pools with a basic structure.

The tools for deriving code from PASS graph refinements depend on the used specification language. Therefore this issue is not discussed further in this paper.

Currently, two generators exist to produce code for PASS graphs, based on two concepts of representing the PASS graph in program code (see figure 2):

- the code driven representation and
- the data driven representation.

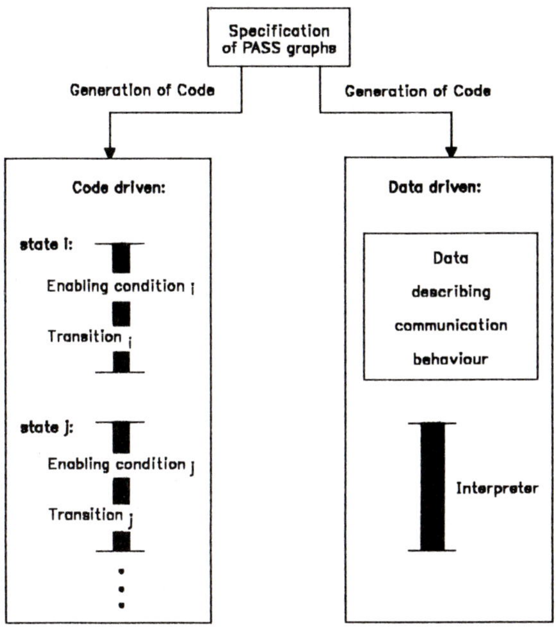

Figure 2. Coding of PASS Graphs

The code driven representation maps the PASS graph completely into program code. Every state of a PASS graph is represented by a sequence of code. Each such piece of code has a label, that corresponds to a state name. After the operations and functions required in a node have been performed, a GOTO to the successor piece of code is executed. For each state type (Transmit-, Receive-, Operation- and Function state) the sequences of code have the same structure. Those sequences include variable parts, that can be determined from the PASS graph.

The data driven representation maps the PASS graph into a data structure that is interpreted at runtime. Instead of having sequences of code for every state, each state type is represented by one sequence of code. The variable parts of the code are determined at runtime from the data structure representing the PASS graph.

Both generators use the line-oriented representation of the PASS graph as input. The code for the PASS graph can be completely generated in PASCAL or in C. No manual programming has to be done.

In order to support the implementation of the PASS graph refinements, the generators produce procedure headers for all required operations and functions, representing the receive message specifications, the send message specifications, the internal operation specifications and the internal function specifications. For getting a complete program, the procedure bodies have to be added according to the functions and operations in the PASS graph refinements.

4. Experiences

Practical experience with PASS was gained in implementation of the following ISO/OSI communication protocols:

- The X.25 layer 3 protocol (packet switching layer) was specified and implemented with PASS in the programming language C on an IBM PC.
- Transport layer (layer 4) class 0 was developed on an IBM PC in the programming language Modula 2 under MS-DOS [Frantz86].
- Session layer (layer 5) was implemented in the programming language Pascal under the operating system VM/SP [Pappe86], [FlChEf87].
- Presentation layer (layer 6) was implemented in Pascal under VM/SP.
- Remote operation service element (ROSE, layer 7) was realized in Pascal under VM/SP.
- Remote Database Access (RDA, layer 7) was realized in Pascal under VM/SP [PaEfLa87].

Implementing these communication protocols with PASS tools shows considerable advantages in contrast to a traditional coding. Using PATE helps to avoid incorrect protocol state transition sequences. The plausibility checks of PATE allow to test the specification on PASS graph level.

The Session and Presentation layer standards introduce functional units which have to be negotiated by the communication partners for their specific requirements. These functional units represents a certain functionality provided by certain service primitives. To get an implementation which realizes only a special functional unit subset, the PATE subsetting feature is used. Thus only a master version of the complete specification containing all functional units is maintained. The needed subsets are derived with the PATE subsetting feature.

The generator can be requested to generate a PASS state tracing facility into the program code. This trace reflects the executed PASS states of the protocol automaton. Thus the debugging and maintenance of the implementation is done at the abstract level of PASS and not at programming language level.

PASS was applied by different people who were in the beginning not very familiar with it. PASS and the use of the tools can be learned very easily. PASS tools generate the complete code for the PASS graph and a code frame for PASS graph refinements. The structure of the PASS tools mirrors the distinction of the main aspects of process description (see chapter 1): process communication, process behavior and process data. Thus use of the PASS methodology forces the implementor to a well-structured design.

We implemented a generator producing code driven code and a generator producing data driven code. Both generators were applied to the PASS graph of the ISO Session protocol. The comparison of the produced code has the following results (compiled with PASCAL/VS IBM compiler for VM/CMS systems) [Urb87]:

Storage code driven: 413 KB
Storage data driven: 51 KB

For the time measurement a representative sequence of messages was used (establishing a section connection, data transfer, releasing a connection):

Time code driven: 11,280 microseconds
Time data driven: 7,994 microseconds

First thoughts expected the code driven implementation to be faster than the data driven implementation. Closer analysis has shown that the runtime management which is involved with procedure calls for the code driven implementation takes more time than the management of the data structure for the data driven implementation. The procedure calls in the code driven version are necessary, because the used compiler has (as many compilers do) a limit for the size of code, that can be included in one procedure. Thus the code for the states is spread over many procedures. With further development the procedure calls can be minimized, so that the two implementations will take the same time. But, the data driven version will always be smaller than the code driven.

If data and behavior aspects are mixed in the specification of a process as in ESTELLE, LOTOS and SDL the generation of data driven code will be very difficult. The behavior of a process has to be extracted from the specification which means that the dynamics of a process has to be analyzed. This is a clue that at least process behavior and data aspects should be described separately.

Conclusion

We wanted to point out that the separation of a process into process communication/synchronization, process data and process behavior aspects as it is made by the PASS specification language helps also to structure the development of a corresponding toolkit. The basis of this toolkit was presented which supports the development of a well-structured specification, the validation and implementation of communication protocols. The discussion of application experiences with using this toolkit has shown the value of the PASS methodology and the related tools for developing communication protocols. New aspects like the data driven implementation of PASS graphs were found and are already implemented, others like the generation of a testing environment for an implementation are for further development.

References

[Barr86] H. Barringer, *A Survey of Verification Techniques for Parallel Programs,* Lecture Notes in Computer Science, No. 191, Springer Verlag, Heidelberg, 1986

[ESTELLE] ISO, Information Processing Systems - Open Systems Interconnection -, *ESTELLE - A Formal Description Technique based on an Extended State Transition Model* ISO 9074

[Feder86] C. Feder, *Ein Interpretierer fuer PASS-Spezifikationen basierend auf einem Grapher-setzungssystem (An Interpreter for PASS-Specifications based on a Graph Replacement System),* Diplomarbeit at the University of Erlangen, 1986

[FlChEf87] A. Fleischmann, S. T. Chin, W. Effelsberg, *Specification and Implementation of an ISO Session Layer,* Technical Report of the IBM European Networking Center, No. 43.8706, 1987

[Fleis87] A. Fleischmann, *PASS a Specification Technique for Parallel Processes,* Technical Report of the IBM European Networking Center, 1987 to appear

[Frantz86] K. Frantz, *Generierung von Protokollen aus einer PASS-Spezifikation am Beispiel der ISO/OSI Transportebene (Generation of a PASS specified ISO/OSI Transport Layer),* Diplomarbeit at the University of Frankfurt, 1986

[ISO7498] ISO, Information Processing Systems - Open Systems Interconnection -, *Basic Reference Model,* ISO 7498

[ISO8326] ISO, Information Processing Systems - Open Systems Interconnection -, *Basic Connection Oriented Session Service Definition,* ISO 8326

[ISO8327] ISO, Information Processing Systems - Open Systems Interconnection -, *Basic Connection Oriented Session Protocol Specification,* ISO 8327

[ISO8822] ISO, Information Processing Systems - Open Systems Interconnection -, *Basic Connection Oriented Presentation Service Definition,* ISO 8822

[LOTOS] ISO, Information Processing Systems - Open Systems Interconnection -, *LOTOS - A Formal Description Technique based on the temporal ordering of observation behavior,* ISO 8807

[NMMF87] I. Neumeier-Mackert, L. Mackert, A. Fleischmann, *A Knowledge-based Protocol Engineering Environment,* Technical Report of the IBM European Networking Center, No. 43.8706, 1987

[Pappe86] S. Pappe, *Anwendung einer Implementierungstechnik für Kommunikationsprotokolle auf das ISO-Kommunikationssteuerungs-Protokoll (Application of an Implementation Technique for Communication Protocols to the ISO Session Layer Protocol),* Diplomarbeit at the University of Karlsruhe, 1986

[PaEfLa87] S. Pappe, W. Effelsberg, W. Lamersdorf, *Database Access in Open Systems. Proc. Networking in Open Systems,* Lecture Notes in Computer Science, No. 248, Springer Verlag, Heidelberg, 1987, pp 148-164

[SDL] CCITT *SDL - Functional Specification and Description Language,* CCITT Red Books Volume VI - Fascicle VI.10 and VI.11, 1984

[SPECS87] Specification Environment for Communication Software (SPECS), Document D4, *A Feasible IBC Software Specification Environment; Part 1, State of the Art; Part 2, Critical Evaluation,* RACE Project, 1987

[Urb87] K. Urbschat, *Vergleich zweier Implementierungstechniken von OSI Kommunikationsprotokollen (Comparison of two Implementation Techniques of OSI Communication Protocols),* Diplomarbeit at the Fachhochschule for Technique of Mannheim, 1987

Network Information Processing Systems
K. Boyanov, R. Angelinov (Editors)
Elsevier Science Publishers B.V. (North-Holland)

A WORK-STATION FOR PROTOCOL ENGINEERING

Hartmut KOENIG

Technical University Dresden, Informatics Centre, G.D.R.

Katalin TARNAY

Central Institute for Physics, Budapest, Hungaria

The development of real-life protocols, especially tgose based on international standards, is a process which needs many efforts during all its phases. It seems necessary to provide more practical tools for real protocol realizations. The paper will outline requirements to a work-station for protocol engineering and present the project under realization in co-operation between our organizations.

1. INTRODUCTION

The development of real-life protocols, especially those based on international standards, is a process which needs many efforts during all its phases. Much work has been done in recent years to investigate this process. It has been shown that using a formal, machine-readable specification its phases can partly be supported by automatic tools, e.g. for validating the design, for deriving implementations and for testing their conformance with international standards. On the other hand there are a lot of approaches proposed in literature. Protocol realizers are sometimes confused in making a right choice. Often, the proposed method is not elaborated enough to be appliable in practice. It seems necessary to provide more practical tools for real protocol realizations. Some of the methods seem to be advanced enough for being a base for such tools [Bochmann 85, 87] , [Rudin 85] .

The paper will outline requirements to a work-station for protocol engineering and present the project which is under development in co-operation between our organizations. It summarizes our former experiences in the field of protocol specification, validation, automated implementation, and testing [Bremer 85] , [Koenig 86]. The work-station proposed has the following aims:

- to provide practicable tools permitting an efficient realization of protocols,

- to support the co-operation between several protocol realizers, and

- to offer wide spectre of different methods.

The paper is organized as follows. In the next section the overall structure of the work-station will be introduced. The following sections will deal with special topics of its components discussing the decisions made in the design.

2. THE OVERALL STRUCTURE OF THE WORK-STATION

The work-station reported here is to support the realization of real-life protocols by means of pra-ticable tools tuned to each other. The design of the work station can be based on following assumptions:

- the protocol development process can be aided by the computer in most of its phases,
- the development of communication protocols will often be realized by larger developer teams,
- there will be a coexistence of various methods in all development phases the choice of which depends on different factors.

Therefore, the work-station should provide tools for the whole protocol development process to guarantee the co-operation between the developers and to support different approaches. The structure proposed for the work-station (see Fig. 1) consists of a set of protocol development tools and a protocol library. In a later phase an expert system will also be included.

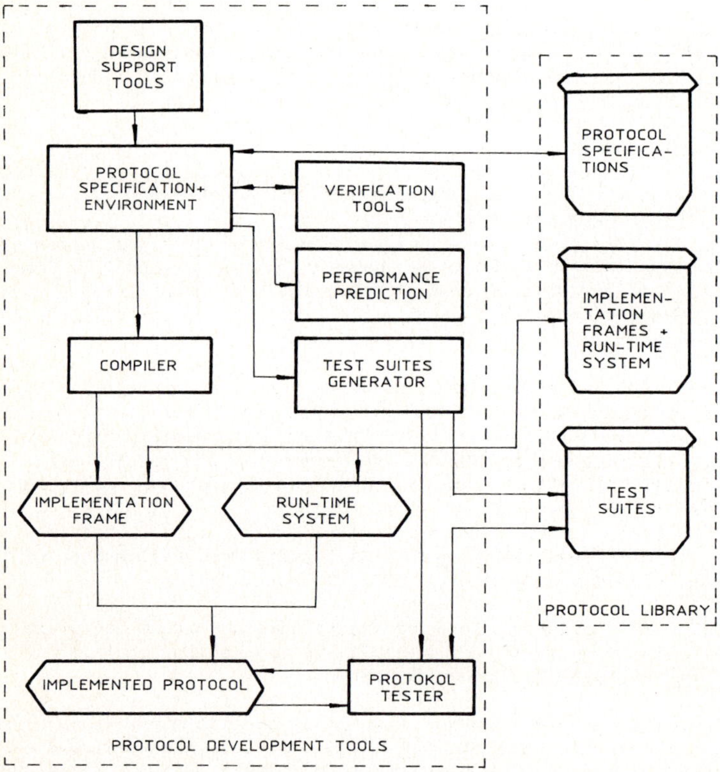

Fig. 1. The overall structure of the work-station

The protocol development tools are to support the protocol realization during all its phases. The base for this is the existence of a machine-readable protocol specification which forms the reference specification for the other tools. Due to the expected coexistence of several specification languages it seems useful to provide seperate technological development lines for the most significant specification languages. We shall discuss this in more detail below.

The protocol library is the connection link between the protocol development tools. It is to support the co-operation between the developers, the use of different methods and the rationalization of the protocol development process including protocol specifications in various representations, implementation frames, test suites and others.

The expert system will be used above all as an adviser system in those phases of the protocol development process where an interaction between the developer and the tools is necessary, e.g. by selecting test suites [Koenig 87c]. The inclusion of expert systems into the protocol development process is still a subject of research with many open questions. It will not be discussed further here.

Besides, such a work-station has to provide means which make its use simple and efficient. Above all there is a need for a small operating system which controls the different components of the work station and realizes the communication with the user. These aspects, although very important for the practical value of the work-station, are not discussed here, too.

3. PROTOCOL DEVELOPMENT TOOLS

3.1. Design support

The protocol design is one of the most important and most creative phases of the protocol development process, but only little attention is focused to it at present because most of the protocols interesting for practical realizations are already designed by international standardization organizations. The protocol developers are more confronted with the following steps than with design problems. Nevertheless, a work-station should provide means to support the protocol design as well as this topic should be more investigated. There will be every time the necessity of designing new protocols, especially in the application field. Other reasons may be the modification of protocols for introducing them in special-purpose communication architectures, for the design of gateways or for protocol maintenance. Methods for the systematic protocol design are a complementary way to develope correct protocols. The availability of such methods is an important precondition for a general computer-aided realization of the protocol development process.

The planned work station will include means for supporting the protocol design. For this purpose we use the software development environment at the Informatics center of the Technical University Dresden which is dedicated to the design of distributed software. It forms the frame system from which specialized environments can be derived. At present, we are realizing such an environment for designing services and specifying them in the formal specification language PDL (see below) [Koenig 87b]. This work is in an experimental phase only and will be reported later.

3.2. Service and Protocol Specification

Machine-readable formal service and protocol specifications are the fundamentals of such a work-station. Most of its components are based on formal descriptions of the services and protocols.

The spectre of methods and languages used for service and protocol specification is very large. The choice of the method will depend on different factors which reach from administrative decisions to the individual experience of the users. The development of standardized FDT's will loosen the multiple approaches used in past to a certain extend. Nevertheless, there will be a coexistence of different techniques in next years. This is partly a consequence of providing different standardized FDT's: ESTELLE and LOTOS by ISO, SDL by CCITT, but above all of the fact, that there is no method, and probably will not be, which completely satisfies all requirements of the service and protocol specification. Therefore, other previous developed techniques will be further used with local importance, in order to profite from their advantages and the gathered experience, particularly as they are often supported by runable software.

For the use of the work-station, which has first of all the task to "work" with the specification, this coexistence of methods may be very useful, because each reflects the protocol in a different manner and this way contributes to a better understanding of the whole protocol. Besides, it is known that the specification techniques favourite methods of the further development phases in a different way. Hence, the work-station should support several FDT's in order to permit the user to chose those techniques which best fit his purposes and promote his thinking. Among the offered languages and methods should be at least one standardized and at least one which may be the base for a technological development line. The transformation from one formal description into another should be possible by means of automatic transformators, as far as this can be realized. Thus it will be possible, for instance, to transform state-oriented protocol specifications into communication-oriented ones, in order to make the communication progress between the interacting entities visible on the monitor.

The work-station we are realizing consists of two development lines at present, one for PDL and one for ESTELLE (see Fig. 2). The Protocol Description Language PDL [Koenig 86] was developed at the Technical University of Dresden. It supports a step-wise protocol development by help of several description levels for the service-, the protocol- and the implementation-specification. The PDL-language-features are strongly connected to the OSI/RM-notions. The description principle is process- and communication-oriented (see Fig. 3). The processes (protocol parts) correspond to subtours in FSM-specifications. They reflect in a goto-free manner the communication progress. PDL supports verifications by means of petri net-analysis [Koenig 86], rapide prototyping [Fischer 87] and automated implementation (see below). The input to the analysis tools is automatically derived from the language representation. The ESTELLE-line will have the same functions, e.g. connection to the petri net-, and rapide prototyping-tools, and automated implementation. The realization of the ESTELLE-compiler has been started, between the two lines transformators are being provided. As first step the transformator PDL-ESTELLE was implemented [Hofmann 87]. Every line will be supplemented by a special language environment including syntax-oriented editors, graphic support and debuggers.

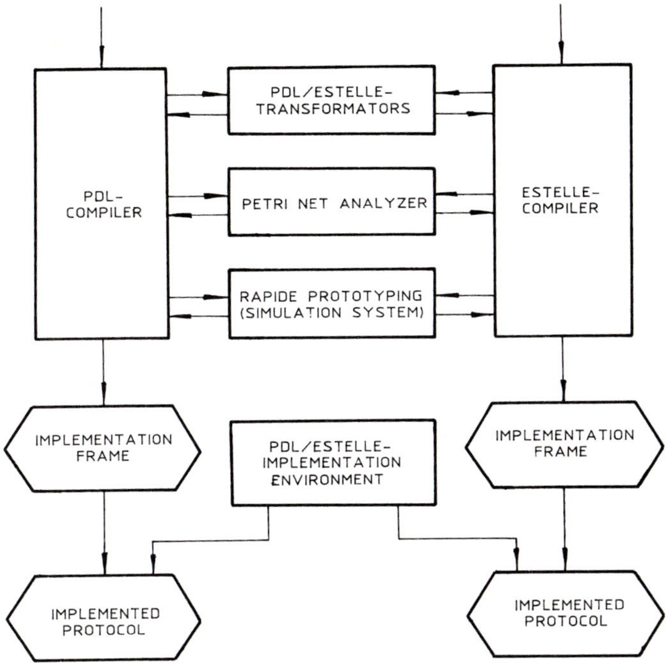

Fig. 2. Structure of the work-station under realikation
(without test tools)

All the transformators mentioned above were realized by help of the meta-language system DEPOT [Loetzsch 86] designed for implementing specialized languages. Our experience shows that such systems are a good tool for the implementation of transformators from one representation into another. The transformators are quickly implemented, usually in few month, without supposing a special knowledge about compilers. The transformator can be realized complete automatically if there is no large difference between the description principles of the methods as in the case of the transformations mentioned above. Otherwise it must be realized in an interactive manner. This is the case for the transformation ESTELLE-PDL [Hofmann 87] because the PDL description structure is a more stronger than the ESTELLE one and, therefore, the mapping has to be supported by the user.

3.3. Verification

In the verification field we find a similar situation. Although many ap-

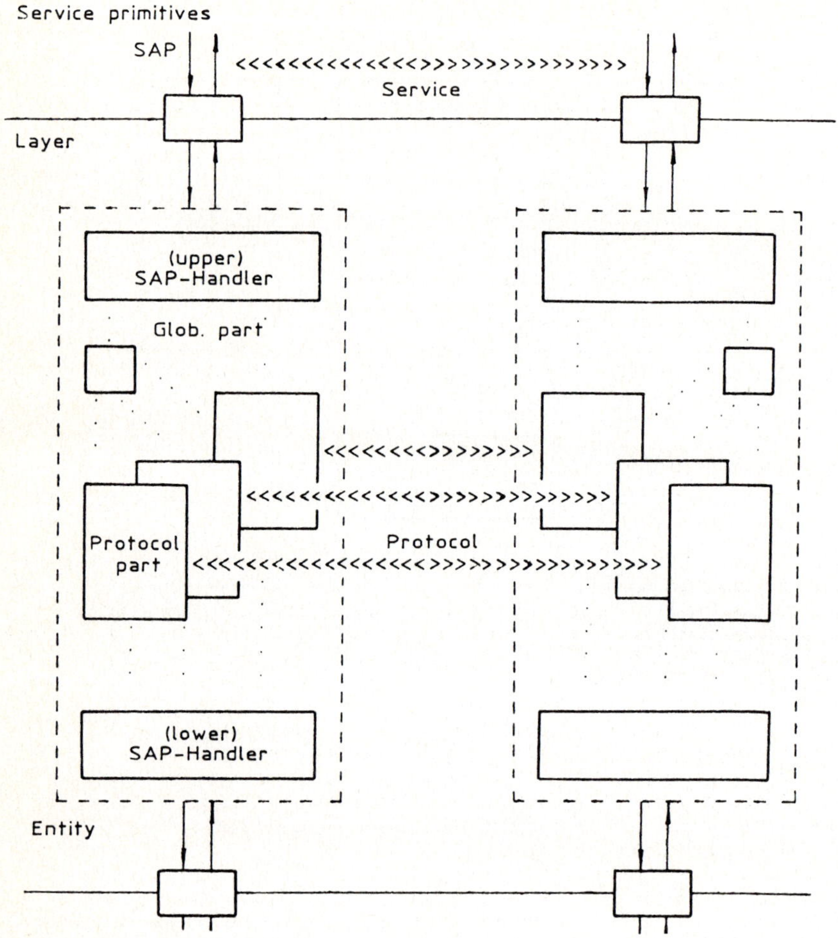

Fig. 3. The PDL-description principle

proaches are persued there is no method which can completely proof the correctness of the protocol design. The handling of complex protocols is also a problem, yet. Therefore, the application of several methods is recommended to decrease the probability of errors. The choice of verification techniques depends on pragmatic aspects as the FDT chosen, the availability of verification tools and the user's familarity with them.

The work-station has to make allowance for this situation and to assure the application of different methods as far as possible independently from the FDT chosen. In this connection it is very important to realize an automatic transformation into the input representation of the verification tools which often differs from the FDT. At moment we provide the laready mentioned petri net-analysis and rapide prototyping which are connected via the PDL-compilers to the formal description. The connection to ESTELLE will be realized within the ESTELLE-compiler-realization. Both tools serve above all for general verification purposes to detect deadlocks, livelocks, uncomplete design, and similar errors. They are tested by several examples, e.g. the transport protocol class 0/2. Now the investigations concentrate on the recognition of the error classes within the FDT's detectable by help of this tools. Furthermore, the simulation system used for rapide prototyping will be also applied for predicting performance based on the FDT.

3.4. Automated Implementation

Automated implementation will be one of the main application fields of such a work station. Computer support for deriving implementations from a formal description can make implmentations of complex protocols much more efficient. Further advantages are the reduction of the implementation error probability, the avoidance of incompatibilities between implementations, a better support of protocol maintenance and the independence from a particular implementor [Aggarwal 85].

The automated implementation approach realized for PDL is based on the concept of a meta-language. This language consists of the implementation language (we use C) extended by specialized functions which are supported by a run-time system. The latter contains, besides such tipical elements as a process- and a subprocess-supervisor, a queue-manager, and a budderpool, features which support the event- and connection-management in protocols. The interface has a very common character. It includes such functions as waiting for events with parallel and selective reactions (guarded commnads), assigning events to queues, starting and resetting of timers, manipulating data structures and others. The PDL-specification modules are transfered into functions of this meta-language which usually are linked to a process for one connection but this can easily be changed. The implementation approach is described in [Koenig 87b] and will be published in more detail in another paper. The ESTELLE-implementation as well as the TTCN-implementation (see below) will be realized in the same manner.

3.5. Conformance Testing

The usage of the work-station for conformance testing depends on the performance of the underlying computer, and on its connection to a test centre. Our work-station is dedicated to the preparation of conformance tests. It is to provide tools for deriving test suites from FDT's, for generating executable test software, and testers for local tests as well (see Fig. 4).

The development of protocol test software needs as much efforts as their realization. Hence, the test tools should be flexible permitting the adaption to different implementation and the realization of various tests. Testers and test scenarios can be interpreted as special kinds of entities and protocols. It seems, therefore, appropriate to apply the principles of automated protocol implementation also to the realization of testers. The approach persued in this connection is based on the implementation of TTCN, the notation described in ISO for describing test scenarios. TTCN has a series of similarities with PDL which allow a straight-forward mapping of TTCN descriptions into PDL/T, a PDL-variant for testing, followed by a generation of executable test code [Koenig 87a,b]. The received tester structure is defined by the PDL-entity con-

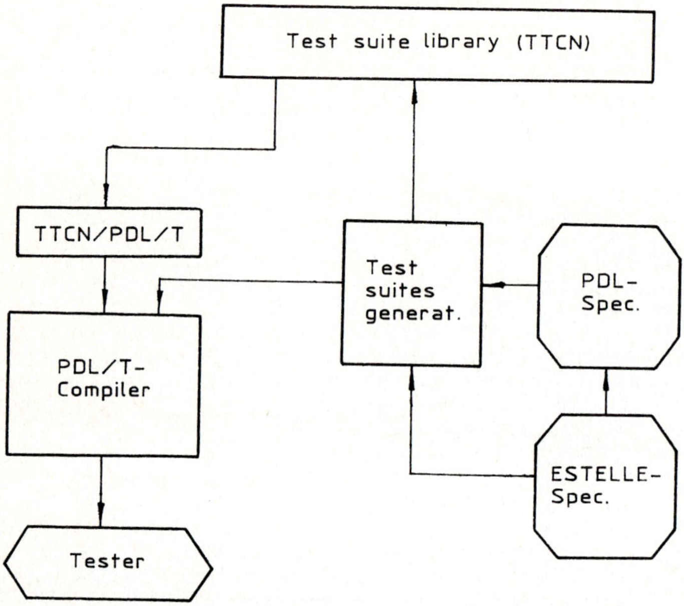

Fig. 4. Test software development tools

cept (see Fig. 3). In this tester structure the protocol parts contain the test sequences whereas the sap handler can be used for adapting to the concrete implementation.

4. PROTOCOL LIBRARY

The protocol library has the key function in this work-station. It is the connection-link between its different components. The protocol library has two functions:

(1) It realizes the exchange of protocol representations between different tools and also between several developers. Thus, it supports the handling of complex protocols by larger developer teams as well as the expected specialization of single members to certain phases and tools.

(2) It is to make future protocol realizations more efficient becoming more and more a "protocol base".

In compliance with our discussion above the protocol library should include protocol descriptions in various formal representations, implementation frames and test suites. Its extension to a protocol base including also specifications, implementations and test suites developed in other organikations would be a contribution to an effective development of communication software. The complexity of protocols and the large efforts necessary for their realization force to exchange and re-use specifications, implementations and test suites. The trend to realize specielized communication architectures as MAP and TOP, which use certain classes or subsets of wide-spread protocols, are a good example for this. The availability of a protocol library simplifies this process because these protocol variants can be derived from the specifications stored in the library using the protocol tools of the work-station.

5. CONCLUDING REMARKS

The work-station proposed will be step by step extended to provide other tools and more comfort to the user. Extensions may be the inclusion of further technological lines based on SDL and LOTOS, other verification tools and graphic support.

REFERENCES

[Aggarwal 85] Aggarwal, S.; Kurshan, R.P.: Automated Implementation from Formal Specification. In Yemini 85 , pp. 127-136

[Bochmann 85] Bochmann, C.v. et al.: Use of Formal Specifications for Protocol Design, Implementation and Testing. In Yemini 85 , pp. 137-144

[Bochmann 87] Bochmann, G.v.: Usage of protocol development tools: the results of a survey. In Rudin, H; West, C.H. (eds.): Protocol Specification, Testing and Verification VII-Participants Proceedings. Zuerich, May 5-8, 1987, 12

[Bremer 85] Bremer, J.; Mondvai, G.; Tarnay, K.; Tibor, T.: Some experiences with Test Sequence Generation in Application Layer. In Yemini 85 , pp. 623-636.

[Sischer 87] Fischer, J.; Koenig, H.: Simulation of Computer Network Protocols Based on Their Formal Description. In Tagungsberichte Problemseminar "Lokale Rechnernetze", Gaussig, Jan. 1987, TU Dresden, Informatikzentrum (to be printed)

[Hoffmann 87] Hoffmann, M.: Entwurf und Realisierung eines Transformators PDL - ESTELLE. Diplomabeit, TU Dresden, Informatikzentrum, 1987

[Koenig 86] Koenig, H.: Heiner, M.: The PDL-System - An Unified Approach to the Specification, Verification and Implementation of Protocols. In Csaba, L.; Tarnay, K.; Szentivanyi, T. (eds.): COMPUTER NETWORK USAGE: Recent Experiences. North-Holland Comp., Amsterdam, 1986, pp. 567-582

[Koenig 87a] Koenig, H.: Developing Protocol Test Software Using the PDL-System. Preprint KFKI Budapest, KFKI-1987-11/M

[Koenig 87b] Koenig, H.: Kommunikationsprotokolle - Prinzip und Entwicklung. Diss. B., TU Dresden, Informatikzentrum, submitted 1987

[Koenig 87c] Koenig, H.; Tarnay, K.: A Intelligent Work-Station for Protocol Engineering. Preprint KFKI Budapest, 1987 (to be printed)

[Loetzsch 86] Loetzsch, J.: The Dresden Specialized Languages Approach. In Proc. of the Workshop "Compiler Compilers and Incremental Compilation", IIR Informatik informationenreporte 12/1986, pp. 35-49

[Rudin 85a] Rudin, H.: An Informal Overview of Formal Protocol Specification. IEEE Communications Magazine, Vol. 23, No 3 (March 1985), pp. 46-52

SPECIAL PURPOSE LANS
AND NETWORK INTERCONNECTIONS

Network Information Processing Systems
K. Boyanov, R. Angelinov (Editors)
Elsevier Science Publishers B.V. (North-Holland)

MANAGEMENT OF RETINE VIDEO TRANSMISSION NETWORK

Abdelali AYACHE and Richard CASTANET

ENSERB - UNIVERSITE DE BORDEAUX I
351,COURS DE LA LIBERATION
33405 TALENCE - FRANCE

The aim of the RETINE project is image transmission using high speed LAN. This paper describes on the one hand the analog sub-network for video transmission, and on the other hand the protocols used to provides these transmissions. We describe the management process for the control of resources and the management of the users. Finally, an overview is given of the evolution of the system within the context of the RETINE project.

I. INTRODUCTION

The need for image transmission has been and still is increasing continously for a large number of users. It was, therefore, included in the ISDN project area[8], but this service needs a very high speed of transmission. This is the reason why image transmission has been studied rather lather than data and voice communication

Local area networks can potentialy provide a wide range of services in the scientific-image field:

- interactive graphics in CAD/CAM applications
- image processing (remote sensing sattelite pictures, medical images...)

But even now local area networks cannot cover all the needs of image processing, especially real time video which expects a channel of at least 50 Mbits/s for a low resolution. Such rates are obviously difficult to provide for a single connection and also finding digital devices operating at these rates isn't any easier

With these considerations in mind, we take a broad band option for the RETINE project. By broad band, we mean there is a sub-network for each kind of data:

- Low speed data transmission (paquet, circuit and voice)
- High speed digigital image transmission (about 100 Mbits/s presently in development)
- Video (or analog image) transmission

In this paper, we focus on on the architecture and management of the video sub-network. With this LAN, we propose a set of video-communication services:

- acces and control of a video-disk data base.
- broadcasting news concerning campus activities.
- broadcasting films, conferences, courses or laboratory experiments.
- digitisation and processing of video images for their diffusion.
- Course illustration tools, in order to present the visual aspect of the subject anywhere on the campus.
- Video-conferenses.

II. LAN TOPOLOGY AND HARDWARE SYSTEM

The retine LAN is presently on a large campus (about 20 km) and in the future it will be extended to a nearby industrial area. It covers the campus and consists of five stations and has a fibre optic ring topology.
The RETINE LAN has been developed with ten optic fibres cables:

- 4 for video transmission
- 2 for voice and low speed data
- 2 for digital image transmission (high speed data)

These fibres are multimode graded index glass with PIN-FET receivers and LED transmitters. They have a 300 Mhz bandwidth belong to class 4.

Video-transmission uses two sub-network, one for the control of the users and the video switching, and the other only for the analog data images without control. The control LAN is a conventional LAN[7], in our case the LCT 6500 providing X25 access ports. Video transmission is provited by a switching system and a connection oriented ptotocol.

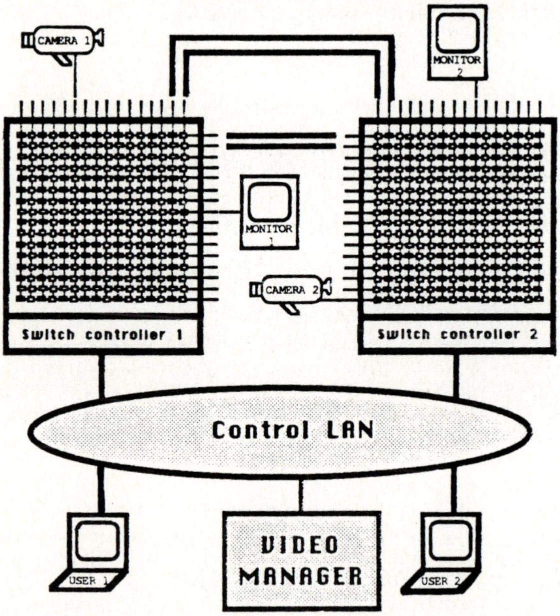

FIGURE 1 : video transmission LAN

The switching matrix is based on 16 wide-band video multiplexers TG536 16*1 with a 300 Mhz bandwitdh. Each switching matrix has 16 inputs and 16 outputs.

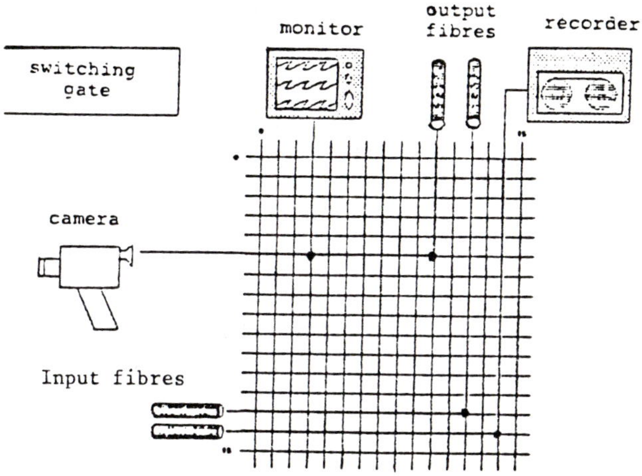

FIGURE 2 : Switching gate

The switching node controller is a 68000 motorola TS-VME 101 microprocessor with the folowings components :

- one switching matrix
- four PIA which control the 16 analog inputs
- one PIA which control the 16 analog outputs
- one ACIA for communication with the video-LAN manager

Switching systems have also been developed in other projects, such as that of IBM [4] , for interconnecting different types of LANs or WANs with gateways or computers. Other solutions have been proposed by IBM[5] for latency minimization in the interconnection control of N high-performance devices, just like processor-memory connection in parallel computing. In these two projects, as in our's, there is a clear separation between the control network and the data network.

III. VIDEO COMMUNICATION PROTOCOL

The video transmission protocol is clearly a connection oriented one. The manager must provide to any user a connection between one source and one (or several) target analog device (s) during a time slice. For certain kinds of source devices, such as video-recorder or video-disk, a controller is included in the kernel manager. In order to provide the connection service, the manager controls two kinds of communication. One is a user connection server with a human-interface, and the other is a monitor which configures the switching nodes involved in the path, computed by the routing algorithm, in order to join with a video-connection the input and ouput analog devices.We focus now in this section on the monitoring protocol of the switching nodes. At this point we have the possibility of controlling these switching nodes following the ring topology, with the manager operating as a master in the folowing protocol:

It sends a packet with the configuration parameters to its following neighbour node and waits for this packet to pass round the loop. Each node processes the incoming packet, possibly executes its switching command, puts its report in the same packet and retransmits the

resulting packet to its following neighbour. When finally, the manager receives the returning packet, depending on its status it would take the appropiate action. But this method assumes that each node knows his own address and the one of his neighbour node and must have the ability to down-load the software of this neighbour node. This would on one hand make heavy demands on the proccessing environment of the switching nodes and on the other hand monopolize permanently the network communication channels of the loop.
The other possible protocol wich has been chosen is that the manager still operates as a master and consists of: after the routing algorithm gives a path through the switching nodes it selects the involved nodes and enters a configuration transaction.This selective transaction configuration can be done with only one network communication channel, due to the LCT 6500. This method, being the opposite of the one above, allows the video manager to down-load the switching nodes software provited it has their network addresses and enables it to select a possible faulty switching controller entity.

To provide a physical analog circuit the video manager must set matrix points in the corresponding switching nodes, in order to have the input row analog signal supplied to the output columns. We saw that this setting procedure is initiated by the manager, and the switching controller is always waiting. So the protocol used is clearly asymmertic. We can give an example of PDU-exchange between these two entities:

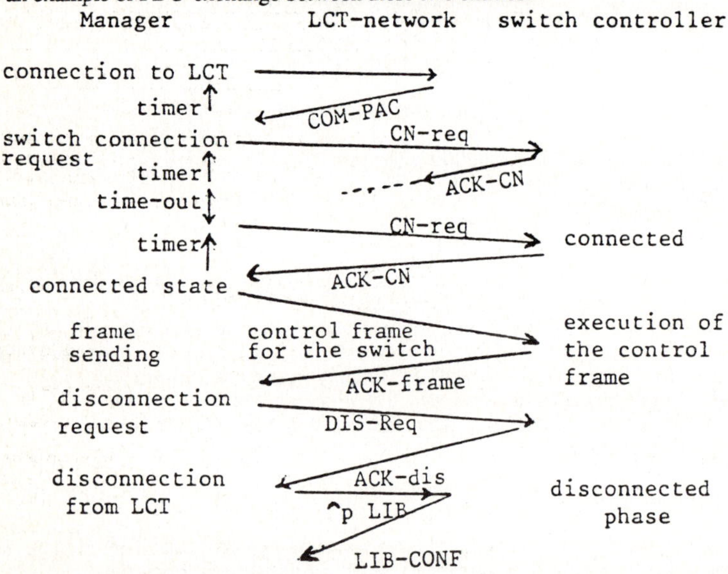

IV. MANAGEMENT SYSTEM

The need has been recognised by ISO, ANSI and ECMA to integrate the special problems of initiating, terminating, monitoring activities and abnormal conditions in the OSI reference model. Management functions in LANs those which, within ISO[6], are denoted:

1 - Configuration management: resources, status and distibution of software
2 - Fault and report management
3 - Directory management: maintenance of mapping between resource-type names, resource names and addresses .

The solutions proposed by A. DANTHINE[3] for the internet management architecture in the OSI architecture model, complete this point of view. Even though we intend to interconnect the actual prototype local video LAN with similar video LANs joined by fibre or sattelite mediums, there is no problem of data conversion because of the analog nature of the data. In our case we plan that all the manager has to do, in order to provide a distant video connection, is to configure the local path and to generate a connection request to the remote video LAN manager exactly as a connection reqest from a virtual user, provided that the local video output is an input analog device for the remote video manager. So we can focus our interest only to the local management issues of the video LAN. These management issues are actually handled by a set of 45 functions. Since the development system is a VME120-MOTOROLA UNIX V, the hierachy of the information and the organisation is based on the principles of UNIX. The complete description of the system functions can be foud in [1].

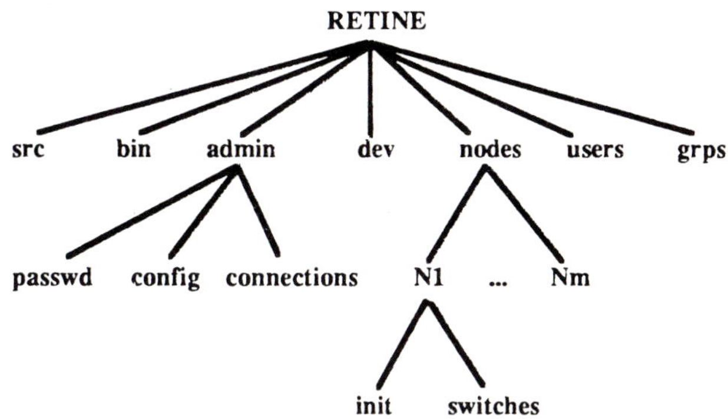

The components of the switching LAN system are handle by a set of command groups. Each group is structured as an ADD element, a LIST element and a remove element with possibly some options. Such groups are built for the switching nodes (or gates), the fibres, the users and the analog devices.

IV.1. Configuration Management

As we said in a previous section only the LAN manager keeps and maintains a list of the network-addresses of the switching nodes. At power-up all the switching nodes operate with a little monitor wich is able to receive a MOTOROLA format S data file and possibly execute it.

The switching node software is compiled and linked in the develoment system in order to be executed on the switching nodes. Therefore the down-loading and the initiating procedures are done in an easy manner, provided that the manager keeps the initial state of each switching martix, especially information relating to the configuration of the network graph.

IV.2. Directory Management

A user is the owner of his set of devices and has access to the set of devices of the users wich belong to his group. A video connection is provided only if the user who initiates this request has the right access to the en-point analog device. The video manager provides, for several users, a protected login for a video connection or disconnection request and, possibly control commands for source-devices which have a controller included in the manager kernel.

Since several users are supported and their actions modify the video LAN configuration, a mechanism of mutual exclusion is provided for each video manager resource, such as routing-tables switching matrix tables or network ports. The login processes communicate to the application manager, by using unix pipes, only the internal parameters needed for the setting

of the video circuit. The conversion of the user commands into the internal application manager requests are the semantic actions of a LEX-YACC process.
For users' convenience a set of services are provided:

- An alias mechanism for naming facilities
- A "motd" at login time gives possible modification in the configuration or notification of maintenance.
- A mailing box for users' communications

For security, there is a special set_access command provided only to the super-user, even though initially, by default, the users can execute all other commands. This powerful command allows the super-user to forbid selectively or globally the axecutions of certain commands.

IV.3. Routing Management

Even though, the video-LAN is presently ring structured, we plan that the network graph and its links would be modified depending upon future traffic reports and statistics. So the routing algorithm must operate in every oriented graph and not necessarilly in the actual multi-cycle graph. We use an adjacency matrix as the basic data structure, and an adapted FORD-FULKERSON algorithm in order to keep the global condition:

- the path is one which leaves free the maximum number of possible paths.

For exemple, if we request an AD circuit, then the ABD path would be chosen.

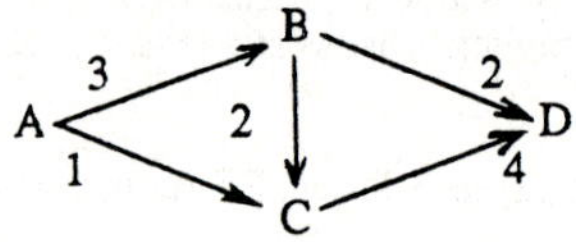

An interesting and important point of this video-LAN is the fact that two (or more) connections can share the initial part of their respective path provided that they have the same source analog device. If there is a path wich is already set up between the A, B nodes, and the AC connection request comes in, then we may possibly choose the BC path instead of a new AC path provided that it verifies the above condition. With this adaptation, only the nodes between B and C have to be switched.

IV.4. Fault And Statistics Reports

For testing and maintenance purposes we record in a trace file a detailed report for each atomic action performed by the video-LAN manager for a specific user. These files are periodically processed and cleaned in order to constitute a global and less detailed report archive file. This archive file is actually used to relate traffic statistics, and would also be used for users billing. The trace files are necessary for the recovery after video-LAN failure to return in a previous coherent state.

V. CONCLUSION

The video-LAN is only a part of the RETINE project. The aim of the project is video image transmission and digital image transmission up to 560 Mbits/s [2]. We propose in the future in a first time to multiplex the voice whith the video signal. And on a second time to multiplex analog channels on the optic fibre, the bandwidth of this medium allows theoretically at least fifty video channels. The former multiplexing would simplify the video-LAN links and would make the number of video connections larger.

VI. REFERENCES

[1] A.BELAMKADEM, P. FUSTIE, O. HEILLES, S. TAILLE
RETINE. rapport DESS. Universite de Bordeaux I. Mars 87.

[2] R.Castanet
High speed LAN for image transmission FOC/LAN. BALE. MAY 87.

[3] A.DANTHINE, B.HAUZEUR
Management of backbone wideband network for LAN interconnection. Symposium on local communication system. Toulouse. France. Nov 86.

[4] D.Diaz, A. Goyal, M.Kumar.
A dynamically reconfigurable swich for integrated communication.Symposium on local communication System. Toulouse. France. Nov 86.

[5] P.A. Franaszed.
Path hierarchies in interconnection networks.
IBM J. Res. Develop. Vol. 31 No. 1 Jan 87.

[6] ISO
OSI Management Framework. OSI/TC97/SC21/W64 N155. April 86.

[7] LCT 6500. Presentation generale du reseau LCT 6500.
Doc. LCT-Matra Communications. Massy. France. 86.

[8] G. Pujolle.
Les reseaux de donnees: reseaux locaux ET reseaux longue distance
TSI.Paris. march 86.

[9] R. Sharp, M. Skov, M.Jensen, J. Sparso
architectural considerations in LAN_dth.
Symposium on Local commucation Systems.Toulouse. frannnce. Nov. 86.

Network Information Processing Systems
K. Boyanov, R. Angelinov (Editors)
Elsevier Science Publishers B.V. (North-Holland)

MULTIOBJECTIVE OPTIMIZATION IN LOCAL AREA NETWORKS FOR REAL TIME APPLICATIONS [+]

Emil I. STOILOV and Emil S. GEORGIEV

Institute of Industrial Cybernetics and Robotics
Bulgarian Academy of Sciences
Sofia, Bulgaria

An algorithm for optimum traffic control in local area networks for real time applications is discussed in the paper. Using the flying horizon method, an optimum control strategy for the coordinator is developed. The presented approach allows the designer to shorten the optimization horizon, and hence to decrease the maximum delivery time for priority messages.

1. INTRODUCTION

Recently, intensive work has been done for the development of algorithms for dynamic traffic optimization in local area networks for real time application. Algorithms for network flow control are described in [1,2,3,4]. They have hierarchical structure and employ the flying horizon method. One of the main shortcomings with these algorithms is the complicated task to be solved in real time by the coordinator. Moreover, short delivery times of priority messages remain an unsolved problem. This deficiency was partially eliminated in the case of the local area networks for process control purposes described in [5], where some specific hardware features are used.

Actually the main problem is the missing uniform optimum criterion for network control. Usually there exist some criteria, however they are often contradictory. A method for multiobjective optimization and "on-line" local area network control is presented in this paper.

2. BRIEF DESCRIPTION OF THE NETWORK

The local area network considered has N stations and a bus architecture. Data transmission is message oriented and the token passing method is used for bus access. At system start up one of the stations generates the token. Further this station will be refferred to as coordinator. The coordinator

----

+ This work was supported by the Committee of Science of the Bulgarian Government under contract 442/09061987 program is stored in the program memory of each station. In case the coordinator drops out of communication, another station takes over its functions. There always exists a coordinator in the network, and only one station is a coordinator.

The coordinator transfers bus control to the individual stations by a special MTF command. Besides the token, this command also contains the time interval, during which the station, having received the token, can be a master in the network. After receiving the MTF command the station starts to transmit the messages having been accumulated in the queue. When the specified time interval is over or if all previous messages are sent, network control is returned to the coordinator by means of the MTF command. Besides the token, in this case the command also contains the current length of the queue of messages to be sent, the value of the income message flow to this queue and the maximum delay of an unsent message in the queue.

Two basic parameters, $x_n(t)$ and $y_n(t)$, presenting the station state, are associated with any station n, n 1,N. $x_n(t)$ is the length of the information message queue in time units, needed for the data to be transferred along the bus. $y_n(t)$ is the maximum delay of a message in the station n queue, waiting to be transferred at time t. The following equation holds for $x_n(t)$:

$$\frac{dx_n(t)}{dt} \equiv v_n(t) - u_n(t), \quad x_n(t_o) = x_{no} \qquad (1)$$

where $v_n(t)$ stands for the arriving flow of information messages in the station n at time t. The station n control at time t is defined as $u_n(t)$

$$u_n(t) = \begin{cases} 1, & \text{when station n controls the network bus and transmits an information message at the time t} \\ 0, & \text{otherwise} \end{cases} \qquad (2)$$

The second state equation of station n, presenting the change of $y_n(t)$ will not be given apparently. It should be noted that when the station transmits information messages ($u_n(t)=1$), $y_n(t)$ decreases at a leap.

Each station continuously identifies its arriving message flow [2]. Hence, at any time t the values of $x_n(t)$, $v_n(t)$ and $y_n(t)$ in the station n are well known. If we assume that at time τ station n returns network control to the coordinator by means of a MTF command, this command will contain $x_n(\tau)$, $v_n(\tau)$ and $y_n(\tau)$.

Generally, the network control problem is reduced to a classical coordination problem: several stations of equal priority require access to the resource distributed, in this case the transport medium. According to the pure token passing method the stations gain access to the bus in a logical loop and each station sends all its messages accumulated by that time. The main disadvantages of this algorithm is the scan time increase at dense input flows and high dynamics [3]. In this case there is an increase of the probability of rejecting a message, due to a queue overflow in the station. On the other hand the maximum delay of a message in the queue considerably increases and can not be dynamically guaranteed for.

To reduce the maximum delay time of a message in the queue in [1,2,3,4] it is accepted that the coordinator should perform its functions in a cycle, solving the dynamic optimization problem for a shortened horizon. The requirements for small values of $y_n(t)$, $n \in \overline{1,N}$, are taken into account as restrictions in the algorithmic structure and are not included explicitely in the target function.

Below a method is presented, where these requirements are part of the target function of the coordinator, thus the artificial restrictions on the decision making process on part of the coordinator drop off.

3. THE COORDINATOR'S STRATEGY

Two functions, describing the worst case network conditions as a whole, are defined:

$$X(t) = \max_{n \in \overline{1,N}} x_n(t) \tag{3}$$

$$Y(t) = \max_{n \in \overline{1,N}} y_n(t) \tag{4}$$

The coordinator's task is to minimize these two functions at any moment of time. It is obvious, that when the message with the longest delay is not in the longest queue, a simultaneous minimization of X(t) and Y(t) is not possible. According to [6,7], we introduce a nonlinear scaling function, the so called Germaier function:

$$Q(t) = \max\left[\lambda X(t), \mu Y(t)\right] , \tag{5}$$

where $\lambda \geqslant 0, \mu \geqslant 0$ are scale factors reflecting the network designer's preferences and are determined by the specific requirements to a certain system.

Let us go back to the network operation mode. We assume, that at the time t the coordinator is to decide which station is to receive network control and for what period of time. Assuming that for the last time prior to the moment t, the coordinator has received MTF commands from the stations at the moments τ_n, $n \in \overline{1,N}$, it has at its disposal the values $x_n(\tau_n)$, $y_n(\tau_n)$ and $v_n(\tau_n)$, $n \in \overline{1,N}$. As shown in [2], the arriving message flow into the station during the time between two consecutive MTF commands from the same station may be considered unchanged. This allow the equation (1) to be solved analytically:

$$\overline{x}_n(t) = x_n(\tau_n) + (t - \tau_n)v_n(\tau_n) \tag{6}$$

Here $\overline{x}_n(t)$ denotes the length of the station n queue at the moment t, as predicted by the coordinator. Similarly, for the predicted maximum delay time of a message in the queue we obtain

$$\overline{y}_n(t) = y_n(\tau_n) + t - \tau_n, \quad n\in\overline{1,N} \tag{7}$$

Since station n has not been receiving bus control during the time interval $[\tau_n, t]$ and the message is still in its queue; thus the value of $\overline{y}_n(t)$, as predicted by the coordinator, completely coincides with $y_n(t)$, i.e. $\overline{y}_n(t)=y_n(t)$, in case $y_n(\tau_n)\neq 0$.

The functions X(t) and Y(t) in (5) are unknown to the coordinator. It can implement only the predicted values, i.e.:

$$\overline{X}(t) = \max_{n\in\overline{1,N}} \overline{x}_n(t) \tag{8}$$

$$\overline{Y}(t) = \max_{n\in\overline{1,N}} \overline{y}_n(t)$$

Substituting X(t) in (5) with $\overline{X}(t)$ and Y(t) with $\overline{Y}(t)$, we obtain:

$$\overline{Q}(t) = \max\left[\lambda\overline{X}(t), \mu\overline{Y}(t)\right] \tag{9}$$

3.1. Choosing the station

The following sets are defined:

$$L = \left\{k\colon \overline{X}(t) = \overline{x}_k(t)\right\} \tag{10}$$

$$M = \left\{k\colon \overline{Y}(t) = \overline{y}_k(t)\right\} \tag{11}$$

An arbitrary element from each set is chosen and respectively denominated with l and m, i.e. $l\in L$, $m\in M$.

The coordinator aims at such a choice of a station to transfer network control to, so that in the following moment the function $\overline{Q}(t)$ will be reduced maximum. This station is denoted by i and the following algorithm for station choosing by the coordinator is formed:

$$i = \begin{cases} l, & \text{when } \lambda\overline{x}_l(t) \geqslant \mu\overline{y}_m(t) \\ m, & \text{otherwise} \end{cases} \tag{12}$$

3.2. Access time-interval determination

To determine the access time-interval of a station to network control, the term time to be shared should be elucidated. We assume that within the interval $[t,t+h]$ every station will receive bus control only once. The sequence of the stations gaining control is of no matter. Denoting the access time-intervals of the individual stations with T_n, we see that the following relationship is to be fulfilled:

$$\sum_{n=1}^{N} (T_n + \Delta) = h \tag{13}$$

Δ is the time necessary for the coordinator to receive a MTF command, to choose a station to transfer control to, to determine its access time-interval and to send the MTF command to it. Hence, within the interval $[t,t+h]$ the stations will alltogether use the time

$$q = \sum_{n=1}^{N} T_n,$$

reffered to as time to be shared.

In the algorithms described in [1,2,3,4], h is called optimization horizon and together with the time to be shared related with it, both are system parameters and meaningful to the system designer. With decreasing time to be shared, the stations gain access of the bus more often, but for shorter time intervals. Accordingly the share of time for commands of the total time increases. If a longer shared time interval is chosen, the maximum length queue in the stations and the maximum message delay time in the network increase as well.

When the station i, which is to receive control is determined at the time t, the coordinator determines its access time interval, denoted in the following with $T_i(t)$:

$$T_i(t) = \frac{\overline{x}_i(t)}{\sum_{n=1}^{N} \overline{x}_n(t)} q = \frac{x_i(\tau_i)+v_i(\tau_i)(t-\tau_i)}{\sum_{n=1}^{N} x_n(\tau_n)+v_n(\tau_n)(t-\tau_n)} (h-N\Delta) \tag{14}$$

Actually the coordinator realizes a proportional impulse regulator with the queue length acting as feedback. From (14) is seen that the time to be shared is an upper limit for the access time interval, i.e. $T_i(t) \leqslant q$. On the other hand with $\mu=0$ we always have

$$T_i(t) = \frac{\overline{x}_i(t)}{\frac{1}{N}\sum_{n=1}^{N} \overline{x}_n(t)} \cdot \frac{q}{N} \geqslant \frac{q}{N} \tag{15}$$

In this marginal case not every station is able to receive network control within one optimization horizon.

For $\lambda = 0$ the stations receive control in a logical loop and at a more intensive traffic message queues are not emptied completely. It can generally be said, that with reasonable values of λ and μ all stations receive network control within an interval slightly different from h.

4. CONCLUSIONS

The algorithm presented for solving the coordinator's task is extremely simple and the time necessary for its processing is minimum. With respect to determining the time interval Δ, the time for the transmission of the MTF commands proves to be crucial here. This time on its part entirely depends on the transmission rate in the system. All this allows the designer to shorten the optimization horizon h, and hence to decrease the maximum delivery time for the priority messages. The choice of appropriate values for h, λ, and μ can be carried out on-line upon installing the network depending on the concrete requirements.

5. REFERENCES

[1] Stoilov, E. and Strugarova, M., The Use of the Flying Horizon Method to Traffic Optimization in Process Control Communication Systems, in: Lecture Notes in Control and Information Sciences, 84, Springer Verlag, 1986.

[2] Stoilov, E. and Strugarova, M., Optimizing Traffic in Local Area Networks, Computers in Mechanical Engineering, January 1987, New York.

[3] Stoilov, E., Kissiov, M. and Strugarova, M., Traffic Control and Optimization in Process Control Communication Systems, in: Proceedings of the International Symposium on Software for Computer Control - SOCOCO'86, Graz, Austria, 1986.

[4] Stoilov, E., On-line Multilevel-Multilayer Control in Local Area Networks, Problems of Engineering Cybernetics and Robotics, vol.28, Sofia, Bulgaria, 1987.

[5] Stoilov, E., Coordination Mechanisms in Local Area Networks for Real-Time Applications, in: Proceedings of the First Iberian Conference on Data Communications - IBERICOM'87, Lisbon, Portugal, 1987.

[6] Germaier, I., Introduction to Operational Research, Moscow Nauka, 1971 (in Russian).

[7] Peschel, M., Multiobjective Optimization, in: System Analysis (ed. W. Findeisen), PWN, Warsaw, 1985 (in Polish)

Network Information Processing Systems
K. Boyanov, R. Angelinov (Editors)
Elsevier Science Publishers B.V. (North-Holland)

Analysis of High Speed Token Rings for a Mixed Traffic Environment

P. Martini, Th. Welzel
Lehrstuhl Informatik IV, Technical University Aachen
Ahornstr. 55, 5100 Aachen, West Germany

Abstract
Local Area Networks have been designed to provide high data rates for communication in geographically restricted areas. Several media access protocols have been standardized in the last few years. To cover broader site environments a high speed backbone network is of common interest for an efficient interconnection of heterogeneous LANs. Progress in fiber optic transmission techniques now enables high speed communication spanning larger distances. In this paper a backbone network based on the token ring access mechanism is analyzed by diffusion approximation as well as by simulation. Results are presented for file transfer and interactive traffic environments. Furthermore, a mixed traffic scenario has been considered which comprises stations transferring files and stations representing interactive traffic. The suitability of the token ring access protocol is studied on the basis of both queue length and packet delay.

1. Introduction

Local Area Networks (LANs) have widely been accepted which is reflected by an increasing number of installations. Standardization bodies proposed several concepts for the medium access (see eg. [IEEE 84], [IEEE 85]). Almost each major manufacturer of electronic equipment supports one or more of these concepts. Designed for small sites (e.g. buildings) most of the LANs typically are not able to cover areas of more than a few kilometers in diameter. Therefore, LAN interconnection becomes inevitable in "campus wide environments", i.e. multi-building sites like university campus or large industrial site. Due to the coexistance of heterogeneous LANs tailored to specific applications backbone networks for multi-vendor LAN environments nowadays are considered an urgent matter. Backbone stations have to provide gateway capabilities for protocol conversion between backbone and attached LANs. Today there is no doubt about optical transmission being the most appropriate medium for communication providing high data rates and covering large distances. Fiber is most easily configured as a one-way medium. Thus, ringlike and starlike bus structures are generally preferred to linear bus structures [RHO 83]. Several medium access protocols have been studied [e.g. BUX 81, DAN 85, MAR 87] and the Multiple Token Ring appeared to be one of the most promising candidates to meet the demands for a high speed backbone. The design requires information about numerous parameters concerning gateways and backbone itself. This must be supported by performance evaluation. This paper deals with the analysis of the token access method with respect to buffer dimensioning and packet delay. We study a realistic scenario with file transfer and interactive traffic reaching a high speed backbone via LANs.

2. Model of a High Speed Token Ring

In a token ring the stations are interconnected by unidirectional point-to-point links. Access to the common medium is controlled by a deterministic algorithm: a special bit pattern (i.e. the "free token") circulates around the ring, giving momentary control over the transmission channel to the station holding the token. Many variations of the token passing protocol have been proposed. According to the standards of IEEE [IEEE 85] and ECMA [ECMA 85] a station ready to transmit changes the incoming free token into a "busy token" without additional delay, i.e. "on the fly", and appends packets to be transmitted. After the station has completed its transmission and the header of the transmitted packet has returned, a new free token is generated and passed to the successor. This procedure simplifies priority mechanisms as well as error detection and recovery functions. However, this strategy may cause significant throughput degradation in High Speed Local Area Networks (HSLANs) operating at data rates exceeding 100 Mbit/s (see eg. [DAN 85]). Therefore, we consider a modified token-passing method: a new free token is released immediately after the end of transmission. This protocol is called "multiple token ring" since now several busy tokens and at most one free token may coexist on the ring.

3. Backbone Station Model

For our analysis the model of the gateways interconnected by the backbone network comprises Medium Access Control (MAC) sublayer only. Stations are assumed to provide full duplex connection between backbone ring and attached LAN according to figure 1. Packets arriving from the source LAN are gathered by the transmit queue in FIFO manner. The corresponding server adds MAC-overhead, waits for the receipt of a free token and transmits the packets on the backbone ring. Packets destined to the station are copied into the receive buffer and retransmitted to the destination LAN. Impacts of processing times in HSLAN-stations are ignored. The token ring itself is modelled by a single cyclic server representing the rotation of the free token. Neither error situations nor recovery procedures are taken into account by our model.

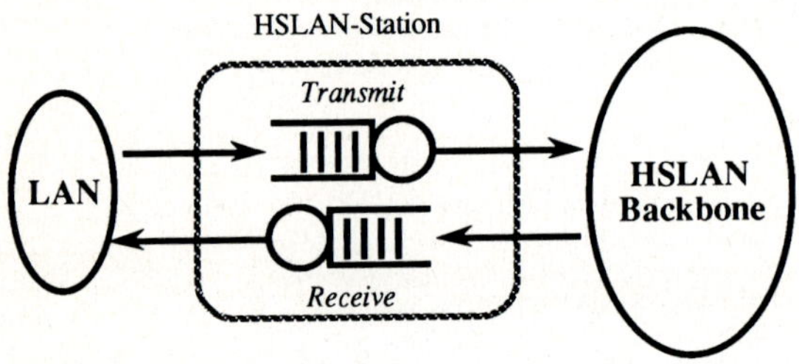

Figure 1: Station Model of the Gateway

4. Source Descriptions

The source model represents applications supported by the interconnected LANs. In this paper we consider a scenario comprising file transfer as well as interactive applications.

Furthermore, at the gateways we assume an average throughput of 2 Mbit/s in each direction [DAN 85] resulting in an internet load of 4 Mbit/s for each LAN. This load imposes very hard demands for the stations.

4.1 File Transfer

This class of sources models transmission of files across the backbone. Files may contain graphics, high/low resolution images or any other kind of data. Figure 2 shows the time diagram of file transfer, which has been modelled by a burst arrival process: during a burst packets follow each other back to back and consecutive files are separated by a relatively long interfile gap.

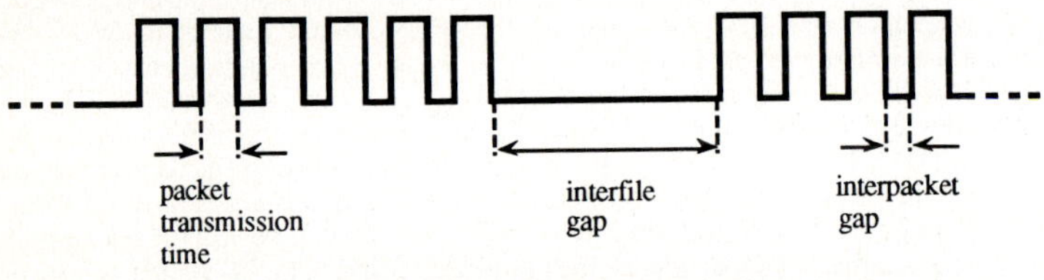

Figure 2: Time Diagram of the File Transfer Source

This kind of sources has to be included in our performance evaluation since file transfer appears to be one of the most important applications of HSLANs in general and high speed backbones in particular.

File transfer arriving at the backbone station may be characterized by the following features [WEL 87b]:

- packets are transmitted at 10 Mbit/s by LANs
- each packet contains an information field (1024 bytes) as well as an internet overhead
- each packet transmission is followed by the CSMA/CD interpacket gap [IEEE 84]
- interfile gaps are exponentially distributed with mean value 56.03 ms chosen for 2 Mbit/s access data rate
- From measurement results we adopt a file length distribution observed in an university computer centre [WEL 87]. Most files are short according to the global mean value of 16.58 kbyte. The coefficient of variation has been computed as 1.6. Remark: this distribution is only an approximation of general file transfer applications and does not meet the requirements of CAD or image transfer!
- destinations of files are uniformly distributed
- flow control mechanisms interrupting the continuous stream of packets are not taken into account.

4.2 Interactive Traffic

Obviously, internet traffic cannot be modelled by file transfer only. Thus, we define another class of sources representing applications based on sequences of interactions. An example for this kind of traffic is the interconnection of terminals with a remote host computer via the backbone network. In this case many packets contain short commands or responses. However, few packets comprise more complex information (listings, reports etc.). The interpacket time is assumed to be exponentially distributed. Figure 3 shows the time diagram of interactive traffic. Destinations of packets are assumed to be uniformly distributed.

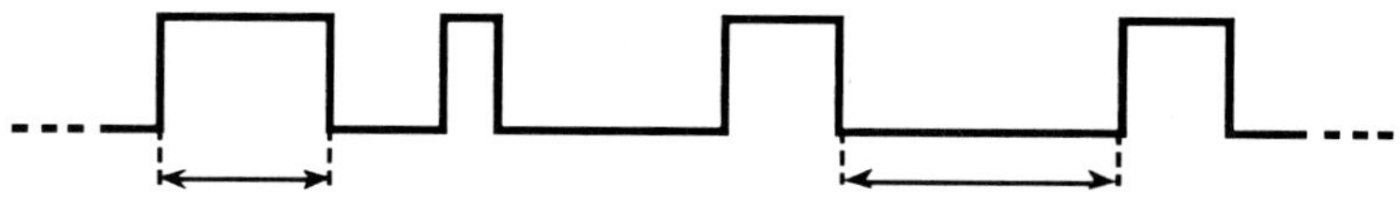

Figure 3: Time Diagram of the Interactive Traffic Source

To get an idea of a realistic distribution of information field length we adopt a distribution derived from the workload study mentioned above. The majority of small packets and few long packets result in a mean information field length of 40.9 byte and a rather high coefficient of variation (2.06).
Packets are generated by source LANs at 10 Mbit/s. Additionally to to the information field each packet contains an internet header [ECMA 84].

4.3 Comparison of Source Classes

The following table shows the main features of the two source classes:

	file source	interactive source
mean information field length [bytes]	1024	40.85
inter-packet time distribution	exp./constant	exponential
mean inter-packet time [ms]	3.389	0.243
packet generation rate [packets/s]	236	3296
mean interarrival time [ms]	4.236	0.303
destination address variation	every file	every packet

Due to larger information field length the file transfer source generates less packets than the interactive source. However, during file transmissions we have a load of 9.9 Mbit/s.

5. Buffer Dimensioning

Buffer dimensioning is an important point for gateway implementation. Buffer space has to be small enough to enable fast and efficient access. On the other hand it has to be large enough to guarantee reliable connections without excessive loss of packets due to buffer overflow. In this section the required buffer capacity is studied in detail. Transmit queues only depend on the properties of arrival process and backbone service capabilities whereas receive queues are also influenced by destination LAN characteristics. Results for receive queues are shown in [MAR 88b].

5.1 Analysis of Transmission Queue Length by Diffusion Approximation

A network with sources as described above does not lend itself to classical methods of analysis. Therefore, we use an approximative approach: each station is modelled by a GI/G/1 system and diffusion approximation is applied for deriving the values we are interested in. According to this technique the number of customers in a GI/G/1 system is approximated by a diffusion process which is described by a differential equation:

$$\frac{\partial}{\partial t} f(x,t) = \frac{1}{2} \alpha \frac{\partial^2}{\partial x^2} f(x,t) - \beta \frac{\partial}{\partial x} f(x,t).$$

Any analysis by diffusion approximation is based on solutions of this "diffusion equation". First of all we have to consider the normalizing condition

$$\int_0^\infty f(x,t)\,dx = 1,$$

Furthermore, we adopt the "instantaneous return model" described in [GEL 80], with an absorbing boundary at the origin. This model yields a unique steady-state solution for the probability density function of the number of customers in the system

$$f = \begin{cases} (1-\rho)\,\delta(x) & \text{for } x = 0 \\ (1-e^{\gamma x})\,\rho & \text{for } 0 < x \le 1 \\ (e^{-\gamma}-1)\,\rho\, e^{\gamma x} & \text{for } x \ge 1 \end{cases}$$

where $\rho = \lambda/\mu < 1$ denotes the utilization and $\gamma = -2(1-\rho)/(\rho K_a^2 + K_s^2)$. Now we may calculate the mean number of customers in the system as a function of mean arrival rate (λ), mean service rate (μ), coefficient of interarrival time variation (K_a) and coefficient of service time variation (K_s).

$$\overline{N} = \rho\,\left(\frac{1}{2} + \frac{\rho K_a^2 + K_s^2}{2(1-\rho)}\right),$$

The p-percentile, i.e. the number of buffer places which is sufficient with probability p, is given by

$$N_p = \frac{\rho K_a^2 + K_s^2}{2(\rho-1)} \ln\left[\frac{2(\rho-1)}{(\rho K_a^2 + K_s^2)\rho}\;\frac{1-p}{1-\exp[2(1-\rho)/(\rho K_a^2 + K_s^2)]}\right]$$

In order to apply the formulae given above we have to determine the first two moments of the departure process which will be described in terms of the following parameters:

- D: Station latency (in bit)
- L_m: Medium length, i.e. circumference of the ring
- L_{gn}: Mean length of packets generated at station n
- σ_{gn}^2: Variance of length of packets generated at station n
- N: Number of stations attached to the ring
- R: Raw bit rate, i.e. number of bits transmitted per second (including overhead)
- T_{rot}: Mean value of free token rotation time
- σ_{rot}^2: Variance of token rotation time
- V: Signal velocity

Assuming that each station may transmit at most one packet upon capturing the token, [VYN 85], we may calculate the service time of packets by summing up token waiting time and packet transmission time. Obviously, it is upper bounded by the rotation time of the free token and in the following we will use these two terms synonymously. After capturing the token each station transmits exactly one packet if and only if there is at least one packet in the transmission queue. Passing the token without transmitting a packet may be regarded as transmission of a packet of length zero. This kind of packets shall be called "virtual packets". We approximate the probability of transmitting a virtual packet by $1 - \rho_n = 1 - \lambda_n/\mu$, where λ_n denotes the mean arrival rate at station n. Therefore, we may calculate the mean length of the packet transmitted by station n upon capturing the token (including virtual packets) by weighing the mean length of generated packets Lgn by the utilization ρ_n. Now, the mean value of the rotation time of the free token may be written as follows:

$$T_{rot} = \frac{N \cdot D + (Lm/V)R}{R} + \frac{1}{R} \sum_n \rho_n \cdot L_{gn}$$

and using $T_{rot} = 1/\mu$ and $\rho_n = \lambda_n/\mu$ we obtain

$$\mu = \frac{R}{N \cdot D + (L_m/V)R + (1/\mu) \sum \lambda_n \cdot L_{gn}} = \frac{R - \sum \lambda n \cdot Lgn}{N \cdot D + (L_m/V)R}$$

The variance σ_{tn}^2 of the length of transmitted packets (including virtual packets) may be obtained from conditional expectations, which may be calculated for the cases "packet sent" and "virtual packet sent" [MAR 88a]. Assuming independence of length of packets transmitted by different stations, we may write:

$$\sigma^2_{tn} = \rho_n \sigma^2_{gn} + \rho_n (1-\rho_n) L_{gn}^2.$$

Thus, we have $\sigma^2_s = (1/R^2) \sum_n (\rho_n \sigma^2_{gn} + \rho_n (1-\rho_n) L_{gn}^2)$ for the variance of service time σ^2_s.

Now, we have given the parameters describing the departure process in terms of parameters describing arrival process and packet length.

5.2 Analysis of Transmission Queue Length by Simulation

In order to validate our analysis and to extend the performance evaluation on packet delay aspects a simulation program has been designed using QNAP2 [QNA 84]. QNAP2 is a programming tool suitable for the evaluation of queueing networks. Due to limited memory capacity and for the sake of realistic modelling the buffer size of each queue has been restricted to a finite value (100 packets). Packets arriving at a filled buffer are lost resulting in throughput degradation (no retransmission procedure has been implemented). HSLAN-stations have been implemented according to our station model. The MAC-protocol has been realized by a single cyclic server giving transmit permission to backlogged stations. Confidence intervals have been computed for a level of 99 % using the batch means algorithm [FIS 78]. The simulation duration has been set to 40 seconds for each run providing the generation of a very great number of packets to achieve statistical significance.

6. Choice of Parameters

The following table sums up parameters chosen to determine the operation of backbone network and related stations:

- medium length	25 km
- signal velocity	$2 \cdot 10^8$ m/s
- data rate of the backbone	140 Mbit/s (at MAC sublayer)
- buffer space limitation	100 packets (for simulation purpose only)
- internet overhead	according to ECMA-92 connectionless internet protocol [ECMA 84]
- MAC-overhead	according to MAC-layer specification [VYN 85]
- free token release after transmission of each packet	
- stations are spaced equidistantly on the ring (for simulation purpose only)	

7. Results for Transmit Queues

The first part of this section presents results for both applications separately. Then we study a mixed traffic scenario comprising 20 gateway stations. We analyze the sensitivity with respect to varying ratios between the number of file transfer sources and the number of interactive traffic sources.

Figure 4 shows mean station transmit queue length versus number of sources for both analysis and simulation. Furthermore, confidence intervals for both applications are included. For file transfer, analysis and simulation yield almost identical results. Mean values are small due to the rather small packet generation rate. In contrast, the great number of packets generated by each interactive source results in high utilization even for moderate numbers of stations. For more than 25 stations simulation indicates packet loss increasing up to 10 % of the offered load (40 stations). Simultaneously, mean values approach buffer limitation (100 packets). However, in typical applications it seems to be quite hard to find 40 LANs interconnected by a single backbone network.

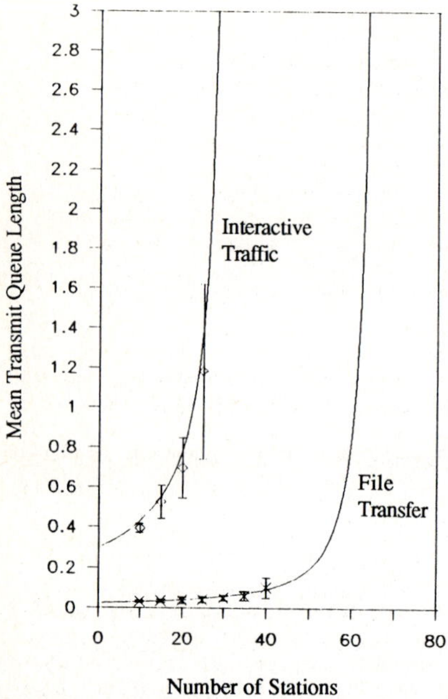

Figure 4: Mean Value of Transmit Queue Length

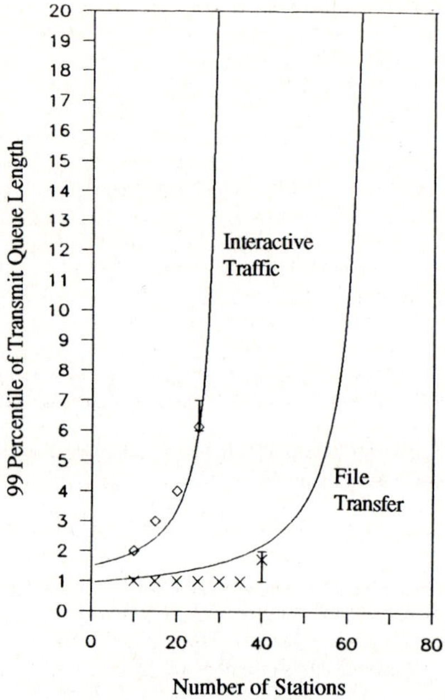

Figure 5: 99 Percentile of Transmit Queue Length

Percentiles obtained by analysis and simulation are shown in figure 5. Our simulation program provides percentiles on a per station basis. Thus, figure 5 includes their average as well as corresponding maximum and minimum values (marked by dedicated symbols) for both applications separately. Note, that the simulation program handles integral numbers of "customers". Values obtained by analysis and simulation are very close to each other. Again, for interactive traffic values obtained by simulation approaches buffer limitation.

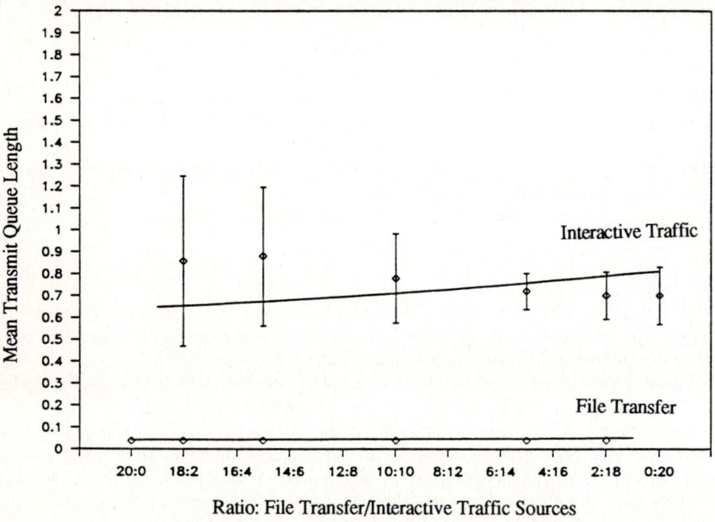

Figure 6: Mean Transmit Queue Length for Mixed Traffic

In order to analyze the sensitivity with respect to varying ratios of the number of file transfer sources and the number of interactive sources we study a mixed traffic scenario comprising 20 gateway stations. Figure 6 shows the mean values of transmit queue length for several selected ratios. The mean transmit queue length of file transfer is not affected by varying traffic characteristics in the HSLAN. This may be regarded as a typical result for a lightly loaded system ($\rho_n = \lambda_n/\mu << 1$). Concerning interactive traffic analytical results are within the confidence interval of simulation. Large confidence intervals for an increasing quota of file transfer indicate that for our mixed traffic scenario simulation goes to its limits: relatively large inter-file gaps result in more and more varying server availability. The higher utilized stations generating interactive traffic are more affected by this irregular service process than the lightly loaded file transfer sources. However, figure 6 points out that the mean transmit queue length is only slightly influenced.

8. Results for Packet Delays

Packet delay has been analyzed with respect to mean value as well as 99 percentile by simulation. We define "backbone delay" as follows: The backbone delay comprises transmission time from source LAN to station transmit queue, queueing delay in gateway transmit part and transmission time to the backbone network. Thus, the backbone delay reflects performance depending on arrival process and backbone characteristics only. It has to be remarked that only the delay of packets not lost due to buffer overflow has been measured. Thus, neither time-out nor retransmission strategies have been considered. Figure 9 shows the results of the mean values.

For less than 25 stations confidence intervals are small (< ±10% of the mean). However, for more than 25 stations they exceed the corresponding mean values. In contrast, in our file transfer application the receive queue length mainly affects source-destination delays due to the bursty arrival process at the destinations. As a consequence, confidence intervals and mean values are only slightly different. Due to short transmit queue lengths the backbone delay is dominated by source LAN transmission time and grows only slightly with increasing load. Confidence Intervals are very small (< ±5% of the mean) for this kind of delay. 99 percentiles of backbone delay are shown in figure 10. For more than 25 stations the results for interactive traffic are mainly determined by our buffer space limitation.

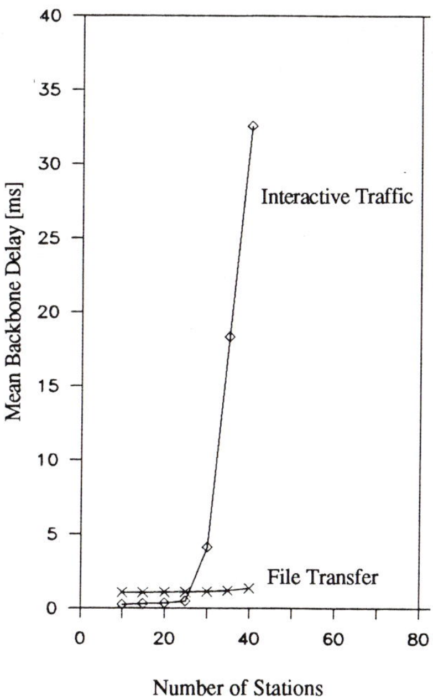

Figure 9: Mean Backbone Delay

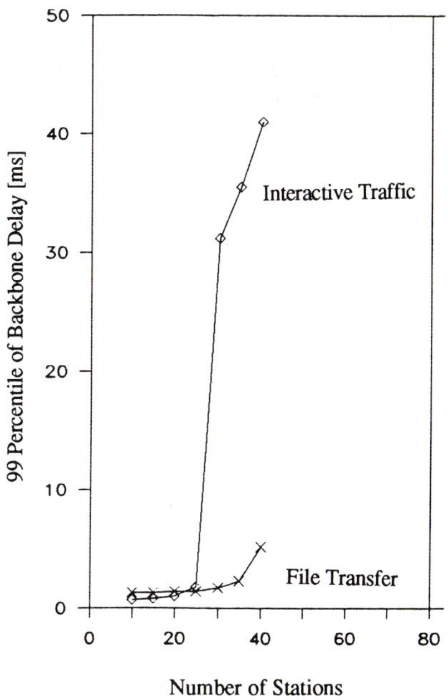

Figure 10: 99 Percentile of Backbone Delay

9. Conclusions and Further Work

Mathematical analysis and simulation results have been presented for both queue length and packet delay in a Multiple Token Ring backbone. It has been shown that this medium access protocol is able to cope with the assumed number of stations very well in mixed application environments. Moreover, the backbone performance for a given application represented by a particular station is almost unaffected by the traffic characteristics of the other stations. For each considered load the results of analysis and simulation have been almost identical. However, for heavy load (> 25 active stations) confidence intervals of our simulation increase indicating sensitive range of load. In order to extend this analysis other medium access protocols have to be taken into account to allow a comparison [MAR 87]. Obviously, protocol overhead of higher layers as well as processing times at HSLAN-gateways have a strong impact on the performance of backbone networks. Thus, these aspects will have to be included for an evaluation of layered communication protocol architectures to predict the performance from an user point of view.

References

[BUX 81] Bux W., "Local-Area-Subnetworks: A Performance Comparison", *IEEE Transactions on Communications*, No. 10, 1981, pp. 1465-1474

[DAN 85] Danthine A., Vyncke E., "Broad Site Local Wideband Network" in *"ESPRIT 84: Status Report of Ongoing Work"*, J. Roukens, J.F. Renuart, Eds, North-Holland, 1985, pp. 337 - 353

[ECMA 84] ECMA, "Standard ECMA-92, Connectionless Internetwork Protocol", March 1984

[ECMA 85] ECMA, "Standard ECMA-89, Local Area Networks, Token Ring Technique", 2nd Edition, March 1985

[FIS 78] Fishman G., "Principles of Discrete Event Simulation", *J. Wiley & Sons*, New York, 1978

[GEL 80] Gelenbe E., Mitrani I., "Analysis and Synthesis of Computer Systems", *Academic Press*, 1980

[IEEE 84] IEEE Project 802, Local Area Network Standards, IEEE Standard 802.3, CSMA/CD Access Method and Physical Layer Specification, Revision F, July 1984

[IEEE 85] "Local Area Networks: Token Ring Access Method", ANSI/IEEE Standard 802.5, 1985

[MAR 87] Martini P., "Protocols for High Speed LANs - A Performance Comparison", *Proc. of the IFIP TC6/WG6.4 Workshop on High Speed Local Area Networks*, Aachen, 16-17 February, North-Holland 1987, pp. 75-88

[MAR 88a] Martini P., "Performance Analysis of Multiple Token Rings", *Proc. of IBERICOM '87*, Lisbon, North-Holland 1988

[MAR 88b] Martini P., Welzel, Th., "Heterogeneous Traffic in High Speed Local Area Networks", *Proc. of EURINFO '88*, H.-J. Bullinger et al. (Eds.), Athens, North-Holland 1988

[QNA 84] "QNAP2, Reference Manual, version V03", *INRIA and Bull*, May 1984

[RHO 83] Rhodes N., "Interaction of Network Design and Fiber Optic Component Design in Local Area Networks", *IEEE J. Select. Areas Commun.*, No. 3, April 1983, pp. 489-492

[VYN 85] Vyncke E., Danthine A., "Broad Site Local Wideband Communication System, Medium Access Control Specification", ESPRIT Project 73, University of Liège, 1985

[WEL 87] Welzel Th., "Analyse und Messung der Workload...", *Proc. of "Communication in Distributed Systems"*, Informatik Fachberichte 130, Springer 1987, pp. 493-505, in German

Network Information Processing Systems
K. Boyanov, R. Angelinov (Editors)
Elsevier Science Publishers B.V. (North-Holland)

THE USE OF LEARNING ALGORITHMS IN DATA NETWORK ROUTING A METHODOLOGY

Dr. Athanasios VASILAKOS and Dr. Stavros KOUBIAS

School of Engineering
Dept. of Comp. Eng. and
C.T.I., University of
Patras, 26500 Patras,
GREECE

School of Engineering
Dept. of Electrical Eng.
Applied Electronics Lab.
University of Patras
26500 patras, GREECE

ABSTRACT

The purpose of this paper is to develop both mathematical models of the network and the probabilistic theory of learning algorithms routing in data communication networks and to verify through simulation that the models and theory are in agreement with the behavior observed in a communication system.

INTRODUCTION

A data communication network is defined by a set of nodes at which messages or packets enter or leave the network, and a set of links interconnecting the nodes.

Messages entering a node from a source or a link are directed by a routing law to one of the outgoing links and transmmited or stored in a queue if the link is occupied.

The message traffic entering a network normally has peak and slack periods, and the topology of a network may change, as when a link failure occurs. Consequently, the adaptive routing of messages as network conditions change is of particular interest.

In learning automata routing, a learning automaton is situated at each node of the network where a routing decision must be made and directs traffic entering the node onto one of the outgoing links. Using network feedback, an automaton modifies its routing stategy to improve its link selections.

NONSTATIONARY ENVIRONMENTS

Network state vectors descriptive of the individual transfers of information parcels between the various nodes have been suggested elsewhere [6] to approximate the network's physical operation by a discrete Markov process. The convergence of the system consisting of the network with its learning automata can then be shown. With convergence of the system established, performance characteristics and equilibrium conditions of the system are determined using stable, mathematically tractable models of the network as an abstract environment in which only general functional properties are assumed of the environment's input-output relationship. In the operation of a real network, the traffic and consequent queue populations vary with changes in the routing probabilities.

The two nonstationary environment models that are now described have a continuous functional dependence on the action probabilities of the automaton. In the first model the environment in an instantaneous function of the routing probabilities:

$$c_i(n) = \Phi_i[P_i(n)] \tag{1}$$

This behavior implies that the network immediately attains its steady state when the traffic is valied. To study the transients in the environment, a fully dynamic modes is introduced:

$$c_i(n+1) = k.c_i(n) + (1-k)\Phi_i[P_i(n)] \tag{2}$$

Each of the environment parameters is now a state variable so the system state consists of the automaton stategy argumented with the r-vector of the environment. We assume $0 < k < 1$ so the environment model is stable.

In both (1) and (2) $\Phi_i(.)$ is defined to have the same properties, which are:

(i) $\Phi_i(p_i)$ is defined every where on $[0,1]$,

and $\Phi_i : 0,1 \to 0,1$ with $\Phi_i[1] = 1$,

(ii) $\Phi_i(p_i)$ is analytic of every point of $[0,1]$, and

(iii) $\Phi_i(p_i)$ is monotonicawwy increasinh. (3)

In addition the following environment model with delay will also be considered:

$$c_i(n) = \Phi_i[p_i(n-\tau)] \tag{4}$$

The system state vector is the automaton state augmented by its τ previous values. The effect of time delay in the environment as exists in actual network is there by represented.

LEARNING AUTOMATA IN NONSTATIONARY ENVIRONMENTS

The learning automaton acting into an environment is illustrated in fig. 1.

The automaton is defined by a quadruble $\{\underline{a},\underline{\beta},\underline{p},T\}$ for which $\underline{a}$ and $\underline{\beta}$ are the output and input sets, $\underline{p}$ is the action probability vector, and T denotes the learning algorithm.

The input set $\underline{a}$ is the action set of the automaton $\{a_1,\ldots,a_r\}$, the output set $\underline{\beta}$ is, taken to be the binary set $\{0,1\}$ (p-model).

The environment is defined by the set

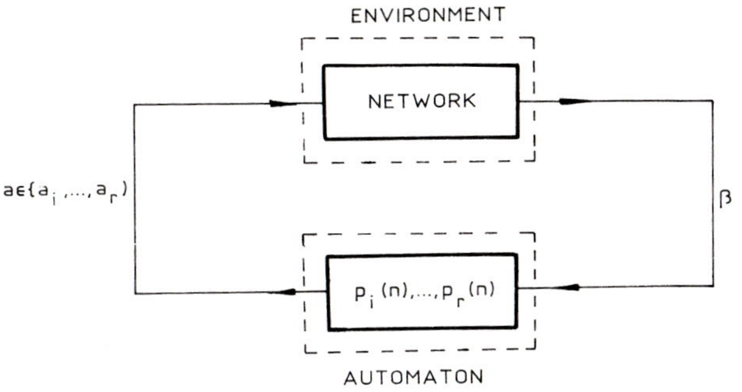

Figure 1

$\underline{c} = c_1, \ldots c_r$ where

$c_i = p\{\beta(n) = 1/a(n) = a_i\}$

c_i is called the i penalty probability of the environment.

For our environment (data network) the output $\underline{\beta}$ is a continuous random variable in the interval [0,1] (S-model). By normalizing the queue delay feedback can be made to correspond.

The learning algorithm with r-actions takes place as follows:

$$p_i(n-1) = p_i(n) - a(1-\beta(n))p_i(n) + b\beta(n)[\frac{1}{r-1} - p_i(n)]$$

$$\text{if } a(n) \neq a_i$$

$$p_i(n+1) = p_i(n) + a(1-\beta(n))(1-p_i) - b\beta(n)p_i(n)$$

$$\text{if } a(n) = a_i \qquad (5)$$

The constans a and b are the reward and penalty parameters, $0 < a, b < 1$. The reward to the selection of action a_i is largest when β is close to 0, and the converse is true for β close to 1. We shall refer to the case when a = b as the L scheme (linear reward-penalty).

The linear reward- in action, L_{RI}, algorithm is given by (5) when b = 0.

The $L_{R\epsilon P}$ algorithm is given by (5) when b = 0[a]. The operation of an s-automaton in either abstract environment has been analyzed in [9].

The details of the converge of our algorithm will be in the final version of the paper. The principal results of the analysis concerning the equilibrium behavior are:

1) The SL_{RP} automaton equalizes the penalty rates:

$$p_i^*(n)c_i^*(n) = p_j^*(n)c_j^*(n), \; i,j \; \{1,\ldots,r\} \qquad (6)$$

2) SL_{RI} and $SL_{R\epsilon P}$ automata equalize the penalty probabilities

$$c_i^*(n) = c_j^*(n), \quad i,j \quad \{1,\ldots,r\} \tag{7}$$

The equilibrium characteristics predicted by the two environments are identical, but the transient responses are quite different. The use of a dynamic abstract environment is of applicability in a variety of network problems. Further the speed and stability with which an automaton adapts at node are important factors affecting such questions as network and automata design, variation in the parameters of an automaton with variable step size, and event the applicability of automata routing in a particular situation. The theory of campact Markov processes and instance diminishing operators are employed to prove convergence in distribution of the state x of the system consisting of the automaton and environment.

Let $e = (a,\beta)$ be a particular event at a given trial and $e^n = (e_0, e_1, \ldots, e_{n-1})$. The algorithm at trial n is indicated by $\underline{x}_{n-1} = T(\underline{x}_n, e_n)$ and the probability of a particular event e at trial n is denoted by $p(\underline{x}_n, e)$.

The following criterion of Norman [7] is applied to prove the algorithm is distance diminishing.

Define

$$l(T) = \frac{d\ T(\underline{x},e),\ T(\underline{x}',e)}{d(\underline{x},\underline{x}')}$$

$$m(p) = \sup_{\underline{x}\neq\underline{y}} \frac{p(\underline{x},e) - p(\underline{y},e)}{d(\underline{x},\underline{y})} \quad \text{where d is the metric}$$

$$d[\underline{x},\underline{x}] = \sum_{i=1}^{r} |x_i - x_1'|$$

Let E denote the event space and K the state space. The operation of the algorithm is distance diminishing if $m(p) < \infty$ and $l(t) < 1\ \forall\ e \in E$ and if, for all $\underline{x} \in X$ there are $j \geq 1$ and 1 and ℓ E such that $1\ u(\underline{x},e^j) < 1$ and $p_j(\underline{x},e^j) > 0$.

It has be shown in reference [9] that these conditions are satisfied by the nosntationary environments described aerlier. The distance diminishing property and the compactness of X assume that $\{X_n\}_{n\geq 0}$ is a compact Markov process. A compact Markov process converges with probability 1 to one of its ergodic kernels.

SIMULATIONS

This section is concerned with the simulated behavior of automata operating in data communication networks. The consistency of the simulated behavior of automata operating in the network with the behavior predicted by the models it is shown. The need for a fully dynamic model is pointed out, and the use of this model to predict transient behavior is demonstrated.

The asymptotic behavior of the SL_{RP} and SL_{RI} automata (0,7) is verified with the forcing function of the environment chosen to be $\Phi_i(p_i) = p_i$.

The transient behavior of the SL_{RP} automaton in an expected sense is illustrated by the averages of simulated ensembles with 300 sample paths is fig. 2 and 3 with the automaton acting in the instantaneous and dynamic environments.

In either case, the asymptote 0.573 is approached by p_1. Simulations of the SL_{RI} automaton also approach the predicted asymptote.

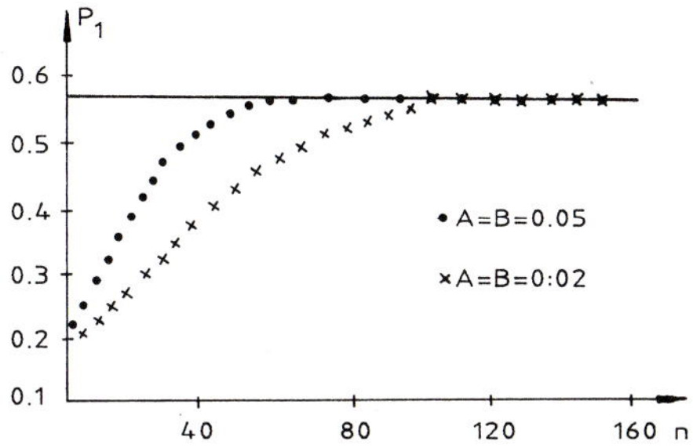

Figure 2. SL_{RP} automaton in Instantaneous Environment

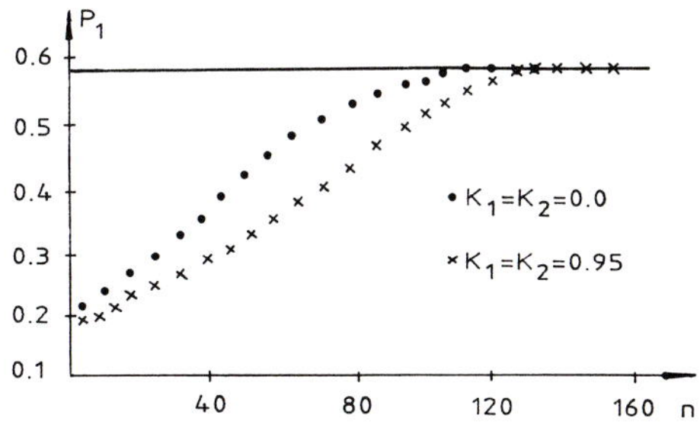

Figure 3. SL_{RP} automaton in State variable Environment

To verify that the models correctly predict the equilibrium performance in networks, simple networks were simulated. The network inputs were modeled with poisson distributed arrivals and exponentially distributed message lengths. A four node network is illustrated in fig. 4.

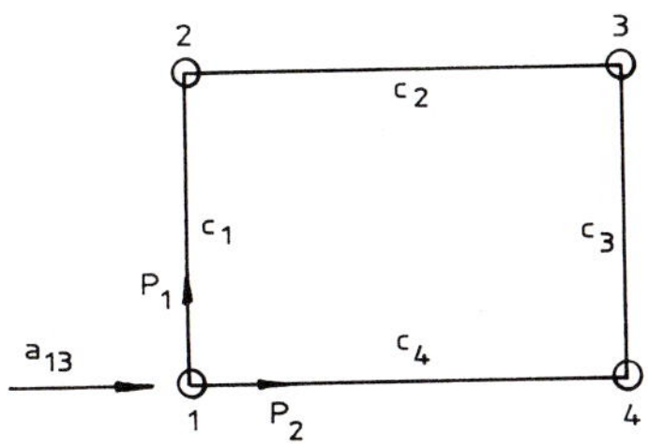

Figure 4. $c_1=c_2=c_3=c_4$ = 10000 bits/sec; A_{13} = 10.0 messages/sec message length = 1000 bits

	λ_{13}	Delay a_1	Delay a_2	Delay x Probability a_1	Delay x Probability a_2
SL_{RP}	2.0	4.331	4.840	2.745	2.738
	8.0	7.992	7.300	3.971	3.930
SL_{RI}	2.0	5.197	5.141	3.780	3.100
	8.0	8.631	8.790	5.242	4.002
$SL_{R\epsilon P}$	2.0	5.220	5.310	3.620	3.368
	8.0	9.211	9.013	4.880	5.170

Table 1

The delay refereed is the sum of the queue contents, in kilobits. In all cases a=b=0.02. For the $SL_{R\epsilon P}$ automaton b = 0.002. It is clear from the table 1 that the simulated SL_{RP}, SL_{RI}, $SL_{R\epsilon P}$ automata acting into the network behave in the theoretically prdicted maner. Now we illustrate the need of a fully dynamic environment.

The instantaneous environment is memoreless and consequently $p_1(n_1) = p^1(n_2)$ at trial n_1, n_2 implies that $c_1(n_1) = c_1(n_2)$.

Transient peaks of $p_1(n)$ were generated with two different source rates in fig. 4. Equal values of $p_1(n)$ have been observed and the corresponding values of $c_1(n)$ were found to be significantly different. The numerical values at these points are given in table 2. It is clear that the network is not memoreless.

λ_{13}	n	$p_1(n)$	$c_1(n)$
10.0	100	0.4980	0.413
	200	0.4971	0.628
15.0	100	0.4960	0.453
	200	0.4969	0.731

Table 2

By varying the time constants of the dynamic environment model (2) it is seen that the transient behavior of the automaton in the dynamic environment and network match when $k_1 = k_2 = 0.95$.

The comparison of our algorithm and other optimal dynamic routing algorithm will be studied in the future.

CONCLUSIONS

The consistency of the simulated behavior of learning algorithms operating in the network with the behavior predicted by the models it is shown. This work indicates that the use of learning automata is a realistic and useful approach to routing in data communications networks.

Simulations show clearly that the dynamic environment can be used to study the behavior of automata with varying reward and penalty parameters. While useful results are obtained from the first order model, higher order models must be investigated to explain, for example, oscillatory behavior. Further, optimality of our learning algorithms have to be considered in the future study.

REFERENCES

1) Narendra, K.S., Mason, L.G., Tripathi, S.S., "Application of learning automata to telephone traffic routing problems", 1974 Joint Automatic Control Conference, Austin, TX, 18-21 June 1974, pp. 753-759.
2) Narendra, K.S., Wright, S.A. and Mason, L.G., "Application of learning automata to telephone traffic routing and control", IEEE Transactions on Systems, Man and Cybernetics, vol. SMC-7, no. 11, pp. 785-792, Nov. 1977.
3) Narendra, K.S. and Thathachar, M.A.L., "On the behavior of a learning automaton in a changing environment with application to telephone traffic, Yale Univ. Technical Report S, IS 7803.
4) Narendra, K.S., Thathachar, M.A.L., "Leanring automata a survey", IEEE Trans. on Sys., Man and Cyb., SMC-4 (1974), pp. 323-334.
5) Tanenbaum, A.S. "Computer networks", Prentice-Hall, N.J., 1980.
6) Kleinrock, L., "Queueing systems: II-Applications", John Wiley, 1976.
7) Norman, M.F., Markov "Processes and learning models", New York and London, Academic Press, 1972.
8) Gallager, R.G., "A minimum delay routing algorithm using distributed computation", IEEE Trans. on Comm. vol. COM-25, pp. 73-84, Jan. 1977.
9) Vasilakos V.A., "Learning Automata for Data Communications Routing Problem", Univ. of Patras and C.T.I., Technical Report.

Network Information Processing Systems
K. Boyanov, R. Angelinov (Editors)
Elsevier Science Publishers B.V. (North-Holland)

AN HIERARCHICAL ADAPTIVE ALGORITHM FOR A DATA TRANSMISSION IN A DISTRIBUTED MICROPROCESSOR'S NETWORK

Todor At.STOILOV and Krasimira P.STOILOVA

Central Laboratory of Control Systems
Bulgarian Academy of Sciences
Sofia, Bulgaria

It is shown an optimal data transmission policy on a microprocessor's network.The network is applied on a wide spread systems as an automatic vehicle's location system.An on line algorithm for a data transmission is presented using a defined optimal problem.A complete mathematical description of the optimal algorithm is given.It is used an hierarchical approach to evaluate the solution of the problem.The data transmission's algorithm obtains adaptive features fulfielled in real time rules.

1. INTRODUCTION

A data transmission policy between the components of a microprocessor's distributed real time operating network is presented.An adaptive algorithm is designed for controling the order of data transmissions,which allows an optimal using and operating of the technical devices for information link and processing.The algorithm's purpose is shown on an application of an automatic vehicle's location system /AVLS/ for tracing the vehicles' motion in an observable region.This kind of systems are used for controling the urban traffic, the taxi vehicles, special kinds of cars etc. The real time automatic vehicle's location system is considered as an hierarchical microprocessor's network with two levels,fig.1. On the lower level are situated microprocessors' units $\mu P_i, i=1,n$ built-on the vehicles.During the vehicle's motion the microprocessor's unit μP_i establishes the vehicle's location or transmits a signal for a measuring the coordinates of the vehicle.The time for a data transmission or sending a signal for measuring is determined by a central control unit /CCU/,situated on the second hierarchical level of the microprocessor's network.In the AVLS the data transmission between the microprocessors units μP_i,i=1,n /n-a number of the watching vehicles/ and the CCU is accomplished by a radio channel.For practical purposes of the investigated system,it takes place the case of using only one radio channel for data transmission between μP_i,i=1,n, and the CCU. The occasion of using n channels is admissible but does not take place and does not use in the conditions of saturated spectrum of frequencies and its restricted limits.Hence the problem,which takes place in this article is to design an optimal algorithm for using a radio channel to perform the data transmission;to determine the necessary and sufficient parameters,which must be transmited from a μP_i,i=1,n,to the CCU, so that in real time the AVLS achieves a maximal knowledge about the vehicles' location For practical purposes I1,2,3,4,5I the normal rule of operation of the microprocessor's network in the AVLS is as bellow. First the CCU calls one of the μP_i,i=1,n.It transmits data for vehicle location or sends a signal for measuring.After this the CCU calls the next vehicle in a cyclic consequence order. In this normal used rule of operation the time cycle T_i for calling each vehicle will be

(1) $$T_i = t_c.n, \quad i=1,n,$$

where t_c is the time when the CCU is unoperable with more than one vehicle.The time t_c is determined by the software's and hardware's possibility of the CCU and the μP_i,i=1,n. It is obvious that with increasing the number n of the vehicles, the cycle's time T_i for consequtive calling of μP_i will increase too.It means that it will take place more rarely vehicle location for each car and the system will loose its real time operations capabilities. To appreciate the influence of (1) on the velocity of the system,we shall estimate aproximately the range of the time cycle t_c of the system.From practical reasons it is known I2,4,5I that for reaching a stability in data transmission using a wireless channel,it must be used 300 bit/s rate for transmission ,in which rate it is not necessary to implement special hardware and software requirements.This rate is recommendated in wide used computer networks,which use radio link for data transmission because of it is applied here. We assume that

(2) $$t_c = t_{TCCU} + t_{call} + t_{\mu P} + t_{T\mu P} + t_T + t_{CCU} ,$$

where:

t_{TCCU} - time delay for switching on the transmit/receiver unit of the CCU to transmit data call ,

t_{call} - time delay to transmit data call of the μP_i ,

$t_{\mu P}$ - time delay for operating of a μP_i and preparing the data for transmission ,

$t_{T\mu P}$ - time delay for switching on the transmit/receiver unit of the μP_i to transmit data ,

t_T - time delay for data transmission from a μP_i to the CCU ,

t_{CCU} - time delay for data processing in the CCU and preparing the new call for the next μP .

The technical possibilities of the wide used transmit/receiver units allow t_{TCCU} to be in a range of 30-80 ms I1I. In this investigation we assume the best occasion $t_{TCCU}=t_{T\mu P}=30$ ms.The time delay t_{call} is determined by the size of the message, which will transmit the CCU and the channel's speed. If we assume that the CCU transmits 2 bytes,according to the presence of one start and one stop bits,the CCU will transmit 20 bits.Hence $t_{call}=20.3,33$ ms=67 ms. Respectively if the μP_i transmits a message,consisting 5 bytes,then $t_{T\mu P}=50.3,33$ ms= 165 ms. If we assume the ideal occasion $t_{\mu P}=t_{CCU}=0$,e.g. μP_i and the CCU do not loose time for information processing , according to (2), we obtain $t_c \approx 300$ ms. If the communication fails because of wrong received data or the vehicle does not transmit its location due to the existance of radioshadow areas,it is organized a dialogue up to three or more calls I1,2,4,5I,which determines $t_c \approx 1$ s.

This examination is done in ideal conditions,but the time delay of the overall system,respectively for the CCU,is not less than 1 s,$t_c > 1$ s.Moving with different speeds,for a time delay t_c,the vehicles will pass a space interval S_i,estimated in a Table 1, where

$S_i = v.T_i$, $T_i = t_c.n$, $n=20$, v-a vehicle's velocity .

v Ikm/hI	30	40	50	60	70
v I m/sI	8	11	14	17	20
S_iI m I	160	220	280	340	400

Table 1. Space intervals as a velocity function

Table 1 shows the values of the space intervals,which the vehicles will pass during the observation of 20 cars in a system with time delay of the CCU $t_c = 1$ s.These space intervals determine the maximal rapidity of the system, which is an ideal according to the speed of the vehicles.It is obvious that with increasing of n the AVLS operating management will be loosen and the system becomes inoperable. In this article is designed an optimal rule of data communication between μP_i,i=1,n, and the CCU.It is determined as a result of solving an optimal problem.

2.A PROBLEM OF THE OPTIMAL DATA TRANSMISSION

We consider that the topic of the AVLS is to decrease the uncertainity about the vehicle location of the examening cars. Let us define the components of the optimal problem by the way:

x_i - the μP_i location ,

$f_i(x_i)$ - the uncertainity (entropy) and a lack of knowledge about the μP_i location ,

S_i - restrictions of the technical and programm features of the μP_i ,

$g(x)$ - restrictions due to the technical and programm features of the CCU.

The optimal problem for data transmission can be defined as

$$\min \sum_{i=1}^{n} f_i(x_i) \quad , \tag{3}$$

$$x_i \in S_i \quad ,$$

$$g(x) \leq 0 \quad ,$$

$$x = (x_1, \ldots, x_n) \quad .$$

The function f_i is an accuracy knowledge about the vehicles' locations.If the real time AVLS reacts actually to every vehicle's location change,we achieve the ideal performance of the system operation.As the vehicles' motion is watched on a display,which consist a scale representation of the observable region,the minimal change,noticeable by the operator, is C_{min}.Hence each vehicle must change its location more than $k.C_{min}$,in order to appear requiring for data transmission of the new position from a μP_i towards the CCU. Hence $f_i(x_i)$ may be defined

$$f_i(x_i) = \min |dx_i - k.C_{min}| ,$$

where:

dx_i - the distance,passed after the last data transmission,

k - a scale representation coefficient of the observable area,

C_{min} - the admissible change of the vehicle's representation on the display.

$$dx_i = x_i(T_i) - x_i(t_i) ,$$

$x_i(T_i)$ - the position of the i-th vehicle,reported on last data transmission,

$x_i(t_i)$ - the current i-th vehicle's location.

The constrain $g(x) \leq 0$ include the possibility of the CCU and formalizes the condition that in a time interval $dt=t_c$ the CCU is inoperable with others μP. Hence $g(x)$ is

$$g(x) : |t_i - t_j| \geq t_c , \forall i,j=1,n, i \neq j .$$

The optimal problem of data transmission in the microprocessor's network becomes

(4) $$\min \sum_{i=1}^{n} |y_i(t_i)| ,$$

$$y_i(t_i) = x_i(t_i) - x_i(T_i) - k.C_{min} , \forall i=1,n ,$$

$$g(x): |t_i - t_j| \geq t_c , \quad \forall i,j=1,n , i \neq j ,$$

$$y_i(t_i) \geq 0 , \quad \forall i=1,n .$$

The solutions of (4) are the moments t_i and the row of consequent indices $J = (i)$, $i \in 1,n$, which determine the order of data communication between a μP_i,$i=1,n$, and the CCU.This formulation of the problem of the data transmission is considerably better than the common used procedure of a consequently calling and data transmission between a $\mu P_i, i=1,n$, and the CCU. In a case of different speeds of a motion, (4) allows better and smoother following and watching the vehicles' locations.

A problem (4) can not be solved analyticaly. That is why $x_i(t_i)$ is aproximated and represented in a polynomial form, using the existing data of the old data transmission by composing a suitable mathematical model and predicting the vehicle's motion. Hence we obtain the analytical formulation

$$x_i(t_i) = x_i | T_i, T_{i-1}, T_{i-2}, \ldots, x_i(T_i), x_i(T_{i-1}), \ldots | ,$$

where $T_i, T_{i-1}, T_{i-2}, \ldots, x_i(T_i), x_i(T_{i-1}), \ldots$, are the old reported data of vehicles' locations. Here is used the interpolation Newton formula to present the vehicle's motion in a polynomial form |6|

$$x_i(t_i) = c_o^i + c_1^i(t_i - T_o^i) + c_2^i(t_i - T_o^i)(t_i - T_1^i) + \ldots + c_m^i(t_i - T_o^i)\ldots,$$

where

$$c_o^i = x_i(T_o^i) \;, \quad c_1^i = | x_i(T_1^i) - x_i(T_o^i) | / (T_1^i - T_o^i), \ldots$$

Hence

$$x_i(t_i) = x_i(T_o^i) + \{ |x_i(T_1^i) - x_i(T_o^i)| / (T_1^i - T_o^i) \} (t_i - T_o^i) + \ldots, \qquad (5)$$

$$T_1^i < T_o^i < t_i \;.$$

To restrict the use of the history of the vehicles' motion, we take into account some conclusions:

a/ The vehicle's motion is an arbitrary and that is why it is useful to take into account only the last transmited data;

b/ The urban network is displayed by the CCU like a linear aproximation and segmentation ;

c/ To accomplish a fast computation in a μP_i and the CCU and to maintain a time delay $t_{\mu P} = t_{CCU} = 0$, it is useful to use the first two terms of (5) ;

d/ The expression $|x_i(T_1^i) - x_i(T_o^i)| / (T_1^i - T_o^i) = V_{av}$ has an exact physical sence and represents an average motion's speed for the definite time interval.

Hence a problem (4) becomes

(6) $$\min \sum_{i=1}^{n} | y_i(t_i) | ,$$

$$y_i(t_i) = \{ Ix_i(T_1^i) - x_i(T_o^i) I / (T_1^i - T_o^i) \} (t_i - T_o^i) - kC_{min}, \; \forall i=1,n ,$$

$$g(x) = | t_i - t_j | \geq t_c , \quad \forall \; i,j=1,n, \; i \neq j ,$$

$$y_i(t_i) \geq 0 , \quad i=1,n.$$

A problem (6) is analyticaly determined and unknown arguments are t_i , i=1,n.

3. A SOLUTION OF THE OPTIMAL DATA TRANSMISSION'S PROBLEM

For solving (6) we use an hierarchical approach.Neglecting the linking restrictions g(x), a problem (6) is decomposed to n subproblems

(7) $$\min | y_i(t_i) | ,$$

$$y_i(t_i) \geq \{ Ix_i(T_1^i) - x_i(T_o^i) I / (T_1^i - T_o^i) \} (t_i - T_o^i) - kC_{min}$$

$$y_i(t_i) \geq 0 ,$$

which have local solutions

$$t_i^* = \arg \{ Ix_i(T_1^i) - x_i(T_o^i) I / (T_1^i - T_o^i) \; (t_i - T_o^i) - kC_{min} = 0 \} .$$

Hence in the hierarchical system,fig.1, after receiving the solutions t_i^*, i=1,n, the coordination unit CCU will chack constrains g(x).

If $g(x) \geq 0$, end.
If $g(x) \ngeq 0$, it is necessary to determine the suitable consequence of data transmission between the CCU and a μP_i, i=1,n.

The expression $|y_i(t_i)|$ is not convenient for analyticaly solving a problem (7).That is why here is chosen the form $y_i^2(t_i)$ for the performence index,which does not change the physical meaning of the problem.

We assume the marks

(8) $$V_i = Ix_i(T_1^i) - x_i(T_o^i) I / (T_1^i - T_o^i) ,$$

$$S_i = I(x_i(T_1^i) - x_i(T_o^i)) / (T_1^i - T_o^i) IT_o^i .$$

A problem (6) takes the form

$$\min \sum_{i=1}^{n} y_i^2(t_i) \quad ,$$

$$y_i(t_i) = V_i t_i - S_i - kC_{min} \ , \ i=1,n \ ,$$

$$y_i(t_i) \geq 0 \ , \quad i=1,n \ ,$$

$$g(x) \ : \ |t_i - t_j| \geq t_c \ , \quad \forall \ i,j=1,n, \ i \neq j.$$

By ignoring constrains g(x) the solutions of problems (7) are

$$t_i^* = (S_i + kC_{min})/V_i \ , \qquad i = 1,n.$$

We form a set of indices $\{p\}$, for which constrains $g(x(t^*))$, is not satisfied and a set $\{q\}$, where $g(x(t^*))$ is fulfield, e.g.

$$\{p\} : |t_i^* - t_j^*| < t_c \ , \quad \forall \ i,j \in \{p\},$$

$$\{q\} : |t_i^* - t_j^*| \geq t_c \ , \quad \forall \ i,j \in \{q\},$$

$$\{p\} + \{q\} = n \ .$$

Hence for the set of indices $\{p\}$, the moments for data transmission t_i, $i \in \{p\}$, must be determined by solving a problem (6), e.g. without neglecting constrains g(x).The optimal problem (6) is reduced to the form

(9)
$$\min \sum_{i \in \{p\}}^{n} I V_i t_i - S_i - kC_{min} I^2 \ ,$$

$$t_i \geq (S_i + kC_{min})/V_i \ , \qquad \forall \ i \in \{p\} \ ,$$

$$g(x) : |t_i - t_j| \geq t_c \ , \qquad \forall \ i \in \{p\} \ .$$

To simplify the condition of the research,we assume that $\{p\} = \{1,2\}$,e.g. the set $\{p\}$ consists only two indices.In a case that $\{p\}$ consists more elements,for example $\{p\} = \{1,2,3\}$, the set $\{p\}$ could be decomposed to a three subsets $\{1,2,3\} = \{1,2\} + \{1,3\} + \{2,3\}$,each consisting a pair indices, and to perform the research three times consequently.Using these simplifications, (9) becomes

(10)
$$\min IF = y_1^2(t_1) + y_2^2(t_2) I \ ,$$

$$y_1(t_1) = V_1 t_1 - S_1 - kC_{min} \ ,$$

$$y_2(t_2) = V_2 t_2 - S_2 - kC_{min} \ ,$$

$$y_1(t_1) \geq 0 \ , \quad y_2(t_2) \geq 0 \ ,$$

$$g(x) : |t_1 - t_2| \geq t_c .$$

Conditions g(x) consist a logical condition and can be written in the form

$$-t_1 + t_2 + t_c \leq 0 \quad \text{or} \quad t_1 - t_2 + t_c \leq 0 .$$

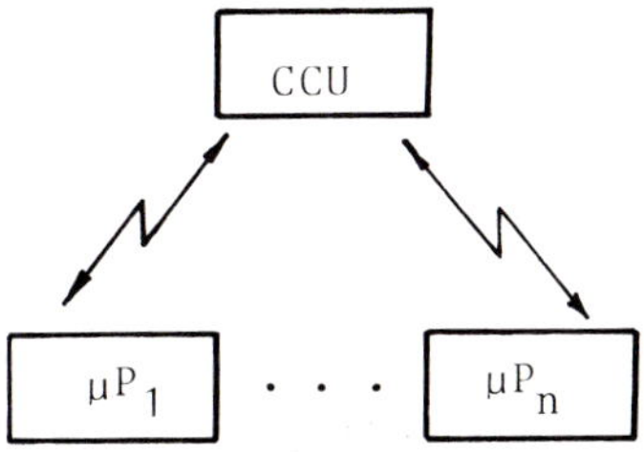

Fig.1.An hierarchical microprocessor's network

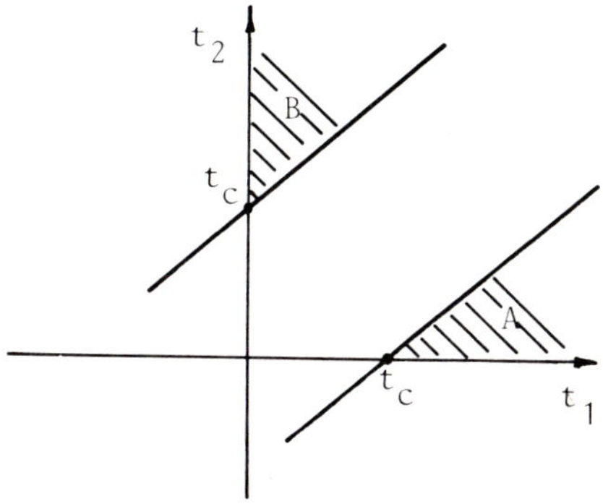

Fig.2.A feasible noncompact area

According to fig.2,the constrains g(x) define a subarea A and B. As the admissible area is not compact, a problem (10) has to be resolved separately for each subset A and B.After substitutions, (10) becomes

$$\text{(11)} \quad \min I\ F=(V_1t_1-S_1-kC_{min})^2 + (V_2t_2-S_2-kC_{min})^2 I \ ,$$
$$t_1 \geq t_c \ , \qquad t_2 \geq t_c \ ,$$
$$g_A(x) : -t_1 + t_2 + t_c \leq 0 \text{ or } g_B(x): t_1 - t_2 + t_c \leq 0 .$$

For solving (11) by using an hierarchical approach,we use a goal coordination method I7I. In this case we form the Lagrange function by a way given bellow.

A case A/ :

$$L_A(1)=F+1g_A(x)=(V_1t_1-S_1-kC_{min})^2+1(-t_1+t_2-t_c)+(V_2t_2-S_2-kC_{min})^2,$$
$$t_1 \geq t_c \ , \qquad t_2 \geq t_c \ .$$

A case B/ :

$$L_B(1)=F+1g_B(x)=(V_1t_1-S_1-kC_{min})^2+1(t_1-t_2+t_c)+ (V_2t_2-S_2-kC_{min})^2$$
$$t_1 \geq t_c \ , \qquad t_2 \geq t_c \ .$$

The right Lagrange problem $\min_t L(1)$ has the following solutions.

A case A/ :

(12) $t_1^A(1)=\max I(S_1+kC_{min})/V_1 + 1/2V_1^2;\ t_c I$,

$t_2^A(1)=\max I(S_2+kC_{min})/V_2;\ t_c\ I$.

A case B/ :

(13) $t_1^B(1)=\max I(S_1+kC_{min})/V_1;\ t_c\ I$,

$t_2^B(1)=\max I(S_2+kC_{min})/V_2 + 1/2V_2^2;\ t_c I$.

The solutions of a problem (11) are a system (12) if $F(A) < F(B)$ or (13), if $F(B) < F(A)$.

The exact definition of solutions $It_1^A(1), t_2^A(1)I$ and $It_1^B(1), t_2^B(1)I$ is done after estimating the lagrange multiplier 1 by the way of solving the dual Lagrange problem I 7 I. But in this particular case of constrains g(x), it is permissible to determine a solution $t_2(1)$ if $t_1(1)$ is known, because

$$t_2(1) = t_1(1) + t_c .$$

Using a system (12), $t_2^A(1)$ does not depend on 1. Hence the solution has a form

$$t_1^A(1)=t_2^A(1) + t_c,$$

$$t_2^A(1)=\max I(S_1+kC_{min})/V_2;\ t_c I .$$

For a system (13) the solution is

$$t_1^B(1)=\max I(S_1+kC_{min})/V_1;\ t_c I ,$$

$$t_2^B(1)=t_1^B(1) + t_c.$$

From (12) follows

$$t_1(1)=(S_1+kC_{min})/V_1=t_1(1=0)=t_1(0) ,$$

e.g. the solution $t_1(1)$ is the same, if the lagrange multiplier is equal to zero /1=0/. Respectively

$$t_2(1)=(S_2+kC_{min})/V_2=t_2(1=0)=t_2(0).$$

Hence the solutions for cases A and B are

(14) $t_1^A(1)=t_2^A(0) + t_c$,

$t_2^A(1)=t_2^A(0)=\max I(S_2+kC_{min})/V_2;\ t_c I$,

or

(15) $$t_1^B(1)=t_1^B(0)=\max I(S_1+kC_{min})/V_1;\ t_c I\ ,$$
$$t_2^B(1)=t_1^B(0)+t_c\ .$$

The right solution is determined by substituting $t_1(1)$ and $t_2(1)$ in the function F, evaluating and chacking the minimal value $FIt_1^A(1),t_2^A(1)I$ or $FIt_1^B(1),t_2^B(1)I$. These conclusions help to design an algorithm of the CCU operation and estimation the consequence of data transmission in the network between the microprocessors' units $\mu P_i, i=1,n$, in the AVLS.

4. AN ALGORITHM FOR SYSTEM OPERATION

Step I. Initial starting of the system.

1 step.The CCU calls the all $\mu P_i, i=1,n$, by an arbitrary manner and receives data $x_i(T_\circ^i), i=1,n$.

2 step.Repeat the action of step 1.

3 step.The CCU forms the sets $\{V_i\}_n$ and $\{S_i\}_n$ using (8) with the data from steps 1 and 2.

4 step.Solving (7) and evaluating the solutions $t_i^*=t_i(1=0)$, $i=1,n$.

5 step.Chacking the constrains g(x) :

if g(x) is satisfied, go to step II ;

if g(x) is not satisfied, go to step 6.

6 step.Estimation the subset of indices $\{p\}$,for which g(x) is not satisfied.

7 step.Determination the first two indices k and 1,which belong to the subset $\{p\}$,e.g.

$$|t_k^* - t_1^*| < t_c\ ,$$
$$t_1^* \le t_k^* = \min\{t_r^*\}\ ,\quad r \in \{p\}\ .$$

Hence a μP_k and a μP_1 have to transmit their information to the CCU, but the times of transmissions t_k^* and t_1^* do not allow the CCU to process and receive this information.

8 step.Evaluating the solutions from the systems (14) and (15) and determining the consequence of indices k and 1 .

9 step. If at a step 7 the subset $\{p\}$ contains more than two components, the rules of steps 7 and 8 are repeated until determination the index r, which must be first.

10 step. Decreasing the subset $\{p\}$ and $\{q\}$ with an index r and forming the index row $J = \{i\}$, $i \in 1,n$ for data transmission. A chack: if $\{p\}$ is empty, go to step II ; if $\{p\}$ is not empty, go to a step 7.

Step II. Normal operation rules.

1 step. Calling the μP_m by the CCU.

$$m = \min J = \{i\}, \quad i \in 1,n ,$$

where m is the first element in the row of indices for data transmission.

2 step. Receiving the data $x_m(T_m)$.

3 step. Actualization the sets $\{V_i\}$ and $\{S_i\}$ with the new evaluated V_m and S_m .

4 step. Computation and prediction the new moment T^m_{i+1} for data transmission:

$$T^m_{i+1} = T^m_o + dt , \quad dT^m = kC_{min}/V_m ,$$

$$V_m \leq |x(T^m_o) - x(T^m_1)|/(T^m_o - T^m_1) ,$$

where

$x(T^m_o)$ - the new received data ,

$x(T^m_1)$ - the data, received before the new ones.

5 step. Chack the constrains g(x):

If g(x) is satisfied, actualization of the row J with T^m_{i+1} and go to 1.

If g(x) is not satisfied, go to step 6.

6 step. Implementation the operation of step I.7.

7 step. Implementation the operation of a step I.8.

8 step. Actualization the row J and go to a step 1.

This algorithm determines the information parameters, which

have to be transmited by the CCU to a μP_i, $i=1,n$, and vice-versa, the consequence and the time moments for a data dialogue and transmission a CCU - a μP_i.

In a fig.3 is done an information exchange in an AVLS.This information structure imposes the hardware and software requirements for the CCU and the μP_i, $i=1,n$, to implement the algorithm for an optimal data transmission.

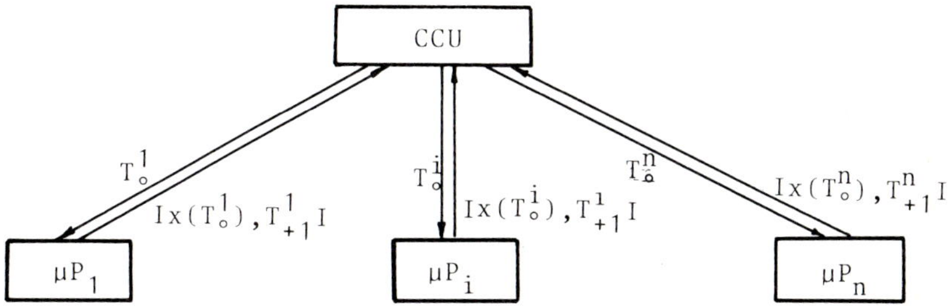

Fig.3. An information exchange structure.

5. AN EXAMPLE

It is watched two vehicles with initial models of motion

$$x_1(t_1) = 10t_1 , \qquad x_2(t_2) = 30t_2 .$$

The admissible minimal sensitive error is

$$kC_{min} = 300 \text{ m}.$$

The optimal problem for data transmission becomes

$$\min I \, y_1^2(t_1) + y_2^2(t_2) \, I ,$$

$$y_1(t_1) = x_1(t_1) - kC_{min} = 10t_1 - 300 ,$$

$$y_2(t_2) = x_2(t_2) - kC_{min} = 30t_2 - 300 ,$$

$$|t_1 - t_2| \geq t_c = 5 \text{ s}.$$

We assume that the CCU is able to execute transactions - a calling and a data transmission at every 5 seconds.

I iteration. The solutions of (7) are

$$t(t_1^*(1=0)) = 30 \text{ s} , \qquad t(t_2^*(1=0)) = 10 \text{ s} ,$$

where $t(t_1^*)$ is the current time after the system's starting. Hence the CCU will call first for a μP_2 at the 10-th s,fig.4a.

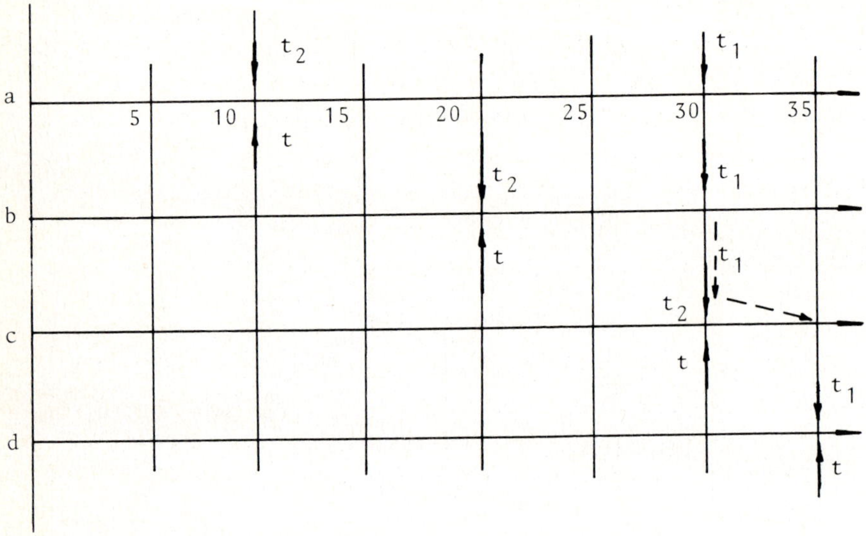

Fig.4. A data transmission's diagram.

II iteration. We assume that the characteristics of the motion is preserved. The solution is presented on a fig.4b. It will report again a μP_2 at a time moment $t(t_2^*(1=0))=20$ s.

III iteration. If the model of the motion is the same, the solution for both μP_1 and μP_2 is to transmit data to the CCU simultaneously. According to (14) and (15) we obtain:

A/ $\quad t(t_1^A) = 30 , \quad t(t_2^A) = 35$;

B/ $\quad t(t_1^B) = 35 , \quad t(t_2^B) = 30$.

As $F(A) = 150^2 > F(B) = 50^2$, the optimal consequence for a data transmission is a case B/, e.g. at the 30-th s will transmit a μP_2 and at the next time cycle will transmit a μP_1, fig.4c, 4d. If the kind of a motion is preserved, the consequence of a data transmission will be

t_2	t_2	t_2	t_1	t_2	t_2	t_2	t_1	t_2 ...
10s	20s	30s	35s	40s	50s	60s	65s	70s

6. CONCLUSION

This procedure allows irregular calling and data transmission between a μP_i, $i=1,n$, and the CCU. At each step the model of the optimal problem (6) is actualized and the algorithm performs adaptive features.This allows the overall computer network to operate in an optimal manner and to execute an optimal data transfer in the sence of a problem (6).

REFERENCES

I1I Младенов,Д.И.,К.П.Стоилова,Т.А.Стоилов,Техническо осигуряване на система за оперативен контрол на клас подвижни обекти,Комплексни системи за управление №1,София, 1984,стр.78-86.

I2I Младенов,Д.И.,К.П.Стоилова,Т.А.Стоилов,Вычислительная система для управления автомобильным парком в движении, Автоматика и вычислительная техника №6,Рига,1983,стр.24-27.

I3I Carter,D.A.,N.C.Kalnitsky,Personal computer based automatic vehicle location and monitoring systems,Cornahan conference of security technology,Lexington,Kentucky, 1984,p.21-36.

I4I Pinpoint - Radio system for locating and monitoring vehicles,Philips Tech.Rev.,vol.35,N1,1975,p.15-22.

I5I Шкирятов,В.В.,Радионавигационные системы и устройства, Радио и связь,Москва,1984.

I6I Корн,Г.,Т.Корн,Справочник по математике,Наука,Москва, 1977,стр.831.

I7I Лэсдон,Л.С.,Оптимизация больших систем,Наука,Москва, 1975,стр.432.

DISTRIBUTED COMPUTING SYSTEMS

Network Information Processing Systems
K. Boyanov, R. Angelinov (Editors)
Elsevier Science Publishers B.V. (North-Holland)

AN APPROACH TO CREATING A SERVICE FOR DISTRIBUTED PROGRAMMING IN COMMUNICATION-ORIENTED OPERATING MEDIA

Ljudmil MANASSIEV, Rumen STAINOV, Kiril BOYANOV

Bulgarian Academy of Sciences
Centre of Informatics and Computer Technology
"Acad. G. Bontchev" str., bl. 25-A
1113 Sofia, Bulgaria

The present paper proposes a new service, which makes possible the automation of the distribution of the processes, constituting a distributed program. It has been implemented in a communication-oriented distributed medium.

1. INTRODUCTION

The first developments of Distributed Computer Systems (DCS) are characterized by a centralized logical structure which allows for passive resources to be shared [1], [2]. Lately, the faster communication media and more powerful microprocessors allowed the distribution of the active resources [3], [4], [5]. The DCS processing capacity is considered as a basic active resource. This new trend is associated with the development of distributed operating system support, providing management and utilization tools for the computational processor resources. Many research projects have been concerned with various approaches to the distribution of tasks among DCS nodes. For some of them, starting a particular process must be preceded by LOGIN in a particular node [3]. With more sophisticated DCS, the operating system provides a CREATE PROCESS primitive, whose parameters specify the location of the new process [5]. The achievement of effective load on the constituent processing capacity of the distributed system is closely connected with the methods and aids for distributed programming [8], [9], [10] . This is natural, taking into account that the distributed program can be considered as an unity of interactive processes on one or more computers (nodes). The constituent processes have two peculiarities: (1) they cooperate to execute effectively the task (2) they compete for the DS common resources. The first makes necessary the availability of free interprocess interactions the second - a control mechanism.

The present paper proposes a new tool (service), which makes possible (to a sertain degree) the automation of the distribution of the processes, constituting a distributed program. It has been experimentally implemented in a communication-oriened distributed operating medium.

2. COMMUNICATION-ORIENTED DISTRIBUTED OPERATING MEDIUM (CODOM)

CODOM is a communication-oriented operating kernel, which is duplicated in every node of the distributed system. The interaction of the operating kernels in the system ensures its logical entity.

The principle underlying the design of the medium requires that its development should not affect the kernel [6]. Its functions and volume remain intact. All supplementary services in the operating medium have been implemented as kernel-based processes, which cannot be distinguished from user processes. This approach has two main advantages. First, this provides a flexible functional specialization of the individual nodes. Some of them may be organized as specialized servers or workstations, others may form a processor pool providing processing power [5]. The second advantage is expressed in terms of enhanced experimental possibilities and search for better solutions.

CODOM is characterized by a decentralized logical architecture. It has been adopted for the purpose of increasing the total reliability of the system and also ensuring direct and parallel interworking of the system processes. We shall define CODOM by its communication features, naming and protecting principles, and provided services [7].

2.1. Communication Features

In communication respect, CODOM consists of active and passive elements. Active are the processes, passive - the ports. The port mechanism is based on the object-oriented approach. Every port is considered as an object of one of the following three classes: communication, system and information. The main responsibility of the system ports is to provide interface of the process with the local operating kernel, and hence the possibility to use the basic functions of the medium. The communication ports are the objects, which form the common address space of the system. Every communication port is a logical input for exactly one of the existing processes (the process-owner) and output for all the rest. Every process has access to the common address space and, if necessary, addresses its element (a communication port), without taking into account its location and the process-owner. Similar to the centralized OS, where part of the address space is allocated for system purposes, here some ports may also be reserved for processes providing system functions. The basic communication primitives SEND and RECEIVE are supported by the operating medium. The SEND primitives are of a nonblocking type, i.e. the process-sender receives exact diagnostics of the result from the operation and does not block during its execution. The RECEIVE primitives are blocking or nonblocking, being buffered in both cases.

2.2. Naming and protection

The main objects managed by the system on an operating kernel level are the ports and processes (the so called basic elements). All remaining objects, linked to creating of services, are composed of basic elements. Separate services are identified by the ports assigned to them. For their part, these are located via a Name-service characterized by its complete distribution. Logically, the Name-servers, representing a part of the operating kernel and running in every station, provide the common address space of the system. To use a particular service, the application process must address its assigned port in an adequate manner. This is possible via an identificator or via generic identificators (i.e. multicast distribution). The local Name-server is responsible for the conversion of this name into a machine equivalent on the basis of its global information. For its part, the Name-server in the destination station locates the port of the process-receiver.

The full distribution of the Name-service in CODOM has two aspects. First, the use of a centralized Name-server is avoided, thereby interprocess communications are speeded and paralleled. Second, system reliability is enhanced. Of course, the distributed Name-service is far more difficult to maintain in an active state, but finally this remains transparent to the user.

2.3. Services

The distributed operating medium consists of two layers: service and system. The service layer is responsible for the provision of definite services for different applications. The services are basic and supplementary. The basic services provide Boot-Service, File Transfer, Remote Procedure Call, Distributed Programming. The supplementary services provide Electronic Mail, Teleconferencing, File Server, Print Server, Gateway Server, etc. The supplementary services can be accessed by the application processes only, while the basic services are available for both application processes and supplementary services (Fig. 1).

3. SYSTEM SUPPORT OF DISTRIBUTED PROGRAMMING IN CODOM

A main issue of distributed programming is the availability of free interprocess links and of control mechanisms, allowing the usage of common resources in DCS (Distributed Computer Systems). CODOM complies with these two conditions in system respect, the primitives for their use being located in the user interface. In this way, every algorithmic language could be extended for the purpose of distributed programming.

3.1. Process Servers (PS)

The problems of distribution, migration and load balancing of the constituent processes in the system has been solved in CODOM via process servers. In the ordinary systems, the server is a specialized process, which manages a certain common resource (file, disk) and provides shared usage by all processes and nodes in the system. With the service for distributed programming in CODOM, the common resource is the aggregate of separate computational resources in the nodes. That is why a particular approach to the organisation and management of the common resources is vital. CODOM lacks an uniform server process, but a set of process servers is available and provides uniform system support of distributed programming and execution, based on their interaction.

To provide a possibility for dynamic changes in the volume of the distributed processing capacity, a processor pool is created. It unlike the processor pool described in [5] is created dynamicaly in terms of size and configuration. A particular node is connected to or disconnected from the processor pool through the activation or deactivation of a PS in the node. As regards the distributed operating medium, the PSs are treated as application processes. Either of them interfaces the operating kernel of the medium via its information and system ports.

There exists, however, certain difference in the creation and use of the communication ports. The communication ports of the PSs belong to the system part of the common address space. In this way the operating kernel of the medium identifies them and provides priority specialized support.

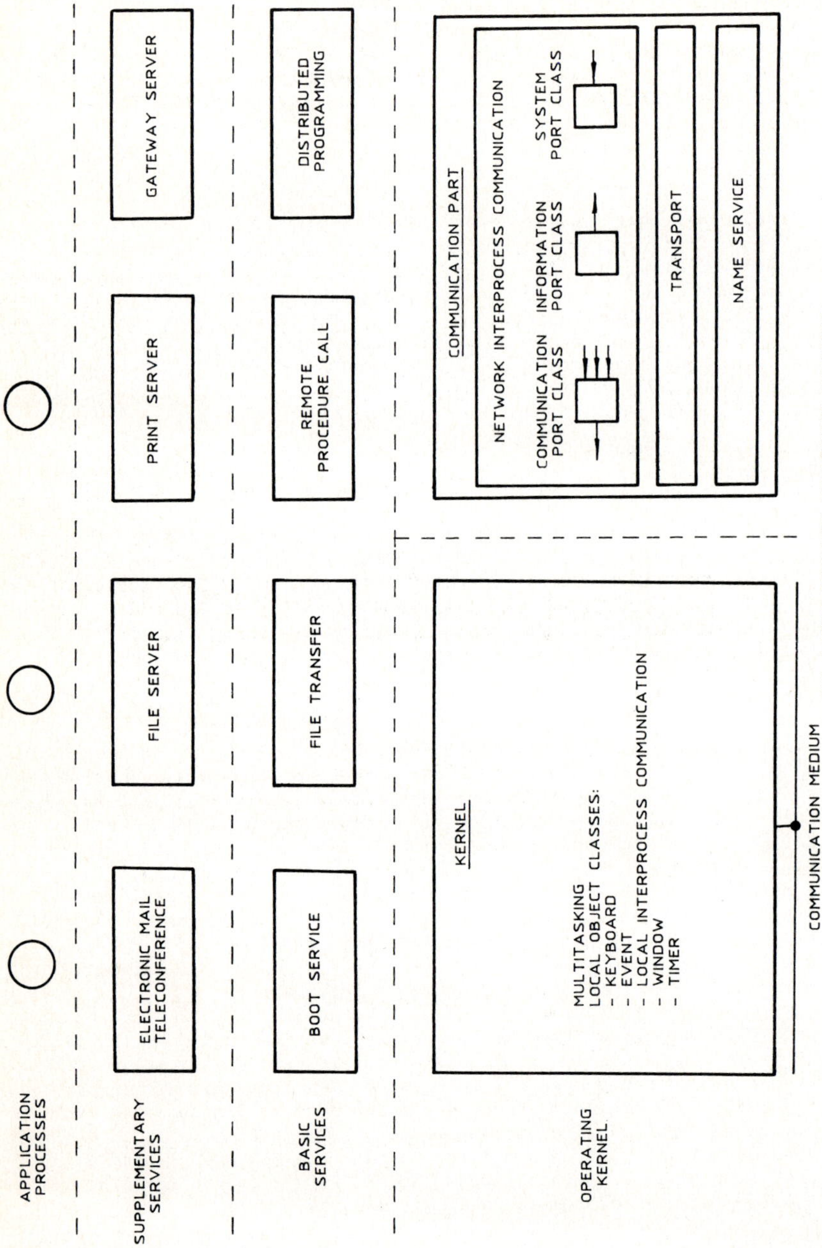

FIG. 1. THE DETAILED STRUCTURE OF CODOM

3.2. Mechanism of Operation and Interaction of the Process Servers

Every PS is assigned exactly one communication port which is an element of the system address space. It represents an access point of the application processes in the system to the service under consideration. In this way, any process based on a node where no PS runs, may use the service via any of its ports, existing at the moment in the corresponding subpart of the system address space.

The structure of the PS consists of the following modules (Fig. 2):

(a) Basic - organizes the execution of the user's request, based on the information provided by the corresponding Load Management Block, and defines the most appropriate node for the execution of the request.
(b) Load Management - estimates the load on the resources in a particular node of the DCS. The choice of the node executor of the user's request is based on this evaluation.
(c) Process-initiator - starts and manages the new process in the node-executor.
(d) Analyzer-dispatcher of the input flow - analyzes the requests for service from the application processes and the messages for provision of interaction among the PSs, distributing then among the three modules above.

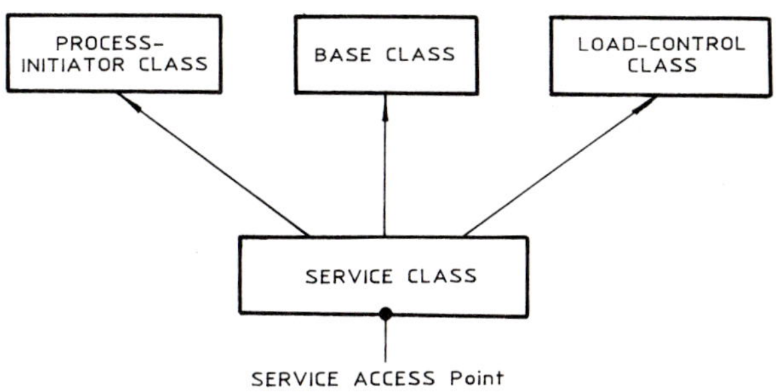

FIG. 2. THE STRUCTURE OF THE PS

The tasks handled by these four modules are independent to a large degree and in a number of cases are parallel. The modules are implemented as separate processes. Access to them is managed via the following four classes of objects:

- Class Service. The objects from this class provide user access to the service for all DCS processes.
- Class Base. These objects provide system access to the base part of the PS.
- Class Load. The objects from this class allow information on the node resources to be made available for all DCS process servers.
- Class Initiator. These objects together with the objects from the two classes above are inaccesible for the application process but allow the process-initiator to be used by all DCS process servers.

The analyzer-despatcher represents the class SERVICE. It is the owner of the system port, unambiguously associated with the PS. The whole server input flow goes through this port. The task of the analyzer-despatcher is to recognize and distribute the messages from the input traffic of the PS among the remaining three constituent service processes.

The basic part of the PS represents the class BASE. It is intended to initialize and, to a certain extent, synchronize the execution of the application requests. Every request expresses the wish of the user process for a new process to be organized somewhere in the system. Of course, "somewhere in the systems" means the aggregate of those nodes where PSs run. The request is extended to any of the input points of the service for distributed execution and describes the elements required for the successful run of the new process. The most important elements are: the file with the execution code; the files to be used as input/output files; the required operating memory; specialized input/output devices. Based on the request, the process server module under consideration generates an enquiry to all available PSs. This is possible through the use of the capabilities of the operating medium for multicast distribution towards a part of the address space.

The sent enquiry is handled by a LOAD MANAGEMENT module in the receiving PSs. It registers the accessible ressources at the moment in the node where it has been located. The purpose is to meet the user requirements in the application request on the one hand and to strike a balance in the distribution of processes between the nodes. Besides, loading the least loaded node has always been aimed at. In the present implementation, the load balancing function is expressed in terms of the number of processes, running in a particular node. It should be noted, however, that the implementation and incorporation of another function, representing other load balancing criteria, is possible. For example, the minimization of interprocess communications, or the location of interactive processes in different computers to secure their maximum parallelism.

The Load Management modules in those nodes that comply with the user requirements send an answer to the process server that has generated the request. The answer also contains the transitory value of their load function. The base part of the enquiring PS receives these answers and selects the node-executor on the basis of the load. Then, the PS in the node-executor is sent a request for starting a new process.

The request is handled by the PROCESS-INITIATOR module in the node-executor. The base part of the originating PS, which has received the initial request, is responsible for providing access of the process-initiator to all necessary files. This is possible either through a file service or sending these files to the executor via a file-message. On starting successfully the new process, the process-initiator in the executor directly informs the user that has sent the request. Or else, the base part in the PS makes a repeated attempt to organize the execution after having received the initial request. Should a new failure occur, the user is informed of the cause. The processes create as a result of the user request do not differ in any way from the other user processes and have the right to use all available system capabilities. As far as the distributed program is concerned, the programmer must express in an algorithmic language the distribution of the constituent processes and the way of their synchronization. The CODOM operating kernel and the service under consideration provide sufficient capabilities for the above expression, using the user interface.

4. SERVICE REALIZATION

The CODOM experimental model has been based on a local network of the type Ethernet (10 Mbit/s), comprising IBM XT/AT personal computers. The service for distributed programming has been implemented in Assembler to ensure maximum high speed. For experimental purposes, the language Pascal, extended with the corresponding primitives comprising the user interface, has been used for the service. The experience from the service shows that the service-based distributed applications, make rational use of the free computational resourse of the personal computers in the local network. The programmer is released from the manual allocation of the processes constituting the distributed program to the network nodes. The distributed programming service may be used for distributed applications and experiments in the parallel algorithms.

5. CONCLUSION

With distributed operating systems, the creation and allocation of new processes is of crucial importance. CODOM solves this problem establishing two hierarchical level in OS. The low level controls the local creation of new processes and is incorporated in the operating kernel. The high level solves general tasks of load balancing and distribution of the new DCS processes. In compliance with the general conception adopted for the construction of the medium, the high level has been designed as a service. Its main characteristics are:

1. Possibility for dynamic change of the configuration of the nodes to accommodate new processes.
2. Multitude of ports for service access available for all user processes.
3. Automatic load balancing with capabilities for dynamic change of the load functions.

ACKNOWLEDGEMENTS

The discussions with A. Petkov, V. Sabev, N. Avramov and other research associates from the Distributed Systems Laboratory at the Coordination Centre of Informatics and Computer Technology at the Bulgarian Academy of Sciences have been essential to the implementation of the above ideas.

REFERENCES

[1] 3Com Ether Series User's Guide, March, 1984.

[2] IBM PC Network Technical Reference, Sept., 1984.

[3] Needham, R.M. and Herbert, A.J. The Cambridge Distributed Computing System, Addison-Wesley, Reading, Mass., 1982.

[4] Van Tilborg, A.M. and Wittie, L.D., Wave Sheduling: Distributed Allocation of Task Forces in Network Computers. In Procedings of the 2-nd International Conference on Distributed Computing Systems, IEEE, 1981.

[5] Mullender, S.J., The Amoeba Distributed Operating System. CWI News Letter, Num. 11, 1986.

[6] Manassiev, L., Stainov R., Boyanov K., Object Oriented and Port Based Distributed Operating Medium, Proc. of the IFIP TC6/W6.4A Workshop on LAN Management, North-Holland, 1988.

[7] Tanenbaum, A.S., and Van Renesse, R., Distributed Operating Systems. ACM Computing Surveys, Vol. 17, No 4, Dec., 1985.

[8] Natarajan, N., Communication and Synchronization Primitives for Distributed Programs. IEEE Trans. on Soft. Eng., Vol. SE-11, No 4, Apr. 1985.

[9] Ng, K.W., A Kernel for Distributed Programming Languages. Interfaces in Computing, No. 3, 1985.

[10] Andrews, C.R., The Distributed Programming Language SR - Mechanisms, Design and Implementation, Software Pract. & Exp., No. 12, 1982.

Network Information Processing Systems
K. Boyanov, R. Angelinov (Editors)
Elsevier Science Publishers B.V. (North-Holland)

WEATHER FORECASTING - DISTRIBUTED IN NATURE

Dag JOHANSEN

Department of Computer Science
University of Tromsø
Tromsø, Norway

Weather forecasting is identified as one area where distributed processing might be convenient. This report describes a distributed application monitoring and exchanging local weather data, and this application is running on the distributed system Amoeba connected through wide area networks.

1. INTRODUCTION

In recent years, advances in observational apparatus and techniques have revolutionized weather forecasting. Computers have been increasingly important in this particular field ranging from collection of weather data to simulation of global weather patterns. Several of the problems weather forecasters are faced with are of a distributed nature, and computerizing these might be dealt with by distributed processing.

This report investigates how an actual problem of getting on-line weather maps currently available on several nodes throughout Europe might be solved. The design and implementation of a distributed weather map is outlined, and experience gained is presented. Future work is identified with important place given to intergration of an artificial intelligence application on top of the weather map application described. A short introduction to weather forecasting is also given to demonstrate the usability of distributed processing in weather forecasting.

2. WEATHER FORECASTING

Weather forecasting is the prognostication of the weather, and virtually every country in the world collects data on weather conditions within its borders and shares these data with the World Meterological Organization. The weather is either observed from points at the surface of the earth or at upper air installations, and weather is considered in terms of such meterological variables as temperature, humidity, cloudiness, precipitation, brightness, visibility and wind.

Weather forecasting has basically been done by weather forecasters aided by a diversity of tools, but a current trend is to turn over almost all of the task to computers. One task that has been computerized is the exchange of observed conditions to nodes wanting to display a weather map. A weather map showing the actual weather situation can be used to verify and control an early weather forecast, and this might lead to improved weather forecasts. Computers running implementations of complex mathematical models might also produce

* This work is supported by the NAVF grant no. D.07.08.001 (The TRACE project).

weather forecast maps. The physical state of the atmosphere can be described or modeled by mathematical equations, and observational data are put into the model to produce a weather forecast.

Weather forecasting is an activity distributed in its nature with several cooperating organizations collecting, processing and exchanging weather data. Even if a lot of the activities involved here have been computerized, another approach than the current ones can be taken. Collecting weather data can be done by a distributed application running on top of a distributed system, and simplicity, extensibility, transparency, and fault-tolerance might be achieved. Such a distributed application can deal with most of the tasks involved in collection of weather data. The design of such a weather map application is outlined in the next section.

3. A WEATHER FORECASTING TOOL

A weather map is an important weather forecasting tool. A weather map shows the meterologizal elements at a given time over an extended area. Normally, the distribution of surface isobars and the location of fronts, centers of high or low pressure, winds, temperatures and other severe weather areas are shown. At certain locations on the map, a standard plotting code might indicate:

- Wind direction and speed.
- Air temperature and dew point.
- Barometric pressure.
- The amount and types of clouds.
- The weather type.
- Prediction of actual or possible situations such as:
    - Excessive rainfalls.
    - Flash floods.
    - Avalanches.
    - Forest fires.
    - Blizzards.
    - Typhones, hurricanes and tornados.

A weather map is based on the collection of weather data from different locations, and collecting and exchanging these data is a process born to distributed processing. The succeding subsections sketch the design of an actual framework in which collection and exchange of weather data can be done.

3.1. Interface to the User.

A first issue to investigate is what kind of interface is to be presented to the user of a weather map application. The interface part is responsible for the user dialogue and displays the data obtained from other parts of the weather map application. No further processing is done in the interfaces to reduce the amount of data transferred. Each interface module displays at least two types of weather maps, one giving a local weather map based on data monitored in a local domain, another based on results exchanged with other local domains. An example of a local domain is northern part of Norway while a global domain is Europe.

3.2. Local Processing.

A local processing module exists at every local domain to be monitored, and every module of this kind can be accessed from interface modules within its own domain or from any other local processing module in other local domains.

When an interface is to display the current weather situation in its own domain, the interface sends a request to the local processing module. This module forwards the request by sending several requests to the modules within its own domain responsible for gathering and collecting the actual weather data. Replies from these modules are processed by the local processing module, and a reply containing local weather data is sent to the interface that issued the original request.

A request for a global view is sent to the same local processing module, and this module interacts with the modules responsible for collecting the weather data in the other domains of interest. The data returned includes only a subset of each local domain, and the local processing module that issued the requests processes the incoming replies and returns a global view to the interface. Fig. 1 shows how the different modules interact. No interaction between an interface in one local domain and a local processing module in another local domain is possible to simplify the interaction between the modules.

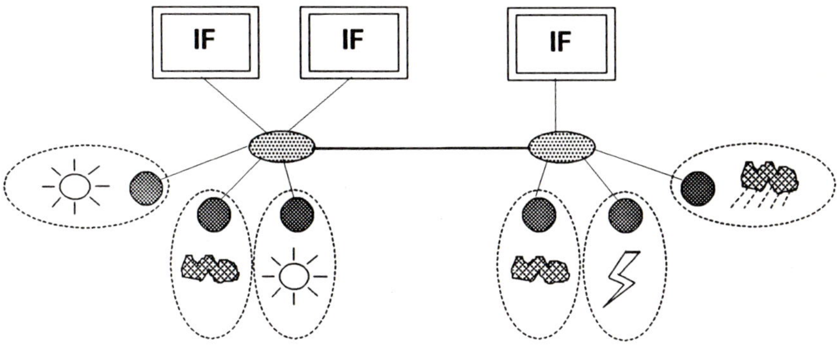

Fig. 1. Possible interactions between modules in the weather map application.

3.3. Collecting Weather Data

The weather map application heavily relies on the collection of weather data, and each physical device collecting weather data has to be connected on-line to a monitor module responsible for obtaining weather data upon request from a local processing module. Several modules of this kind can be located in the same local domain.

The current implementation exchanges only temperatures collected at certain locations, and this kind of data is obtained by interaction with a random generator implemented in one monitor module in each local domain. Several monitor modules are shown in fig. 1, and these modules can be closely tied to real weather observation equipment in the future.

4. IMPLEMENTATION ISSUES

A prototype version of the weather map application is currently running on the distributed system Amoeba. A brief presentation of necessary hardware and software is given in the succeding subsection.

4.1. Amoeba

Amoeba is an object-oriented distributed system [1], and semantically, client processes perform operations on objects managed by server processes. Associated with each object is a capability giving the owner the permission to carry out operations on the object. The operations are initiated by using a blocking message passing mechanism which form a simple kind of remote procedure calls [2].

Amoeba runs on a hardware configuration consisting of personal workstations, pool processors, specialized servers and gateways to other Amoeba systems. Locally, the components of the system are connected by a 10 Mb/s local area network.

4.2. Cost-11 ter MANDIS.

The Cost-11 ter MANDIS project [3] is involved in management of distributed systems in local and wide-area network environments. In this project, Amoeba is chosen as the distributed system to be interconnected, and Amoeba is now running on five different places in Europe. Using wide-area networks and gateways [4], these Amoeba installations are connected into a single coherent system.

4.3. The Distributed Weather Map

The initial weather map application was implemented in C, and on each node it consisted of a single or a set of Unix+ processes. Interprocess communication between the different modules was possible by use of the transaction layer from Amoeba on top of Unix.

Initially, collection and exchange of temperature is done, but this can be easily extended if necessary. The framework for building a more sophisticated weather map is present with all the interaction between the different modules intact. If other types of weather data is to be collected and sent between the different modules, it might be necessary to pack as much data as possible in every message since this operation does not consume much time-dependent resources, while the alternative is to reduce packing and increase the network traffic. Coding is necessary for transmission of data to reduce the amount of data exchanged. Processing is also done in each local processing module to exchange results and not raw data, which would lead to a significant amount of data exchanged and overhead in processing the same data several times.

A more refined interface will be developed when Amoeba software has been ported to Hewlett Packard-360CH workstations with high-resolute rastergraphic colour screens.

+ Unix is a Trademark of AT&T Bell Laboratories.

5. DISCUSSION

Weather data might be collected in several ways, and one alternative is to collect it continously, another is to collect it on demand. A main advantage with the former is a weather map always available, even if communication costs will be dominating. The Cost-11 ter MANDIS work has shown [4] that transactions suffer from the poor performance of wide-area networking as opposed to local networking. This might indicate that a continous collection of weather data should be multicasted at fixed intervals in time to guarantee fast response time by the weather map application.

The second approach benefits by demanding less communication, but has the drawback of a larger average response time. Nevertheless, this solution gives more up-to-date data and decreases the network traffic dramatically, and this last approach has been chosen.

We have also chosen the same modularity as in [5] with three different kinds of modules, one collecting local weather data, another processing data possibly based on several collecting nodes, and a third type providing a flexible and extensible interface to its users. We have chosen this modularity for the following reasons:

- Generally, modularization is a convenient software engineering technique, and collecting, processing and displaying weather data are three separate tasks giving this modularization.

- The interface can be used on different I/O-devices without having to modify other parts of the weather map application. Heterogeneous I/O-devices might then be used in the application. The interface part of the application can be located at nodes with rastergraphic displays, i.e. workstations in a distributed system. These workstations can then be used to provide environments for interactive parts of distributed applications. Another example might be a distributed document composer application running command shells and editors locally and the other parts remotely.

- Process migration might be used to share the load across nodes in a distributed system and thus reduce average response time. This is to be done in a user transparent manner, even if the processes are interactive in its nature. One solution to this problem is to separate the user interface from the actual processing, and to some extent, the user might be unaware of where the actual processing takes place. The cpu-bound part of the weather map application might then be migrated to idle or lightly loaded nodes to achieve load sharing. Typically, a pool of processors in a distributed system can be used for this purpose.

- By having a separate module collecting weather data, only this part of the weather map application has to be replicated to obtain the data at several physical locations.

A drawback with this modularization is that the local processing module might be a bottleneck for processing purposes, but also for availability and reliability. Replication or use of leight-weight processes in Amoeba might solve this problem.

The weather map application can run on top of distributed systems connected transparently over wide-area networks [4]. It is not necessary to use an interconnection of distributed systems to realize the weather map application, and local operating systems using virtual circuits for communication might have been used. Nevertheless, this type of communication does not hide machine boundaries since intra-machine communication will be different from inter-machine communication. In addition, another level of fault-tolerance and resource sharing might be introduced with a distributed system supporting a distributed application.

6. WEATHER FORECASTING BY AN EXPERT SYSTEM

Weather forecasting relies on increasingly more sophisticated mathematical models constructed with the aid of high-speed computers. Increasingly more tasks normally done by human experts are now being taken over by expert systems, and one result with the work with the weather map application is the identification of a binding between distributed computing and artificial intelligence. Generally, weather forecasting requires a considerable amount of human expertise. This action is based on certain variables that can be computerized, and an expert system on top of the weather map might be used to predict the weather. The knowledge of weather forecasters can be represented in this expert system, but how this knowledge is to be represented, is still an open question.

Interconnection of several distributed systems into one coherent system provides management issues, and the distributed weather map uses these operating system services. The weather data collected by the weather map application might be used as raw data for an expert system outputting weather forecasts. Then the data base for weather forecasts consists of as complete a description as possible of all the interrelated parameters that defines the atmosphere. Fig. 2 shows the layered relationship described.

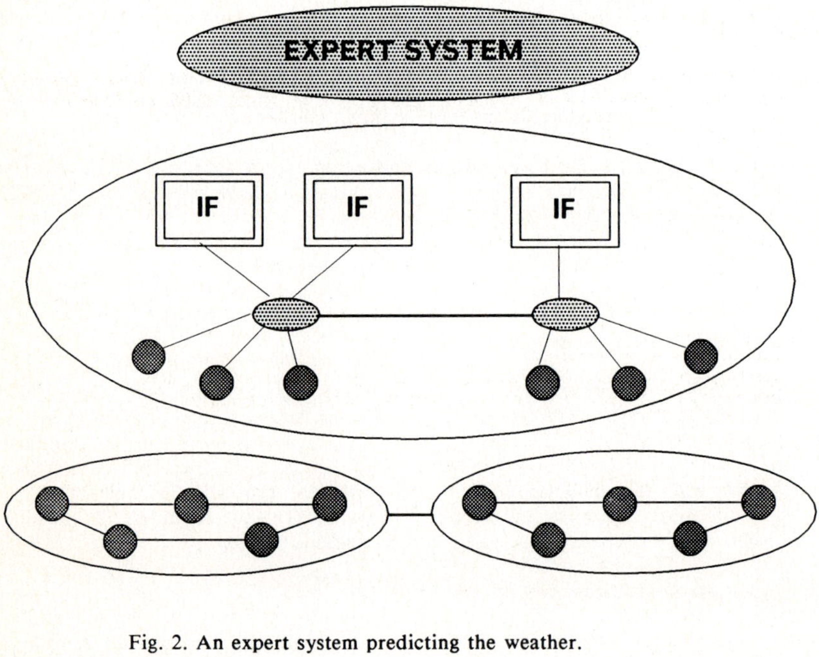

Fig. 2. An expert system predicting the weather.

7. CONCLUDING REMARKS

The main purpose with the design and implementation of the distributed weather map application has been to demonstrate the usability of a distributed system so that it can be used as a virtual machine for more than just traditional sequential processes. The range of applications for distributed systems is very wide, and a distributed weather map is one realistic distributed application to be run on top of a distributed system. Other examples of distributed applications can be found in i.e. office automation and factory automation.

All user interaction is handled by an interface module located at the users workstation, while the rest of the distributed application deals with the actual processing. Separation of the interactive part of the distributed weather map application has shown to be useful if the distributed application is to be dynamically located on several nodes throughout its lifetime.

The distributed weather map application is responsible for collecting weather data while reasoning about and predicting the future weather might be handled by an expert system to be built on top of the weather map application.

ACKNOWLEDGEMENTS.

The author would like to thank members of Cost-11 ter MANDIS for preliminary discussions. Special recognition should be given to Otto J. Anshus and Terje Fallmyr.

REFERENCES

[1] S.J. Mullender, A.S. Tanenbaum, "The Design of a Capability-Based Distributed Operating System," in *The Computer Journal*, Vol. 29 No. 4, 1986, pp. 289-300.

[2] A.D. Birell, B.J. Nelson, "Implementing Remote Procedure Calls'" in *ACM Trans. Comp. Syst.*, Vol. 2, Feb 1984, pp. 39-59.

[3] A. Langsford, " MANDIS: An Experiment in Distributed Processing ," in *Research into Networks and Distributed Applications*, R. Speth (editor), Elsevier Science Publishers B.V., Euteco '88 conference proceedings, pp. 787-794.

[4] R. van Renesse, H. van Staveren, J. Hall, M. Turnbull, B. Jansen, J. Jansen, S. Mullender, D. Holden, A. Bastable, T. Fallmyr, D. Johansen, Sj. Mullender, W. Zimmer, "MANDIS/Amoeba: A Widely Dispersed Object-Oriented Operating System," in *Research into Networks and Distributed Applications*, R. Speth (editor), Elsevier Science Publishers B.V., Euteco '88 conference proceedings, pp. 823-831.

[5] D. Johansen, O.J. Anshus, "A Distributed Diary Application", in *Computer Communications Systems, Proceedings of the IFIP TC 6 First Iberian Conference on Data Communications, IBERICOM '87*, A. Cerveira (editor), Elsevier Science Publishers B.V., pp.73-82.

Network Information Processing Systems
K. Boyanov, R. Angelinov (Editors)
Elsevier Science Publishers B.V. (North-Holland)

A CONCEPT OF GROUP-WORK WITH DSS IN NETWORK ENVIRONMENT

Péter GELLÉRI and Ferenc MARTINEZ

The first experiences about GDSS are not without ambiguity. The literature finds the Decision Room environment to be more questionable while the Office Automation environment is claimed to be more promisful. For the sake of reducing the hazards of introduction we recommend to find conditions of application where disadvantages and expenses do not originate from the use of GDSS. A model is devised for the survey of hardware, organizational and task conditions. In this context the various GDSS types are defined.
Beside the apparent benefits particular importance is attributed to the specification and building of a GDSS version matched to the given conditions in a multiactor iterative development process set out of the actual provisions of organization, hardware (network) as well as decision culture and management culture. A portrait is given of Bid MEDI-T-ATOR, a new GDSS. The task it discharges (selection of tenders and alternatives) and the situation of evaluation are an area that lends itself to GDSS application in network. It was made in pursuance of a system actually suited to the probable situations of cooperation and task organization, knowledge types and sets of tasks. This objective and the need to quickly construct decision aids for the purpose of other task types and situations needed the establishment of a DSS building environment (MEDI-T-ATOR) to be fulfilled.

1. IT IS BORN - BUT WHAT SHOULD IT BE? (Reflexions at the cradle of GDSS)

1.1. Does it really have a name?

This time we suggest to skip the hard task of trying to define group DSS (GDSS). Especially as there is no generally accepted definition for DSS, probably because the content of the DSS notion has steadily expanded over time (McLean and Sol, 1986). On the other hand he definitions proposed by Huber (1984) and by DeScantis and Gallupe (1985) are known and provide useful basis for the time being.

In our approach the notion of GDSS will be hereinafter complete with the following in addition to its strict interpretation: "Group Decision Support" and "Distributed DSS" (Jarke, 1986). At this point we may venture to state that the proper definition, that is, the capable form of GDSS, will be seen in the near future.

We have now arrived to the question of DSS acceptance or, more precisely speaking, to the experiences and inferences so far published about GDSS.

1.2. Joys and fears

Beside joy, the birth of anything new gives rise to fears as well. Our analysis of GDSS is based on recent publications. For the sake of convenience the practical experiences that can be treated as advantages/disadvantages of the system are summarized in a table in an array according to the conditions of use (see Table 1 and 2).

Table 1

GDSS in Office Automation	
Advantages	Disadvantages
a. Enhanced interactivity of decision makers - more depth of analysis - more concentrated discussion (Whistter, 1970; Sanders et al., 1984) b. Proliferation of "Office Automation" (OA) associated with specialization of decision makers (Huber, 1984) c. Support of decision meetings used more and more widely enables - smaller - professionally less heterogeneous groups to cooperate (Huber, 1984) d. This is one of the possible ways toward the more thorough use of OA (Jarke, 1986) e. It can be suited to couple various types of participation in decision making (Jarke, 1986) f. Can be treated as open systems where persons not known earlier can contribute to each phase (Hewitt and DeJong, 1984) g. Encourages the sharing of knowledge, the exchange of opinions and discussion itself (Johansen et al., 1979).	a. Decision maker isolation. (Perrow, 1970; Naylor, 1982)

Table 2

GDSS in Group Decision Meeting	
Advantages	Disadvantages
a. Extremely suitable for - preparing - capability development, - preparing for solving predictable critical situations of participants, especially in the frameworks of gaming (Gray and Borovits, 1986). b. The group situation is more suitable for the development of ideas (Gray, 1986) c. Decisions made in this manner are more elaborate and represent a higher quality (Gallupe, 1986)	a. In hierarchic organizations disagreeing opinion often meets retaliation (Gray, 1986) b. It is too expensive to set up an adequately equipped Decision Room for this single purpose (Gray, 1986) c. Waiting time is much longer than in the case of DSS, moreover, the implications of any failt are much graver (Gray, 1986) d. Participans are to be much thoroughly prepared and there are more problems caused by reconciliation (Gray, 1986) e. Decreasing satisfaction with the decision process (Gallupe, 1986) f. After about 5 years of experience it is not yet known exactly - what is the way of its effective use, - how to train managers for its use (Gray, 1986) g. The use of this tool strongly depends on the preferences of individual decision makers. The tool is usually abandoned after their departure (Gray, 1986).

It is apparent that a number of fears were expressed about the group versions of the generally successful and fast growing DSS.

1.3. Are we talking about the same thing?

The analysis of the two tables suggests that there is no justification to considering GDSS advantages/disadvantages in general, without the context of their conditions of use.

Numerous anxieties were expressed on basis of experience about GDSS used under the conditions of "Decision Room" in the frameworks of "Decision Meeting".

On the other hand, optimism prevails about GDSS operated in the frameworks of "Office Automation". This marked difference in itself deserves special attention.

2. "CAREER" OPPORTUNITIES

The second inference suggested by the analysis of the tables is that the symptoms defined as advantages or disadvantages usually manifest themselves in different dimensions. In other words a factor defined as an advantage does not appear with opposite content even under different circumstances.

From this follows a possible strategy of stating the GDSS "career opportunities": situations must be found where positive attributes assert themselves while negative ones are either missing or are neutral to or acceptable in the given environment.

2.1. Starting from the decision task

Finding decision situations where the strategy statement of the last paragraph holds requires a task analysis.

The decision task of selection between tenders, offers, etc., or bidding in general, is considered to be such a situation.

In bidding, the situation of decision-making implies codified and consequently accepted facts that would otherwise provoke the aversion or objections of at least some of the participants. The most important ones are the following:
- the decision-maker is not allowed to keep outside of the decision process and he may not rise above it,
- involving of outside experts is typically inevitable,
- the decision process is imposed by existing "rules of the game",
- the implemenation of the decision making process and the observation of rules are externally controlled,
- the issue is typically a serious and critical one,
- decision making is a must.

In such conditions, among others, the decision maker is restricted and his scope of making a decision according to his interests is strongly limited. (Gelléri and Martinez, 1987.)

2.2. Starting from the characteristics of the computer environment

As it could be expected after the above reasoning, we find it reasonable to follow the same logic also concerning the problem of the computer environment, that is, we recommend to utilize the technical assets already existing on the spot for the purpose of group decision support and not to install a special system for this particular purpose. A computer environment set up specifically for the operation of GDSS is namely too big a risk to run or to recommend except in special cases.

Another reasoning also arrives at the same conclusion. As it is shown by the references quoted in Tables 1 and 2, the operation of GDSS entails typical difficulties in certain environments, partly just because of the situation determined by the technical conditions. On the other hand the GDSS cannot be "blamed" for all these disadvantages if the technical conditions are ab ovo given, irrespectively of the use of GDSS.

For instance the synergetic, brainstroming kind of effects that cannot assert themselves except in face-to-face situations, are prophylacted or discouraged by the use of the existing system of office automation. The same problem is likely to exist also in the case of GDSS operations and it must need strong and powerful efforts to be alleviated. At the same time the preconditions of access (database, expert system, etc.) are given for resolving any task where the function of the system asks for group decisions.

Not only the types of the technical environment vary from the point of view of GDSS application. The question can be obviously asked the other way round too. Group decision support systems can be similarly analysed from he point of view of running in a given technical environment because the available decision aids also show many different features. The different froms of "Decision Room" application was scrutinized by Gray (1986) also with respect to the computer environment and the experiences gained in that field. However, the essential difference is not between these versions but between the softwares, showing substantial differences from one another, run in this kind of environment vs. those run on the network quoted by Jarke (1986).

For the purpose of the task of matching it is sensible to classify the tools of decision support on basis of hardware interfaces. Such a classification is shown on Table 3.

It can be seen from the table that it has become justified to make a new classification and definition of content of the decision support tools.
- DSS is the name of means created for supporting individual decisions that are actually used for processing group opinions with the combined application of various socio-techniques such as voting, generation of group averages, etc. Although these tools are not intended for group operations, they are nevertheless used, and in lack of a better one are actually useful, tools of decision support.
- GDSS Non-Network - GDSS(NN) - signifies the group decision support methods suitable for receiving, handling and aggregating several opinions in non-network mode.
- GDSS Decision Room - GDSS(DR) - defines the tools of group decision support typically specified for being run in "Decision Room" environment or in another mini network.

Table 3

Software tools of decision support suitable for the consideration of opinions of several persons and their hardware correlations

Software types from the point of view of hardware interfaces	The hardware environment		
	Single computer	Mini network or DR network	Office Automation
DSS	(X)	X	X
GDSS(NN)	(X)	X	X
GDSS(DR)		(X)	X
GDSS(OA)			(X)

X = possible use
0 = matching use

- GDSS Office Automation - GDSS(OA) - comprises the software engineered for group decision support in office automation environments.

It is also apparent from the table that a software designed for a less developed hardware environment can be run in more sophisticated technical environments as well. The use of the term "matching" is nevertheless appropriate. We namely assume that a software reckoning with the provisions of a more advanced environment represents a challenge concerning the quality of decision support and an opportunity for offering more qualified service.

The table does not contain patterns of communication available for the decision making process. In fact any hardware environment is suitable for several ways of organization and information transmission. Practically every version can handle the resolution of participation in time and space or the breakdown of carrying our single tasks. There is a variety of ways for the flow of complementary information and interactivity between participants as well.

The more advanced technology offers, or ought to offer, certain additional opportunities (such as electronic mail etc.) in lieu of the lost ones.

Communication is a cardinal aspect in any group. We will, however, not indulge in it here because it is not decisive in our train of thoughs.

Nor are we going to cover some essential aspects of the principle of software operation or the approaches of supporting the consideration and aggregation of individual opinions that are accomplished on several levels from the point of view of both comfort and principle. At any rate it should be noted that in this respect a sophisticated hardware environment does not necessarily imply he use of a more sophisticated approach of decision support.

2.3. Looking for promising constellations

It is naturally not the isolated study of the decision task and the computer environment but the specific interplay of the two which, along with further circumstances, give the true alternative or "career guidance" for GDSS.
The most important factors are illustrated in the model of Figure 1.

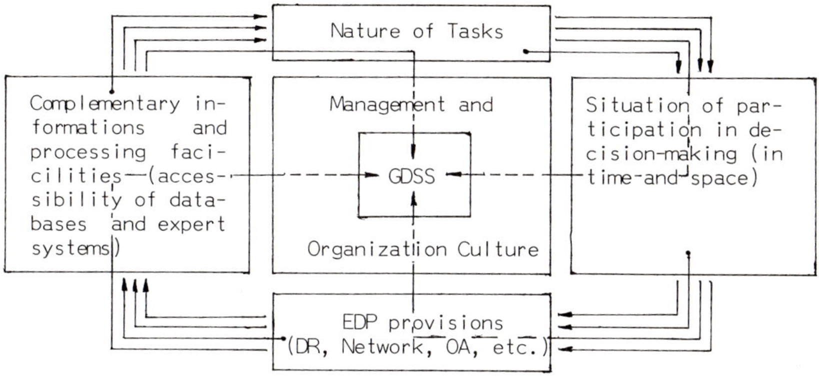

Figure 1. Constellation model of conditions justifying the use of GDSS.

Some elements of the model were mentioned before. In the routine of group decision making the importance of complementary informations and processing facilities availability is as high as of the aforesaid ones. In extreme cases the expert system itself can become a "member" in the decision-making group (Huber, 1986).

The search can be started in any group of factors of the model. The start should be obviously followed by the assessment of other factors and this cannot dispense with the consideration of the factor of management and organization culture. Each of these conditions suggest a matching type of GDSS - GDSS(NN), GDSS(DR), GDSS(OA) - where appropriateness needs to be established for each of the factors figuring in the model.

The process of analysis is exemplified as follows:

When bidding or other proposal evaluation is a recuring task of an organization it probably stands to reason to recommend the use of GDSS. This work typically involves several external consultants. The different external and internal consultants are likely to need parallel access to a specific database or eventually an expert system for their particular tasks. In this case, unless the articulation of discharging the task in time requires simultaneous effort, GDSS(NN) can be an adequate support to group decision making. In a suitable hardware environment, however, the same task can be solved by means of a GDSS(DR) or even a GDSS(OA) provided with the necessary additional facilities. On the above basis the most suitable one of he available tools should be selected with due regard to the management and organization culture that describes the environment. In other cases the availability of an Office Automation system can provide the starting point for the search. This local condition can be grasped for the purpose of analysis of management and organization culture. If the management proves to be "receptive" the chances of he use of GDSS are powerfully increased and the provision of the rest of conditions can be safely prognosticated.

3. PRINCIPLES OF "EDUCATION"

The title makes it clear that in this chapter we should like to discuss the problem of GDSS specification. In other words: we try to answer the question of what is the matching GDSS of a given environmen and task. Our assessment will be set out of the range of existing and available GDSS.

What will not be deal with in the context of "educational" effects is the inverse correlationship vs. the aforesaid, that is, the "moulding" effect of the environment where GDSS is used, some faces of which were covered during the IFIP Conference held in Budapest in 1987 (Gelléri and Martinez, 1987).

3.1. The aim - as we see it today

Jarke stresses the advantages of an integrated computer communication facility as against the meeting facilitation method, based on personal and telephone communication. He claims the first one to be more suitable for sharing of knowledge, exchanging views as well as coordination. (Bui and Jarke, 1984; Bui, 1985; Jarke, 1986).

Also Jarke emphasized the importance of enabling decision participant groups distinguished by function to cooperate in the course of GDSS application in accordance with the natures of their respective roles, not forgetting that such participants are not necessarily cooperative with respect to motivations. He advocates the presence of a "mediator" function in charge of assigning competences in GDSS application and of coordinating this through the whole process (Jarke, 1986).

In the above connection Hewitt and deJong (1984) proposed to consider the group of decision participants an "open system" as the membership is often unknown when a process is initiated whereas the facility is expected to be ready to accept the opinions.

Jarke (1986) postulates that the coming GDSS generation should perform the following:

- give users simultaneous access to different data,
- allow changes of user views or opinions at any moment through the process,
- facilitate cooperation of users with different professional specializations,
- accept disagreeing user considerations and concepts (by providing the socalled "metadata" system to the knowledge base in order to avoid any inconsistency),
- let users have their own secret aids and data for their deliberations,
- be capable of considering and supporting the conditions of the organizational environment in group decision making (security of data of individual and group concern, distribution of information, communication with other organizations, clarification of organizational objectives).

The objective of this subchapter, namely, the summary review of recommendations already given in the literature about the development of GDSS, can be concluded with the following emphatical statement: Gray (1986) finds the present approaches of group process support - such as voting, the Delphi method or NGT - to be rough and sketchy even in case of optimum application. New ways must be developed for supporting group interaction and query of group opinions and these ways must utilize the attributes of and the opportunities offered by GDSS.

3.2. Let it be moulded by the environment

According to Carlson (1983) it is necessary but at least desirable to adjust the DSS to certain personality, intellectual and environmental characteristics of the user group.

The feasibility of one of the following solutions is an obvious precondition to approximate this and many other requirements mentioned earlier:

1. A degree of intrinsic flexibility of GDSS whereby it is enabled to immediately adjust to any appreciable difference on basis of its own diagnosis or through being set.

2. The software facility itself is prepared in an evolutionary process (1978) in permanent iterative interaction with the targeted reality area. It follows from the above that the process of cooperation between designer and user should deserve special analysis and support in the course of parameter specification.

The following axiomatic statement can be made irrespectively of the problem of creation: in any approach a GDSS can be a success only if it always conforms the emerging concrete demand.

The guarantee of accomplishing this seemingly obvious objective must be naturally given by ideas that are technically feasible and economically reasonable. From this point of view another approach of software building is worth noting:

3. Sol (1984) and Sol and McLean (1986) propose to consider the concept of DSS generator or, more generally, of the environment of DSS planning and building where the entire process of problem perception and solution is covered and supported in addition to the interface function.

4. A TENTATIVE "TRAINING COURSE"

An environment was set up for DSS building in part of the establishment of the background for a complex program of research and application. The system family developed by that facility is named MEDI-T-ATOR GDSS. The name is a fortunate contentual reference to the philosophy of this DSS family: to assist the birth of the intellectual child of decision makers. The MEDI-T-ATOR building environment supports the creation of GDSS-s that are open to communicating with other, existing and currently used information systems (e.g. they can be integrated with databases or expert systems). The building of decision support software matched to various types of hardware environments is facilitated and consequently the GDSS developed in this manner can be run in any framework of network and office automation.

Bid MEDI-T-ATOR, the first GDSS product that equally supports the invitation, evaluation and documentation of biddings, seems to have good chances of application according to the criteria detailed above. The following are the essential characteristics of this tool, first used in the selection of an international bidding of banking LAN system carried out with World Bank credit:

- aids of assessment are provided and developed on basis of user decision culture,
- it can be applied according to the style of users (users can also select the range of complementary information and the internal sequence and rhythm of carrying ou the task),
- users can use a shared and an exclusive information base and assessment aids,
- the algorhythm of assessment is interchangeable according to user needs,
- decision participants are enabled of the following in the different phases:
    . to work in groups of any number and composition of members,
    . they can be assigned personal "voting powers" ("weights") also in identical phases (e.g. on basis of professional competence), moreover, this weight can be variable and dedicated to aspects and alternatives (Gelléri and Martinez, 1988),
    . work in environments of GDSS(NN), any network and GDSS(OA),
    . when they do not work simultaneously on the task they can have their dedicated tasks on data medium for processing; the system is capable of accepting it after the task is done, etc.
- the phases and levels of information available to participants about each others work and about the outcome of their collective effort can be controlled,
- aspect charts of practically unlimited size and breakdown can be drawn up,
- utility functions can be assigned to aspects,
- ex post analysis as well as impact and responsivity study can be made on user request,
- amendment or revision is possible at any time and in any phase of the decision-making process; in a supervisor function the relevant consequences are also monitored by the system,
- lengthy comments can be assigned to alternatives, aspects as well as participants for the purpose of explanation, documentation, etc.
- each phase of the process is supported by a multistage dynamic help system controlled by a menu which also gives access to examples.

The application, deliver or sale of Bid MEDI-T-ATOR naturally includes the accurate assessment of user requirements for a custom-made system.

REFERENCES

1. Brookes, C.H.P. (1986): Requirements Elicitation for Knowledge Based Decision Support Systems, in: McLean, E.R. and Sol, H.G. (eds): Decision Support Systems: A Decade in Perspective, Elsevier Science Publ. B.V. (North-Holland).

2. Bui, X.T. and Jarke, M. (1984): A DSS for Cooperative Multiple Crite-Criteria Group Decision-making, Proc. 5th Intl. Conf. Informations Systems, Tucson, AZ, pp. 101-113.
3. Bui, X.T. (1985): Co-oP, a DSS for Cooperative Multiple Criteria Decision-making, Ph.D. Dissertation, Graduate School of Business Administration, New York Univ.
4. Carlson, E.D. (1984): An Approach for Designing Decision Support Systems, Chapter 2 in Building Decision Support Systems, ed. Bennet, J.L., Addison-Wesley.
5. Gallupe R.B. (1986): Experimental Research into Group Decision Support Systems: Practical Issues and Problems, Proc. of the 19th Hawaii International Conference on Systems Science, Honolulu, HI, pp. 513-523.
6. Gelléri, P. and Martinez, F. (1987): Culture of Decision-making and Use of DSS in Municipal Organizations, Paper for the IFIP TC8 Conference on Govermmental and Municipal Information Systems, Budapest.
7. Gelléri, P. and Martinez, F. (1988): How to Handle Differences in Importance among Participants with GDSS, in: Lee, R.M., McCosh, A.M. and Migliarese, P.: Organizational Decision Support Systems, North-Holland, Netherlands.
8. Gray, P. (1986): Group Decision Support Systems, in: McLean, E.R. and Sol, H.G. (eds): Decision Support Systems: A Decade in Perspective, Elsevier Science Publ. B.V. (North-Holland).
9. Gray, P. and Borovits, I. (1986): Gaming and Group DSS, Transactions of the 6th Intl. Conf. of Decision Support Systems, Washington, DC.
10. Hewitt, C. and deJong, P. (1984): Open Systems, in: Brodie, M.L., Mylopoulos, J. and Schmidt, J.W. (eds): On Conceptual Modelling, Heidelberg, Springer, pp. 147-164.
11. Huber, G.P. (1984): Issues in the Design of Group Decision Support Systems, MIS Quarterly, 8, pp. 195-204.
12. Jarke, M. (1986): Group Decision Support through Office Systems: Developments in Distributed DSS Technology, in: McLean, E.R. and Sol, H.G. (eds): Decision Support Systems: A Decade in Prespective, Elsevier Science Publ. B.V. (North-Holland).
13. Johansen, R., Vallee, J. and Spangler, K. (1979): Electronic Meetings, Addison-Wesley, Reading, Mass.
14. Keen, P.G.W. and Scott-Morton, M.S. (1978): Decision Support Systems - An Organizational Perspective, Addison-Wesley, Reading, Mass.
15. McLean, E.R. and Sol, H.G. (1986): Decision Support Systems: A Decade in Perspective, in: McLean, E.R. and Sol, H.G. (eds): Decision Support Systems: A Decade in Perspective, Elsevier Science Publ. B.V. (North-Holland).
16. Naylor, T.H. (1982): Decision Support Systems or Whatever Happened to M.I.S.?, Interfaces, 12, pp. 92-94.
17. Perrow, C. (1970): Organizational Analysis a Sociological View, Wadsworth Publ., Belmont, Ca.
18. DeSanctis, G. and Gallup, B. (1985): Group Decision Support Systems: A New Frontier, Database, Winter, pp. 3-10.
19. Sanders, G.L., Courtney, J.F. and Loy, S.L. (1984): The Impact of DSS on Organizational Communications, Information and Management, 7, pp. 141-178.
20. Sol, H.G. (1984): The Emerging Role of Simulation Based Inquiry Systems, in: Bemelmans, Th.M.A. (ed): Beyond Productivity Information Systems Development for Organizational Effectiveness, North-Holland, Amsterdam.
21. Whistler, T.L. (1970): The Impact of Computers on Organizational Communications, Praeper Publ., New York.

Network Information Processing Systems
K. Boyanov, R. Angelinov (Editors)
Elsevier Science Publishers B.V. (North-Holland)

A DISTRIBUTED ALGORITHM FOR MUTUAL EXCLUSION USING DYNAMICAL DISTRIBUTED STRUCTURES IN AN ARBITRARY NETWORK

Miloud FOUZI and Michel TREHEL

Laboratoire d'informatique, Université de Franche-Comté
BESANCON, 25000 FRANCE

ABSTRACT A distributed algorithm for mutual exclusion is presented. No particular assumptions on the network topology are required except connectivity. The algorithm does not require a logical clock; it's based on the idea of distributed data structures: a logical rooted tree and a waiting queue. A site which invokes a critical section, sends a request message to the previous site which has requested. All the variables are bounded. The path of the messages is studied to minimize the number of transfers.

INDEX TERMS Distributed algorithm, mutual exclusion, logical rooted tree, distributed variables .

SUPPORT This work was financed by the Université de Franche-Comté and by the CNRS: U.A. 040822 and Greco C^3

1. INTRODUCTION

1. 1 . Mutual exclusion

Consider a distributed system: the sites interact only by means of message transmission. The task of mutual exclusion is to ensure that at most one site, at any moment, can access a resource, called a critical section.

There are algorithms, concerned by complete networks, using the broadcasting of request messages for entering the critical section .

In the algorithms of Lamport [4], Ricart and Agrawala [9], Carvalho and Roucairol [1], Suzuki and Kasami [11], the number of messages is proportional to the number n of sites.

Dijkstra [2] and Le Lann [5] organize the sites in a logical ring with a circulation of a token. The number of messages may be very great.

Maekawa [6], divides the set of sites into subsets such that, between a pair of subsets, it exists one common site, serving as an arbitrator. To enter a critical section, a site sends a request message to every site of its subset and obtains permission from all of them. The number of messages is about $2\sqrt{n}$.

We have studied an other algorithm [7], concerned also by complete networks, the average number of messages of which is H_n (in the order of Log(n)). We are going to describe quickly this algorithm and to present the generalization to an arbitrary network.

1. 2. Description of the Log(n) algorithm [12]

The first aim consists in minimizing the number of messages. We avoid the broadcasting of the request messages. This algorithm is based on the fact that a site sends its request to only one other site and awaits its permission.

It would be a centralized algorithm if the receiving site were always the same, but the receiving site will change at every request. Intuitively, the receiving site is the previous site which has requested

One and only one site has a token. The site which owns the token may enter the critical section.

There are two data structures.

The first is a logical rooted tree which is modified as request messages to enter the critical section are received. Every site knows its successor in the tree structure. A request message issued by a site travels down a path leading from the site to the root.

If the root is waiting for entering the critical section, the requesting site is placed in a waiting queue else the requesting site obtains the token and enters the critical section.

After a request, the tree is reorganized so that the "last" site which has requested be the new root of the rooted tree.

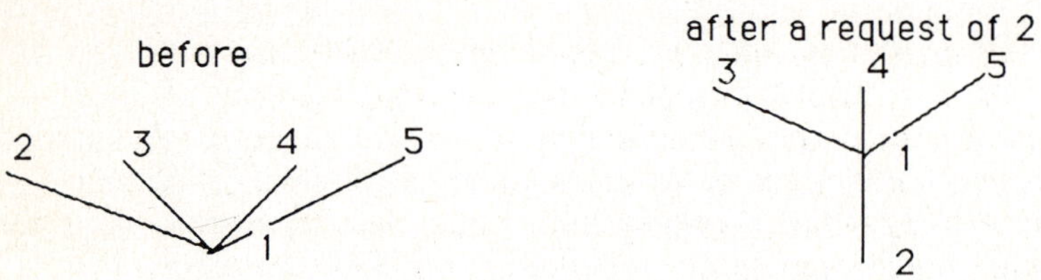

The second is a waiting queue.

The head of the waiting queue has the token and may enter the critical section. The following ones are waiting. The tail is the root of the rooted tree. Every site knows its successor in this queue. When there are some requests at the same time, it is possible we obtain some trees and some queues. When the request messages are all arrived, we have only one tree and one queue.

We are now presenting a generalization to any network.

2. ARBITRARY NETWORK

2. 1. Previous works

In our knowledge, the first distributed algorithm for mutual exclusion in an arbitrary network has been proposed by Hélary, Plouzeau, Raynal [3]. The number of messages necessary to obtain mutual exclusion is between n and 2e +n-1 (e is the number of edges). Another algorithm has been presented by Tréhel and Naimi [13]: It has the inconvenient that the paths of the messages are static. The algorithm we present here uses continual reorganizations of the paths to minimize the number of transfers.

2. 2. Assumptions

Assumptions on the network

The network is described by an undirected graph (V , E) where the set of nodes V represents processes of the network and the set of edges E represents bidirectional communication channels operating between them.

We shall do no difference between the sites corresponding to the nodes of graph and the processes of the algorithm.

- The graph of communications is connected
- Every site knows only its name and its neighbours
- Links between sites are two-directional

Assumptions on the communications and the critical section

- There is no loss, duplication or modification of messages.
- Transmission times are random and finite.
- No assumption is made concerning the order of arrival of messages compared with the order of their transmission.
- A site entering the critical section releases it within a finite time.

3. ALGORITHM

As the Log(n) algorithm, it uses 2 distributed data structures: a logical rooted tree which will be modified following the request , and a queue.

Initial rooted tree

We consider a rooted tree on the set of nodes (It is possible because the network is connected). The edges are oriented towards the root. Every site knows only its father. Initially, the root owns the token.

Principle

a) The process owning the token and invoking to enter the critical section, may enter it if there is no waiting request in its queue.

b)The process S_d which is not a root and which invokes to enter the critical section sends a request message. This request message will transit along a path leading from this process S_d to the root S_r . The path is known because every site knows its father in the rooted tree.

The process S_r can be in one of these 3 situations:

i) S_r owns the token and doesn't use it. In this case, S_r sends the token; the requesting site will receive the token and will enter the critical section.

ii) S_r owns the token and uses it (it is in the critical section): the requesting process S_d is put in a waiting situation.

iii)S_r doesn't own the token (i.e. the process S_r has already made a request and finds itself now in a waiting situation): the process S_d is also put in a waiting situation.

In these 3 cases *the rooted tree is changed:* S_d is the new root.

If S_i is on the way going from the requesting site to the old root, the new father S_v of S_i will verify the 2 following conditions:

C1) S_v was on the path of the request message.

C2) S_v is the nearest site from S_d, and S_v is a neighbour of S_i in the network.

These conditions permit to accelerate the travel of the token.

The other edges of the rooted tree are not modified.

As in a complete network, when there are some requests at the same time, it is possible we obtain some trees and some queues. When the request messages are all arrived, we have only one tree and one queue.

waiting queue

The waiting queue is distributed in the network (every site knows its next, if it exists).

When a site has released its critical section, it sends the token to its next.

Example

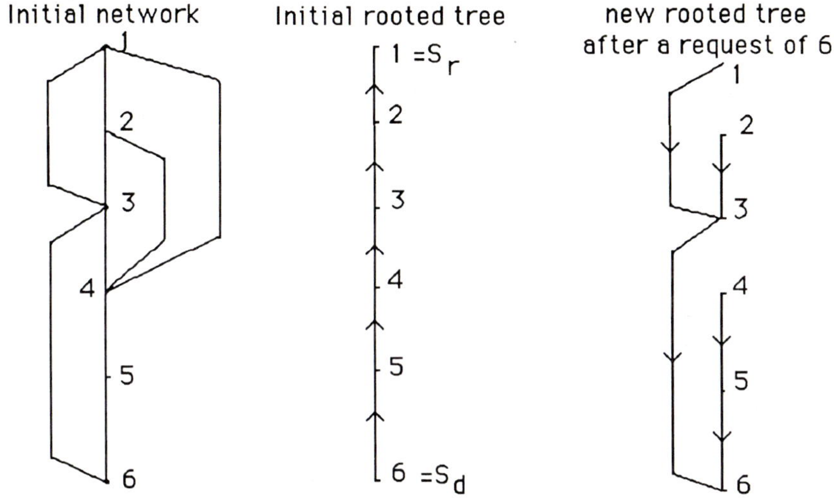

4. STRUCTURE OF THE MESSAGES AND TABLE OF ROUTING

Structure of the messages

For this algorithm, we need 2 kinds of messages: request and token .

1) The *request message* is sent by a process which wants to enter the critical section when it does not own the token.

The message is structured in: (REQ , L , Req-array)

where Req-array is an array of lenght L. It contains the name S_d of the requesting process and the name of the processes visited by the message from S_d.

Req-array is partitionned in levels:

S_d is at the level 0

If S_v is the new father of S_i and S_v is at the level p, then S_i is at the level p+1.

In the example, the successive levels contain: 6; 3,5; 1,2,4;

When the message reaches the process S_i, S_i checks the levels contained in the req-array, beginning by the first one, and determines the lowest level containing one of its immediate neighbours S_v. S_i inserts itself in the following level and sends the message to its old father if it is not the root.

The request message arrives to a root S_r; S_r sends the token to the requesting site at once or waits before sending it. In any case, it sends the token to the requesting site S_d.

2) The adressee of the *token message* is the requesting site. The path has been determined during the transmission of the request. This path is registered in the local routing table first-array. When a site receives the token and is not adressee of this token, it must transmit it to the next site of the path. The routage of the token doesn't change the rooted tree. The token message is structured in: (token, adressee).

Routing table

The routing table is constituted with 2 arrays: first-array and long-array. At S_i, first-array [S_j] gives the first site on the path from S_i to S_j and long-array [S_j] gives the lenght of the path from S_i to S_j. These tables are reorganized at every request.

5. PROTOCOL

Every site S_i executes the same protocol and has the same variables.

A request for the critical section is performed by the procedures

REQUEST_C_S
WAIT until the token is here
CRITICAL SECTION
RELEASE_C_S

furthermore some actions are performed upon receiving REK or TOKEN (presentation by events). These actions are indivisible.

Meaning of the constants and variables

maxn : overvalues the number of sites
me : it is the identity of the process
neighbours : set of processes, initialized with the names of the neighbours.
token-here : this boolean variable is true if and only if the site has the token. At initialization time, token-here is false for every process but one.
requesting-c-s : this boolean variable is true after invoking and before releasing the critical section. At initialization time, requesting-c-s is false.
next : when a site releases the critical section, it sends the token to its next. At initialization time, next is nil.
father : describes the tree. A request message is sent to the father.
requesting : indicates the requesting site during the travel of the requesting message.

For programming, we use the couples: (if,endif), (do,od), (begin,end).

```
PROCEDURE INITIALIZATION
 father :=...; neighbours:=...;  --one process has nil for father--
for i:=1 to maxn do  long-array [i] := ∞; first-array  [i]:=nil; od;
requesting-c-s := false; next := nil; token-here := (father = nil);
```

```
PROCEDURE REQUEST_C_S
requesting-c-s:= true;
if father ≠ nil then
begin req-array [1]:=me;
      req-array [2]:=nil; L:=2;
      send (REQ,L,req-array) to father;
      father:=nil
end endif
```

```
PROCEDURE RELEASE_C_S
requesting-c-s:=false;
if next ≠ nil then
begin token-here:=false;
      send(token,next) to first-array [next];
      next:=nil
end endif
```

```
PROCEDURE REACH-FATHER ;
--this procedure determines the new father and updates the routing table--
new-father:= nil; i:=1; long:=0; requesting:=req-array [1];
 while new-father=nil  do

        if req-array[i] ∈ neighbours then new-father:=req-array[i]
        else if req-array[i]=nil then long:=long+1 endif endif;
        i:=i+1          od;
```

```
while req-array[i]≠nil    do i:=i+1    od;      long:= long+1;
 if i=L then  begin req-array[i+1]:=me; req-array[i+2]:=nil; L:=L+2
              end else begin
                             for j:=L downto i+1 do req-array[j+1]:=req-array [j] od;
                             req-array[i+1]:=me; L:=L+1
                           end endif;
  if long < long-array [requesting] then
            begin first-array [requesting]:=new-father; long-array [requesting]:=long
             end endif;

 UPON RECEIVING A MESSAGE(REQ,L,req-array)
do REACH-FATHER ;
   if father=nil then  if requesting-c-s then next :=requesting
          else begin token-here:=false; send(token,requesting) to first-array [requesting]
               end    endif
   else send(REQ,L,req-array) to father
   endif;   father:=new-father;
od

UPON RECEIVING A MESSAGE (token,requesting)
do if requesting = me then token-here := true
                           else  send (token,requesting) to first-array [requesting]
   endif od
```

6. PROOFS

We give only the outline of the proof. The complete proof will be written in an internal report.

Mutual exclusion

In the initial state, only one site (the root) owns the token. The token is necessary to a site for entering critical section and, at any time, at most one site owns the token. Then mutual exclusion is assured.

Absence of deadlock and of starvation.

The request message is sent from a site S_d to a root S_r . If S_r has the token, it sends it to S_d, otherwise S_d becomes the "next" of S_r and S_r will send the token to S_d when it has obtained and released the critical section.

Then the properties to prove are:

1) The request message of S_d will arrive to a root S_r after a finite delay.

We verify that the message cannot pass twice by the same site.

2) S_r owns the token or will obtain it after a finite delay.

For that, we verify that S_d will be served and, depending of the time necessary for request messages to arrive at a root, some sites which request after S_d may be served before S_d, but their number has an upper limit.

7. CONCLUSION

This algorithm contains new ideas: it does not use a logical clock, which has frequently the inconvenient to be an unbounded variable. It uses dynamical data structures.

Otherwise, the efficiency is good. We have computed it for some topologies. In a complete network, the average number of messages is H_n (O(Log(n)) instead of O(n) or O(√n)). In a line, it is about 2*n/3. In a ring, it is 7*n/12. In a tree a-ary, it is $\log_a(n)$

The algorithm is fault-tolerant. We study different approaches to reorganize the network in case of failure.

8. REFERENCES

[1] O. Carvalho and G. Roucairol, "On mutual exclusion in computer networks," Comm. ACM. Vol 26, 2, (Feb. 1983), pp. 146-147.

[2] E. W. Dijkstra,"Self-stabilizing systems in spite of distributed control," Comm. ACM. Vol 17, 11, (Nov. 1974), pp. 643-644.

[3] J.M. Hélary, N. Plouzeau, M. Raynal, "A distributed algorithm for mutual exclusion in an arbitrary network", IRISA, Université de Rennes, int. rep. n° 281, (jan 1986).

[4] L. Lamport, "Time, clocks and the ordering of events in a distributed system," Comm. ACM. Vol. 21, 7, (Jul 1978), pp. 558-565.

[5] G. Le Lann, "Distributed systems. Towards a formal approach," IFIP Congress, Toronto, (Aug. 1977), pp. 155-160.

[6] M. Maekawa, "A √n algorithm for mutual exclusion in decentralized systems," ACM. TOCS, Vol 3, 2, (May 1985) pp. 145-159.

[7] M. Naimi "Une structure arborescente pour une classe d'algorithmes distribués d'exclusion mutuelle," Thèse de l'Université de Franche-Comté, Besançon, France, (March 1987).

[8] M. Raynal, "Algorithmique du parallélisme. Le problème de l'exclusion mutuelle," Dunod, Paris, (1984).

[9] G. Ricart and A. Agrawala, "An optimal algorithm for mutual exclusion in computer networks," Comm. ACM. Vol. 24, 1, (Jan. 1981), pp. 9-17.

[10] G. Ricart and A. Agrawala, "Author's response to <on mutual exclusion in computer networks> by Carvalho and Roucairol," Comm. ACM. Vol. 26, 2, (Feb 1983) pp.147-148,.

[11] I. Suzuki and T. Kasami, "An optimality theory for mutual exclusion in computer networks," Proc. of the 3rd Int. Conf. on distributed computing systems, Miami, (Oct 1982), pp. 365-370.

[12] M. Trehel, M. Naimi, "A distributed algorithm for mutual exclusion based on data structures and fault tolerance," 6th annual international IEEE Phoenix conference on computers and communications, Scottsdale, (Fev 1987), pp.35-39.

[13] M. Tréhel, M. Naimi, "A distributed algorithm for mutual exclusion in an arbitrary network using the lift strategy," Computers and communications technology towards 2000, IEEE, Seoul, Korea, (Aug 1987).

Network Information Processing Systems
K. Boyanov, R. Angelinov (Editors)
Elsevier Science Publishers B.V. (North-Holland)

PARALLEL COMBINATOR REDUCTION ON A WAFER

Paul ANDERSON*, Chris HANKIN** and Paul KELLY**

* Dept of Computer Science, City University, Northampton Sq, London EC1V 0HB, UK
** Dept of Computing, Imperial College, 180 Queen's Gate, London SW7 2BZ, UK

Declarative languages have been identified as one of the foundations of advanced information technology. Functional languages are at one extreme of the declarative language spectrum. Their simple semantics raise the real possibility of routine, formal derivation and verification of programs; moreover there appear to be plenty of opportunities for parallel evaluation of such languages. In this paper we describe a novel approach to the parallel implementation of functional languages that attempts to exploit the potential of wafer-scale integration. This new technology offers us the possibility of building massively parallel systems on a single wafer at a fraction of the cost of existing machines. In this paper we describe compile-time techniques for identifying parallelism, a computer architecture capable of exploiting such parallelism and some details of a proposed implementation using wafer-scale integration. In the implementation section, we introduce a novel, fault-tolerant routing algorithm that is of general applicability to wafer-scale architectures.

1. INTRODUCTION

Functional Programming Languages [9,13] form one of the cornerstones of the current fifth generation projects. They are important because:

- (a) they are *descriptive* rather than *prescriptive* giving shorter, "specification-like" programs and increasing programmer productivity
- (b) they have simple semantics allowing formal verification of programs and formally-based program transformation techniques

In this paper we describe how compile-time analysis can be used to detect potential parallelism and describe an architecture, called Cobweb [2], which exploits wafer-scale integration to provide parallel execution. Combined with the advanced compiler technology, parallel evaluation will allow functional programs to be executed orders of magnitude faster than their imperative counterparts.

WSI technology [11] provides a good match with the Cobweb architecture because:

- (a) An array of identical elements with nearest neighbour communications implies low design cost since the same mask can be used for all elements
- (b) Reduction does not require a fixed topology, which implies that we can achieve fault tolerance at the processing element level
- (c) A narrow interface at the edge of the wafer implies low pin count, low bonding and packaging costs and low system assembly and maintenance costs
- (d) Implementation using self-test and self-configuration [4] implies low testing and maintenance costs

One of the major bottlenecks in tightly-coupled parallel machines is the communication network. By exploiting wafer-scale integration the communications overhead is a less significant factor since most communications will be on-wafer and hence extremely fast. We expect to be able to produce a prototype that runs faster than any of the current prototype declarative architectures at a fraction of the cost.

We will describe the compile-time techniques in Section 2, the architecture in Section 3 and implementation techniques in Section 4. Section 5 contains some conclusions and directions for further work.

2. COBWEB CODE

The driving force of functional programming systems is function application. During application, some representation of the argument (either a value or closure/suspension) becomes associated with the formal parameters of the function. These associations are used in the evaluation of the body of the function. There are two standard approaches to functional language implementation: environment-based machines (e.g. the SECD machine) and combinator-based machines [9, 13]. In environment-based machines the binding of actual parameters to formal parameters is represented by an association list which is globally accessible and updateable. In contrast, in combinator-based machines the need for an association list is replaced by compiling the program into code which is essentially variable-free and which directs the actual parameters to where they are used. This avoids a major potential bottleneck in parallel implementations.

Directors are a form of combinator code [8, 12]. They are used to annotate applications to indicate where parameters are used (notice that in a language with curried functions, such as the λ-calculus, application is a binary operator):

^	function and argument
\	argument only
/	function only
-	not used

For illustration, we will use a type-free lambda calculus [5]. An example of a program is:

let f = λx.λy.+ (* x x) y **in** f 2 3

which in directors becomes:

let f = [/,\] ([\] + ([^] ([\] * **I**) **I**)) **I** **in** f 2 3

The [...] brackets are list brackets and we will use : to represent the list construction operator (CONS in Lisp). The abstraction algorithm which produces such director code is given in [10].

An evaluation of the above program would proceed as follows:

f 2 3 → [/,\]([\] + ([^] ([\] * **I**) **I**)) **I** 2 3 → [\]([\] + ([^] ([\] * **I**) **I**) 2) **I** 3
→ ([\] + ([^] ([\] * **I**) **I**) 2) 3 → + ([^] ([\] * **I**) **I** 2) 3
→ + (([\] * **I** 2) 2) 3 → + ((* 2) 2) 3 → + 4 3 → 7

This illustrates normal-order reduction which, when combined with a memory to remember the value of sub-reductions, is equivalent to lazy evaluation. Unfortunately, in normal-order reduction there is only one choice of what to do next (the leftmost outermost reduction) which makes it essentially sequential. Rather than compromise the safety of the evaluation mechanism (a mechanism is *safe* if it accords with the semantics of the language; call-by-value is not safe for lazy languages because some evaluations may fail to terminate while the lazy semantics assigns a defined value to the expression), we instead employ a compile-time analysis to identify the places at which we can use parallel evaluation without introducing the possibility of non-termination.

A unary function is strict in its argument if:

$$f \perp = \perp$$

where ⊥ (bottom) represents undefined (non-terminating) values. Thus if the argument is undefined, so is the result of the application; this implies that either the argument is used in the evaluation of the application or that the result is always undefined. This notion generalises naturally to functions of more than one argument. The arguments in which a function is strict may safely be passed by value and thus evaluated in parallel with the application. We cannot detect all of the arguments in which a function is strict, if we could we would have a solution to the halting problem. Instead we use a technique called *strictness analysis* to determine a subset of them [1].

When we have higher order functions, we might find that a function is always strict in an argument (context-free strictness) such as f and y below:

λf.λx.λy.+ y (f x)

or only strict in an argument depending on the value of some other arguments (context-sensitive strictness). The latter is the case for argument x above; x will only be needed if the actual parameter associated with f, in a particular application, is a strict unary function. Context-free information is associated with the function whereas context-sensitive information is associated with individual applications. We use a new annotation on applications (#) and a new parallel combinator (**P**) to control the spawning of parallel tasks [10]. The previous director example becomes:

P([\] **P**([/,\,#]([\,#] + ([^,#] ([\,#] * **I**) **I**)) **I**))

where we have shown all of the context-free and context-sensitive information. Since the example is a first-order one, there is a certain amount of duplication in this information. While the code is obviously more complex it retains the basic structure of the earlier translation. Cobweb uses a lazy evaluation mechanism modified by these new "directors".

3. THE COBWEB ARCHITECTURE

Cobweb code is stored as tagged tokens in the processing elements (PEs) memory. Each bracketted subexpression in the director representation becomes a separate token and may be referred to by its tag. An application message consists of a tag and an argument, it is communicated to the appropriate PE and the tag in the application is replaced by its body creating a new message which may be reducible. A reducible message is one that starts with a director or operator with the appropriate number of arguments. Reduction may spawn new tagged tokens and almost always leads to the production of a new application message.

One of the major spin-offs from the project has been a methodology for mapping requirements into silicon. We currently use a variety of different notations at different stages of the design. In the next phase of the research we intend to integrate these different notations and develop a proof theory that will enable the formal verification of each step in the design. Here, we give a fairly high-level description of the machine using the notation of graph rewriting systems [6]:

(^:d f a) t:x	=> ! (d (f t) t_1:(a t))	**P** f a	=> ! (f (!a))
(^:d **I** a) t:x	=> ! (d t t_1:(a t)	**K** x y	=> !x
(^:d f **I**) t:x	=> ! (d (f t) t)	**Y** t:f	=> ! (f t_1:(**Y** t))
(^:d **I I**) t:x	=> ! (d t t)	+ m n	=> m + n
(/:d f a) x	=> ! (d (f x) a)	+ x y	=> $ (+ (!x) (!y))
(/:d **I** a) x	=> ! (d x a)	t a	=> $ ((!t) a)
(\:d f a) x	=> ! (d f t:(a x))		
(\:d f **I**) x	=> ! (d f x)		
(-:d f a) x	=> ! (d f a)		
(#:d f a)	=> ! (d f (!a))		

The ! indicates that the evaluator should proceed to execute this term and $ represents suspension. As indicated earlier, the bracketted sub-expressions correspond to the code tokens in Cobweb; the identifier which precedes the bracket represents the tag. We assume that, except where modified by !, execution proceeds by leftmost outermost reduction. For example, the small program from Section 2 would be represented by tokens:

f = **P** t_1	t_1 = [\] **P** t_2
t_2 = [/,\,#] t_3 **I**	t_3 = [\,#] + t_4
t_4 = [^, #] t_5 **I**	t_5 = [\,#] * **I**

and an application would be:

f 2 3

Evaluation proceeds in the following way:

f 2 3	≡	**P** t_1 2 3		
	=>	t_1 2 3 **and** 2	≡	[\] **P** t_2 2 3
	=>	**P** t:(t_2 2) 3		
	=>	t:(t_2 2) 3 **and** 3	≡	[/,\,#] t_3 **I** 2 3

=> [\,#] (t_3 2) **I** 3
=> [#] (t_3 2) 3
=> t_3 2 3 **and** 3 ≡ [\,#] + t_4 2 3
=> [#] + t':(t_4 2) 3
=> + t':(t_4 2) 3 **and** t':(t_4 2) ≡ [^, #] t_5 **I** 2
=> **suspended and** [#] t_5 2 2
=> **suspended and** t_5 2 2 **and** 2 ≡ **suspended and** [\,#] * **I** 2 2
=> **suspended and** [#] * 2 2
=> **suspended and** * 2 2 **and** 2
=> **suspended and** 4 **and** 2
=> 7

The **and** operation represents parallel reduction of its two operands. For clarity, this example lacks worthwhile parallelism, but replacing the parameters 2 and 3 by more substantial expressions would yield some significant opportunities for parallel evaluation. The => symbol is used to represent reduction whereas ≡ is used to represent the replacement of a tag by its definition.

4. IMPLEMENTATION

Cobweb is a distributed memory architecture. This provides a good fit with the technology and is ideal for the support of combinator reduction. The architecture consists of a large cartesian grid of PEs. Each PE is connected to its nearest neighbours only. Figure 1 shows a 3x3 defect-free segment of a wafer. A selection of PEs are fabricated with bonding pads for communication with a front end processor, which is used for initial configuration and testing. During program execution these PEs are used for input and output.

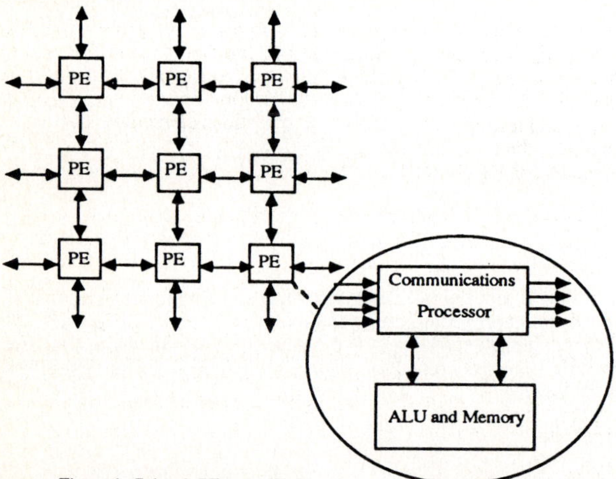

Figure 1. Cobweb PEs on a Wafer

A schematic diagram of a single processing element is shown in Figure 2. The communications processor and the ALU/memory subsystems are logically and physically distinct as indicated by the broken line in the figure. This is so each may yield independently. The communications logic, shown in the upper portion, is very simple and we expect high yields (of the order of 95%). Even if the yield of working ALUs is low, the high density of working communications processors ensures near optimal routing. The other major benefit derived from the high yield of communications processors is that the probability of a good ALU/memory being associated with a faulty communications processor is close to zero; thus the harvest (the proportion of working components which can be used) of ALU/memory subsystems will be high.

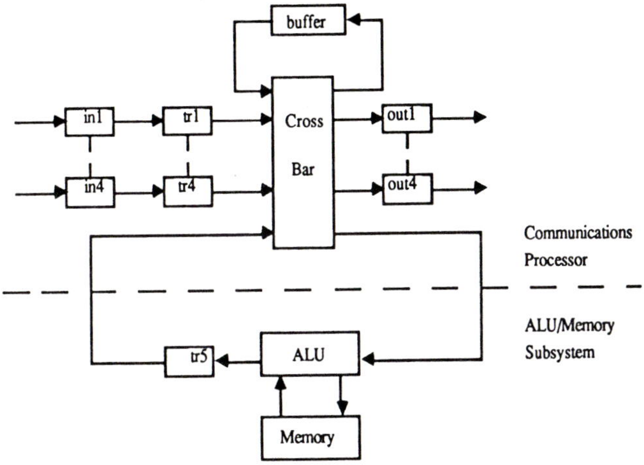

Figure 2. A Processing Element

4.1 Configuration and Test

At power-up, the system goes through a test and configuration sequence. This proceeds in two phases. Firstly, the network of communications elements is tested, providing reliable access to every connectable ALU/memory subsystem. In early prototypes the front-end will control and monitor the testing of each communications element in turn; for production devices it is planned to speed this process by initiating parallel testing where each communications element would test its neighbours autonomously. Secondly, the test phase for the ALU/memory subsystems is initiated. This second phase can be done remotely by the front end using relatively conventional methods.

When both test phases are complete, the front-end processor will have a map of working communications and ALU/memory subsystems. The front-end uses the map to construct a free space pool for every PE. The free space pool consists of a collection of addresses in the memory of the machine. These addresses are made up of the x and y coordinates of the PE plus an offset into that processors memory. To load a program into the machine, the front-end allocates each token of the program graph to a tag taken from the free space pool of a processing element. These tokens are then injected by the front-end into the communications network, which routes them to their allocated PE, which in turn places them in the appropriate memory cell. Application messages are routed through the machine, according to the tag at the head of the message, in an attempt to marry up with the corresponding resident token.

4.2 The Communications Processor

The role of the communications network is to provide arbitrary point-to-point communications between PEs. The role of the individual communications processor is to make a local decision on how to route incoming messages.

There are a number of message types. The primary type of message is the application message, and this is the only type which we are considering in detail in this paper. All messages have a header. In addition application messages have two subfields, the first of which is a tag identifying the function to be applied, and the second containing the parameter information. The header carries information needed by the fault tolerant routing algorithm. It consists of:

a blocked/unblocked bit
a handedness bit (Left/Right)
displacement bits

Each message has two modes: blocked and unblocked. The mode is defined by the blocked bit. When the message is unblocked it always moves in one of the directions that decreases its displacement from its destination. If the message is faced by a wall of duds, there is no such direction. This situation causes the message to go into blocked mode. When the message goes from unblocked mode to blocked mode it records its distance from its destination in the displacement field. The message then follows the edge of the wall of duds until it finds that it is closer to its destination than it was when it became blocked. At this point the message becomes unblocked and its behaviour returns to normal. Figure 3 shows the path taken by a packet through a faulty network.

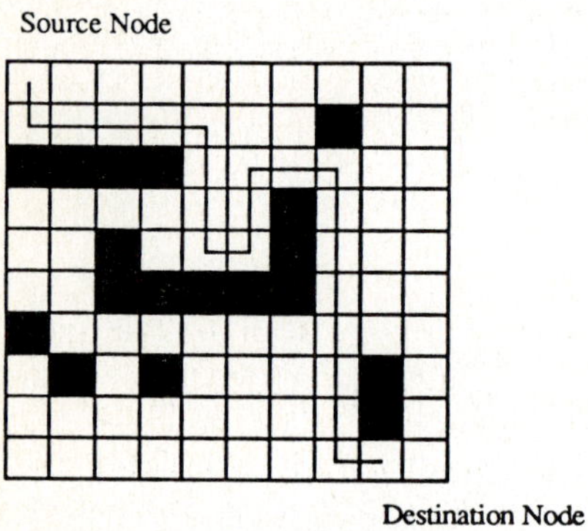

Figure 3. The routing algorithm in action

There is an important optimisation that can be made to the basic algorithm. When the message finds itself blocked it can go left or right depending on its handedness. Occasionally the message follows a wall of duds that leads directly to the boundary of the wafer. Normally the message would traverse the boundary as if it were a concave region of duds and this is almost always inefficient. A better approach is to allow the message to "bounce" off the boundary. This is realised by flipping the handedness bit when the message has found that it is both blocked and is facing the boundary.

This algorithm has been proved correct in that if there is a route between a source and a destination, it is guaranteed to find it. The algorithm also allows 100% harvest of connectable communications processors. Another important feature of the algorithm is that it means that there are no critical elements without which the architecture will not work. Its performance has also been extensively studied by simulation [3].

Figure 2 shows the logical structure of the communications processor. The components marked tr1 through tr5 contain routing logic and allow for the routing of tokens through the machine. The buffer on the crossbar is used to store tokens that cannot be forwarded through the network because of congestion, it alleviates the effects of the congestion building up back through the network and thus prevents deadlock.

4.3 The ALU and Memory Subsystem

The ALU/memory subsystem is depicted in the lower half of Figure 2. It is responsible for three distinct activities: responding to incoming messages, performing local reductions, and memory management. We deal with each activity in turn.

4.3.1 Responding to incoming messages

Messages of several kinds may be received, concerning testing, configuration, debugging, garbage collection, as well as the reduction process itself. For simplicity we deal only with the application message type described in section 4.2 above. An application message has the format:

Header (described in section 4.2), *Tag* (identifying the function), *Parameter information*.

The "tag" component is treated as a destination address by the communications network, so that on delivery, the token representing the function being applied resides in the destination PE's memory subsystem. The ALU examines the application message together with its function part, and decides whether a local reduction can be performed (by referring to the graph rewriting system to find a matching left-hand side; this corresponds to the => rewrites in the example of Section 3) or whether further communication must take place (for example when the body of the function starts with another, non-local tag; this corresponds to ≡ rewrites in the example of Section 3). The details of the parallel reduction mechanism in message-passing terms is the subject of a forthcoming paper.

4.3.2 Performing local reductions

A local reduction can be performed on an arriving application message if the graph fragment comprising the application message, combined with the function, matches a left-hand-side in the graph rewriting specification. Examples of such rewrites include basic operations, such as arithmetic and comparison, as well as director reductions ("/", "\", "^" and "-") and data constructions (e.g. CONS). "CONS" and the "^" director are examples of operations which require free storage cells in which to construct the resultant graph.

4.3.3 Memory Management and Garbage Collection

There is enough memory on each PE to store a number of "resident" token definitions. To satisfy the demand for free space arising during local reductions as fast as possible, each PE maintains a pool of pointers to free memory locations, in its own and in neighbouring PE's memory. The pools are initially created by the front end processor prior to program loading. As claims are made, during reduction, a PE's pool may become empty. When this happens, pointers to free space must be acquired from neighbouring PE's. Meanwhile, outstanding storage claims must be suspended. As functional program objects have highly-dynamic lifetimes, tokens are returned to a PE's free space pool automatically. This occurs when no active token contains a pointer by which it might make access to the token in question.

In earlier, sequential implementations of Cobweb, it was intended to use a classical reference counting scheme. One benefit of such a scheme is that the garbage collection can be done on the fly. Unfortunately, in a parallel system based on a packet-switched communications network, it is no longer possible to use reference counting because there is no way to guarantee that the increment messages will arrive before decrement messages (meaning that some objects might be re-used before all of the references have disappeared). In [7] an alternative reference counting scheme is proposed, called fractional reference counting, which avoids the need for increment messages. We intend to use fractional reference counting as the basic garbage collection strategy in Cobweb.

5. CONCLUSIONS

We have described an architecture which exploits wafer-scale integration in the parallel execution of functional programs. The use of this new technology significantly changes the communication/computation ratio that is acceptable in such machines. We expect to produce a machine that is considerably faster than existing declarative machine prototypes at a fraction of the cost.

We have designed a general purpose communications architecture for wafer-scale machines. This has been proved correct and extensively simulated. We expect it to have application to other declarative architectures and also in areas such as neural computing. We have also made some headway in developing a rigorous methodology for mapping high-level requirements down to silicon. One of the advantages of the structured design approach is that it is possible to produce runnable versions of the specification at an early stage of the design. We are currently using this approach to produce a simulation of the Cobweb architecture which will run on an array of transputers.

ACKNOWLEDGEMENTS

The work reported in this paper is the result of a collaborative project funded by the Alvey Directorate of Great Britain. The authors would like to thank Dave Bolton, Peter Osmon, Malcolm Shute and Phil Winterbottom for their comments on earlier drafts of this paper.

REFERENCES

[1] Abramsky S.and Hankin C. L.(eds), "Abstract Interpretation of Declarative Languages", Ellis Horwood, 1987.

[2] Anderson P., Hankin C. L., Kelly P. H. J., Osmon P. E. and Shute M. J., "COBWEB-2: Structured Specification of a Wafer Scale Supercomputer" in PARLE Volume I de Bakker J. W., Nijman A. J. and Treleaven P. C. (eds) , LNCS 258, Springer Verlag, 1987, pp51-67.

[3] Anderson P., "Performance of a heavily congested two dimensional cartesian routing communications architecture in the presence of faults", forthcoming.

[4] Aubusson R. and Catt I., "Wafer-Scale Integration - A Fault Tolerant Procedure" IEEE Journal of Solid State Circuits, Vol SC-13, 1978.

[5] Barendregt H. P., "The Lambda Calculus: Its Syntax and Semantics (2nd edition)" North Holland, 1984.

[6] Barendregt H. P., van Eekelen M. C. D. J. and Plasmeijer M. J., "Specification of Reduction Strategies in Term Rewriting Systems" Preprint, The Catholic University of Nijmegen, The Netherlands, 1986.

[7] Bevan D. I., "Distributed Garbage Collection using Reference Counting" in PARLE Volume II de Bakker J. W., Nijman A. J. and Treleaven P. C. (eds) , LNCS 259, Springer Verlag, 1987, pp176-187.

[8] Dijkstra E. W., "A Mild Variant of Combinatory Logic", EWD735, 1980.

[9] Glaser H. W., Hankin C. L. and Till D. R., "Principles of Functional Programming", Prentice Hall International, 1984.

[10] Hankin C. L., Burn G. L. and Peyton Jones S. L., "A Safe Approach to Parallel Combinator Reduction (Extended Abstract)" in ESOP 86 Robinet B. and Wilhelm R. (eds), LNCS 213, Springer Verlag, 1986, pp99-110.

[11] Jesshope C. R. and Moore W. R. (eds), "Wafer Scale Integration", Adam Hilger Ltd., 1986.

[12] Kennaway J. R. and Sleep M. R., "Director Strings as Combinators", University of East Anglia, England, 1981.

[13] Peyton Jones S. L., "The Implementation of Functional Programming Languages", Prentice Hall International, 1987

Network Information Processing Systems
K. Boyanov, R. Angelinov (Editors)
Elsevier Science Publishers B.V. (North-Holland)

AN OBJECT-ORIENTED DATA MANAGEMENT SERVER

Elisa Bertino* and Roberto Gagliardi**

*IEI-CNR, **CNUCE-CNR
Pisa, Italy.

Comandos is an ESPRIT project aiming at the development of an infrastructure for the design and support of distributed office applications. In this work the object oriented type model and a partial view of the architecture of the Comandos system are presented. The main goal of the type model is to integrate the database and the general programming language concepts in a single, coherent environment while including facilities for the distribution of objects. The function of the major architectural components that support the type model entities are discussed.

1. INTRODUCTION.

The increasing power and the decreasing cost of personal computers and workstations is making practical a wide range of new types of applications, such as office applications. Moreover the cost of computer networks, which enable computers to exchange informations and share services, is decreasing drastically. This leads to systems consisting of several workstations and specialized devices connected through high speed local network. The sharing of resources and in particular of data is crucial since a number of devices such as optical readers, digital image scanners, and laser printers are too expensive to be located at the user workstations. As far as management of data is concerned several issues should be observed. In environment such as the offices the increasing amount of informations due to the introduction of tools and devices for creating electronic documents can be tremendous, particularly if data contain images and digitized voice.

Further on, the complexity of the data objects that advanced office systems should support has increased with respect to data managed by traditional data management systems. Several object oriented models have been proposed that appear to provide the modeling power needed to describe *complex objects*, such as multimedia documents or VLSI circuits [2], [11], [14], [20]. However first attempts to support such models have consisted of building an object oriented interface on top of a traditional DBMS. As pointed out in [15] this solution does not provide adequate performance.The management of complex objects requires in fact that a number of database techniques must be reconsidered, if not extended or completely re-designed. Effective sharing of data is required by the applications. Locating data at the various user's work stations is not in general the best solution to provide effective sharing of data. An alternative solution is the usage of *server* machines to manage shared resources and support applications running on *client* workstations. Since servers are specialized to support a specific service, the server hardware and software architecture can be built aiming to the optimum ratio performance/cost. Other requirements derive from the evolutionary nature of office environments. As an office organization grows it tends to accumulate informations, to develop different uses of this information, and to acquire over time different tools. It is therefore important that the system provides the capability of supporting pre-existing data management applications and at the same time allowing the development of new distributed applications. Therefore the major requirements concern the capability of keeping the old application running, while allowing the integration of the different data management tools, so that new distributed applications can easily access also data managed by pre-existing applications. An approach to satisfy these requirements consists of leaving the local information systems unmodified and to add software layers on top of them to provide mappings between the local data model and the global data model.

A system aiming to satisfy these requirements is the project Comandos which is part of the European Strategic Programs for Research in Information Technology (ESPRIT). The overall goal of this project is to design an infrastructure for the design and support of distributed office applications. This includes the development of tools for data management and for the support of pre-existing applications. To satisfy this goal, an object oriented type model and a distributed architecture have been designed [7]. In particular the object oriented paradigm has been chosen since it provides users with access to abstract objects in such a way that the distributed nature of their implementation is hidden. In this paper we focus on the tools for the management of data. The data management in Comandos is based on a number of servers that provide the basic functions of complex object storage and associative retrieval by means of an object query language.

The remainder of this paper is organized as follows. In Section 2 an overview of the Type Model is presented. In Section 3 the Server Architecture is presented. Finally in Section 4 some conclusions are presented.

2. TYPE MODEL OVERVIEW.

This chapter summarizes the Comandos type model. The main goal of the type model is to integrate the type system of programming languages and the database schema in a single programming environment. At this purpose the Object Oriented approach has been chosen.

The type model makes a distinction between type interface and type implementation. In addition it allows types to have several implementations. This feature is a good support for the system heterogeneity and flexibility. Type hierarchies and parametric types are additional features of the model allowing the system upgrading while maintaining compatibility with the past. In particular the inheritance concept offers a trade off between the static typing of languages and the dynamic changing of the database schema.

The Object Oriented paradigm assumes the data abstraction as a fundamental principle.The notion of data abstraction is purely intentional [13] in that it handles the behaviours of the object by only applying the operations defined on its type. The Comandos type model adds the extensional aspect to the intentional one, by viewing the objects as *sets* of entities belonging to *classes*. The notion of class has been introduced in the Database Conceptual Models and in Database Programming Languages [1]. Comandos handles classes as generic types having a set of primitive for scanning or testing the membership of a given object to the the class . Classes are distinct between *abstract* and *implementation* classes. Abstract classes are visible to the user. Implementation classes specify how the generic operations defined for the abstract class are implemented at a given site and how objects must be stored in secondary memory. At a given time an abstract class can be bound to one or more implementation classes. Implementation classes are useful for integrating pre-existing data management applications. The idea is to give the uniform view of the underlying systems in terms of one type model. This is accomplished by mapping class operations on operations provided by the existing systems. Implementation classes contain also the specifications of the class physical design inside the database. At present Comandos provides the support for clustering, grouping and indexing.

Comandos uses types for describing the database logical schema and classes for capturing database physical aspects inside the programming environment. Data abstraction obstacles the database design since it hides the internal data structure of types. The Comandos type system has been designed to capture both type abstraction and data structures. At this aim the notion of *property* has been included. The concept of property is analogous to that presented in [20]. Properties can appear in the interface of user defined types together with the operations that are applicable to the type.Therefore the internal object state can be made partially or globally visible to the external world. If no properties appear in the type interface then the type is a *pure abstract data type.*

3. SERVER ARCHITECTURE

In this section the architecture of the server is presented. The server is decomposed at a first level of detail in two major components: the Object Data Management Subsystem (ODMS) and the Object Storage Subsystem (OSS). ODMS deals with logical entities like types , classes and indexes, while the OSS knows only single objects in terms of chunks of bytes. The fundamental functionality of the OSS is to store or retrieve an object in an efficient way, as specified by its low level (unique) identifier. The ODMS is decomposed in several modules. For the purpose of this paper only the following components will be discussed: the Type Manager (TPM), the Class Manager (CLM), the Placement Manager (PLM) and the Query Processor (QPR).

3.1 Type Manager.

The TPM handles types and relationships between them. As stated before the database schema is described in terms of types and classes. Therefore the TPM interacts with the language environments tools and the database side. In both case its function is restricted to give information about the type structure without dealing with syntax parsing or type checking actions. From the language point of view the TPM acts as a library.The libraries of languages like ADA [16] are equipped with sophisticated data management procedures. The idea here is to use the ODMS for storing and retrieving type's data. From the database side the TPM handles the schema (in terms of objects) and makes the structure of types available for the enquiry. This last function is a key feature of Comandos. In fact it has been shown [3] that the retrieval of the office documents based on *document types* increases the selectivity of queries. At this aim the ODMS stores type information on classes (the *type descriptor* classes) as any other value.This operation is performed by interacting with the *CLM*. Structurally the TPM represents types and type relationships as trees (see fig.1). The tree root represents the abstract type declaration (i.e. the type interface). The second level features the type representation (i.e. the object state).The third level is related to the code part (i.e. the methods). A type can have only one declarative part. The possibility of allowing multiple implementations brings to have a 1-N relationship between the declarative part and the representation part and between the representation part and the code part. This organization makes the type management very flexible.

As stated in Section 2 *subtyping* links may exist between types. A particular case of subtyping is the IS_A relationship. TPM keeps track of the IS_A relationship as well. Therefore the type world is represented as a hierarchy of trees as depicted in fig.1 (at present the multiple inheritance is not supported). An additional relationship maintained in the type graph is the *instantiation* of parametric types that gives a non-parametric type as result. Parametric types can be specified as subtypes of already existing parametric types.

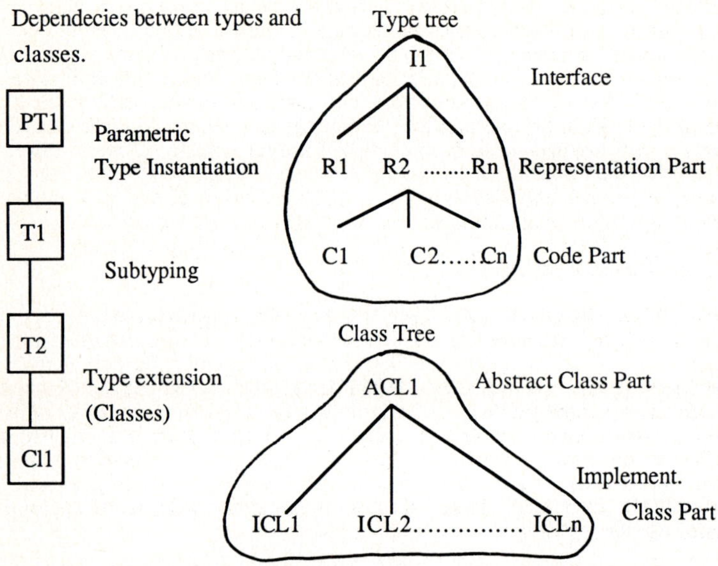

Fig. 1. relationships between types, classes, type parts and class parts.

The TPM takes care also of types dependecies due to the IS_PART_OF hierarchy. For example if a property of a type T1 is of type T2 then T1 depends on T2. The knowledge of dependencies is needed when performing type deletions. The TPM performs the following operations on types:

• Creation. All the type are subtypes of the predefined *Top* type. Top is the only non parametric type that can be supertype of parametric types. Distinct primitives are provided by the type manager in order to create the interface, representation and code part. Additional functions are available in order to manipulate the relationships discussed above (create subtype, create parametric type, instantiate parametric type etc..).

• Freezing. A type is frozen when a class of that type is created. A frozen type cannot be deleted. Updating is legal only if representation or code parts are added but not replaced. The last constraint allows the type to be always consistent with its instances.

• Deletion. The type deletion has the cascade effect on its subtypes. The operation fails if the type or some of its subtypes are frozen. Type representations and code can be deleted separately.

• Update.The declarative part of the type is not updatable. Modifications to representation and to code parts are allowed.

3.2 Class Manager

The CLM handles both abstract and implementation classes. It performs the generic operations on classes namely: get_first object , get_next object , is_empty, get class metadata, read and write objects. The CLM handles also the storage strategies for the object storing. These specifications are described in the implementation class declarations. In particular the CLM activates the mechanisms for clustering, distributing and indexing. In order to execute the generic operations mentioned above the CLM selects automatically the access strategy depending on the active implementation class attributes (for example indexes and/or clustering criteria) . The CLM does not deal with transitive closure of objects, i.e. the components of the Is_Part_Of hierarchy must be inserted exsplicitily. Other operations performed by the class manager are :

• Class Creation. Abstract and implementation class creation can be performed separately. The creation of an abstract class needs the specification of its abstract type that must be a TPM registered type. The creation of the implementation class requires the related abstract class being already inserted in class catalogs.

• Class freezing. A class is frozen if it contains at least one instance. Under some circumstances a frozen class can be forced to be unfrozen.

• Class Deletion. Abstract and implementation class can be removed separately from the class descriptor. However removing an abstract class automatically brings all the related implementation classes being removed. A frozen class (either abstract or implementation) cannot be deleted.

Likewise the TPM , the CLM keeps track of dependencies between abstract and implementation classes as two level trees (see fig 1.).

3.3 Placement Manager

The main function of the PLM is to provide high level support for object distribution on the various sites. It supports the *object distribution schema*, which describes the distribution criteria for objects, and makes available this schema to other components, such as the Query Processor, so that the current object location can be determined. An important requirement is that distribution criteria are associated to object classes. In particular distribution criteria for a given class should possibly be defined in terms of predicates defined on that class. The concept of distribution based on predicates is very similar to the concept of horizontal fragmentation for Distributed Databases . We distinguish two types of distribution/replication:

• Partition: object in a given class can be stored in only one sites, among those associated to the class.

• Replication: each object in a given class is replicated at all the sites storing instances of the class (full replication), or in a subset of these (partial replication).

To illustrate the previous concepts, we present an example of a statement for the definition of distribution criteria (vertical bar is used to separate choices):

```
DISTRIBUTION SCHEME OF Class_name:
REPLICATION AT sequence_of_sites |
PARTITION AT sequence_of_sites |
FOR Condition_1: STORE AT sequence_of_sites
FOR Condition_2: STORE AT sequence_of_sites
.........
FOR Condition_n: STORE AT sequence_of_sites.
```

The conditions are specified as predicates on object properties. We call these conditions *placement conditions*. An important requirement on conditions is that they must cover the whole set of instances of a class. This prevents the possibility of having instances that do not verify any of the conditions.

The type of distribution/replication used has an impact on the way a query is processed. In particular when the option of FULL REPLICATION is used, then a query is sent only to one among the sites storing instances of the class. When the option PARTITION is used, this means that objects are partitioned on the sites, but no placement conditions are specified. Therefore, since no conditions are specified, a query referencing this class is broadcasted to all sites associated to the class. Also upon creation of a new object the site(s) must be specified among those associated to the object class, where the object is to be inserted.

Finally object distribution (and replication) predicates can be defined by using placement condition. Objects satisfying a specific condition are replicated at the set of sites in the associated sequence. When conditions are specified the system can automatically determine the appropriate sites where to store the object. Also conditions allow to further restrict the sites on which the query must be processed. In fact by matching the query predicates against the placement conditions it may be possible to eliminate from the set of sites to be accessed, the ones having conditions that are mutually exclusive with respect to some of the query predicates.

Distribution primitives based on conditions on objects are very powerful and flexible in conforming to application needs. In particular it allows to restrict the number of sites to access to execute a particular query. However it can increase the complexity of certain operations. For instance modifying an object component on which one of such predicate is defined, would allow to check whether the object has to be moved to another site. The primitives provided at the Placement Manager interface perform the following functions: definition of distribution schemas, retrieval of distribution schemas, modification of distribution schemas. In particular the last primitives may involve object migration among the various sites

3.4 . Query Processor

The functionality provided by the QPR is to support the query language defined at the ODMS interface. The query language allows to specify both queries on instances and on types.

The major requirements for the QPR concern the performance and the support for distributed queries. In particular optimization issues on LAN environments differ with respect to WAN, since communication is not a bottle-neck in LAN environments [18]. Also application requirements toward the query processor are quite different with respect to WAN. In fact in LAN data are stored by servers and it is expected that data semantically related are stored together on the same server. Therefore issues such as distributed joins [17] do not appear to be relevant in such environment. Therefore we can expect that queries will be addressed in most of the cases toward one or more specified sites. An important issue here concerns instead the integration of pre-existing applications. For example it may be necessary to translate the queries written in Comandos in terms of the query language provided by the data management system installed at a given site.

The interface provided by the query processor allows to specify two basic types of queries: queries on objects and queries on types. Queries on objects have the following main clauses :

- SCOPE: the scope specifies a site (or a set of sites).This clause is optional.

- CLASS: the class clause specifies a class (or a set of classes) to which the query must be restricted.

• CONDITION: the condition clause specifies a boolean combination of predicates to be satisfied by the retrieved objects.

Queries on types have the following main clauses:

• TYPE: the type clause specifies that the query must be restricted to subtypes of the specified type.

• CONDITION: the condition clause specifies a boolean combination of predicates to be satisfied by the retrieved types. In particular predicates for types are restricted to be predicates on the type structure.

The task of query processing has been decomposed in five phases: parsing, type checking, query decomposition, query optimization, and query execution. During the parsing the query is translated into an internal format (parse tree) and its syntax verified. The type checking phase has the task of processing and modifying the query according to the type definitions of classes involved in the query. This last activity is performed by interacting with the CLM to collect information about type definitions of classes and class hierarchies.The query decomposition phase has the task of determining the sites involved in a given query. It uses the SCOPE and CLASS clauses (if these are specified in the query) and the distribution schema to determine the sites to be accessed. A query is therefore decomposed in a set of local sub-queries. Each sub-query is sent to the appropriate site to be optimized and executed locally. The query optimizer phase has the task of deciding the execution strategy for a given local query. This phase is carried out by interacting with the CLM to fetch information about data statistics and access mechanisms. Furthermore, the query optimizer performs query decomposition in terms of the operations provided by the CLM. Finally during the query execution phase the query is executed according to the strategy defined during the previous phase. This phase is carried out by interacting with the CLM, that in turns interacts with the Storage Subsystem, to request the execution of the operations in which a given query has been decomposed and to fetch objects when needed.

Each one of the previous phases is implemented by a specific sub-component of the Query Processor, that therefore is internally decomposed into the following sub-components: parser, type checker, query decomposer, query optimizer, and query execution manager.

3.5 . Object Storage Subsystem

As stated before the main function of the OSS is to access objects by their low level identifier which is used by the storage system to identify physical storage space. However objects can be clustered. In this case a cluster caching mechanism may be activated that returns possibly all the objects of the cluster. The OSS includes simple versioning and replication primitives as well. However the management of the replication and versioning mechanism themselves would be the responsibility of higher architectural components. For the aims of this paper the descriptions of the OSS is restricted to the discussion of some aspects to the object storing. These issues will be discussed in the following section.

3.6 Complex Object Manager.

This component provides the functions of complex object storage and retrieval by interacting with the Simple Object Store. Therefore this component must support the object storage schema, describing how complex objects are stored in terms of storage objects.

In general several storage strategies can be adopted. The choice is crucial since the system performance depends heavily on the efficiency of object accesses. In particular a storage strategy should provide an efficient support for: objects having both simple and complex properties; objects having multi-valued properties, where each value may be in turn complex; objects with long-fields.The last requirement derives from the need of supporting multimedia data types (text, image, voice) that are essential in advanced applications, such as the management of multimedia office documents [4].

The major problem in designing a storage organization for complex objects is that the efficiency of such an organization depends on the access patterns. In general we can distinguish two basic types of accesses:

• Access based on the whole object.This type of access is in general appropriate for applications that perform complex manipulations on objects by means of specialized programs or editors. In such case the whole object is copied into the application virtual memory (possibly at a different machine) and manipulated by the application.

• Access to object properties. This type of access is used to retrieve properties of objects and not entire objects. This type of access may be appropriate when accessing very large objects.

Various storage strategies have been proposed lately [12],[8], [9]. Although it is difficult to make a comparison among them, storage strategies for complex objects lie between two extreme approaches : the Direct Model and the Normalized Model.

In Direct Model objects are directly as they are defined in the conceptual schema. In other words the unit of storage coincides with the semantic unit. Objects belonging to the same class are stored in one file, where each record is a member of the class. The main advantage of this approach is that the retrieval of entire objects is very efficient, since no "join" operations are needed to rebuild objects. The major disadvantage of this strategy is that the access to a subset of object properties may be very expensive, especially when objects have long-fields, because the presence of such properties affect the performance of operations based on other properties.

In the normalized model, objects are decomposed in atomic components, that are stored in different files. The correspondence among the various object components is kept by means of the object identifier. In such way objects are decomposed in sets of binary files. In particular in the implementation of this approach proposed by [19] two copies exist of each binary file. One copy has records clustered on the value of the atomic property, while the other is clustered on the object identifier. This type of approach has the major advantage of supporting in an efficient way partial accesses to objects. However, accesses to entire objects may rather inefficient due to the large number of "join" operations needed to recompose objects. To alleviate this problem, a special access structure, called "join index" has been proposed in [19], supporting materialization of joins needed to rebuild the objects.

In general between these two extremes, an intermediate approach is possible. In such cases, the objects are still decomposed, but the object properties are grouped together on the base of the access patterns, in such a way that properties most frequently referenced together are stored i n the same file. In addition the same property may be replicated in several files.

A language for storage schema specification is under definition in the framework of this architecture. Such a language will allow the definition of the storage schemas for object classes, so that applications can tailor object storage on the base of their accesses. However a default storage schema will be also provided.

4. CONCLUSIONS

The definition of part of the logical architecture of the Object Server designed for the Comandos Esprit project has been presented. The discussion has been firstly focused on the Comandos type model then the architectural components that handle the type model entities have been described. The type model has been designed to capture the intentional and the extensional aspects of objects. Query facilities have been added as well. Therefore the type model provides the concepts of user-defined types, abstract types and classes. Furthermore both the concepts of implementation types and implementation classes have been introduced. These are crucial in supporting applications in distributed environments, since they allow different implementations for a given type or class at different nodes. The type manager, class manager, query processor and placement manager components support all the concepts above. Finally some issues on the object storing have been discussed.

ACKNOWLEDGEMENTS.

This work has been carried out under ESPRIT contract 834, COnstruction and MANagement of Distributed Office Systems. The authors gratefully acknowledge the contributors to the Comandos O-O Working-Group: Bull -R.Balter, J. Bernadat, E. Paire, G. Vandome; INESC - .Alves- Marques, J.P. Cunha, P. Guedes; LGI - S. Krakowiak, M.Meysembourg, C. Roisin, X. Rousset de Pina, R. Scioville; Olivetti - A.Billocci, A. Converti, M. Farusi, L. Martino, C. Tani; TCD - V. Cahill,A. Donnelly, A. El-Habbash, E. Finn, N. Harris, C. Horn, G. Starovic, B.Tangney, I. White.

REFERENCES.

[1] Albano A., Cardelli L., and Orsini R.,"Galileo: A Strongly Typed, Interactive Conceptual Language",ACM TODS, Vol.10, N.2, 230-260, 1985.
[2] D.S. Batory, W.Kim, "Modeling Concepts for VLSI CAD Objects"TODS 10.3,1985.
[3] Bertino E., e Rabitti F., "Accesso a DocumentiMultimedia in Workstations Avanzate", Atti Conferenza IDI-AICA,Mondovi' [CN], 16-18 Maggio, 1985.
[4] Bertino E., Gibbs S., Rabitti F., Thanos C.,Tsichritzis D., "A Multimedia Document Server", Proc. AdvancedDatabase Synposium, Japan, August 29-30, 1986.
[5] Bertino E., Gagliardi R., Meghini C.,Negri M., Pelagatti G., Sbattella L., White I.,"The Comandos Type Model", Working Paper Task T2.1, ProjectComandos (ESPRIT), August 1987.
[6] "Object Oriented Architecture",Comandos (ESPRIT Project 834),Project Report, D1-T2.1-870904, September 1987.
[7] "Kernel and System Services Functional Specifications",Comandos (ESPRIT Project 834),Project Report, D1-T3.2.1.1-870904, D1-T3.2.2.1-870904,September 1987.
[8] Deppish U., Paul H.B., Schek H.J,"A Storage System for Complex Objects", Proc. IEEE Workshop onObject Oriented DBMS, Asilomar (Calif.), September, 1986.
[9] Ege A., and Ellis C., "Design and Implementation ofGORDION, an Object Base Management System", ThirdInt. Conf. On Data Engineering (IEEE), Los Angeles (U.S.A.),
[10] Horn C., Krakowiak S.,"Object-Oriented Architecture for Distributed Office Systems",in Proc. fourth ESPRIT Technical Week, Brussels, September, 1987.
[11] Kersten M., and Schippers F.,"Towards an Object-Centered Database Language",Proc. Workshop on Object OrientedDBMS, Asilomar (Calif.), September 1986.
[12] W. Kim et al., "Enhancing the Object-Oriented concepts for Databasesupport",Proc. Workshop on Object OrientedDBMS, Asilomar (Calif.), September 1986.

[13] Levesque H., Mylopoulos J.,"A procedural semantic forsemantic networks", in Associative Networks , Academic Press 1979.
[14] Manola F., Orenstein J.,"Toward a General Spatial Data Model for an Object-Oriented DBMS",Proc. of the Twelfth International Conference on Very Large DataBases, Kyoto, August, 1986.
[15] O'Brien P.,"Trellis Object Based Environment", DEC-TR-373vers. 1.1, November 15, 1985.
[16] S. H. Saib and R.E. Fritz, "The ADA programming language", IEEEComputer Society Press, IEEE Catalog Number EHO 202-2
[17]Selinger P., Adiba M., "Access Path Selection inDistributed Database Management System",Proc. International Conference on Data Bases, Deen and Hammersly(eds.) July 1980.
[18]Stonebraker M, et Al.,"Performance Analysis of Distributed Data Base Systems",in Proc. Third IEEESymposium on Reliability in Distributed Software andDatabase Systems, October 17-19, 1983.
[19] Valduriez, P."Join Indices", ACM TODS, Vol 12 n.2, June1987.
[20] Zdonik S.,"Object Management Systems for Design Environments", IEEE DatabaseEngineering, Vol8 n4, December 1985.

Network Information Processing Systems
K. Boyanov, R. Angelinov (Editors)
Elsevier Science Publishers B.V. (North-Holland)

LINEAR HASHING FOR SIGNATURE FILES

Pavel Zezula

Computing Centre
Technical University
Brno, Czechoslovakia

The signature approach is an access method for partial-match retrieval especially successful in office environment. In this method signatures serve as a filter for retrieval in order to save accesses to nonqualifying objects in the storage file. However, sequential processing of signatures is for large files time consuming. We suggest to apply the linear hashing for organizing signatures. We show how such approach can reduce the number of accessed signatures while the semi-consecutive access of the pages of signatures can still be preserved. An analytical formula for estimating the number of discarded pages is derived. Simulation results show a very high percentage of discarded pages especially for large files and query signatures with higher weights.

1. INTRODUCTION

The signature file access method is a retrieval method. The very idea of it is to encapsulate properties of objects in terms of abstractions, signatures, which are much smaller to be organized and processed by computer. It is a two-level hierarchy. The first level, called the access level, provides filtering capability. It contains the signatures while the second level, called the storage level, contains the corresponding objects.

The main problem that we have to face when applying the method is the control of false drop. The false drop is the situation in which a signature in the access level of the file seems to qualify while the corresponding object in the storage level of the file does not actually qualify. It affects the number of physical page accesses, I/O time, on the storage level. The most important papers dealing with the false drop probability estimation and the signature design are /1, 4, 5, 6/.

Single level signature files have been analysed in /13/. Tsichritzis et. al. describe in /14/ a prototype multimedia office filing system that applies the signature file approach both for attributes and text. Christodoulakis /2/ adopts this approach for image captions and text selections related to images in order to handle queries on images. Alternative storage structures for signatures are the bit-sliced storage /12/ and the recent method called S-tree /3/.

In this paper we suggest a new method of organizing signatures. It is based on linear hashing. We summarize the signature approach in chapter 2 and the linear hashing in chapter 3. The application is described in chapter 4 accompanied by its performance analyses. An evaluation of the method can be found in the conclusions.

2. SIGNATURE FILES

Even though more than one technique for signature extraction can be used in practice, we will concentrate on superimposed coding which has been recognized as the most promising one /4/. This method works as follows. Each object is divided into logical blocks. A logical block is defined as a piece of text that contains a constant number D_{bl} of distinct non-common words. Each non-common word yields a bit pattern of size f. These word bit patterns are OR-ed together to form a block signature. The concatenation of the block signatures of an object forms the object signature.

To create a word signature, more details are needed. Each non-common word yields m bit positions, not necessarily distinct, in the range 1 ÷ f. Bits corresponding to these positions are set to "1" while all the other bits are set to "0". For example, as we can see in Figure 1, the word "distinct" sets to "1" the 3-rd, 7-th, 8-th, and 11-th bits. That means that number of bits which we set to "1" per a word is 4.

Word	Signatures
distinct	001 000 110 010
word	000 010 101 001
block signature	001 010 111 011

Figure 1. Superimposed coding method
$D_{bl} = 2$, $f = 12$, $m = 4$

Searching for a word is handled in an easy way. The signature of a searched word or a set of words is created in exactly the same way as the signatures of the logical blocks. Suppose that the signature contains "1" in the positions 2, 3, 6 and 9. If the above bit positions, i.e. 2, 3, 6, and 9, of a block signature also contain 1\`s then the block qualifies and the document containing the block is retrieved. Otherwise it is discarded. It is important to say that the value of the other bit positions of the block signatures, i.e. 1, 4, 5, 7, 8, 10, 11, and 12 are, in this case, immaterial.

For the sake of simplicity we will suppose in the following that each objectconsists of only one logical block. This means that the block signatures are equal to the object signatures. We will also suppose that all our signatures are, in the sense of /4/ optimal, it is with the minimum false drop and as a consequence of this with the same proportion of ones and zeros.

3. LINEAR HASHING

The dynamic hashing scheme for organizing files having single attribute keys called linear hashing, LH, has been presented in /7, 8, 9/ and later in many other works, e.g. /10, 11/. Let each key, K_i, $i = 1, 2, \dots, N$, is supposed to be a sequence of f binary digits $b_1, b_2, \dots, b_f$ and let n be the number of allocated pages addressed from 0 to n-1, where $2^{h-1} < n <= 2^h$ for some integer h. A hash function g maps the keys onto the addresses /0, 1, 2, ... , n-1/ and is defined for h grater than 0 as:

$$g/K_i,h,n/ \; = \; \begin{cases} \sum_{r=0}^{h-1} b_{f-r} \cdot 2^r \, , & \text{if} \quad \sum_{r=0}^{h-1} b_{f-r} \cdot 2^r \quad n, \\ \sum_{r=0}^{h-2} b_{f-r} \cdot 2^r & \text{otherwise.} \end{cases} \qquad /1/$$

The value of h is termed the file level and varies from 0 to f. As the initial conditions , h is 0, n is 1, and we define $g/K_i,0,1/$ to be 0.

A variation in h and n induces a variation in g. The function g corresponds to the split functions discussed in /7, 8, 9/. According to this, g is the split fuction because for any key, K_i,

$$g/K_i,h,n/ = g/K_i,h-1,n/ \qquad \text{or,}$$
$$g/K_i,h,n/ = g/K_i,h-1,n/ + 2^h.$$

In fact, the computation of $g/K_i,h,n/$ is equivalent to taking the h-bit suffix of the key K_i and interpreting it as a binary integer.

Briefly, the idea of linear hashing scheme involves a set of n primary, addressable, pages each with zero or more overflow pages chained to it to form a list of pages. Assuming that the file level is h, then to insert a record with key K_i, the page address, p, is computed as the value of the function $g/K_i,h,n/$. The record is stored in the primary page p except when overflow occurs. In this case it is stored in an overflow page linked to p. The occurence of the overflow triggers an expansion of the address space from n to n+1 primary pages.

The expansion of the address space progresses by page splitting whenever an overflow occurs in a primary page. A pointer, denoted by SP, designates the primary page that is to be split next. Suppose a collision occurs in page p. The key, being inserted, is stored in an overflow page chained to p. Besides, a new primary page, number n, is allocated and the keys in the primary page SP, as well as its overflow keys, are rehashed and distributed between the pages SP and n. The number of primary pages now becomes n+1. The values of SP and h are synchronized as follows.

1. The file level h is increased just befor the primary page 0 is split.
2. The pointer SP is advanced according to the assignment $SP = /SP+1/\text{mod}2^{h-1}$.

4. LINEAR HASHING FOR SUPERIMPOSED SIGNATURES

The application of the described modification of LH which deals with superimposed signatures, LHSS for short, is obvious. Since each signature is a sequence of f bits, they can be considered as keys for the function g.

Sequential processing is easy. The only thing we must do is to generate the page characteristics p from 0 to n-1 and access the pages in this order. Nevertheless, LHSS is less efficient than sequential organization, because the consecutive processing of pages in the LHSS organization can be interrupted by accessing signatures in the overflow area. Fortunately, the expected overflow is not high. Since signatures are usually not large, mostly less than 100 bytes, we can store many signatures in a page. For this case Litwin /9/ reports practically no overflow records with uncontrolled load and the storage bucket capacity of 50% records per a page, and only 5% of overflow records for the same storage bucket with the guaranteed load of 75%.

Furthermore, we can adopt a more efficient access strategy. All the primary pages can be accessed first in the most efficient way, i.e. with the increasing page number. Since the order of accessing signatures is not in this case important, the overflow signatures, if any, can be read in the second step, preferably in a batch access mode. However, exhaustive search is time consuming because it requires all signatures to be accessed and tested for qualification.

Before explaining how the LH scheme can be exploited for a more efficient query processing, let us consider the queries first. The queries are transformed into query signatures, which are again bit patterns of size f. The number of 1\`s in query signatures ranges from m to f/2, supposing the block signatures are optimal. In this case the number of 1\`s in a block signature, called the signature weight, is f/2 while the number of bits that each distinct word sets to "1" is m. The weight of a specific query signature depends on the number of words specified in the query. To distinguish among the document signatures, designated as keys K_i, i = 1, 2, ... ,N, and the query signature we will use the symbol Q for the query signature.

However, even though the number of 1\`s in Q is for a typical query substantially smaller than in $K_i$, we can compute a characteristic key of Q such that p = g/Q,h,n/. If there are no 1\`s among the last h-bits of Q then p = 0. In this case all n pages, including their lists of overflow pages, must be read and tested for qualification. In other words, the exhaustive search must be used. But if there are some bits with value "1" within the last h bits of Q, the number of accessed pages can be decreased.

For the sake of simplicity we will suppose now that $n = 2^h$. Let us further assume that there is just one bit with value "1" in the h-bit suffix of Q. Then the number of accessed pages can be reduced to 2^{h-1}. This means that 2^{h-1} primary page accesses can be saved. The reason is obvious because in general any h-bit binary integer with j bits having a fixed value, e.g. "1", can have at most 2^{h-j} integer values.

According to this we can say that if there is a query signature Q with j 1\`s in its h-bit suffix, h/Q/, it is enough to read only 2^{h-j} primary pages and their overflow areas instead of 2^h primary pages as well as all the overflow signatures of the file. In other words, since the number of possible h-bit binary integers with j fixed bit positions is 2^{h-j}, this is also the number of page characteristics the signatures of which can contain qualifying signatures. We can be sure that any other page as well as its overflow area cannot contain a qualifying signature, it is a signature with the j prespecified 1\`s in its h-bit suffix.

Actually, the pages with signatures which must be evaluated are not necessarily consecutive now. But they can be accessed in the increasing order of page number, starting with the page number g/Q,h,n/.No page with a smaller number can include a qualifying signature. That is why we call this processing the semi-consecutive processing.

We have restricted the range of pages with possible qualifying signatures to g/Q,h,n/ ÷ n. But as we have explained, we can skip some pages also in this range. Let P be an h-bit binary integer. Then to evaluate the query Q, assuming the number of primary pages is n and the level of the file is h, the following algorithm can be used.

Algorithm 1.

1. P := g/Q,h,n/
2. IF h/Q/ AND P IS h/Q/ then access the page P to match its signatures
3. P := P + 1
4. IF P < n THEN GOTO 2.

It is easy to understand that the number of accessed pages is proportional both to the level of the file h and to the query signature weight w/Q/. A more detailed analyses is the subject of the following section.

4.1. Performance analyses

Before we start we present together all the symbols which we are going to use. For convenience, they can be found in Table I.

Table I. Specification of symbols

Symbol	Specification
N	Number of signatures in the file
K_i	i-th key, signature, i = 1, 2, ... ,N
D_{bl}	The number of non-common words in a logical block
f	Signature size in bits
m	The number of bits that each non-common word sets to "1"
Q	Query signature
w/ /	Signature weight. The number of bits which are set to "1", $w/K_i/ = f/2$ for all i, m <= w/Q/ <= f/2
h	The file level, 0 <= h <= f
n	The number of addressable pages, $2^{h-1} < n <= 2^h$
S/h/	The number of addressable pages hashed with the level h
P/j/	The probability that exactly j bits with the value "1" appear in the h-bit suffix of the signature Q
h/Q/	h-bit suffix of Q
w/Q,h/	The weight of the h-bit suffix of signature Q
E/w/Q,h//	The expected number of bits with the value "1" in the h-bit suffix of the query signature Q
P/Q,h/	The probability of saving a primary page access
N/n,h,Q/	The total number of discarded primary page accesses

The main aim of this analyses is to try to understand the performance of the query evaluation for signatures organized under the LHSS scheme. We will take the exhaustive search of the LHSS file as the basis for comparison, since in this special case we have the least effective search. As we have shown, depending on the query Q, the file level h, the signature size f and the number of addressable pages n, not all pages must be accessed. For this reason an analytical formula for estimating the number of saved accesses will be derived in the following.

4.1.1. Performance estimation formulas

According to the procedure described above, the most important factor which reduces the number of page accesses is the weight of the h-bit suffix of query signature Q designated as w/Q,h/. That is why we are going to estimate the expected value of w/Q,h/ first. The expected value, E/w/Q,h//, can be computed as

$$E/w/Q,h// = \sum_{j=1}^{\min/h,w/Q//} j \cdot P/j/, \qquad /2/$$

where j is the number of bits with value "1" and P/j/ is the probability that in the h-bit suffix of Q are exactly j bits with the value "1". The value of j is changing from 1 to the minimum value of h and w/Q/. Since the bit positions with ones are generated by using a random number generator, the distribution of ones within a signature is for the individual non-common words uniform. Supposing that all the words in the query are different and functionally independent, this implies that any combination of ones is in a query equally probable. According to this:

$\binom{f}{w/Q/}$ is the total number of query signatures with the weight w/Q/,

$\binom{h}{j}$ is the number of possibilities of storing j ones in h bits,

$\binom{f-h}{w/Q/-j}$ is the number of combinations of w/Q/-j bits within f-h bits.

Then we can write the probability that j bits with value "1" appear in the h-bit suffix of the query signature Q, as

$$P/j/ = \frac{\binom{h}{j} \cdot \binom{f-h}{w/Q/-j}}{\binom{f}{w/Q/}} \qquad /3/$$

Another formula for estimating E/w/Q,h//, which is more suitable for computation and which can be derived from /2/ and /3/ is

$$E/w/Q,h// = \sum_{j=1}^{\min/h,w/Q//} j \cdot \prod_{i=1}^{j} \frac{/h-i+1/\cdot/w/Q/-i+1/}{i\cdot/f-w/Q/+i/} \cdot \prod_{i=1}^{w/Q/-j} \frac{f-h-i+1}{f-i+1} \qquad /4/$$

Let us now define the proportion of the number of storage locations generated by the Algorithm 1, provided the h-bit suffix of Q have E/w/Q,h// positions occupied by 1`s, to the total number of storage locations which can be produced by the suffix as the probability of access saving. Let us designate this probability as P/Q,h/. According to the definition, we can write

$$P/Q,h/ = 1 - \frac{1}{2^{E/w/Q,h//}} \qquad /5/$$

Now it is convenient to return to the description of linear hashing. As we mentioned in chapter 3, the number of addressable pages is related to the level of the file h. Namely, $2^{h-1} < n <= 2^h$. The value of n is also important for the hash function /1/ which in fact hashes some keys with the level h while the others with the level h-1. When $n = 2^h$, all the pages are

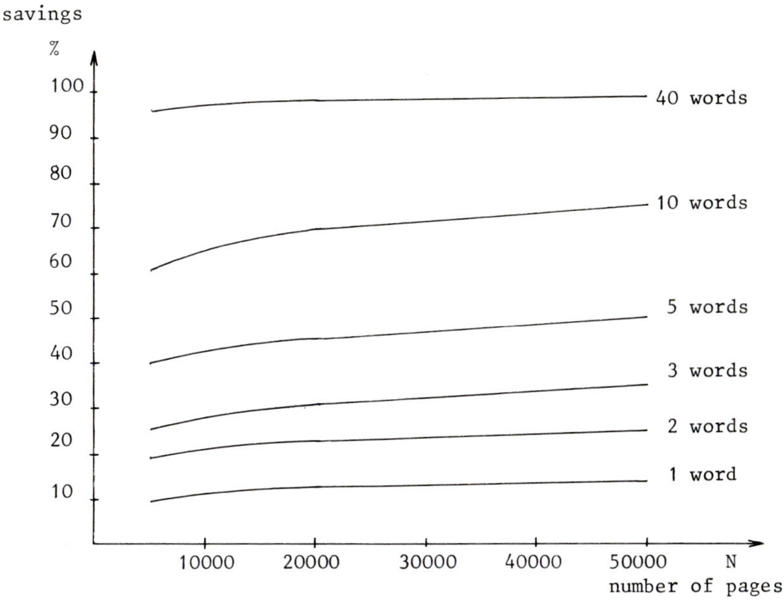

Figure 2. Percentage of savings, D_{bl} 40, f 600, m 10

hashed with the level h. But as soon as a new page is added, the level is increased and the new page, as well as the page number 0, are rehashed with the increased level. All the other pages remain to be hashed with the original level. In general, each extension of the file causes that one of the original pages determined by the pointer SP and the new page are filled with keys hashed with the increased level.

If there are n addressable pages, the number of pages hashed with the level h, designated as S/h/, can be computed as

$$S/h/ = 2n - 2^h, \qquad /6/$$

and the number of pages hashed with the level h-1 as

$$S/h-1/ = 2^h - n. \qquad /7/$$

Finaly, the total number of savings can be writen as

$$N/n,h,Q/ = S/h/\ P/Q,h/ + S/h-1/\ P/Q,h-1/. \qquad /8/$$

4.1.2. Performance evaluation

For our experiments we have chosen parameters which are typical for office environment. Actually, we use the same assumptions as in /4/. The most important one is the number of distinct words per a logical block $D_{bl} = 40$. Then according to /4/, m = 10 and f = 600.

To illustrate the performance of LHSS, we have decided to compute the savings, it is the number of discarded primary page accesses for files containing from 100 to 50000 pages of signatures. We express the savings as a percentage of the total number of addressable pages. The specific values can be found for different queries in Figure 2.

5. CONCLUSIONS

Under the above considerations, the LHSS seems to be a reasonable structure. Insertions and deletions can be handled easily because the file can grow or shrink linearly. Since the signature patterns are generated by using a random number generator, the distribution of 1`s and 0`s within the signatures is uniform. There are also not significant functional dependances among the individual block signatures because the common words are omitted and the number of words in a logical block is large. This makes signatures nearly ideal for LH. The expected overflow is low and as a consequence of this, exhaustive search is nearly as good as the exhaustive search of a sequential file. Moreover, LHSS can save a substantial number of accesses while the semi-consecutive processing of pages can still be preserved. As we can see from Figure 2, the percentage of discarded primary page accesses is dependent both on the size of the file and the number of words in a query, the query weight. In other words, the higher the weight and the size of the file the higher the percentage of discarded pages. Notice that this percentage does not depend on the distribution of document signatures. The non-uniform distribution of document signatures can increase the overflow but cannot change the number of discarded primary page accesses for a query.

These characteristics make the linear hashing for superimposed signatures the best method for organizing signatures in dynamic environment, because no other methods, attaining such or better processing characteristics, are known.

6. REFERENCES

/1/ Christodoulakis, S. and Faloutsos, C., Design Considerations for a Message File Server, IEEE Transactions on Software Engineering, Vol. SE-10, No.2, pp. 201-210, March 1984.

/2/ Christodoulakis, S., A Framework for the Development of a Mixed-Mode Message System for an Office Environment, Proc. 3rd ACM-BCS Symposium on Research and Development in IR, Cambridge, 1984.

/3/ Deppisch, U., S-Tree, Proc. of 1986-ACM Conference on Research and Development in IR, Pisa, Italy, 1986, pp. 77-87.

/4/ Faloutsos, C. and Christodoulakis, S., Signature files, ACM TOIS, Vol. 2, No. 4, October 1984, pp. 267-288.

/5/ Faloutsos, C. and Christodoulakis, S., Design of a Signature File Method that Accounts for Nonuniform Occurrence and Query Frequencies, Proc. of VLDB-85, Stockholm, Sweden, Sept. 1985.

/6/ Faloutsos, C., Integrated Access Methods for Message Using Signature File,Proc. of the IFIP Working Conference on Methods and Tools for Office Systems, Pisa, Italy, 1986, pp. 135-157.

/7/ Larson, P.A., Linear Hashing with Partial Expansions, Proc. of VLDB-80, Montreal, pp. 224-232.

/8/ Larson, P.A., Performance Analysis of a Single File Version of Linear Hashing, TR No. CS-83-28, University of Waterloo, 1983.

/9/ Litwin, W., Linear Hasing, Proc. of VLDB-80, Montreal, pp. 212-223.

/10/ Orenstein, J., A Dynamic Hash File for Random and Sequential Accessing, Proc. of VLDB-83, Florence, Italy, pp. 132-141.

/11/ Otoo, E.J., Symetric Dynamic Index Maintenance Scheme, Proc. of FODO-85 Kyoto, Japan, pp. 283-296.

/12/ Roberts,C., Partial Match Retrieval via the Method of Superimposed Codes, Proc. IEEE Vol.67,No.12, pp. 1624-1642, Dec. 1979.

/13/ Tsichritzis,D., Message Files, ACM TOIS Vol.1, No.1, pp. 88-98, 1983.

/14/ Tsichritzis,D., A Multimedia Office Filing System, VLDB-83,Italy,1983.

COMPUTER MESSAGING SYSTEMS

Network Information Processing Systems
K. Boyanov, R. Angelinov (Editors)
Elsevier Science Publishers B.V. (North-Holland)

A MESSAGE SYSTEM FOR THE OFFICE ENVIRONMENT

Frank Foersterling, Claus Sattler, Christine Tessmer

Academy of Sciences of the GDR
Institute of Informatics and Computing Technique
Berlin, GDR

In 1984 the CCITT confirmed the X.400 recommendation series for Message Handling Systems (MHS). But there was a gap between the X.400-model of the application layer and the application layer view of the ISO. The MHS model is under development to overcome some problems in integrating PC's as user agents. The paper gives an overview of a functional model and implementation aspects of a message system with an integrated message store and user agent functions related to office message handling tasks.

1. INTRODUCTION

Message handling as one of network applications in present is subject of many research and implementation work. In 1984 the CCITT confirmed the X.400 recommendation series for Message Handling Systems (MHS). But there was a gap between the X.400 model for the application layer, containing the Message Transfer and the User Agent Sublayers, and the ISO work on the structure of the application layer, based on Common and Specific Application Service Elements.

For comprising personal computers as user agents the functional MHS-model was expanded by a Message Store, capable for long-term storing of messages until their retrieval by the User Agent.

2. FUNCTIONAL MODEL

Personal computers in the office environment are used not only for message handling, but a lot of other office tasks, too. By using a PC with a single task operating system, the PC isn't able to receive messages all the time. Recognizing this problem, we developed a functional model (fig.1), containing User Agents (UA) and Message Transfer and Store Agents (MTSA). Because of the office needs the MTSA contains

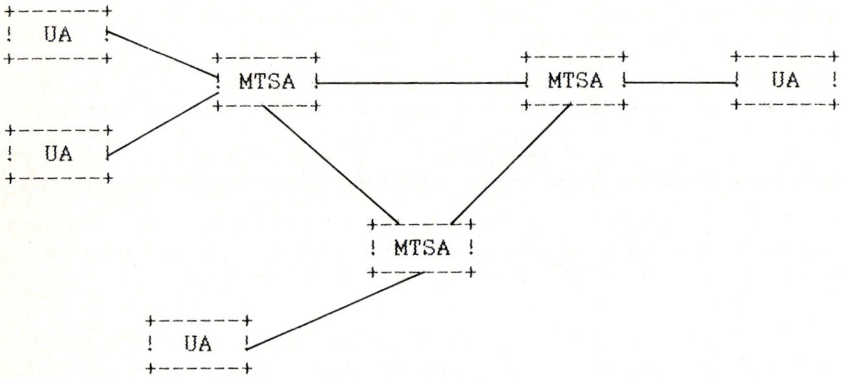

FIGURE 1
Functional Model

electronic archives functions, too. Although this may be not a object of standardization, we felt the close relation between the message transfer and store function and the message archives function. To send a message, a copy, usually, is put down in the electronic archives. The received message, or a copy, of such a message, usually, must be stored in the electronic archives, too. Because of the limited storage capacity of personal computers the archives function must be located outside the PC's.

So, in our system the MTSA contains a lot of storing objects. One of them is the mailbox, containing received messages. Other objects are classified boxes of the electronic archives. A special object is the input/output registration book. In our application it is related not to an individual user, but to an organizational unit with special access rights for its individual members.

The retrieval protocol contains the specification of the object (box), where the retrieval is to be performed.

In the submission protocol there is a possibility to specify objects of the electronic archives, in which a copy of the submitted message should be stored.

The entries of the input/output registration book are generated automatically.

Therefore, the UA-MTSA-protocol is not the standardized P3-protocol, but a special one. It contains a registration, submission and retrieval port with different attributes.

The registration part identifies the user agent in connection with a password. The individual rights can be set up and changed by the MTSA-manager. Only a password change can be done by the user.

The submission part contains as attributes the originator, a list of recipients, the submission date and time, the priority and a specification of delivery notification, and, in addition, a list of electronic archives objects, in which the submitted message is to be stored.

The retrieval part contains a specification of the storing object (box), and some filter attributes, e.g. the submission date and time interval, a list of recipients, the priority.

The UA-UA-protocol, which is comparable with the MHS P2-protocol, supports the cooperating UA, and is based on typical office mail forms, containing such attributes as original/copy specification, our/your sign, our/your journal number, your date and time, subject, and a list of notes. "Our sign" is the identifier of the UA submitted the message (not necessarily the originator, which in our system is treated as the authorized person), "Your journal number" is the entry number of the submitted message in the input/output registration book. "Your sign", "your journal number" and "your (submission) date and time" are reference attributes in answering messages. The idea behind the attribute "list of notes" is, in the case of forwarding or sending a copy, to add formalized notes, what is to do with the received message, e.g., give a comment, or answer, or for personal information, or to decide something.

The MTSA-MTSA-Protocol will be implemented in the standard MHS-P1 manner.

3. IMPLEMENTATION ASPECTS

At present the UA functionality is implemented on a 8-bit PC connected to a LAN via a transport station (fig. 2). The application protocols use the transport interface directly. This is caused by the limited main storage of the 8-bit PC's. The user interface of the UA is a menu-driven interface, including the call of and return from a Wordstar compatible text processor for preparing messages. It includes a simple line-oriented editor for short messages, too. It supports the creation and the maintenance of distribution lists stored on the local PC, and a lot of activities for answering and forwarding messages.

The MTSA functionality is implemented on a 16-bit PC under a UNIX-compatible operating system.

It contains a specialized message file system supporting the

```
  8-bit PC                 8-bit PC                  16-bit PC
 +--------+               +---------+               +----------+
 !  UA    !               !  UA     !               !  MTSA    !
 +--------+               +---------+               +----------+
      !                        !                         !
      !                        !                    +----------+
      !                        !                    !          !
      !                        !                    +----------+
      !                        !                         !
+-------------------------------------------------------------+
                     !
              +------------+
              !  Gateway   !-----
              +------------+     /
                              /-----> X.25
```

FIGURE 2
Physical Structure

organization of the storing objects and the access to them, but also the organization of a simple management information base.

The application manager of the MTSA can use a menu-driven interface with a lot of functions for maintaining organizational units, its members and the access rights, and for controlling the MTSA activities.

Network Information Processing Systems
K. Boyanov, R. Angelinov (Editors)
Elsevier Science Publishers B.V. (North-Holland)

INTELLIGENT MESSAGES or When Messages Come Alive.

Per Wiggo Richardsen[*] & *Thore Danielsen*[†]

[*] *FORUT, P.O. Box 2806, Elverhøy, N-9001 Tromsø, NORWAY, tel.: +47 83 80150, ean: per-wiggo-richardsen @ forut.uit.uninett*

[†] *Computer Science Department, University of Tromsø, P.O. Box 953, N-9001 Tromsø, NORWAY, tel.: +47 83 44040, ean: thore-danielsen @ df.uit.uninett*

This paper deals with the concepts of *active* and *intelligent* messages. Messaging systems have been around long enough for us to consider them as being less than our own visions some years ago. What they have made us do, is to start rethinking the notion of required functionality - *what the user (should) want.* A description of these needs and visions supports a redefinition of the concept *messages.*

1. INTRODUCTION.

Electronic communication plays a particular important part in our way of communicating. A steadily increasing number of messaging systems are introduced and in daily use all over the world, and interferes with most every social aspect of our lives. But all these messaging system are rather imperfect systems!

At this stage, maybe we should moderate our statement and describe the existing systems as not as good as they could be. The systems of today are based on messages as passive objects. In these systems it is possible to perform operations on the message, but it is not possible for the message itself to initiate and manage operations.

We would here like to discuss the effects of changing messages into objects which may operate themself. Such a change of the message paradigm would make the message play a more important role in the communication process. In this context, we would like to describe:

- messages as living objects
- messages as communication partners
- messages as their own guide
- messages which make their own decisions
- messages as a support for the receiver

Such a communication will reduce todays messaging problems and make electronic messaging systems more like face to face communication, and enhance the service made available to the communication partners.

2. THE MESSAGE CONCEPT OR VANILLA MESSAGES.

Todays messaging systems use what we refer to as ordinary (vanilla flavour) messages. An ordinary message includes a content, an envelope and a set of parameters. The parameters are given as both contentheading-parameters and envelope-parameters. For instance, the sender and the receiver of a message are given as such parameters. The content embodies the information which the sender wants to pass to the receiver.

The Message Content

Some of the existing systems include a bit more. For instance, the EAN implementation of the CCITT's X.400 standard includes contentheading-parameters: receiver(s) of "carbon copy", the message subject, the importance of the message subject a.s.o. This implementation also support sorting of messages into folders.

Message inbox: 32 - Read
From: Thore Danielsen <thore@xps.gmd.dfn>
To: <dfpr@hugin.uit.uninett> [confirm]
Importance: high
Subject: IFIP-paper

Everything OK!
Our work is accepted by IFIP.
Well done!

See you later.

A message in the ean MHS-implementation.

The next version of the X.400 standard will include both some group communication services and directory services. Some of the existing implementations offer both facilities already. But even though, use of ordinary messages is just an electronic way of handling short notices!

The presentation of the X.400 standard describes the services which may be provided as simple and straightforward to learn and to use. It is an electronic mail service built upon the same principles as yellow mail. And it is really simple. It is communication using passive or ordinary messages.

3. ACTIVE MESSAGES.

An ordinary message is, as we have described it, a passive object, a notice handed from the sender to the mail system and eventually from the mail system to the receiver. An active message is something more. It:

- is a living object
- has a restricted self-determination
- is allowed to make its own decisions
- is allowed to have children
- has knowledge regarding its own family

An Active Message

3.1. RESPONSE - ROUTING.

An ordinary message is not allowed to visit other receivers than the addressee(s), including distribution list. The active message itself may accept the response/answer from the receiver. Depending upon the response, the active message itself may choose a new route, either back to its own creator or to another receiver. We will bring an example below.

3.2. MESSAGE CONTENT.

The message content is a set of guidelines and questions. Among the pure informative constructs (e.g. plain sentences) there exist a set of questions which the message itself is aware of. The questions are presented to the receiver by the message itself, and the message collects and stores the answers.

The guidelines, which is the second, important part of an active message content, define the continuation of the conversation. The guidelines define which information-part and which questions are the next to be raised, depending upon the answer the receiver just gave.

3.3. From ordinary to active message.

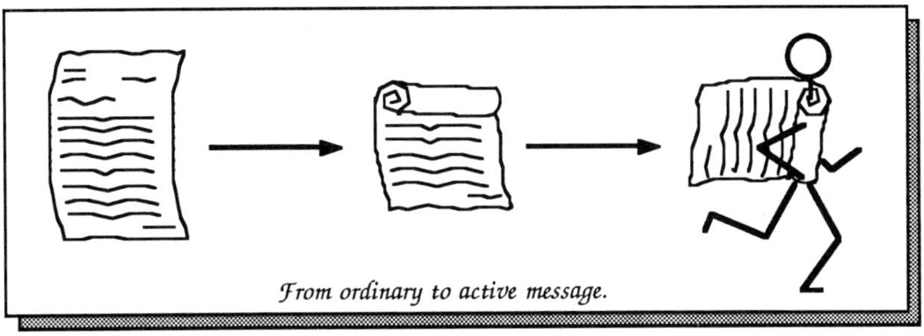

From ordinary to active message.

As described above, an ordinary message is a passive object. Messaging systems using ordinary messages is an electronic way of handing over notices between the partners in the communication process. Contrary, the active message is a living object. It is not only a content and an envelope which the courier delivers, it is the courier itself. While the ordinary message is a static set of sentences, the active message is a dynamic set of information and questions. Reading an active message is like running a computer program. The performance of a computer program may depend on the input from the user. In a similar way, the active message depends on the answer(s) from the receiver.

Distribution of an ordinary message depends upon the listed receiver or on the receivers listed in a distribution list. The use of active messages allow a dynamic routing either in a parallel or sequential order.

3.4. When to use an active message.

In our opinion, there is no question of designing a system supporting ordinary or designing a system supporting active messages. We need the availability of both in any system. Depending upon the application, the user choose either an ordinary or an active messages. These three examples should show the need for active messages:

1 a connected set of different questions
  1.1 depending upon the answer, the further traversal is defined
2 date-planning
  2.1 a set of possible/not possible dates
  2.2 the active message selects one date frome the final, possible set
3 shopping list
  3.1 including a set of what has the highest priority
  3.2 including a set of what has second priority

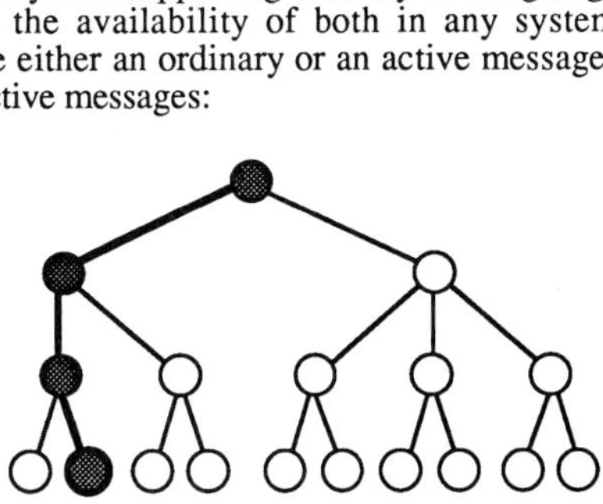

3.5. Active message - an example.

The figure below shows an example of an active messages using problem type 1 - a connected set of questions. The generator of the conversation has bought 8 tickets for a consert. He wants to distribute both information of the concert and announce for sale the tickets he has left.

Distribution of tickets for the "Rotten Ronalds" concert

(1)

This is an inquiry about 'Rotten Ronalds' concert. Do you want to answer now?
I am sorry, not yet.
OK, but don't forget to answer. Deadline is Monday at 10.00 a.m.

The sender receives a message which indicates that the receiver doesn't want to be disturbed

(2)

The 'Rotten Ronalds' concert.
I have bought 8 tickets, but I just want to use 1 of them by myself. Are you interested?
Yes, of course.
How many tickets do you need?
Two - 2 - tickets.
OK, they are yours. Do you know if somebody else of the gang want tickets?
Willy Brandt, I suppose.
I'll send a message for him.

- next one to be reached is Willy Brandt
- tickets to be distributed are reduced from 7 to 5
- when no tickets are left, the active message terminates and returns to the original sender.

(3)

The 'Rotten Ronalds' concert.
These have reserved tickets.
- *Gro Harlem Brundtland: 2*
- *Willy Brandt: 2*
- *Margaret Thatcher: 1*
- *Georges Mitterand: 2*

4. THE QUEST FOR INTELLIGENCE IN MESSAGING SYSTEMS.

So far we have considered the notion of enhancing the user services in a messaging system by introducing the active messages, messages which carry a description of a set of actions they perform themselves. The actions discussed so far have been more or less simple logic descriptions, e.g. await user becoming active maximum 4 hours & if not then return to sender. All these logic expressions interrogate simple status variables of the communicators, the users of the message system(s). In addition, these expressions have to be given by the initiating user in an algorithmicly correct manner - they may be visualized as a set of orders performed by the message.

Actions given in messages is then the users way of expressing parts of the knowledge s/he has or would like to establish through communicating. When designing message systems there have been, maybe not too consciously, attempts at grouping the message objects into entities suiting the users needs. Examples are meetings/conferences and distribution lists. These are mainly a shot at defining topics which might be dealt with during conversation. Our claim is that the imaginative and creative mind does not only deal with topics.

When communicating, the human being would normally - if actively interested - search through her/his vast memory for all pieces of information relevant to the discussion. So why not use the same method in any computer-supported communication as in face to face communication. Truth is, that a steadily increasing number of personal workstations are employed. Most users of such workstations try to collect most of their machine-readable information either on the workstation or on a server permanently connected to the workstation. Frequently, we recognize the concept of integrating the user's applications, or at least: some applications allows for fetching information from other applications. Lots of the information which could play a part in any information process, this means information which give rise to *associations* with information exchanged through the communication, is available. The problem reduces to a problem of establishing the right links, i.e. *making the associations*, and utilizing the pieces of information in the right manner, i.e. *acting intelligently*. This means taking advantage of the users *knowledge on communication.*

Once the knowledge on communication have been recognized, we may be able to establish a knowledge base integrated with all of the users information bases. With knowledge on communication we refer to the questions what, how, when and why regarding exchanged message objects and stored information objects. In short, the concepts understood by the user and the relations of these concepts are stored in a structure which is manipulated by a set of methods and/or rules which embodies the startegic knowledge of the user. This strategic knowledge covers the users understanding on how to utilize the concepts and the concepts' relations in the process of making the appropriate associations and, on such a basis, how to generate information from information.

This should give a "layout" description on what we expect to find by studying general communication processes.

5. INTELLIGENT MESSAGES.

An active message is a living object - a living being. An intelligent message is a living being too, but it is a living being of higher rank. Both kind of messages are able to make their own decisions and to work out an answer-dependent communication. In addition, the intelligent message is able to make associations (see above) on behalf of the receiver - prior to involving the receiver in the process. It is able to build references to related communication processes, as background information, and to stored litterature or alternative information.

Introducing intelligent messages is introducing objects which operate themselves. An ordinary message will be operated, an active message is able to operate itself in a restricted way, and an intelligent message is operating by itself and brings the electronic communication closer to a face to face communication process. This enhancment of the services provided to the users of a messaging system is important.

Each communication partner may be a member of several communication prosesses. It indicates that s/he is a receiver of a lot of different messages. If (as an example) communication prosess A is archived in a "red box", an intelligent message in this process will make it possible for the receiver to get relations to the "red box" and to the interesting information in this "red box". During the communication between the receiver and the intelligent messages, each intelligent message will select the appropriate parts of information and guide the receiver during her/his decision processes.

The intelligent message is able to:
- give a presentation/summary of earlier communication.
- give basis information about the subject of the communication.
- select interesting information during the internal communication.
- be the receivers guide while making up her/his mind.
- list possible solutions and vote for the best.

5.1. From active to intelligent messages.

The main difference is:

- an active message interrogates the receiver
- an intelligent message interrogates the receiver´s informationbase and archives prior to interrogating the receiver

An inteligent message is able to extract the appropriate information from the available sources, in order to releave the receiver of some tasks - prior the communication.

In this paper the receiver is a human being, an ordinary human being and no expert. S/he has some books in a personal library, s/he has a collection of records and so on... The information exchanged during different communication prosesses is archived, and it is possible for an intelligent message to extract information from these archives and from the informationbases as for example the library´s titles.

Intelligent messages will make it less difficult for the receiver to make its her/his decisions. The intelligent message will, based on the information the receiver itself has produced and the informationbase, produce a set of solutions and vote for one of those.

5.2. When to use an intelligent Message?

There is no choice between providing either intelligent or ordinary messages. A messaging system must support both ordinary, active and intelligent messages. The active messages are a supplement for the ordinary messages. The intelligent messages are a supplement for the both.

If background information is to prefer, intelligent messages is the first choice. But there are also a set of other applications were we envisage increased functionality by the use of intelligent messages. A lot of reports are produced as a team-work by a set of authors. An intelligent message is able to collect, produce headings and summarize the complete report. Another application is control management. During a lot of communication processes, a previous communication is mentioned. If for example a copy for Mr X is forgotten, the message itself will recognize the fault (missing information) and produce a copy for him.

Intelligent messages may be difficult to generate. One solution may be that the intelligent message itself is a part of a team generating another message in cooperation with the sender. If a scheme has to be produced, the intelligent message can propose another scheme used in another communication process as a template. Or if an intelligent message content is a large set of questions, the intelligent message itself will check if any answer will cause bugs.

Finally it is possible for the message to detect faults. If it is impossible to reach a receiver, either because of a node failure or because the receiver stays inactive for a longer period of time, the intelligent message itself will check out the reason why.

So when to use intelligent messages?

- everywhere when background information is to prefer
- during report generation
- when we have a well-known model
- when fault(s) is (are) discovered

5.3. Intelligent messages - an example.

Let us return to the example of distributing concert tickets. The use of intelligent messages as a supplement for active messages makes it possible to give the receiver information about "Rotten Ronald", selected from the receiver´s information base. It is also possible to help the receiver to make up his mind using information from the same base and from his answers.

Another solution to distribution of tickets.

(4) *The 'Rotten Ronalds' concert. I have 8 tickets for the concert, and I just want to use one of them myself. Are you interested in some of the leftover tickets?*

In case no is the answer: The sender receives a message which indicates that the receiver does not want to be disturbed.

(5) *If you don't know what to do, I may help you. Among your LPs I have recognized 'Rotten Ronalds' two latest recordings: 'Rotten Eggs for the Prime Minister' (PZ 52) and 'The Rotten Rats and Father Christmas' (PZ 53). I have also found the 'Rotten Ronalds' biography: 'How to become a Rotten Star.'*
If you still don't know what to do, just one more argument: When you were 17 years old, you visited 'Rotten Ronalds' first concert in Europe!

If the recipient need help to make up her/his mind, the intelligent message may vote for one solution.

(6)

Meetings together with the sticking doctors?	**** DROP*
Dinner together with the Prime Minister of Finland?	**** DROP*
The 'Rotten Ronalds' concert?	**** GO-FOR-IT! ****

5.4. REQUIREMENTS AND PROBLEMS.

There is always at least one "but"... We have mentioned two: requirements and problems. Such a system - a messaging system providing intelligent messages - have to be a system for ordinary users. This implies that the interface between the message and the user plays a very important role. Users may come from rather different cultures. Everything which is more powerful may in some situations increase danger and initiate faults. The intelligent message itself interrogates the receivers informationbase(s), and strict rules governing such access have to be supplied by the user acting receiver. Information acting as "mail bombs" have to be stopped before reaching the information base.

Both an active and an intelligent message is allowed to have children - give birth to new messages. This hierarchy of messages has to be kept under control. The parent message should always have the relevant information on all children, and deletion of a parent message should affect all child messages as well. This has to be done in order to prevent the uprising of an anarchy of messages.

6. CONCLUSIONS.

What we aimed at describing in this paper, was that the process of diminishing the shortcomings in functionality of the message systems of today requieres a redefinition of the concept messages. We have shown that through formalizing the set of operations on messages which a user normally would perform, and thereby making it possible to define a representation scheme for such operations available for the communicating processes embodying the message system, we could use the message themselves not only as a carrier of the description of functions to be performed, but also as the entity initiating and performing the functions.

We would stress that this discussion is more a description of a future research direction than any description of implementation. The process of gathering more sound and basic knowledge on general communication processes has been started. When this is achieved, we should be able to find a suitable representation scheme. Only then may the ideas be realized.

An introduction of intelligent messages will put electronic communication closer to a face to face communication:

- the information will be of better quality
- the information will be supported
- the information will be close to complete

Acknowledgements.
Thanks to the members of the AMIGO Advanced Group (project sponsored by COST 11 ter) and to John Churcher and John Bowers of the COSMOS project (part of the Alvey action programme). Last, but not least, thanks to Frode and Truls for being there.

References

[Aiello84] *Modeling the Office Structure: A First Step towards the Office Expert System.* Luigia Aiello, Daniel Nardi, Maurizio Panti, ACM - Office Information Systems.

[AMIGO87] *AMIGO Group Communication Model for a Computer-Based Communication Environment.* ed.: Thore Danielsen, Uta Pankoke-Babatz et. al. <to be publ.>

[Brotz83] *Message Systems Mores: Etiquette in Laurel.* Douglas K. Brotz, ACM - Transactions on Office Information Systems, vol. 1 no. 2, April 1983.

[Bundy84] *Intelligent Front Ends.* Alan Bundy, pp 193 - 203 in: Research and Development in Expert Systems, ed. M.A. Brahmer.

[Byrd80] *Intelligent Forms Creation in the Systems for Business Automation.* Roy J. Byrd, Peter de Jong, IBM T.J. Watson Research Centre.

[Chi82] *Advances in Computer Mass Storage Technology.* Chao S. Chi, IEEE Computer, 15 (5) pp. 60 - 74, May 1982.

[Danielsen86] *The AMIGO Project: Advanced Group Communication Model for Computer-Based Communications Environment.* Danielsen, Pankoke-Babatz et. al. CSCW'86: Conference on Computer-Supported Cooperative Work, Austin, USA, Dec. 1986.

[Danielsen87a] *Relation and Inheritance in Group Communication.* T. Danielsen, T.Folkow, P.W. Richardsen, IFIP 6.5 Intl. Working Conference on Message Handling Systems, München, Fed. Rep. of Germany, April 1987.

[Darden87] *Viewing the History of Science as Compiled Hindsight.* Lindley Darden, AI Magazine, vol. 8 no. 2, 1987.

[Dretske81] *Knowledge and the Flow of Information.* Fred I. Dretske.

[Fikes81] *Odyssey:A Knowledge-Based Assistant.* Richard E. Fikes,Artificial Intelligence,no. 16,1981.

[Good81] *Etude and Folklore of User Interface Design.* Michael Good. Proceedings of the ACM Sigplan Sigoa Symposium on Text Manipulation.

[Hofstadter81] *The Mind's I.* Douglas R. Hofstadter, Daniel C. Dennet, Harvester Press Ltd. 1981.

[Hogg83] *Imail: An Intelligent Mail System.* John Hogg, Murray Mazer, et. al. IEEE Database Engineering, vol. 6 no. 3, September 1983.

[Hogg84a] *An Active Mail System.* John Hogg, Stelios Gamvroulas, Sigmond 1984 Proceedings.

[Hogg84b] *Intelligent Message Systems.* John Hogg, Computer Systems Research Group, Univ. of Toronto.

[Holland86] *Electronic Mail - Future Directions.* Lydia Holland, Computer Communications, vol. 9 no. 2, April 1986.

[Hæmmæin86] *Intelligent Forms, Intelligent Mail and Distribution.* Heikki Hæmmæin, Reijo Sulonen, Laboratory of Information Processing Science, Helsinki.

[Ottery86a] *Benefits of the X.400 Protocol.* Tony Ottery, Sydnes Ltd., London.

[Ottery86b] *How X.400 Works.* Tony Ottery, Peter Westwood, Sydnes Ltd., London.

[Padgham86] *LINKC: Linkøpings Intelligent Knowledge Communication System.* Lin Padgham, IFIP - Office Systems: Methods and Tools, 1986.

[Prinz86] *Office Automation and Group Communication Systems.* Wolfgang Prinz, AMIGO Working Document, 1986.

[Richardsen87] *From Electronic Mail to Intelligent Message Systems.* Per Wiggo Richardsen, thesis for the degree of cand. scient., University of Tromsø, April 1987. (in Norwegian).

[Tsichritzis84] *Message Addressing Schemes.* Dionysios Tsichritzis, ACM - Transactions on Office Information Systems, vo. 2 no. 1., pp. 58 -87, January 1984.

[Tsichritzis85] *Office Automation.* Dionysios Tsichritzis, Springer 1985.

[Vittal81] *Active Message Processing: Messages as Messengers.* John Vittal, Bolt Beranek and Newman Inc., Cambridge.

Network Information Processing Systems
K. Boyanov, R. Angelinov (Editors)
Elsevier Science Publishers B.V. (North-Holland)

A JOB SUBMISSION SERVICE WITHIN THE MESSAGE HANDLING SYSTEM

S. AL BADINE *C. KINTZIG* *M. OKOKO*

CNET/PAA/TIM
38,40 rue du Général Leclerc
92131 Issy-Les-Moulineaux

Abstract

In 1984, the International Telegraph and Telephone Consultative Committee (CCITT) issued a set of recommendations, the X400 series, defining standards to interconnect electronic mail systems throughout the world. The purpose of the Message Handling System (MHS), subject of X400 standards, is to provide capability for a user-defined message of any content to be transparently encapsulated within a standard envelope for subsequent delivery to any defined electronic mail destination. The X420 [1] standard defines the InterPersonal Messaging as one application of the Message Handling System. In 1985 Architel, which is in charge of promoting international standards in France, initiated work on a new messaging application: Soumission de Travaux en Mode Messagerie (STMM), which will offer job submission services in the MHS context. This paper gives an overview of this new messaging application.

1 INTRODUCTION :

Users of computing systems have a wide range of information processing applications that need the use of various resources for computing, data storage, data communications as well as data input and output. It is hard for the user to have all needed resources (very fast processors, rapid high quality printers, large storage capacity, etc.) provided by his local system only.

Thus user, especially one belonging to research communities,needs frequently the use of some vital resource on some system, and preferably with a minimal technical knowlege about that system. In order to meet these needs some facilities are provided by some computer networks; Remote Command Execution (a special case of which is Remote Job Execution) is an example. These facilities which partially meet user needs are system and network dependant (HASP (IBM), UUX (Unix), etc.).

Some standardizing activities concerning Job Transfer and Manipulation (JTM) [2] within the scope of Open System Interconnection (OSI) [3], have been initiated by ISO/TC97. The notion of *job* introduced by JTM comprises all the activities related to some specific and self-contained information processing requirement. JTM assures only a transparent transfer of documents between open systems along with control information related to these documents and offers monitoring and manipulation facilities of the job. JTM considers out of its scope the modelling of the processing concept and the standardization of a system command language which means that user must know the remote system features.

STMM proposes another approach to provide job submission and execution services based on message transfer services provided by the Message Transfer System (MTS) of the MHS. STMM in no way attempts to replace JTM, rather it suggests simple, performant, protocole providing job submission services that meet frequent user needs with a minimal investment cost and a reduced implementation effort due to the use of MTS.

Shortcomings due to the use of MTS connectionless-transfer services (delays, absence of on-line monitoring functions) can be counterbalanced by architecture simplicity and overheads minimization of connection-oriented communications (frequent handskakings, processing handshakes and holding connection state in memory).

STMM will offer *query*, *work submission and execution* and *work progress notifications* services on open systems supporting X411 conforming MTS [4]. This paper first presents the STMM model and the Unified Operating System concept (UOS), which is an STMM users environment virtualizing an operating system that supports job submission and execution. Next, service elements and the protocole used to provide them are described. A full description of the protocole is given in appendix I and a job submission example is given in appendix II.

2 STMM MODEL

2.1 FUNCTIONAL VIEW

STMM users are *submitters* and *executers* and may be people or processes. Submitter is one who submits a job on his local system to be transferred and executed on one (many) remote(s) system(s). Executer(s) is(are) person(s) on whose behalf the job execution(s) on the remote(s) system(s) is(are) achieved. The *job results* are sent back to the submitter from the remote(s) system(s).

To the MTS the submitters and the executeurs are originators and recipients of messages. The *broadcasting* feature inherent to the MTS is used by STMM. It allows the submitter to send *a* job to one or many executers. This might be intersting in some applications like updating a multiple copy distributed date base. In the following we consider the case of *one* executer.

For a job execution to take place on a remote system, the executer who is one user of the remote system, must *allow* the submitter and *determine an execution environment* for him on the system. The job is executed on the remote system in the environment determined by the executeur and under his responsability.

Each STMM user is associated with a *user agent* which is functionally distinct from the one attached to the IPM user. This STMM user agent is termed Job Submit User Agent (JSUA). The JSUA belonging to the submitter (termed JSUA-S in the following), comprises all the functions of preparing, storing and sending *job specification.* It contains also functions of receiving and presenting execution results and execution progress notifications. The JSUA belonging to the executer (termed JSUA-E in the following), comprises all the functions of receiving and executing jobs, sending notifications of job execution progress, sending results back to the submitter and informing its user on the job done on his behalf. Local functions supported by STMM JSUA such as journaling, displaying and manipulation job requests are not described. The functional components of STMM model are presented in figure 1. A layered description of STMM is presented in figure 2.

2.2 JOB, RESULT AND NOTIFICATION NOTIONS

Two kinds of **job**, are distinguished, *query* and *work*.
Query allows the JSUA-S to verify the possibility of a future work execution (recipient existance, execution permission in a certain environment) before sending an important work.
Work is composed of :

- user reference,
- destination data,
- work attributes,

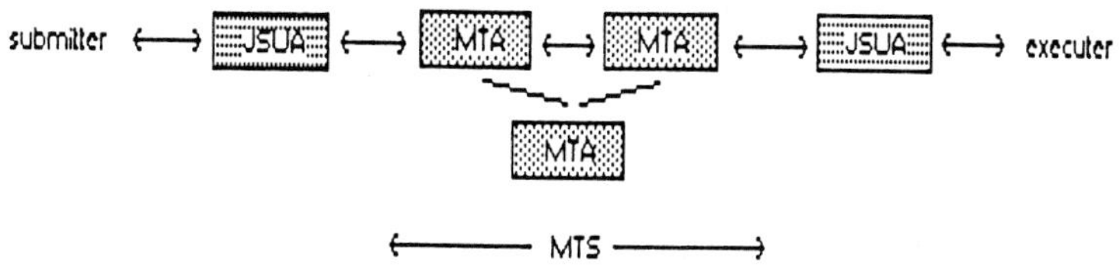

MTS : Message Transfer System
MTA : Message Transfer Agent
JSUA : Job Submit User Agent

Fig. 1 : STMM functional model

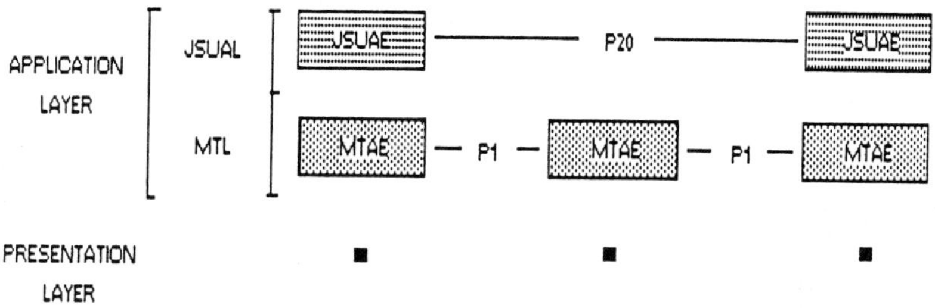

MTL : Message Transfer Layer
MTAE : Message Transfer Agent Entity
JSUAL : Job Submit User Agent Layer
JSUAE : Job Submit User Agent Entity
P1 : Message Transfer Protocol
P20 : STMM Protocol

Fig. 2 : Layered description of STMM model

- transferred files,
- commands.

User reference is a name given by the user that he subsequently uses to refer to a work, results and notifications.
destination data comprise executer name, execution environment name and a brief message to the executer.
work attributes comprise execution priority, execution date and obsolete date.
transferred files are,

- files to be transferred from the submission environment (JSUA-S) to the execution environment (JSUA-E),
- files to be transferred from the execution environment to the submission one once the work execution terminated.

commands are the commands to be executed on the execution system. They belong to the unified operating system command language.

Job execution result reports on query or work. Query result comprises the execution permission verification result. Work result can be positive or negative,

A **negative work result** comprises :
- user reference given to the submitted work,
- problem encountered (execution permission denied, obsolete work,maximum processor time exceeded, file transfer problem).

A **positive work result** comprises :
- user reference,
- result attributes (work execution status, cost, execution start time, execution termination time),
- commands execution results (status, UOS response message),
- files.

Notification is the means by which the submitter follows the progress of the work execution. When specifying a work, the submitter may ask for some commands execution notifications to be sent to him. When the execution of the *referenced* command is initiated, a notification comprising the command reference and execution start time is sent to the submitter.

2.3 UNIFIED OPERATING SYSTEM

In keeping with the goal of OSI to minimize the amount of technical knowledge about a system that one needs before comminucating with it, STMM must establish a common model for the processing concept on different systems to meet job submission requirements. The model used by STMM is called Unified Operating System (UOS). For uniformity reasons this model applies to both JSUA-S and JSUA-E. This means that both submitters and executers when interacting with their JSUAs have the impression to deal with a virtual operating system which is the STMM services provider.

In a job submission process three major requirements can be distinguished :
- . file transfer between submission and execution systems (input and output data),
- . execution system resources manipulation,
- . execution of commands that manipulate files and resources.

To meet these requirements the UOS model defines three concepts: *files*, *resources* and *commandes*.
These three concepts are defined through the presentation of the UOS three functional components : *JS* (Job Scheduler), *UFMS* (File Management System) and *URMS* (Resource Management System). Note that when UOS models the JSUA-E it comprises just two functional components JS and UFMS.

1) JS

This UOS component has in a JSUA-S the following functions:
- structuring and sending work specification in a submission environment,
- informing the user of work execution progress notifications received,
- informing the user of work execution result received.

In a JSUA-E, JS contains the following functions :
- access control and execution environment establishment,
- UOS commandes interpretation,
- reporting on work progress,
- sending work execution result,

A work execution is defined to be a sequential execution of UOS commands,
A UOS command is composed of :

- a name,
- arguments,
- attributes,

Name indicates the type of the command (file creation, resource acquisition, printing ..), Arguments can be files, resources or character strings,
Attributes are :

- a command reference given by the submitter that is used in the notification,
- a sequencing attribute that can be *aborting* or *non-aborting*, an erroneous execution of an aborting command terminates the work,
- paralleled processing attribute which indicates the possibility of the command parallel executions in respect to other commands.

Recognizing that the definition of a complete set of UOS commands demands an important effort [6], STMM defined a few numbers of them that can be used in a first implementation (appendix I). A more complete set of commands will be supported in a future extension.

2) UFMS

The need to transfer files between heterogeneous systems and their manipulation in the job submission process, has led to the definition of a virtual file management system, called Unified File Management System (UFMS).

UFMS defines :

- a model for file system organization called Unified File System (UFS),
- operations on file system objects.

A UFS file is defined to be a named collection of information. A UFS file system is a tree structure in which files are leaves. A UFS directory is a node in the ufs file system tree structure. It references files or other directories. A directory in the UOS model is considered to be a special kind of file. A UFS file or directory referenced by a directory is said to be contained in that directory. A UFS name is a sequence of directory names terminated by a file name. The UFS name has two types : submission and execution ufs names. The first one references a file in the submission environment while the second references it in the execution environment.

A UFS file is composed of :

- UFS name,
- File attributes (creation, last access and modification dates)
- contents (T73,text-lines, binary)

Other contents may be supported in future extensions.

Operations on UFS file system objects defined in the present STMM draft are files operations, other operations (directory operations) will be supported in future extensions. These operations include create,write,read,delete,availability and ufs names mapping operations.

3) URMS :

Resources in a computing system can be either *consumable* or *usable.*
Consumable resources are generally resources necessary to computing process (cpu times,memories ..).
Usable resources are used by the system commands (printers, tapes ..).

URMS defines :

- a model for usable resources designation called URS,
- operations that manipulate resources (acquisition,attachement ..).

A resource designation contains :

- resource type,
- resource name,
- resource attributes.

resource type indicates the nature of the resource (tape, disk, printer ..).
resource name is the resource local name.
Resource attributes define the physical features of the resource (tape density, impression speed, etc.).

Operations defined on resources comprise acquisition, liberation, attachement and detachement of resources. Other operation may be defined in future extensions.

3 OVERVIEW OF STMM SERVICES

In the following an overview of STMM services offered to both submitters and executers.

3.1 JSUS-S SERVICES:

STMM services offered to submitters through their JSUA-Ss are,

job specification (work and query): This contains the following service elements (only the first two concern query job) :

- **user job reference**
- **access list(s) name(s):** is(are) the name(s) of the execution environment. An access list playszs a role in authenticating and authorizing STMM submitters,
- **File Transfer from JSUA-S to JSUA-E:** are UFS names of files to be transferred within the work specification and that will be used as input data. User can optionally specify the UFS names of target files on the execution system and whether or not to erase these files from the execution system once the work execution terminated.
- **File transfer from JSUA-E to JSUA-S:** are UFS names of files to be transferred within the result and whether or not to remove these files from the execution system.
- **comments:** to be sent to the executer after a work execution.
- **execution start date**
- **obsolete date**
- **commands specifications**
- **execution priority**

Notification:

- **work progress indications:** are sent to submitter when execution of the referenced commands is initiated.

positive work result: It contains the following service elements:

- **work execution status**
- **commands execution results**
- **File transfer:** Files effectively transferred from JSUA-E to JSUA-S or problems preventing the transfer.
- **date at which job execution started**
- **execution termination date**
- **charges:** execution cost. Considering billing a local matter, STMM offers the service of conveying it to the submitter as logical points.

query result:

- **authorisation indication**

negative work result:

- **error indication:** this service element informs the submitter of either the submission failure (file trsnsfer problem, MTS problem) or the execution failure (file transfer problem, permission denial,obsolete work).

3.2 JSUA-E SERVICES

STMM services offered to executers throurgh their JSUA-Es are,

access lists: they define the execution environments. Each list contains many execution environments (one per submitter), so a submitter can have one or more environments , but just one environmnet in a list. The environment execution comprise : submitter O/R name, base directory (all execution UFS names are referenced by it), cpu maximum time allowed. These access lists play a role in authenticating and authorizing STMM submitters.

work execution information It contains the following service elements:

- **comments indication:** comments sent by the submitter within the job
- **execution work status**
- **charges**
- **UOS general informations:** these might be resources acquired by the submitter during the execution.

4 STMM PROTOCOLE

In order to provide STMM services to users (submitters and executers), JSUAEs cooperate with each other through P20 protocol. This protocol is (as P2 [1]) a content-specific protocol; that is, it defines a standardized message content structure. The STMM protocole has transactional features. Sending jobs, queries, notification can be considered as transactions or operations. In fact the JSUA-S entity sends work or query opertrations to JSUA-E which performs them and sent the outcome. During the execution of the operation JSUA-E can send notification operation to the JSUA-E without waiting for an outcome. So the specification of P20 protocol uses the concept of remote operation and remote errors defined in X410 [6] (remote operation server). In other terms, remote operation data units encapsulate P20-data-structures and it is these data units that form the p1-message content. Appendix I contains a full description of STMM protocole that uses the presentation transfer syntax and notation [7].

5 CONCLUSION

A technical notice describing STMM model, services and protocol is issued by Centre National d'Etude de Telecommunication in France in july 1986 [8]. A first implementation of this protocole in an X25-Based Local Network (SMARTIX) [9] that supports an X400-conforming Message Transfer System, will be available on a UNIX system (V5) by the end of this year.

APPENDIX I

```
P20 DEFINITIONS ::=
BEGIN
-- the following type, used in P20 DEFINITIONS, is defined in X.411 (P1)
 -- P1.ORName
-- the following macros are used, as defined in X.410
OPERATION                    ::= RemoteOperations.OPERATION
ERROR                        ::= RemoteOperations.ERROR
```

```
--operations

work    OPERATION
        ARGUMENT SET {
                SubmitterReference  OPTIONAL,
                DestinationData,
                Work,
                FileTransfer OPTIONAL}
        RESULT SET {
                SubmitterReference  OPTIONAL,
                WorkData,
                CommandsData,
                ResultFiles}
        ERRORS {accessDenied,fileError,obsoleteWork}
        ::=1

query   OPERATION
        ARGUMENT SET {
                SubmitterReference  OPTIONAL,
                DestinationData}
        RESULT SEQUENCE {
                        authorized BOOLEAN,
                        reason INTEGER {
                                unknownSubmitter(0),
                                unknownExecuter(1)} OPTIONAL,
                                                -- present if authorized is
                                                -- FALSE
                                }}
        ::=2

notification            OPERATION
                         ARGUMENT SET {[0] IMPLICIT SubmitterReference  OPTIONAL,
                                -- same reference used within the work
                                invokeID [1] IMPLICIT INTEGER,
                                        -- same invokeID in work operation
                                commandReference [2] IMPLICIT IA5String,
                                executionStartTime [3] IMPLICIT GeneralizedTime}
                         ::=3

--errors
accessDenied ERROR
                PARAMETER INTEGER {
                        unknownSubmitter(0),
                        unknownExecuter(1)}
                ::=1

errorFile ERROR
                PARAMETER SEQUENCE OF SEQUENCE {
                        FileProblem,
                        file            FileGeneralInformation}
                ::=2

obsoleteWork ERROR
                PARAMETER INTEGER {obsolete(0)}
                ::=3

-- various P20 data units
```

```
--destination data
DestinationData ::= SEQUENCE OF SEQUENCE {
                        comments [0] IMPLICIT IA5String OPTIONAL,
                        recipient P1.ORName,
                        listName [1] IMPLICIT IA5String}

-- Work argument data units
WorkData ::= SET {
                WorkAttribute,
                SEQUENCE OF COMMANDE}

WorkAttribute ::= SET {
                executionDate [0] IMPLICIT GeneraliziedTime OPTIONAL,
                obsoleteDate [1] IMPLICIT GeneralizedTime OPTIONAL,
                cpuTime       [2] IMPLICIT INTEGER OPTIONAL,   -- in seconds
                priority [3] IMPLICIT INTEGER {
                                        normal(0),
                                        nonUrgent(1),
                                        urgent(2)} DEFAULT normal}

--commandes
COMMAND MACRO ::=
    BEGIN
    TYPE NOTATION ::= "NAME" CommandID
                        "ARGUMENT" Arguments
                        "ATTRIBUTE" Attributes
    VALUE NOTATION ::= valeur(VALUE SEQUENCE {
                                        commandID,
                                        Arguments,
                                        Attributes})

    CommandID ::= INTEGER {
                        execute(0), --local system command file execution
                        delete(1),  --delete UFS file
                        access(2),  --verify accesibility to UFS file
                        acquire(3), --acquire URS resource
                        liberate(4),--liberate URS resource
                        attach(5),  --attach URS resource
                        detach(6),  --detach URS resource
                        wait(7)          --synchronisation command
                                         --other commands will be added in
                                         --a future extension}
    Arguments ::=NamedType

    Attributes ::= "ATTRIBUTE" SET {
                        commandReference [0] IMPLICIT IA5String OPTIONAL,
                        sequencing [1] IMPLICIT INTEGER {
                                                nonAborting(0),
                                                aborting(1)}
                                                        DEFAULT aborting,
                        paralled [2] IMPLICIT  BOOLEAN DEFAULT FALSE,
                        notified [3] IMPLICIT  BOOLEAN DEFAULT FALSE }

    NamedType::= identifier typ|type
  END

-- Type Notations for commands defined in the present version
```

```
--execute
Execute ::= COMMAND
                NAME INTEGER{execute(0)}
                ARGUMENT SEQUENCE {
                        ufsName CHOICE {
                                -- command file containing execution system
                                -- local commands
                                submission [0] IMPLICIT UFSNameDesignation,
                                execution [1] IMPLICIT UFSNameDesignation},
                        Parameters OPTIONAL}
                ATTRIBUTE --same as in Macro definition}
                Parameters ::= SEQUENCE OF ParameterElement
                ParameterElement ::= CHOICE {
                        ufsSubmitName [0] IMPLICIT UFSNameDesignation,
                        ufsExecuteName [1] IMPLICIT UFSNameDesignation,
                                        [2] IMPLICIT ResourceLogicalName,
                        characterString [3] IMPLICIT IA5String}
--delete
Delete::= COMMAND
                NAME INTEGER {delete(1)},
                ARGUMENT UFSNameDesignation,
                ATTRIBUTE --same in Mmacro definition
--access
Access::= COMMAND
                NAME INTEGER {access(2)}
                ARGUMENT SEQUENCE {
                        UFSNameDesignation,
                        modes BIT STRING {
                                        execute(0),
                                        write(1),
                                        read(2)}
                ATRIBUTE --same as in Macro definition
--acquire
Acquire::= COMMAND
                NAME INTEGER {acquire(3)}
                ARGUMENT SEQUENCE {
                                [0] IMPLICIT ResourceType,
                                [1] IMPLICIT ResourceName OPTIONAL,
                                [2] IMPLICIT ResourceAttributes OPTIONAL,
                                [2] IMPLICIT ResourceLogicalName OPTIONAL}
                ATTRIBUTE --same as in Macro Definition
--liberate
Liberate::= COMMAND
                NAME INTEGER {liberate(4)}
                ARGUMENT CHOICE {
                                [0] IMPLICIT ResourceLogicalName,
                                [1] IMPLICIT IMPLICIT SEQUENCE {
                                                ResourceType,
                                                ResourceName}
                ATTRIBUTE --same as in Macro Definition
--attach
Attach::= COMMAND
                NAME INTEGER {attach(5)}
                ARGUMENT CHOICE {
                                [0] IMPLICIT SEQUENCE {
                                                ResourceType,
                                                ResourceName,
```

```
                                                 ResourceLogicalName OPTIONAL},
                              [1] IMPLICIT ResourceLogicalName}
--detach
Detach::= COMMAND
            NAME INTEGER {detach(6)}
            ARGUMENT CHOICE {
                              [0] IMPLICIT SEQUENCE {
                                                 ResourceType,
                                                 ResourceName},
                              [1] IMPLICIT ResourceLogicalName}
--wait
Wait::= COMMAND
            NAME INTEGER {wait(7)}
            ARGUMENT commandReference IA5String
            ATTRIBUTE --same as in Macro definition

-- file transfert data

FileTransfer ::= SET {
             [0] Ftse OPTIONAL,  -- files transferred to the
                                    -- execution system
             [1] Ftes OPTIONAL,  -- files to be transferred to the
                                    -- submission system
                              }
Ftse ::= SEQUENCE OF SEQUENCE {
                    FileGeneralInformation,
                    File}
Ftes ::= SEQUENCE OF SEQUENCE {
                    FileGeneralInformation,
                    authorizingCommand IA5String}

-- Worg result data units
WorkData :: SET {
            status [0] IMPLICIT INTEGER {
                              normalTerminaition (0),
                              abandoned (1),
                              commandAborted(2),
                              cpuTimeExceeded(3)}
            charges [1] IMPLICIT INTEGER, -- in logical points
            startTime [2] IMPLICIT      GeneralizedTime,
            terminationTime [3] IMPLICIT GeneralizedTime}
CommandData ::= SEQUENCE OF SEQUENCE {
                    number  INTEGER,          -- the sequential number
                    id INTEGER,
                    reference [0] IMPLICIT IA5String,
                    execStatus INTEGER {
                                    successful(0),
                                    failed(1),
                                    aborted(2),
                                    notExecuted(3)},
                    uosMessage [1] IMPLICIT IA5String          OPTIONAL}
```

```
ResultFiles ::= SEQUENCE OF SEQUENCE {
                                [0] IMPLICIT  FileProblem  OPTIONAL,
                                [1] IMPLICIT  FileGeneralInformation,
                                [2] IMPLICIT  File OPTIONAL}

-- errors

FileProblem ::=INTEGER {
                impossibleCreation(1),
                unknownFileStucture(2),
                badFileStructureType(3),
                impossibleFileRead(4),
                impossibleDelete(5),
                authorizingCommandNotExecuted(6)}

-- various data units
-- file general information
FileGeneralInformation ::= SEQUENCE {
                                logicalStructure [1] IMPLICIT INTEGER {
                                                                text(0),
                                                                t73(1),
                                                                binary(2)},
                                submitName [2] IMPLICIT UFSNameDesignation,
                                executeName [3] IMPLICIT UFSNameDesignation OPTIONAL,
                                lifeTime [4] IMPLICIT INTEGER {
                                                                temporary(0),
                                                                permanent(1)}}

--UFS Name
UFSFileDesignation ::= SEQUENCE OF IA5String

-- File
File::= SET {
    [0] FileContents,
    creationTime [1] IMPLICIT GeneralizedTime  OPTIONAL,
    lastAccessTime [2] IMPLICIT GeneralizedTime  OPTIONAL,
    updateTime [3] IMPLICIT GeneralizedTime  OPTIONAL}

FileContents ::= CHOICE {
                [0] TextLine,
                [1] IMPLICIT T73Document,
                [2] IMPLICIT Binary}

TextLine::= SEQUENCE OF Line
Line ::= CHOICE {IA5String,
                OCTET STRING}

T73Document::=SEQUENCE OF T73.ElementsOfProtocole

Binary::=OCTET STRING

-- resource general information

ResourceType ::= INTEGER {
                                tape(0),
                                disk(1),
```

```
                    ond(2), -- optical numerical disk
                    tapeDrive(3),
                    diskDdrive(4),
                    printer(5),
                    console(6),
                    cardReadeR(7),
                    punch(8),
                    specail(9)}

ResourceName ::= IA5String
ResourceLogicalName ::= IA5String
ResourceAttribute ::= SEQUENCE {
                    [0] IMPLICIT TapeAttributes,
                    [1] IMPLICIT DiskAttributes,
                    [2] IMPLICIT OdnAttributes,
                    [3] IMPLICIT TapeDriveAttributes,
                    [4] IMPLICIT DiskDriveAttributes,
                    [5] IMPLICIT PrinterAttributes,
                    [6] IMPLICIT ConsoleAttributes,
                    [7] IMPLICIT CardReaderAttributes,
                    [8] IMPLICIT PunchAttributes,
                    [9] IMPLICIT SpecialAttributes}

TapeAttributes ::= SET {
                    length [0] IMPLICIT INTEGER OPTIONAL,
                    density[1] IMPLICIT INTEGER OPTIONAL,
                    tracks[2] IMPLICIT INTEGER OPTIONAL}

DiskAttributes ::= model IA5String
OndAttributes ::= model IA5String
TapeDriveAttributes ::= SET {
                    model [0] IMPLICIT IA5String,
                    density[1] IMPLICIT INTEGER OPTIONAL,
                    tracks [2] IMPLICIT INTEGER OPTIONAL,
                    speed [3] IMPLICIT INTEGER OPTIONAL}
DiskDriveAttribute ::= model IA5String
PrinterAttributes ::= SET {
                    model [0] IMPLICIT IA5String,
                    speed [1] IMPLICIT INTEGER OPTIONAL}
ConsoleAttributes ::= model IA5String
CardReaderAttributes ::= model IA5String
PunchAttributes::= model IA5String
SpecialAttributes ::= IA5String

END -- end of P20 definitions
```

APPENDIX II

```
work:
destination: john,list1
             /* Will tape MT3027 be ready by
             the end of this month ? */
reference:   NewCCompiler
cputime:     300
transferPriority:   normal
executionPriority:  urgent
startTime:   6/5/87   6:00:00
obsoleteTime:       6/5/87  12:00:00
ftse:        S:compile     C:permanent  T:text
             S:quicksort.c T:text
             S:randomData  E:inputData  C:permanent
ftes:        S:sortResult  E:sortedData C:temporary
commands:
1:cmd1:BN    execute        S:compile  S:quicksort.c
               E:quicksort  E:inputData E:sortedData
2:           delete E:quicksort.o
```

In the above exemple the work is to be sent to an execution system in order to be executed on behalf of user (John) in the execution environment defined in (list1). Notice that the destination address is the alias (john). In fact some directory service on the local system assures the mapping to a full ORname. Submitter comments are to be sent to john once the work terminated. All work attributes are shown. The file transfer between submission and execution system is specified. Three files are to be transferred from the submission environment to the execution one :

compile: this text file will have the same name on the execution system and will not be deleted once the work terminated.
quicksort.c: same as compile but it will be erased from the execution environment when work execution terminates.
randomData: this text file will be saved under the inputData name on the execution system. It will stay in the execution environment.

One file is to be transferred from the execution environment to the submission one :
sortedData: this file will have the name sortResult in the submission environment. It will be erased from the execution system.
There are two work commands :

the first one is the execution of file command (compile). This file contains native execution system commands and will accept four parameters. The command is aborting (presence of B). A notification (presence of N) is to be sent to the submit system once the execution initiated. The notification is to contain the reference (cmd1).

The second one is to erase a file from the execution system.

REFERENCES

[1] Message Handling System : Interpersonal Messaging User Agent Layer. X420 Recommendation.

[2] Information Processing System-Open Systems Interconnection-Job Transfer and Manipulation (JTM).
ISO/TC97/SC21 N210 (services) ISO/TC97/SC21 N211 (protocole)

[3] Information Processing System-Open System Interconnection-Basic Reference Model. ISO 7489/IS.
[4] Message Handling System : Message Transfer Layer. X411 Recommendation.
[5] Operating System Command And Response Language (OSCRL). ISO/TC 97/SC 21 N 965.
[6] Message Handling System : Remote Operations and Reliable Transfer Service. X410 Recommenation.
[7] Message Handling System : Presentation Transfer Syntax and Notation. X409 recommendation.
[8] NOTE TECHNIQUE NT/PAA/TIM/DRI/1803 Centre Nationale d'Etudes des Télécommunications (CNET). July, 1986.
[9] C.kintzig, "le reseau de communication: SMARTIX",convencio informàtica latina. Barcelona March 1987.

Network Information Processing Systems
K. Boyanov, R. Angelinov (Editors)
Elsevier Science Publishers B.V. (North-Holland)

The Directory - Evolution of a Standard

Kai Jakobs

Technical University of Aachen, Informatik IV
Ahornstr.55, D-5100 Aachen, FRG

This paper deals with history and state-of-the-art of the ISO/CCITT directory standard. This standard recently has received much notice. With some characteristic examples we will depict the development of the directory and explain major differences between the various documents. The present version is discussed and problems are pointed out. Some final remarks are given on a general problem that still remains unsolved.

1. Introduction

Networks grow - in size and in complexity. As a result, there is a growing need for user-friendliness in networking and for information about the network itself. To fullfil this requirement, directories - providing information about a network's objects - are an important means.

Starting in 1983, the directory proposal has seen several major changes. Thus, the remainder of the paper is organized as follows:

To introduce the topic, section 2 surveys the directory's functionality.

Section 3 introduces what may be regarded as the ancestor of today's directories: Xerox's Clearinghouse.

Sections 4 four to 6 describe work done by several standardization bodies.

Finally, section 7 gives some comments on a general problem concerning the present directory approach as a whole.

2. Directories - A Survey

The need for a sophisticated information service providing enhanced user-friendliness initiated work on *Directory Services* (DS) [Jak 88]. Inter alia, the DS provides a uniform naming scheme for and information about a network's resources, the *Objects*. One of the main design goals is to achieve a maximum of *user-friendliness* in naming. Two main principles are identified:

- a person should be able to correctly guess a name from information he usually possesses.

- the system must recognize an ambiguously specified name as not being sufficient for identification.

In general, a DS has to provide three services:

- mapping *name --> information*
- mapping *name --> set of names*
- mapping *information --> set of names*

Usually, the DS is described as a *Client-Server System*.

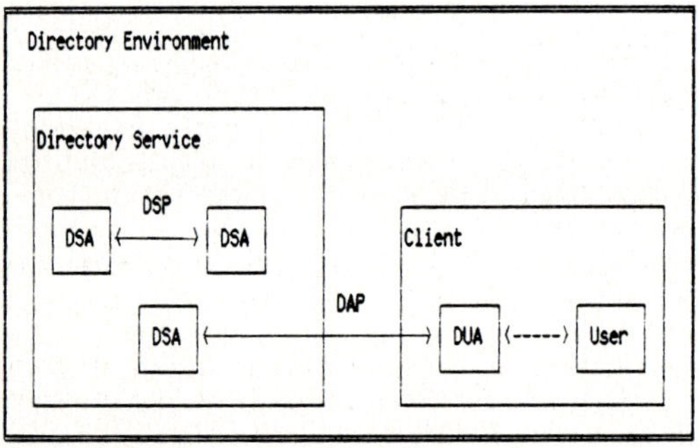

Fig.1: Functional Model of a Directory System

The *Client* - the user and his private *Directory User Agent* (DUA) - communicates with the *Service* via the *Directory Access Protocol*, DAP. The *Servers* - the *Directory System Agents*, DSA, hold services' data. Since data may be replicated and/or distributed, there is a necessity of communication between DSAs. They use the *Directory System Protocol*, DSP.

Information about objects is stored in the *Directory Information Tree*, DIT. Every DSA holds part of the DIT including:

- data about objects within some part of the network
- knowledge about objects known by its colleagues

3. The Ancestor - Clearinghouse

Xerox Clearinghouse [Oppen 83] supports "naming and locating of network-objects in a large, distributed environment". In general, it provides a mapping of object names onto a set of properties. The main features:

- Naming
  Any object within the network is identified by a *Name*.
- Distribution
  Clearinghouse is organized in a decentalized and replicated manner.
- Properties
  Information is composed of properties, held in an *Entry*
- Aliasses
- Yellow Pages

- Object Classes

It will, however, come clear that Clearinghouse's services are not sufficient for OSI requirements (cf. next sections).

4. Some Early Work

The first related document to be published officially is ECMA Technical Report TR/32 [ECMA 85], dated 1985. Generally, this system provides the same services as Clearinghouse does. But there is one important difference:

Each name is constructed as a name part sequence of arbitrary length. A *name part* is a tuple *<NamePartType, NamePartValue>*. However, there are no standardized NamePartTypes defined in the report.

Anyway, it is noticeable that no services are provided to support management of the directory's contents:

- although there may be different classes of objects hierarchical relations (eg. *Country* superior to *Locality*) between them are ignored.

- no relation is defined between different types of objects (eg. *Device* or *Application Entity*) and information allowed in the respective entries.

- structure and contents of an entry is not specified.

There are two more serious shortcomings:

- distributed operations are not specified
- no authentication methods are described

All these details show that this system specified by ECMA will not be able to work well in an extremly large and heterogeneous network with widely distributed administration (it is, however, currently being implemented within the ESPRIT framework [THORN 88a]).

5. The Draft Proposals

5.1. Egham

In October 1986, the first ISO DP [ISO 86] is adopted at ISO SC21 plenary meeting in Egham, UK.

Most shortcomings of the ECMA report are handled, but not always satisfying. Some important modifications are:

- names are composed of *Attributes*. An attribute is a tuple *<AttrType, AttrValue>*. A *Relative Distinguished Names*, RDN, is allocated to every entry. The RDN is unambiguous for all entries with a particular superior. The full name consists of two parts: the *Distinguished Name*, DN, and the *Descriptive Name*. The DN is composed of an ordered sequence of RDNs and may thus be used to route through the Name Tree.

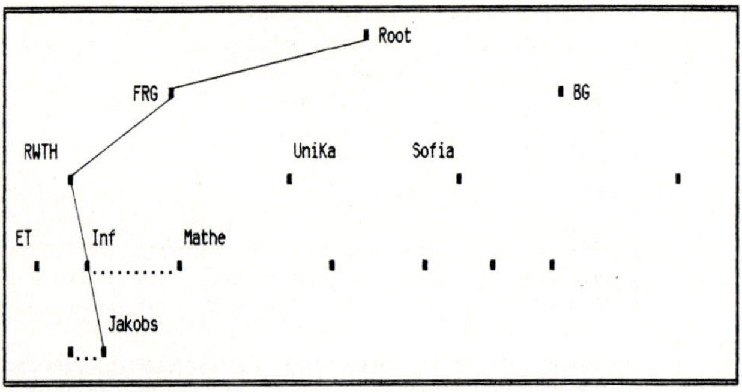

Fig.2: Example of a Name Tree
The DN of the marked object is {C=FRG, O=RWTH, OU=INF, OP=Jakobs}

- standard *Object Classes* are defined (cf. Fig.3). This definition describes hierarchical relations between object classes and information required for every class. In particular, an object class definition contains:
  - the object class, to which the superior object should belong
  - a set of Attribute Types, indicated as either mandatory or optional
  - an indication for each Attribute Type whether it may be present in an object's distinguished name.

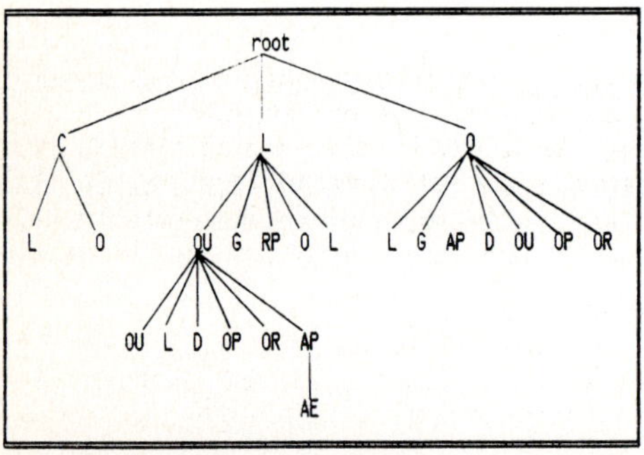

ASN.1 notation of an object class may look as follows:

```
residentalPerson OBJECT-CLASS
    SUBCLASS OF Person
    MUST CONTAIN {
        localityName}
    MAY CONTAIN {
        localeAttributeSet,
        postalAttributeSet,
        preferredDeliveryMethod,
        telecommunicationAttributeSet,
        businessCategory}
    ::= {object-class 10}
```

Fig.3: Hierarchy of Selected Object Classes
C=Country; O=Organization; L=Locality; G=GroupOfNames; RP=ResidentalPerson;
OU=OrganizationalUnit; OR=OrganizationalRole; OP=OrganizationalPerson;
D=Device; AE=ApplicationEntity; AP=ApplicationProcess

- the structure of entries is specified (cf. Fig.4; this figure, however, shoes the present specification differing slightly from the Egham definition).

- to provide for distribution of information, a DSA must have *Knowledge* about data hold at other DSAs. Thus, every DSA maintains a *Knowledge Tree*, KT, containing *References* to information hold by some "colleagues". Like the DIT, a Knowledge Tree is organized hierarchically.

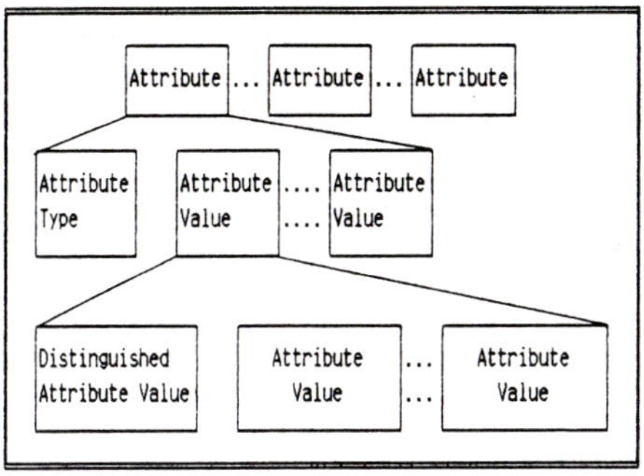

Fig.4: Structure of an Entry

It has been a great progress from the ECMA Report to the first DP and this DP is strongly supposed to be stable. Nevertheless, it is disapproved for various reasons:

- missing authentication services
- non-ambiguity of names is not guaranteed (especially due to the fact that descriptive names are permitted)
- no mechanisms are provided for management of object classes and attribute types

5.2. Munich

A second meeting on the 1st DP takes place in February, 1987. The delegates decide that it will be impossible to pass a standard of the intended scope during the 1984-88 CCITT study period. As a result, a so called "Strawman" - a list of items with high and low priority and of items to be removed - is produced during the meeting. The most important details of this strawman are, [ISO 87a]:

- the DS is reduced to a "Read-Only-Database".
  The *Modify* operation is removed. The only services now provided are:
  - Read: provides information about an entry specified by its name
  - Compare: checks for the existence of a specific Attribute Value in a particular entry
  - List: lists a subtree relative to a speecific entry
  - Search: lists all entries within a subtree containing a specific attribute

- distinguished names become the only kind of name.
  removal of descriptive names is a result of management problems arising with the use of descriptive names.

- directory systems may be distributed
  However, due to this topic's complexity, no final document on distributed services is produced. One remarkable detail is the removal of information replication.

- directory Schema is supported
  The Schema consists of:

- Object Class definition
- Attribute Type definition
- Attribute Syntax definition

including related rules.
The Schema is used for management purposes. Using schemas, the Directory will, for instance, be able to
- prevent creation of subordinate entries of a wrong object class (eg. *Country* subordinate of *ResidentalPerson*, cf. Fig.3)
- prevent addition of Attribute Types forbidden for entries of that particular class

- users may have to be authenticated

5.3. Tokyo

The 2nd DP is registered after ISO TC97/SC21 meeting in Tokyo, June 87. Open questions of the Munich version (cf. sec.5) are handled, resulting in three major alterations of the documents [ISO 87b]:

<u>DIT structure definitions are decoupled from object class definition</u>

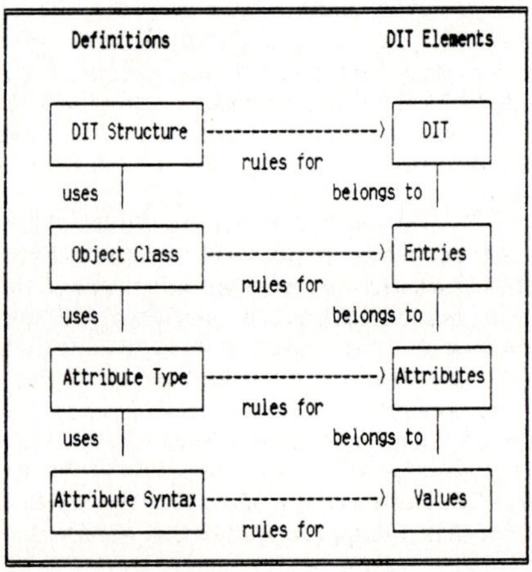

Fig.5: Directory Schema

The DIT-structure describes the (hierarchical) arrangement of entries. Fig.5 shows the relation between DIT-structure, object classes and attributes.

Previously, the DIT-structure definition has been included in the object class definition (cf. sect.5.1.). The new approach assumes that object class- and DIT structure definition are decoupled. There are mainly two points in favour of decoupling:

- it is possible to define new object classes without knowledge of other object classes
- responsibility for DIT-structure definition and definition of an entry-structure may be distributed

distributed operations are specified

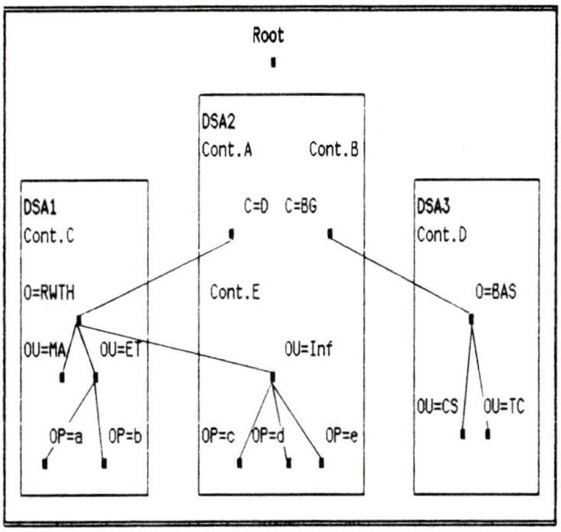

Fig.6: A Hypothetical Distributed Directory Information Tree

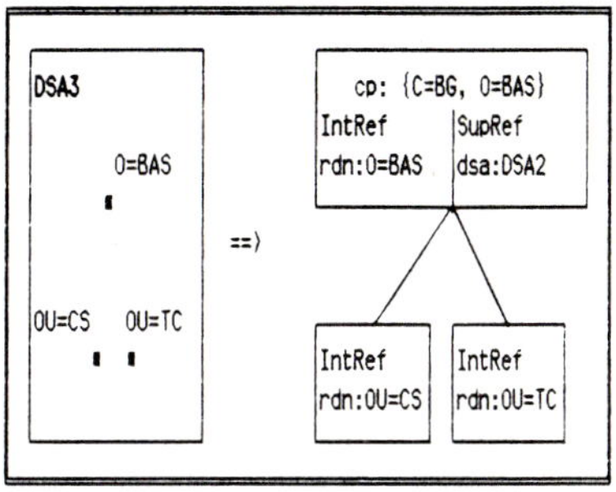

Fig.7: DIT Fragment and Knowledge of DSA3
O = Organization; OU = Organizational Unit
Cont. = Context
cp = Context Prefix; rdn = Rel.Dist.Name
IntRef = Internal Reference
SupRef = Superior Reference

Output of the Munich meeting left most topics related to *Distributed Operations* "for further study". The present version specifies the *Distributed Name Resolution Process* (verifying purported names) and distributed Read, Search and Modify operations. In addition, different modes of DSA interaction are specified:

- Chaining: the DSA forwards a request to *one* other DSA
- Multicast: the DSA forwards a request to *several* DSAs
- Referral: the DSA returns *hints* at responsible DSA(s)

Knowledge is now defined as a set of *References*, pointing at some entry Knowledge Information is based on *Contexts*. A Context simply is a prefix of the Distinguished Name of the respective root vertex of a DSA.

Fig.6 shows an example of a distributed DIT. DIT and Knowledge of a DSA are depicted in Fig.7. In this example, DSA3 holds references pointing at

- a DSA holding the immediate superior entry of O=BAS
- internal entries

a draft proposal for an *Authentication Framework* is added to the document

For the first time, an *Authentication Framework* is included in the directory proposals. Two different levels of authentication are specified:

- Simple Authentication
  based upon a user's Distinguished Name and a password
- Strong Authentication
  using *Public Key* cryptosystems

Services described within the framework are:

- peer entity authentication
  ensures that a user really is the one he claims to be
- access control
  protects against unauthorized use of resources
- data confidentiality
  protects data from unauthorized disclosure
- data integrity
  detects and protects against manipulation of data

Unlike the other parts of the document, the authentication framework's status is 1st DP. However, its contents is already considered stable.

Furthermore, Munich's read-only approach is removed again; leaf entries now may be modified.

6. The Draft International Standard

The 2nd DP is accepted as DIS at the ISO/CCITT collaborative meeting at Gloucester, Nov. 1987 [ISO 87c]. There are a number of modifications of the DP documents, most of them dealing with questions of detail and eliminating defects of the DP (so, this chapter will be quite short). The most important modifications deal with distributed operations, particularly *Distributed Directory Service* and *Procedures for Distributed Operations*. Some other more important modifications concern schema and object classes, the latter due to the fact that this is the only specification of which information is to be stored by the directory. (Although modifications are in detail rather than basic they caused considerable trouble to implementors [THORN 88b].)

The DIS is intended to be passed as an International Standard by the end of 1988. Thus, the last meeting prior to this date (Washington, March 1988) [ISO 88] mainly discusses necessary enhancements to be included in future versions of the standard. As a result, a priority list of enhancements is produced [Thoma 88]:

- support of short names
- access control
- information replication and distribution of knowledge
- schema
- name integrity
- enhanced search
- descriptive names

All these topics are considered as being handled not adequately by the present standard.

7. Some Final Remarks

The present status of the directory standards may be regarded as satisfactory, although there are still several problems left. A number of these problems have been recognized by the standardization bodies (see above) and will hopefully be solved within the next two years or so. However, one really fundamental question remains: in how far does the present system meet the original demand for user-friendliness? Today's situation is characterized by the priority of system management aspects to user-friendliness; a global name space with distributed naming authority may not be adequately coped with by today's systems. Thus, it's the user who is left to carry the can. One possible solution might be to use descriptive names only and to treat today's RDNs as simple attributes. However, searching in a system like this brings up problems (inter DSA communication, ambiguity of names, data management) that - at least today - can not be solved. Thus, it is very likely that this dilemma will not be solved within the next years, but standardization bodies may not lose sight of this problem.

8. References

[ECMA 85]: European Computer Manufacturers Association
ECMA TR/32: Directory Access Service and Protocol, 1985

[ISO 86]: International Standards Organization
Information Processing Systems - Open Systems Interconnection - The Directory - DP 9594/1-7, Egham, 1986

[ISO 87a]: International Standards Organization
Information Processing Systems - Open Systems Interconnection - The Directory - DP 9594/1-7, Munich, 1987

[ISO 87b]: International Standards Organization
Information Processing Systems - Open Systems Interconnection - The Directory - 2nd DP 9594/1-8, Tokyo, 1987

[ISO 87c]: International Standards Organization
Information Processing Systems - Open Systems Interconnection - The Directory - DIS 9594/1-8, Gloucester, 1987

[ISO 88]: International Standards Organization
Information Processing Systems - Open Systems Interconnection - The Directory - DIS 9594/1-8, Washington, 1988

[Jak 88]: Jakobs, K.:
Towards User-Friendly Networking
Proc. EURINFO '88, North Holland, 1988

[Oppen 83]: Oppen, D.C., Dalal, Y.K.:
The Clearinghouse: A Decentralized Agent for Locating Named Objects in a Distributed Environment
ACM Trans. Office Automation Systems, Vol.1, No.3, July 83

[Thoma 88]: Thoma, G.:
ISO SC21/WG4 Meeting on The Directory
Report for DIN NI 21.4.1

[THORN 88a]: Sirovich, F., Antonellini, M.:
The THORN X.500 Distributed Directory Environment
Submitted for ESPRIT Conference 1988

[THORN 88b]: Antonellini, M.:
THORN Status Report July 1988
Thorn Document OLI52, 1988

Network Information Processing Systems
K. Boyanov, R. Angelinov (Editors)
Elsevier Science Publishers B.V. (North-Holland)

Network-Based Information Systems

Joseph F.P. Luhukay

NETLAB University of Indonesia

1. Introduction

As computing becomes increasingly accepted as a means to communicate, computer networks continues to gain importance in the development of information systems. Newly industrialized countries, including those on the southwestern rim of the Pacific, are encountering this fact as a significant issue in their move into automation. Faced with the realization that traditionally centralized information systems impose high telecommunication costs *vis-a-vis* the relatively rapid decrease in the cost of computer hardware and software, new strategies need to be developed [**PoMi85**, **Frie86**, **Luhu88**]. More and more users in this environment are finding out that the promise of the traditional Management Information System is more myth than reality, especially when one takes into consideration the low management use of computer processed information. Moreover, management often prefers to get on-line to external information sources rather than to get connected directly to his/her own corporate data processing facilities. Reasons such as the unavailability of up-to-date information on their own machines, unfriendly user interfaces, or simply the unavailability of internal links have been quoted by several senior managers in the region.

A number of information systems development activities implemented in the past few years have resulted in a general strategy which became broadly named "network-based information systems". The improved strategy is discussed in this paper and a sample case presented.

2. Trends in Information Systems

2.1. Information Technology Investment Patterns

A modern company can be modelled as having three levels of organization, namely the Management Level, the Administration and Production Level, and the

Point of Service Level, as shown in **Figure 1**. The Management Level (Level 3) encompasses top staff and line functionaries within the corporate structure, whereas the Administration Level (Level 2) may be thought of as including all internal administrative and support units. The Point of Service Level (Level 1) consists of all interface units which interact with the company's customers.

Current data processing environments commonly show heavy investment patterns in administration-oriented applications on Level 2. A result of past automation efforts, some of these systems have not yet fully exploited features offered by the computer. Caused mainly by increases in work volume, manual tasks were automated through the use of computers. This is usually combined with some investments on Level 1, and almost none at the Level 3, thus creating an "investment bulge" in the middle corporate tiers. Latest developments, however, show some movements in management-level investments in the form of office automation facilities. Moreover, point-of-service levels are absorbing increasingly heavier investments, mainly due to competition-driven moves to improve service at the customer interface [**Dick88**, **Luhu88a**].

2.2. Movements towards Network-Based Information Systems

There are various reasons behind the move to use networks in corporate information systems. The first reason is *user demands*, causing interlevel communications through some form of computer networking. Demand-driven interactions between Levels 2 and 3 may be in the form of office automation, decision-support systems, and other forms of management support. Levels 1 and 2 may interact through various forms of database access, application access, remote data entry, and other forms of service support.

Another reason is *technology push*, which tends to cause some form of task distribution within corporate data processing. The availability of smaller systems which are more affordable, portable and come with more capabilities, is spreading the use of computers even further. This with time turns into a push to connect the computers together into a network. Dedicated servers are seeing more use in networks performing the tasks of providing users with database, computing or communication services. Networking techniques are becoming increasingly stable through the development of standards and the availability of products.

The third reason is related to corporate policies to improve management style through the distribution of data processing tasks. Most commonly used is the "centralized control and distributed operations" approach. Centralized control is implemented as centrally defined data dictionaries, formats, algorithms, data structures, authentication and other security measures, operational procedures, etc. This centralization is augmented by some degree of distribution of information technology resources to support local processing in order to better meet customer needs in an increasingly competitive market. *Policy-driven* moves are often implemented in a top-down fashion which may require some time before it touches the more remote nodes in the network.

3. Categories of Information Requirements

In order to design the proper network-based information system, it is important to properly recognize the different information requirements within an organization. In the model shown in Figure 1 each of the three levels have slightly unique requirements:

Level 3 requirements:

a. Highly unstructured, mainly to answer "what if" queries

b. Very non-periodic, often even quite unpredictable

Level 2 requirements:

a. Well-structured with almost no variation

b. High-degree of periodicity (e.g. inventory reports, pay slips, etc)

Level 1 requirements:

a. Highly structured, almost always in the form of predetermined interactions

b. Scheduled with very high periodicity

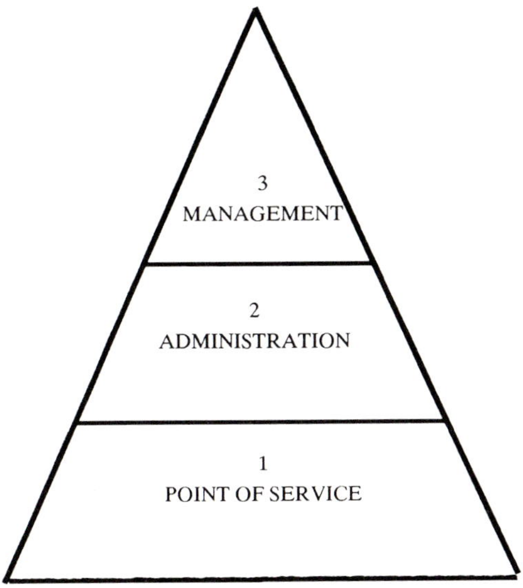

FIGURE 1
The three levels of
Information Requirments

Levels 1 and 2 are predictably similar in their requirements, although Level 1 usually involve much simpler application systems. In some cases, Level 1 requirements may result in dedicated systems because of its simplicity, which in turn may complicate network design. Level 3 requires quite unique information handling and should thus be dealt with differently.

4. Implementation Strategy

As reported earlier, mixing applications for the different levels may not be a good implementation strategy. The following list shows some guidelines for implementing a network-based information system encompassing all three levels:

Level 3 implementation:

a. Requires effectivity, ease of use, and should be directly of value to the end-users

b. Interactive mode supporting end-user queries

c. Data may often be down-loaded from a centralized file-server

d. Usually makes use of relational data-base management techniques with fourth-generation language support on microcomputers.

Level 2 implementation:

a. Requires efficiency in high-volume processing

b. Batch-work scheduling (often quite complex)

c. Data entry may often be on-line

d. Usually supported by non-relational data-base management techniques on mainframe and minicomputers.

Level 1 implementation:

a. Requires predictable response-times

b. Prescribed tasks with simplified user interface

c. May be used for data entry or remote access stations

d. Often dedicated to a predetermined set of applications

As can be readily seen from this list of implementation idiosyncracies at each level, so that running all of the levels on the same computer may not give the best results.

5. Case Studies

The First case involves a manufacturing company with 8 sites scattered over 4 cities in Java. The company is the largest non-automotive diesel engine manufacturer, and holds production licences from various corporations in Europe, Japan and the United States. A corporate-level information technology strategy is being developed wherein computer networks, both local-area and wide-area, will play a decisive role. Half of the company sites are to be connected through a network based on the public packet-switching facilities and a number of LANs will be developed to serve various information needs at the company headquarters.

The network-based information strategy will be utilized and a small prototype technical office automation system is being tested out. This involves the linking of the company's base of engineering drawings, currently stored in a PC-based format on microcomputers, and a number of advanced engineering workstations. The latter will be used for more complicated engineering tasks such as simulations and graphics manipulations. An electronic document interchange format is developed to enable 2D and 3D drafting software running on both classes of computers to share design files, thus distributing the engineering design task over a heterogeneous set of equipment. Efforts are continuing to link into the manufacturing environment, which ultimately will bring the network onto the shop-floor.

On the administrative and management sides of the organization, aforementioned techniques of linking the batch-mode servers with interactive stations will also be implemented. A sales and marketing office in Jakarta will be linked across over 800 kilometers with the administration and production centers in East Java.

The initial stages of a second case study has been reported previously: a financial institution with large number of branches throughout the country [**Luhu88**]. In order to improve its competitiveness the bank has acquired a number of Automated Teller Machines, which are installed in main branches. This typifies a Level 1 acquisition to improve the quality of customer service. Because of its dedicated nature, the ATM's are handled by a turnkey minicomputer through dedicated lines. This minicomputer is in turn connected to the headquarter's LAN, through which it accesses account databases distributed on branch machines. Since a high degree of ATM accesses are performed at the branch where the account is opened, network traffic created by this application is quite small. Moreover, ATM's have relatively long response times, making remote accesses quite bearable to the customer already used to waiting for a few seconds.

The gateways are currently programmed to perform more intelligently, They are now designed to be capable of performing terminal oriented transactions when remotely triggered through a valid active message by another gateway. The bank has decided to reduce the number of vendors supplying its branch machines in 1989, thus somewhat reducing the complexity of network design and management.

Conclusion

This paper reports improvements on a previously publication by the author. A simple model was developed and the information requirements identified. An implementation strategy for network-based information systems is developed and a number of case studies briefly discussed.

References

[Dick88] Brian N Dickie, *Integrating Technology & Banking Strategy*, Seminar on Electronic Banking in Indonesia", 12-13 April 1988, Jakarta, Indonesia.

[Frie86] Joel P Friedman, *Information Technology: The Path to Competitive Advantage*, Bank Administration, January 1986.

[Luhu88] Joseph F P Luhukay, *A Development Strategy for Network-Based Information Systems*, Information Network and Data Communication, 14-17 March 1988, Copenhagen, Denmark.

[Luhu88a] Joseph F P Luhukay, *Information Technology: An Implementation Strategy in Financial Institutions* (in Indonesian), Seminar on Electronic Banking in Indonesia, 12-13 April 1988, Jakarta, Indonesia.

[PoMi85] Michael E Porter and Victor E Millar, *How Information Gives You Competitive Advantage*, Harvard Business Review, July-August 1985.

APPLICATIONS

Network Information Processing Systems
K. Boyanov, R. Angelinov (Editors)
Elsevier Science Publishers B.V. (North-Holland)

A CLASSIFICATION FRAMEWORK FOR OIS METHODOLOGIES

Mauri Leppänen and Vesa Savolainen

University of Jyväskylä
Department of Computer Science
Jyväskylä, Finland

In the literature, numerous models and methodologies have been presented for modelling and analysing office information systems (OIS) and office work. In this paper we construct the OIS Framework, a hierarchical, three-level tool for modelling and analysing office data and activities, development work, and construction of models, tools and methodologies for the development. On the basis of this universal framework and the notion of an approach, the Classification Framework for OIS models and methodologies is constructed and applied. It offers a tool for analysing perspectives, views and principles supported strongly or weakly by methodologies.

1. INTRODUCTION

Office information systems (OIS) have recently been an object of quite intensive research. Dozens of models have been developed for modelling various features of offices. The methodologies constructed have been purported for operationalizing the use of models. Such models and methodologies have been offered e.g. by Dumas et al. [11], Ellis [12], Conrath et al. [10], Zisman [29], Zloof [30], Barber [4], Ladd and Tsichritzis [17], Mumford and Weir [21], Lundeberg et al. [18], Tapscott [26], Sutherland et al. [25], Pava [22], Konsynski et al. [16], Aklilu [3], and Checkland [8].

The relationships between these models and methodologies as well as their perspectives and focuses have been shown by many classifications, e.g. by Bracchi and Pernici [6] and Hirschheim [14]. However, there is no framework to prove a classification complete or valid, or to reveal the relations of classes in a consistent way. The purpose of this paper is to develop such a framework. The framework can be used to indicate the features supported either strongly or weakly by a methodology, and the relationships between the methodologies. Further, the framework is to give the inner structure for analysing other classifications.

In Section 2, a hierarchical three-level OIS Framework is constructed to provide the reader with a holistic tool for the analysis of office data and activities, their development, and the construction of development methodologies. In Section 3, the notion of approach and its subconcepts, viz. perspective, view and principle, are first introduced and analysed. Then the OIS Framework and the notion of approach are utilized to construct a comprehensive classification for OIS models and methodologies. The Classification Framework is also applied to show its applicability. The Framework can be used for distinguishing different models and methodologies from each other, for choosing an appropriate model or methodology, and for developing a new model or methodology for specific purposes. Further, the framework provides an inner structure for analysing other classifications.

2. OIS FRAMEWORK

Our framework presents various office information activities within a hierarchical structure. The two main theories behind the principles of constructing the levels of the framework have been derived from systems theory and linguistics. The approaches used as the foundations of this framework are (1) systems theoretical control structure and (2) linguistic abstraction [1]. In the systems theoretical approach, the systems in offices include *control systems* which create models for the *operative systems,* control their implementation and modify them if necessary.

The linguistic abstraction refers to the *hierarchies of languages* used in offices, in office modelling and in methodology and tool construction. A language for defining another language is called a meta language [19]. The definition of a language includes the definition of syntactics, semantics and pragmatics of the language.

The fundamental conceptual component of an office information system can be constructed in accordance with above approaches and the theory presented in Auramäki et al. [1]. We call it here *OIS Triangle,* though it is a general concept suitable for information systems modelling independent of the contexts. The OIS Triangle describes *informing* i.e. office situations where people inform themselves or one another in order to make possible or to improve their own actions or those of the others.

The hierarchical framework is constructed on three levels. The first level is called an *office information system* (OIS). The OIS Triangle on that level consists of *office data* (OD), *OD processes* (ODP) including the necessary facilities, and *actors* (A). Another essential element of the triagle is a *model* (M), which is used for describing and prescribing the other elements and the connections between them (see Fig. 1).

Office work can be characterized by data-intensive activities supporting operative functions and decision making, by interactiviness, by unstructuredness, by a multitude of exceptions and by frequent changes. The purpose of an office information system is to support the office work.

The office data processes are considered operative subsystems of the OIS and are connected to the upper level processes by interactive relations, such as couplings, signals, impulses and triggers. Those upper level processes are called *OIS development processes* (OISDP). An OISDP has, as the process above, a logical relationship to its data (M), which is, on this second level, called *meta OD* (mOD), though mOD has a role of a model from the lower triangle point of view. Correspondingly, the model of OISDP and mOD is called *meta meta OD* (mmOD), and it includes e.g. the tool and methodology base which is utilized in OISDP. The actors on this second triangle are *OIS developers* (OISD).

The purpose of the OISDP's is to produce the OIS model and to acquire the necessary resources for the OIS. These development processes and their environment can be regarded as a *meta office information system* (mOIS). The development activities in form of OISDP's follow the applied models of mmOD and include the necessary facilities.

The meta OD denotes a logical set of those meta expressions which define the contents, structure and use of the OD. The mOD, in fact, contains a model of the office information system, and it can be divided further into models of office information and its processing. Besides the final version of the OIS, it also contains all partial solutions and checkpoint results as well as different utilization versions and backup system versions. All the OISDP

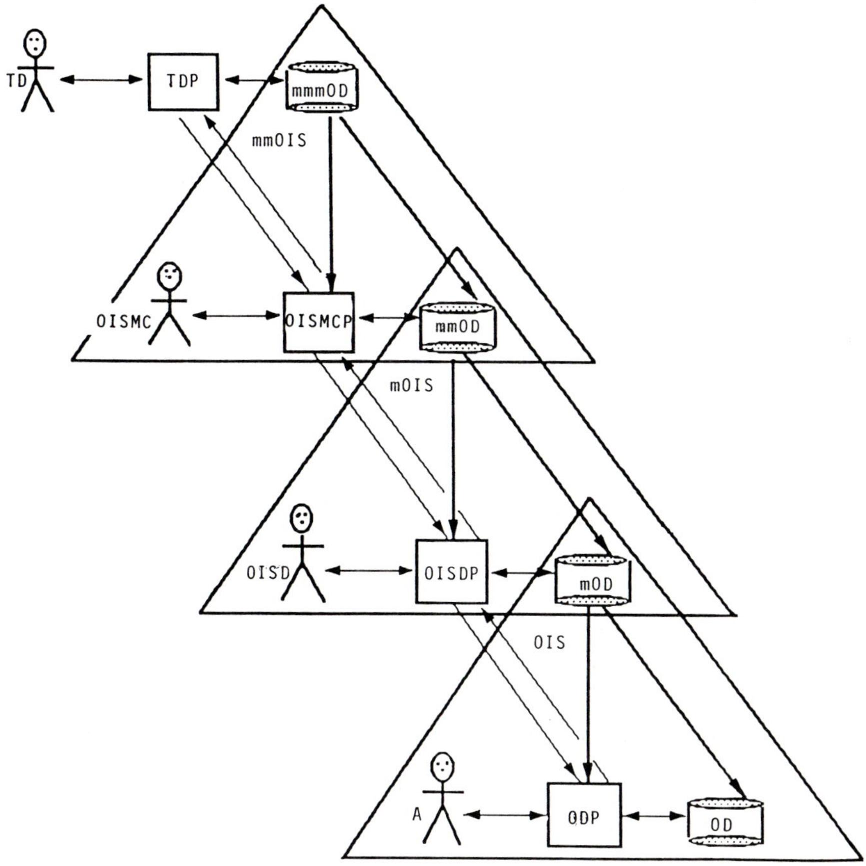

Levels of Office Information Systems:

mmOIS: meta meta Office Information System
mOIS: meta Office Information System
OIS: Office Information System

Roles of People (Actors):

TD: Theory Developer
OISMC OIS Methodology Constructor
OISD: OIS Developer
A: Actor, Office Worker

Information Processes:

TDP: Theory Development Processes
OISMCP: OIS Methodology Construction Processes
OISDP: OIS Development Processes
ODP: Office Data Processes

Levels of Data Bases:

mmmOD: meta meta meta Office Data
mmOD: meta meta Office Data

mOD: meta Office Data
OD: Office Data

Figure 1. OIS Framework

results, such as models for office support systems, are thus included in the mOD.

The third level consists of *OIS methodology construction processes* (OISMCP) and *methodology constructors* (OISMC). The mmOD contains OIS development methodologies, models and tools, from which the OIS developers choose those to be used. The mmOD also defines the contents, structure and use of the mOD.

The construction of OIS development methodologies is a scientific research which aims at producing normative rules and procedures for office development. A methodology includes an *office model* which offers concepts and languages for modelling and describing real offices.

3. Classification of models and methodologies

It seems to be a habit to introduce a new model or methodology and to emphasize its dissimilarities and contributions by relating it to some approach (e.g. dynamic, holistic, socio-technical, humanistic, systematic, comprehensive or structural). However, hardly any of the presentations states what is really meant by an approach. It is rather confusing to study classifications based on the stated approaches without the coherent background. In this section, the notion of approach is first discussed. Then the OIS framework and the notion are used to present a comprehensive classification for OIS models and methodologies.

3.1. Notion of approach

Generally, an *approach* can be considered a starting point for a task, or a path or other means of reaching a destination, i.e. performing a task (cf. Webster's New World Dictionary). The tasks in our OIS Framework are on the three levels. As the tasks are so different in their nature, we define three subconcepts for more specific purposes: a perspective, a view and a principle.

A *perspective* means a fundamental conception of the phenomena to be analyzed, e.g. conceptions of their nature and behavior. The forming of a perspective is effected by the theory basis applied. For instance, the ontological and epistemological assumptions of engineering sciences or social sciences limit and shape the conceptions of an office and office work quite differently. In our framework, the concept of perspective is connected to the meta meta OIS level.

A *view* reflects those aspects of the discourse which are thought to be the most important in the eyes of a perceiver. For example, if the aim is to emphazise the features of the discourse which are connected to the processes, to the rules behind them, and to the temporal and logical relationships between them, a process-based view is applied. A view follows from the choice of the perspective and it should be in harmony with the basic assumptions of the perspective. In our framework, the concept of view is connected to the meta OIS level and the OIS level.

A *principle* is a normative expression, connected to a local target of analysis, describing the final state of the target to be charged (i.e. a static target), or the way to perform the target (i.e. a dynamic target). The choice of the view limits the possibilities for and directs the principle definition. An example of principles, within the process-based view, is concurrency control. In our framework, the concept of principle can be connected to the meta OIS level and the OIS level.

3.2. Classification

The OIS framework and the notion of approach will be used as the basis of classification. A set of well-known office models and methodologies has been chosen for discussions. Also some presentations having remarkable contributions on the area of general information systems research have been included. The results of our analysis are presented in Table 1. It should be noted that the location of the instances of models and methodologies is due to our subjective evaluation which will be completed later.

In Table 1, only two levels of our framework are presented, i.e. OIS and OIS Development levels because it goes beyond this paper to deeply analyse the backgrounds of theories and sciences on the third level. Both the levels encompass the basic elements: data, processes and actors. Data on the upper level (meta data) is a model describing and prescribing the structure, the contents and the use of the data on the lower level.

Table 1. Classification based on views

	Views	Main focus	Subtypes	Instances
O I S development	Developer-oriented methodologies	Functions, roles and actors as role holders in development	- Designer-oriented methodologies - End-user-oriented methodologies	OAM (ref. 24) ETHICS (21), Pava (22)
	Development-oriented methodologies	Phases and activities of development process	- Phase-oriented methodologies - Proto-oriented methodologies	MOBILE (11), ISAC (18) Boar (5)
	Model-oriented methodologies	Model or language for describing the results of development	- Concept-based "methodologies" - Language-based "methodologies"	OSL (13) SOS (7), ICN (12), SCOOP (29), OBE (30)
Office information system	Actor-based models	Functions, roles and actors as role holders on an office	- Role models - Cognitive models	ETHICS (21) Aiello et al. (2)
	Process-based models	Office activities in a coordinated way	- Context independent models - Context dependent models	ICN (12), IML (23), SCOOP (29) Ciborra (9), Lyytinen et al. (20)
	Data-based models	Objects manipulated by office workers	- Form based models - Picture based m. - Voice based models - Multimedia models	OMEGA (4), OFS (27), OFFIS (16), OBE (30) - - Woelk et al. (28)

A rough classification according to the views is obtained by analysing what characteristics, from the viewpoint of the upper level OD, are regarded as the most important ones to be described and prescribed. On the OIS level, this leads to the following categories: data-based models, process-based models and actor-based models (cf. [6]).

The main emphasis of the *data-based models* is placed on data. The basic elements are data types and data manipulation operations (retrieval, storage, manipulation, transmission). Office tasks are seen as series of operations on data. Usually the data are represented by forms like in the traditional office. Besides forms and documents, other media can be used. The data can be in the form of pictures or voice. Depending on the form of data, models are classified into the *form-based models, picture-based models, voice-based models,* or *multi-media models.*

In the *process-based models* the relevant elements are activities, which are performed in a cordinated way by the office workers. The emphasis is mainly on producing an integrated vision of all the activities in an office and its control. The models in this category can be further grouped into sub-classes according to the extent by which contextual issues are embedded in the basic concepts. In one end of extreme there are models with abstract and pure mathematical concepts (cf. Petri net-based models). In another end, there are models which encompass a large set of semantically rich concepts. Richness is based on the categorization of elementary tasks found in an office (e.g. typing, negotiation, mailing, phoning) or on treating activities as logically connected functions, as some kind of roles to be held by actors.

An *actor-based model* describes an office from the viewpoint of the office workers, the domains within which they are authorized to act, and the relations to other actors. The aim of the models is to examine roles and the delegation of them in an office. Data and processes are considered only in relation to their executors. A sub-classification into *role models* and *cognitive models* can be made according to how the subjective and intersubjective issues of real actors (e.g. attitudes, motivation) are considered in the models. On the other hand, the models can be regarded as "personal" or "collective". In the former case, activities are seen to be related to a single actor or a group of actors doing the same. Complementary to this is the collective models referring to the human activity as the combined effort of a group of actors. The models in this category focus on how each individual contributes to the activities and on the connections between individuals.

Furthermore, there are a set of mixed models which are based on two or more aspects mentioned above.

On the OIS Development level the classification contains methodologies; model-oriented methodologies, development-oriented methodologies and developer-oriented methodologies. In a *model-oriented methodology* the descriptions of final results, their forms and contents, are stressed more than the development processes. This is usually the first phase in the construction of an OIS methodology. In the simplest form, only a model together with some language for the OIS or its part are given (cf. ICN [12]). There are also methodologies which contain modelling facilities on several abstraction levels but no transformation rules for levels.

In a *development-oriented methodology* the emphasis is set on development tasks, structure of tasks, methods and tools for the tasks. Models and languages have minor roles. These methodologies can be further classified into classical, prototyping, and evolutionary methodologies depending on their control structure. The methodologies can cover the development tasks partially or totally.

A *developer-oriented methodology* particularly concentrates on actors which take part in the development.

The perspectives could be located above the levels presented in Table 1. A perspective affects the contents, structure and usage of a methodology (cf. meta meta OD). It also affects the research process. A mathematical-conceptual perspective favours conceptual-constructive research methods [15]. On the other hand, a social sciences perspective emphasizes the research methods that facilitate immediate cooperation with the reality to be analysed (e.g. action research).

4. CONCLUSION

In this paper the OIS Framework was constructed to cover the OIS activities on three levels. It was used to build a classification of the well-known OIS models and methodologies. The Classification Framework is complete due to the fact that the OIS Framework embraces all the OIS activities on the three levels. It facilitates the analysis of the relations of the approaches. For instance, from the aim to construct a developer-oriented methodology it must necessarily follow that the social science perspective is prefered and the end-user orientation is emphasized. Further, it can be concluded that a model has to possess many features of actor-based models. It also seems reasonable to expect that the research process is firmly based on methods like action research.

The Classification Framework dictates the main contingencies of the development and usage situations according to which the model or methodology can be chosen. Thus, an appropriate model or methodology for a given situation can be found. Likewise, the Framework can be used to reveal the shortcomings of the present state of the art in the area of office systems, and also as a basis for research efforts in constructing new models and methodologies.

REFERENCES:

[1] Auramäki E., Leppänen M., Savolainen V., Universal framework for information activities, Data Base, Vol. 19, No. 1, Fall/Winter 1987/1988, 11-20.

[2] Aiello L., Nardi D., Panti M., Structural office modelling: a first step toward the office expert system, in: Proc. of 2nd ACM Conf. on OIS in Toronto, 1984.

[3] Aklilu T., Office automation - office productivity - the missing link, Office Automation Digest, AFIPS, Houston, 1984.

[4] Barber G., Supporting organizational problem solving with a work station, ACM Trans. on Office Inf. Syst., Vol. 1, No. 1, 1983, 45-67.

[5] Boar B. H., Application prototyping, John Wiley & Sons, 1984.

[6] Bracchi G., Pernici B., The design requirements of office systems, ACM Trans. on Office Inf. Syst., Vol. 2, No. 2, 1984, 151-170.

[7] Bracchi G., Pernici B., SOS: a conceptual model for office information systems, Data Base, Winter, 1984, 11-18.

[8] Checkland P., Systems thinking, systems practice, John Wiley & Sons, Chichester, 1981.

[9] Ciborra C., Information systems and transactions architecture, Policy Analysis and Information Systems, Vol. 5, December, 1981.

[10] Conrath D. W., De Antonellis V., Simone C., A comprehensive approach to modelling office organization and support technology, in: Pernici B., Verrijn-Stuart A.A. (eds.), Office Information Systems: the Design Process, North-Holland, Amsterdam, in print.

[11] Dumas P., du Roure G., Zanetti C., MOBILE Burotique: prospects for the future, in: Naffah H. (ed.), Office Information Systems, North-Holland, Amsterdam, 1982.

[12] Ellis C., Information control nets: a mathematical model of office information flow, in: Proc. of ACM Conf. on Simulation, Modelling and Measurement of Computer Systems, Boulder, 1979, 225-240.

[13] Hammer M., Kunin J., Design principles of an office specification language, in: Proc. of Int. Conf. AFIPS 80, AFIPS Press, 1980, 541-547.

[14] Hirschheim R., Office automation - a social and organizational perspective, John Wiley & Sons, Chichester, 1985.

[15] Jenkins A. M., Research methodologies and MIS research, Discussion Paper No. 277, Indiana University, 1984.

[16] Konsynski B., Bracker L., Bracker W., A model for specification of office communications, IEEE Trans. on Comm., COM-30, No. 1, 1982, 27-36.

[17] Ladd I., Tsichritzis D., An office form flow model, in: Proc. of Int. Conf. AFIPS 80, AFIPS Press, 1980, 533-539.

[18] Lundeberg M., Goldkuhl G., Nilsson A., Information systems development: a systematic approach, Prentice Hall, Englewood Cliffs, 1981.

[19] Lyons J., Semantics, Cambridge Univ. Press, 1977.

[20] Lyytinen K., Lehtinen E., An action based model of information systems, Information Systems, Vol. 11, No. 3, 1986.

[21] Mumford E., Weir M., Computer systems in work design - the ETHICS Method, Associated Business Press, London, 1979.

[22] Pava C., Managing new office technology: an organizational strategy, Free Press, New York, 1983.

[23] Richter G., Durchholz R., IML - inscribed high-level Petri nets, in: Olle T.W., Sol H.G., Verrijn-Stuart A.A (eds.), Information Systems Desing Methodologies: a Comparative Review, North-Holland, Amsterdam, 1982, 335-368.

[24] Sirbu M., Schoichet S., Kunin J., Hammer M., OAM: an office analysis methodology, MIT, Office Automation Group Memo, OAM-016, 1981.

[25] Sutherland J., An office analysis and diagnosis methodology, Unpublished M.Sc. dissertation, MIT, Mass., 1983.

[26] Tapscott D., Office automation: a user-driven method, Plenum Press, New York, 1982.

[27] Tsichritzis D., OFS: an integrated form management system, in: Proc. of Int. Conf. on Very Large Data Bases in Montreal, 1980, 161-165.

[28] Woelk D., Kim W., Multimedia information management in an object-oriented database systems, in: Proc. of Int. Conf. on Very Large Data Bases in Brighton, England, 1987.

[29] Zisman M. D., Representation, specification, and automation of office procedures, Ph.D. Thesis, Wharton School, University of Pennsylvania, 1977.

[30] Zloof M. M., Office-By-Example: a business language that unifies data and word processing and electronic mail, IBM Syst. Journal, Vol. 21, No. 3, 1982, 272-304.

Network Information Processing Systems
K. Boyanov, R. Angelinov (Editors)
Elsevier Science Publishers B.V. (North-Holland)

KNOWLEDGE BASED DOCUMENT CLASSIFICATION SUPPORTING CONTENT BASED RETRIEVAL AND MAIL DISTRIBUTION+

Helmut EIRUND§

TA Triumph-Adler AG, Research Lab
Hundingstr. 11b, D-8500 Nuernberg, FR Germany

Abstract:

In this paper we give an overview of a knowledge based office system, realized as a prototype in the framework of an experimental office system currently being developed at Olivetti research. The prototype integrates two major requirements of office work: content based document retrieval and mail distribution. In this system documents are described and classified by their semantic structure.

The derivation of the semantic structure of a document supports both an efficient retrieval by content and an intelligent mail filtering through document semantics. After a short review of the document model used for an abstract representation of documents semantics, the classificationsystem is presented. The knowledge based classificationsystem automatically generates the conceptual description of a document to be inserted into the system by means of content analysis, and associates the document to an appropriate predefined type. This task is conducted by the given typehierarchy where the relevant content for each conceptual component of a type is defined by a set of content description predicates. With the classification system we close the gap between electronic document entry systems and processing of (semi-) structured document content.

1. Introduction

Office documents show a wide range of structures, extending from highly formatted forms, business letters with standardized structures like quotations or purchase orders to totally unstructured memos. Classes of *conceptually similarly* structured documents can be observed frequently, e.g. quotations, purchase orders etc. Classical document classification systems that represent documents by a subset of a predefined set of descriptors do not satisfy the office requirements [Sacc84]. Especially the principle of word matching is not sufficient. E.g. consider an application from a purchase department where all computer offers from company "Selly" offering the computer "M32" should be retrieved or should be

+ This work has been funded in parts by the Commission of the European Communities as ESPRIT-Project No. 28 "MULTOS" and by the German Ministry of Research and Technology in the joined project "WISDOM".

§ Authors present address:
Helmut Eirund, University of Oldenburg, FB 10, Postfach 2503, D-2900 Oldenburg

sent automaticly to the clerk, who is concerned with computer offers[1]. The system then must be able to differentiate offers from orders or invoices and to distinguish names of offered computers from names of comparable products that can be found in the offers as well.

1.1 Early Experience With a Mail Distribution Prototype

With the EPIKUR system [Krep86] we developed a system in theWISDOM project that performs a document analysis, interweaved with the mail distribution process. The system provides a *recognition of exactly one type* of document (itidentifies the concepts "sender", "recipient", "date" and "topic", plus keywords from a given thesaurus -if present). This works well on this level of document analysis. With the demand of *changing* the analysis process for the identification of the given concepts or specifying user profiles on a higher level of abstraction (see example above), problems arise. The reason is in the description of the analysis target *directly in a program*, not specifying the relevant concepts ("sender", "recipient" and more) separatly.

What we need is a *more abstract view* of the documents, an identification of conceptual components in documents analogous to the conceptual schema of database systems. Referencing those components in mail distribution rules can allowe a higher complexity and varity of mail filtering on document content (see e.g. [Malo87]).

1.2 A Semantic Document Model

In [Barb85,Bert85,Cons86] a document model is proposed to cope with the task of describing documents and their semantics. A key point of this model is the notion of *weak typing* that is a means for describing classes of similarly structured documents as opposed to strong typing that requires identical structures for all instances. In this model a *conceptual structure* as an instance of a conceptual type is associated with each document. Via the conceptual structure semantically relevant components of documents may be accessed. Chapter 2 gives an overview of this model, more details can be found in [Barb85]. In the 3rd chapter we show how to refere to the conceptual structure in a retrieval system and in mail distribution rules.

With adopting this document model there is the problem of *creation of the conceptual structure* . Although it can be constructed step by step by an editor during the creation of the document, this possibility is not sufficient. An open system must be capable of handling documents from arbitrary sources, including documents without a conceptual structure. Therefore our knowledge based office system provides a classification subsystem that analyses the document content and automatically constructs a conceptual structure based on a given set of type definitions. For this creation process the type definitions can be viewed as templetes for possible document conceptual structures that are instantiated according to a set of specialization rules and document analysis rules that may refere to application domain knowledge. The classification unit allocates the document to an appropriate type. Currently we restrict the classification to the textual part of the documents.

1.3 An Integrated Document Handling System

In figure 0 we show our approach to an integrated intelligent document handling system. The global architecture is based on the "*client / server* " paradigm [Svob84]. This has been choosen as it leads to an open system, composed of loosly coupled components. There will be a number of clientsystems that provide document handling tools interacting with human users, as well as passive server systems specialised on a set of applications. The

---

[1] the 'sending of mail' can be seen more general as a primitive office procedure

separated classification module craetes the documents conceptual structure that can be used in several other applications, like *mail filtering* (general: for global distribution, or local: for a further privat processing) and the support of access structures for *retrieval by content* in a document archiv system.

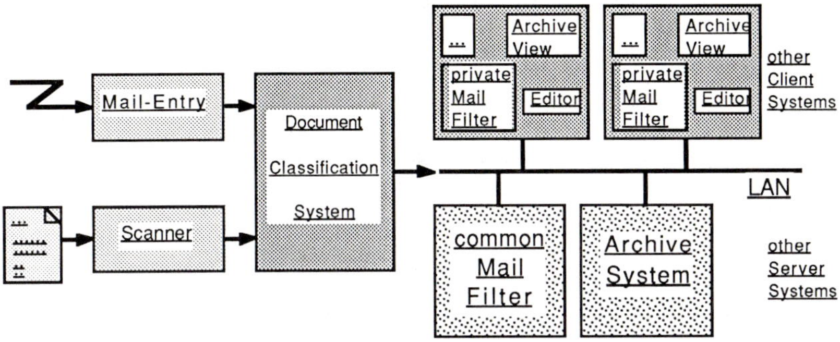

Figure 0: Integrated Document Handling System

2. The Document Model

For purposes of document editing and exchange some more or less standardized models have been developed, e.g. DCA/DIA by IBM, SGML by ISO, ODA by ECMA. Most of them provide a type concept different from type concepts found in database systems. A type in these models can be viewed as a skeleton that supports the creation of new instances by predefined document structures and content parts. Additionally it enables different layout styles of the same document [Furu82]. On the other hand a type in database systems specifies the structure common to all instances (strong typing).

For modelling office documents the strong type concept is too restrictive, since even documents with similar contentstructures should be grouped into one class e.g. a documentclass "quotation". We need a weak type concept for the description of the common properties of all instances that allows a far more specific and complex structure on the instance level [Barb85, Lame85].

2.1. The Conceptual Structure

Following the issue of analysing the document content for an "intelligent" processing of the document, we see there presentation of the document in the conceptual view that describes the semantics of a document by the "*conceptual structure definition*" (CSD). The conceptual structure identifies and allocates a name to all those components of a document that are relevant for the further processing, i.e. mail distribution or retrieval.

Three modelling principles form the essentials of the proposed document model: aggregation, typing , and specialization. A CSD is composed of conceptual components that maybe aggregations of other conceptual components. Thus we get a tree conceptual structure.

For modelling semantic units of a document, we distinguish three kinds of conceptual components:

basic components that will be linked to content portions in the document, belonging to different value domains like string, integre, text, image, voice.

complex components that are constructed by subcomponents. A complex component may be a sequence of subcomponents (AGG), possibly with iterations, as well as a possibly selected choice of a set of subcomponents.

spring components as special CSD tree leaf nodes that are used for a later refinement of the structure.

We distinguish *type-CSD* from *document-CSD*. Typical document structures are described a priori by type-CSD's that define the type set (catalog). For a dynamic extension of this set we introduce a refinement operation on the type-CSD's. Thus we get a hierarchy of specialized types. The refinement operation can be also used for deriving instances of document-CSD's from a type-CSD. For an overview of the specialization / instantiation rules possible in the document model see table 1.

Refinement Rules	Subtype	Instantiation
substitute spring by CHOice, AGGregate or Basic concept	possible	possible
selection of CHOice	possible	mandatory
iteration of AGGregation sequence	possible	mandatory
link content to Basic concept	not allowed	mandatory

Table 1: CSD-Refinement Rules

Figure 1 shows an example of a type hierarchy, with a simple conceptual structure defined for each type. Figure 2 gives a document with its CSD as an instantiation of <COMPUTER-OFFER-TYPE> with document portions allocated to all basic components of the CSD.

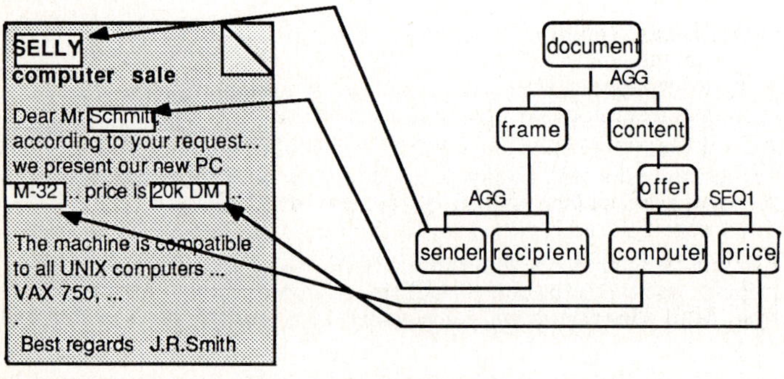

Figure 2: Document with Document-CSD

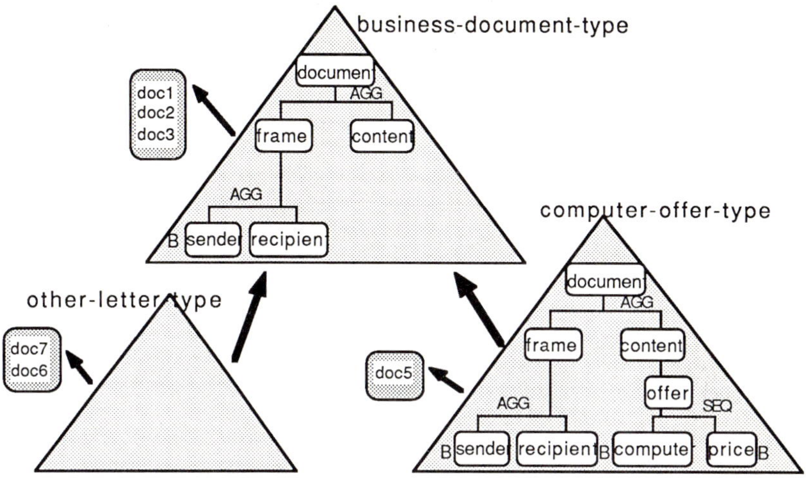

Figure 1: Type Hierarchy and Type-CSD's
(B:basic component, S:spring, AGG:aggregate)

3. The Use of the Document Conceptual Structure in an Integrated Office System

With the definition of the conceptual document types the view on the document semantics is described. This view depends on the use of the conceptual components, e.g. for retrieval purposes or automatic control of office procedures, like mail distribution.

3.1. Content Based Retrieval

The query language allows the specification of conditions of the content and on the conceptual structure itself. *Conditions on the conceptual structure* specify the existence of special conceptual components where *conditions on content* specify the existence of special data values, e.g. attribute values, or the existence of special words in text content parts.

The query processor is based on the presumption that each document is associated to the most specific type available in the type catalog. Then the processing may be restricted to the instances of a subset of the type catalog. Besides a directly mentioned type all its subtypes are included in the subset, but not more general types. This a priori restriction improves the performance of the query processing, especially the evaluation of textual conditions.

The user of the system need not be bothered with a complete knowledge of the type catalog. If she/he does not specify a type name, the system automatically identifies all type definitions that contain the names of the specified conceptual components of the query.

3.2. Automatic Mail Distribution

In the application area of office procedures the interchange of information is performed through documents with in general typical and semanticly well structured documents (e.g.official travel form, purchase order, mail distribution). In many cases the continuation of a procedure depends on the values of well defined semantic units of the document. E.g.the mail distribution may be controled by the sender and recipient(-value) and the general type of the document (see also [Malo87] on this topic). These issues determine the view of the document semantics that is relevant for this special application, i.e. the type definition.

We see the knowledge that *control the distribution procedure* in three levels of abstraction:

the *type association* of the mail document that determines the general semantics of the document

the *values* of the document conceptual components, i.e. the content portions linked to the basic components of the document CSD (e.g. value of 'recipient' component)

additional *user profiles* that describe the special interpretation of the document classification results for each user(-group) (e.g. "all documents of type "computer-offer-type" with 'recipient' equal ... should be distributed to ..."). Those profiles may also include the use of backround knowledge ("...'recipient' equal clerk_of 'sales-dept'..").

The common mail filter in figure 0 accepts the mail, comming from outside the system through the classification system. To adopt this filter to a special office environment, the organization structure of the specific office world should be mapped on it: a general filter, activating subfilters foreach department etc..

The *action* s that are triggered by the selection rules are: "send to", "activate subfilter" (only common filter), "insert into privat filesystem" (only privat filter), "reject" and "assign internal attribute of mail" (e.g.importance).

4. The Document Classification System

As we have outlined before, one assuption of our approach to a semantic based mail filtering or retrieval system is the "proper" *construction of conceptual structures of documents* . With this structure a document is allocated to the type that describes the semantics (i.e. the structure) of the document most precisely (e.g. the document in figure 2 is linked to <COMPUTER-OFFER-TYPE>, not to <BUSINESS-DOCUMENT-TYPE>).

Providing those prerequisites the document content is to be analyzed in a sufficient way. Automatic indexing or abstracting use technics like similarity measurement, based on statistical methods. Such methods investigate the document word set as a whole.

In the office environment it is not sufficient to identify documents as a whole, but the *values* of the smallest semantic units should be recognized in the context and identified (i.e. the name of the offered computer). This task requires *document analysis facilities* beyond the syntactic level, but because of the extreme complexity of this (unsolved) problem must fall short of total 'text understanding'.

In our project a middle course is adopted. With the use of apriori defined conceptual types that contain document content constraints, documents are analyzed, structured and classified. This approach is explained in more detail insection 4.1. In section 4.2 we give an overview of the used knowledge. Section 4.3 subsumes the architecture of the classification component in the proposed integrated office system.

4.1. The Classification Approach

The basis of the proposed classification process is a predefined type, whose conceptual components the system tries to recognize in the document. By the instantiation of the type CSD we get an appropriate document CSD with the instantiation rules applied (see table 1) and all basic components linked to the relevant content parts. To *find the best fitting type* , the type hierarchy is investigated top-down. Foreach type the system tries to recognize if the document includes its specified components. If this is the case, all subtypes of this type are investigated. With this procedure we get the best fitting type for a document, together with a most specialized document CSD that can be constructed for this document as an instantiation of this type.

To identify content portions, relevant for a conceptual component, the description of those concepts by a name and a domain is not sufficient. For this reason *predicates are added* to the concepts of a type to describe the "*relevant content* ". Their use is as follows:

(a) The content satisfying the predicate of a basic conceptual component is just allocated to that basic component.

(b) The content that complies with the predicate of a complex component serves as the search scope of its subcomponents. Within this scope the predicates added to the subcomponents are tried to be verified, i.e. an appropriate document part is to be identified within this scope.

(c) With this constraint we implicitly have introduced a relation between the subcomponents $SC_1,..,SC_n$ of a complex component CC: the relevant content allocated to all the SC_i is within the same content part, i.e. in the content allocated to the complex component CC.

(d) We get a gradual refinement of content portions from the root component to the basic content portions.

The description of concepts is also provided in the document retrieval system RUBRIC [McCu85]. In a query the resulting set of documents is specified by word match constraints, layout predicates and a synonym relation. The I3R system presented in [Crof86] supports powerful specifications of concepts in a query (e.g. references between concepts, simple parsing). Barbi et al. [Barb84] presented a system for the extraction of concepts from documents using a semantic network representation of the documents' subjects. While their approach starts with the lexical analysis of the document followed by the inference of concepts from the knowledge base, we use a type-directed approach restricting the search space for patterns describing concepts as far aspossible.

In the proposed classification system predicates are specified in a "Content Description Language" (CDL), presented hereafter. Within this language content description predicates can be formulated not only on the syntactic and layout level, but also semantic and linguistic relations are provided. The knowledge used in the classification process can be adressed in those predicates on a high level of abstraction. Table 2 summarizes the main features of CDL predicates.

CDL predicates specifying "relevant content" may include:

- layout predicates (sentence*, word*, line*, title*, ...)
- position constraints (TOP, FIRST, AFTER, ...)
- wordmatch, pattern - semantic relation (instance_of* <domain>, part_of* <object>,...), refering to application domain knowledge
- grammatical relation (possessive*, ...)
- reference to relevant content of other components (VALUE_OF)

and

- combinations of CDL predicates by set and/or logic operators

Table 2: Main Features of the Content Description Language (CDL)

Besides the issue of describing concepts as exactly as possible, we pursue two goals with this approach:

Flexibility : Concepts may be identified in a different context or different document types in different ways. This can be modelled by associating different CDL predicates to identically named conceptual components.

Uniformity : Knowledge, common for all CDL predicates (e.g. document layout forms, semantic relations of backround knowledge), may be addressed by built-in CDL predicates (marked with '*' in tab. 2).

The following simple *example* based on the <COMPUTER-OFFER-TYPE> of figure 1 gives an insight into the main features of identifying content portions by CDL predicates:

• the relevant content part of the root component 'document' is the whole document, without further restrictions.

• for the 'frame' the content of the first layout form "paragraph" united with the content of "line" form containing a "salutation"-phrase (e.g. "Dear Mr...") is taken.

• the 'content' component inherites the relevant content of 'document' (i.e. no content restriction).

• a document portion relevant for 'offer' should include the set of paragraphs following the first (address-)paragraph, but containing a synonym of "offer"(-phrase).

• the basic component 'sender' is linked to the company name within the scope associated to 'frame'.

• the content relevant for the component 'recipient' is the word exactly after the "salutation" within the given scope.

• the content associated to 'computer' is that word equal to a computer name, in a possessive context[2] with the company, identified in the component 'sender'.

---

[2] We investigate the use of "partial parsing": Such linguistic predicates are searched in a small context scope (sentence, with resolved references). They are described by simple context free grammars plus sets of keywords.

• the 'price' content has a specified price-pattern within a sentence containing the name of the offered computer.

In figure 3 the adequate CDL predicates associated to components of the <COMPUTER-OFFER-TYPE> are presented. An example of the CDL predicates for <COMPUTER-OFFER-TYPE> is given in figure 3.

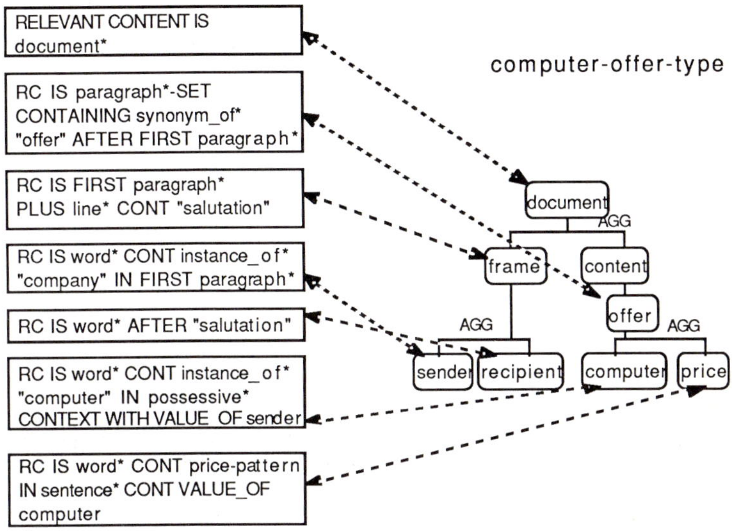

Figure 3: CDL predicates of <COMPUTER-OFFER-TYPE>

4.2. The Classification Knowledge

The knowledge the system operates on, can be subdivided into three different classes:

Actual Data: In the *preprocessing* phase special knowledge about the document is to be inferred that can be addressed in the content analysis phase, controlled by the CDL-predicates.The preprocessing aims three goals: (1) Uniform representation of the document. (2) Identification of layout (e.g. page, block, line) and logical structure (e.g. paragraph with title, sentence). (3) Identification of words and their normalization.

Structural Knowledge: The description of the goal of the classification process, i.e. to find and instantiate a best fitting conceptual type for a given document, is given in three levels of abstraction: (1) the *typehierachy* as a set of types, ordered according to the "is_a" relation. (2) Each type defined by a *structure of conceptual components*, represented by the type-CSD. (3) For each conceptual component an added *CDL-predicate*, specifying the range of relevant content.

Backround knowledge: The backround knowledge can be seen as the expert knowledge about the *application domain* (e.g. the organization and products of the company) as well as the general knowledge used in the *linguistic analysis* (e.g. synonym relation, substitution rules for reference solving). Both forms of knowledge are modelled within the representation mechanism "pro_Ludwig" , [Heye87] a structured inheritance network similar to the KL-ONE system [Brac85].

4.3. Architecture of the Classification System

The classification system, composed of the *classificationhandler* and the *knowledge bases*, gets the type definitions and a document as input and produces the document's conceptual structure as an instantiation of one of the types (see figure 4). The classification handler itself is realized in PROLOG. It consists of a classification control unit and a document analysis component. The classification control unit traverses through the type hierarchy, controls the construction of the document conceptual structure and calls the document analysis component to satisfy the CDL predicates, i.e. to interpret the CDL program code. Thus, the controlunit totaly depends on the type information.

In section 4.1 we have shown, how the type information (including the content describing predicates) serves as a description of the classification process on a high level of abstraction. To take from the user the task of reprogramming (in PROLOG) the classification handler while updating types, the type definitions are automatically transformed into a PROLOG predicate representation. With this we can see the classification control unit automaticly *generated from the type information* . The CDL predicates are compiled into logical programs in clause form (called CDL code) for efficiency reasons.

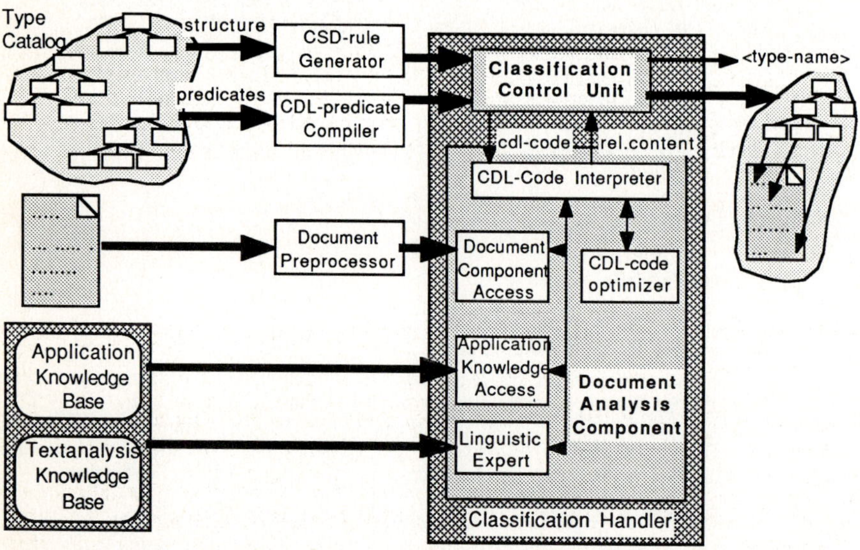

Figure 4: Architecture of the Classification System

5. Conclusion and Status

We have presented a document handling system that integrates two major tasks in the office environment: content based document retrieval and mail distribution. We use a document model designed to satisfy the special requirements of office environments. This document model enables the creation of semantic document structures, allowing the content dependent specification of queries and mail filters aswell, on a high level of abstraction.

The pertinent prerequisites are created through the generation of a conceptual structure and classification of the documents in accordance with the document types defined a priori. Within our funded project an integrated system is developed as a prototype. The knowledge based classificationsystem is developed which performs automatical creation of the document structure and effects document classification. The semanticly structured and classified documents serve as input for the document archive system and mail filter system that are both connected with the classification system.

Status

Our mail distribution system is implemented on top of the UNIX mail system, with a primitive user interface for filter definition. The document archiv system is implemented, but will be extended with optical disk storage medium.

Tests with the classification system have shown the feasability of the description method. The classification of over 200 similar documents (e.g. UNIX-manual entries, project correspondence) has shown a precision of about 90%. To cope with less formatted documents (e.g. offer documents) more sophisticated description features like weighted analysis and linguistic methods are currently under development.

Many persons contributed to the concepts and realization of the three subsystems described above. The author would like to *acknowledge* all the MULTOS staff members. At the TA-lab, Ernst Lutz, Helge Rieder, Mathias Lindner and Susanne Kleemann made mutch of the work developing the classification system. Hans von Kleist-Retzow, Karl Hoernig and Thomas Zechel implemented the mail filter system. Significant conceptual input on all topics came from Klaus Kreplin.

References

Barb84. E. Barbi, F. Calvo, C. Perale, F. Sirovich, and F. Turini, "A Conceptual Approach to Document Retrieval," Proc. 2nd ACM SIGOA Conf. on Office Information Systems, Toronto, 1984.

Barb85. F. Barbic and F. Rabitti, "The Type Concept in Office Document Retrieval," Proc. 11th Conference on Very Large Data Bases, Stockholm, 1985.

Bert85. E. Bertino, S. Gibbs, F. Rabitti, C. Thanos, and D.Tsichritzis, "Architecture of a Multimedia File Server", Proc. 2nd ESPRIT Technical Week, 1985.

Brac85. R.J. Brachman and J. G. Schmolze, "An Overview of the KL-ONE Knowledge Representation System," Cognitive Science, vol. 9, 2, 1985.

Cons86. P. Constantopoulos,Y. Yeorgaroudakis, M. Theodoridou, D. Konstantas, K.Kreplin, H. Eirund, A. Fitas, P. Savino, A. Converti, L. Martino, F. Rabitti, E. Bertino and C. Thanos, "Office Document Retrieval in MULTOS," Proc. 3rd ESPRIT Technical Week, 1986.

Crof86. W. B. Croft, "User-specific Domain Knowledge for Document Retrieval," Proc. ACM Conf. on Research and Development in Information Retrieval, ACM, Pisa, 1986.

Furu82. R. Furuta, J. Scofield, and A. Shaw, "Document Formatting Systems: Survey, Concepts, and Issues," Computing Surveys, vol. 14,3, ACM, 1982.

Heye87. G. Heyer and B. Schneider, "Conditions on a Knowledge Representation for Processing Natural Language Semantics," Proc. Expertensysteme '87, Teubner, 1987.

Krep86. K. Kreplin and H. K. Rieder, "Wissensbasierte Post-Klassifikationssysteme," WISDOM Forschungsbericht, no.FB-TA-86-28, TA Triumph-Adler AG, 1986.

Malo87. T. W. Malone, K. R. Grant, F. A. Turbak, S. A. Brobst, and M. D. Cohen, "Intelligent Information-Sharing Systems," CACM, vol. 30, 5, 1987.

Sacc84. G. M. Sacco, "OTTER -An Information Retrieval System for Office Automation," Proc. 2nd ACM SIGOA Conference on Office Information Systems, Toronto, 1984.

Lame85. W. Lamersdorf, "Semantische Repräsentation komplexer Objektstrukturen," Informatik Fachberichte 100, Springer Verlag, 1985.

Svob84. L. Svobodova, "File Servers for Network-Based Distributed Systems," Computing Surveys, vol. 16, 4, ACM, 1984.

McCu85. B. P. McCune, R. M. Tong, J. S. Dean, and D. G. Shapiro, "RUBRIC: A System for Rule-Based Information Retrieval," IEEE Trans. on Software Engineering, vol. 11, 9, Sept. 1985.

Network Information Processing Systems
K. Boyanov, R. Angelinov (Editors)
Elsevier Science Publishers B.V. (North-Holland)

AN EXPERT SYSTEM APPROACH TO THE HUNGARIAN BUILDING REGULATIONS

Gábor RÉDEY*, Ernő G. NAGY* and Petranka ZS. GEORGIEVA*

Computer Centre
Hungarian Institute for Building Science
Budapest, Hungary

The Hungarian Institute for Building Science has a three year project supported by the Ministry of Building- and Urban Development and the State Office for Technical Development to develop an expert system concerning the Hungarian Building Regulations which contains the technical and legal requirements for building design and construction. The project started in 1986, and we now wish to present the results we achieved since then. We describe in outline two expert systems and also a keyword searching system, and discuss our conception about the knowledge representation methods of these systems.

1. INTRODUCTION

The information concerning the Hungarian building regulations is specified in text form (ocassionally in tables). As for a natural language text like this, two complementary ways of knowledge representation can be followed:

- the knowledge can be representeded in propositional form, that means the text itself or a completed formalized version of it;
- or by putting questions to the text, and extract the possible answers from it.

We used both of these knowledge representation methods, and summarized our experiences in the 2nd and 3rd Sections.

The knowledge representation method using propositional sentences follows the formal characteristics of the original text; a general formalism is used to carry the contents, in other words, syntactical characteristics are mostly in focus. As to the method using questions, we set out from a meaning

* H-1113 Budapest, Dávid F. u. 6., Hungary

analysis of the text, that is the semantical aspects are in the centre of interest. It is obvious that the consecutive questions cover not only the basic meaning of the text, but also the knowledge concerning the application of it. This is the knowledge that is unconsciously considered to belong to the text even by its well experienced appliers.

One of the main characteristics of the result of the knowledge representation method using propositional sentences is the closeness to the original version of the text, which is ascribable to the accurate formal logical analysis. This is a rather difficult job, because the text is full of logical incorrectness delivering imperfect information and ambiguities, and besides the logical formulation is sometimes difficult to "decode". On the other hand its advantages are that the formulation is easy to modify, and usually there is no need to understand the meaning of the text properly.

The knowledge representation method using questions requires thorough knowledge about the meaning of the text. In case of a respectably complicated text, the structured processing is a fundamental requirement with respect to easy modification possibilities and readability.

An essential expedient of the textual knowledge processing is a well constructed subject index. At the present level of text processing much more flexible and concept definition friendly systems are available. We will be giving some short information about a keyword searching system based on the text of the Hungarian Building Regulations in the 4th Section that also supplements the other two systems described in the 2nd and 3rd Sections.

2. AN OUTLINE OF AN EXPERT SYSTEM BASED ON THE LOGICAL ANALYSIS OF THE TEXT

The purpose of this approach is to integrate the knowledge covered by the Hungarian Building Regulations into a knowledge base to which any kind of questions can be put within a wide range, and the answer is deduced by a suitable inference machine making use of the stored knowledge. Apparently, a text procession with this intention must be based on logical analysis, because it can reliably guarantee the sufficent flexibility of the knowledge base.

Fig. 1 shows the outlined structure of the expert system. It can be roughly divided into two main parts: the knowledge base and the inference machine. The knowledge base evidently contains elements which are not explicit, but without them the system would not be complete. There is unwritten information belonging to this class that is quite natural or well known by any experienced applier of the text, and there is also some supplementary knowledge arising during logical analysis that comes from the elimination of latent inconsistencies in the text. The stored knowledge is written in a communication language that more or less resembles the structure of natural languages preserving the logical structure of the referred knowledge. The user communicates in the same language with the system which is to infer all the conclusions concerning the given question. There are no restrictions against the strategy of putting the questions.

It is a prototype system at the moment, the knowledge base consists of some paragraphs of the Regulations. The implementation language is PROLOG.

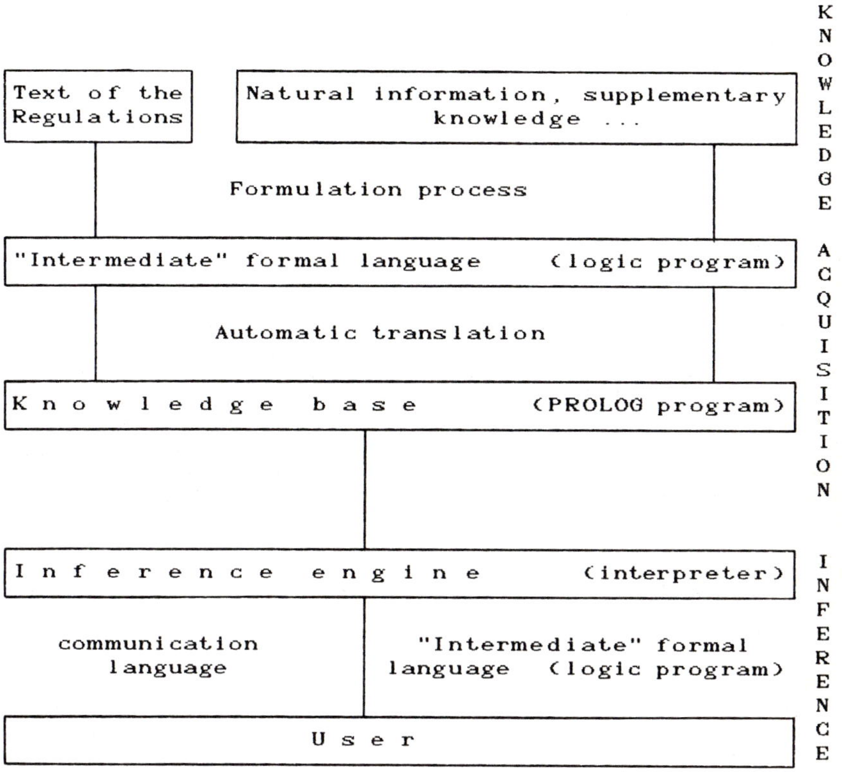

FIGURE 1
The structure of the expert system based on the logical analysis of the Hungarian Building Regulations

The dialogue between the man and machine can be demonstrated by the following example:

? { FORM piece_of_ground 'i-st_building_area' }
The question put to the system: (can) I form a piece of ground in the i-st building area ?

? { INDIVIDUAL piece_of_ground } ?
The question of the system: is that piece of ground

individual ? ("Individual" is one of the ways a piece of ground can be formed in a certain building area.)

substitution:
The register of the variable substitution is empty until now.

yes
The user's answer.

{ Possible <what1> }
<what1> --> FORM { FORM <what2> 'i-st_building_area' }
The answer of the system: it is possible to form a piece of ground in the i-st building area.

substitution: piece_of_ground/<what2>
"Piece_of_ground" stands for "what2" in the previous sentence.

is this answer satisfactory ?

no

? { MINIMAL_WIDTH ? piece_of_ground } ?
Collecting further information: what is the minimal width of that piece of ground ?

20
(meters)

? { MINIMAL_LENGTH ? piece_of_ground } ?

30
(meters)

? { MINIMAL_AREA ? piece_of_ground } ?

600
(square meters)

? { MAXIMAL_BUILDING_UP ? piece_of_ground } ?

20
(%)

? { WAY_OF_THE_BUILDING_UP 'separate' piece_of_ground } ?

substitution: 20/Width 30/Length 600/Area 20/Building_up_measure

yes

? { CODE_OF_BUILDING_AREA 'i_s_1' piece_of_ground } ?
In 'i_s_I' "s" stands for "separate", "I" refers to some special characteristics of the upbuilding.

yes

```
{ POSSIBLE <what1> }
     <what1> --> PLACE : { PLACE <what2> <where> }
     <what2> --> Object : { DWELLING_HOUSE <A> }
     <where>  -->  Piece_of_ground  :  {  FORM  <C>  'i-st_
                                              building_area' }
     <A> --> Object : { RANGING_WITHIN 12.5 <B> 22.5 }
     <B>  -->  Facade_height  :  {  FACADE_HEIGHT_TO_THE_STREET
                                          Facade_height Object }
```

The answer of the system: it is possible to place a dwelling house of facade height to the street ranging from 12,5 to 22,5 meters on a piece of ground formed in the i-st building area.

substitution: 20/Width 30/Length 600/Area 20/Building_up_measure piece_of_ground/<C>

is this answer satisfactory ? ...

3. PROCESSING OF THE HUNGARIAN BUILDING REGULATIONS SUBJECT TO THE CIVIL BUILDING AUTHORIZATION

Quite another approach to the processing of the Hungarian Building Regulations is the reformulation of the knowledge in a so-called question net. The system using this method initiates a dialogue with the user applying the knowledge formulated in the text, and the knowledge necessary for the proper application of the text, which always follows a prearranged order. A knowledge representation method like this obviously needs a great familiarity with the text. Moreover, as it interpretes the textual knowledge from a certain point of view, this expediency always determines the knowledge representation structure of the system in preparation.

Contrasted with the text procession, based on logical analysis, we could not attempt to prepare the whole text. So the system is going to cover only the most frequently applied parts of the text, that is those paragraphs which are in connection with the civil building authorization.

The intended aim of the system is to guide the user through all the problems which must be solved before authorization. In the beginning of the session, global questions are put so that the general principles are kept, and questions regarding the more detailed prescriptions come afterwards.

As we specified the main principles of the system structure, we tried to consider the user's requirements as much as possible. For instance, questions considered to be boring or have little importance can be avoided in return for later emphasizing its conclusions, ('I do not know' type of answers can be given etc.).

The system is worked out in a prototype level at the moment, the implementation language is PASCAL.

3.1. The system structure

The outline of the structure of the expert system supporting the building authorization process and having the knowledge base formulated by the question net method is shown in Fig. 2. Comparing Fig. 1 with Fig. 2 the difference is conspicuous, namely there is no need for an inference machine in the latter system, because it is eliminated by a rigid control mechanism.

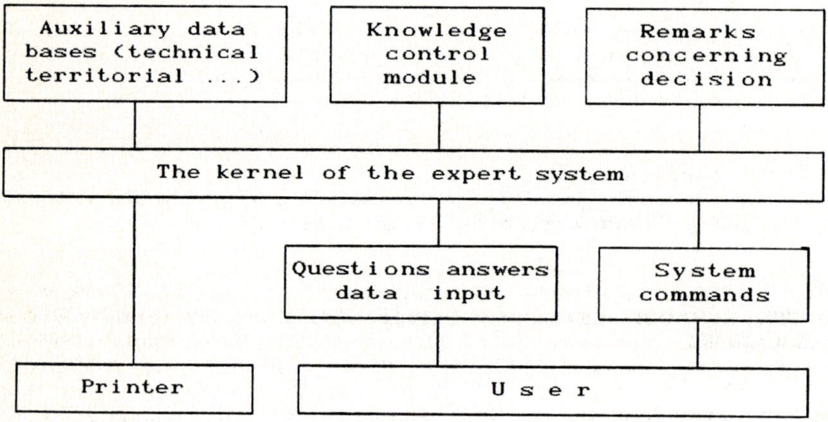

FIGURE 2
The structure of the expert system based on the processing of the Hungarian Building Regulations subject to building authorization

The system works as follows: the user has to answer the questions put by the system choosing options of the enclosed lists, then further questions are put, and so on. The user has the choice to give a command to continue instead of answering. Such kind of answers are e.g. 'I do not know' that means a postponed answer, or 'back to the former question' that can result in a change of the previous answers etc.

The system can use technical, territorial etc. data bases, if they exist. Collecting the notes concerning the decision, it can print its objections and remarks, if there are any. These functions are all optional.

3.2. The knowledge base of the system

The knowledge base is stored by a so-called knowledge/control module. We create this, using not only the text of the Building Regulations itself, but also its application rules as well (e.g. the hierarchical classification of the concepts occuring in the Building Regulations), see Fig. 3. The knowledge stored in the knowledge/control module also includes the question net control mechanism, that is it controls the order of the questions to be put.

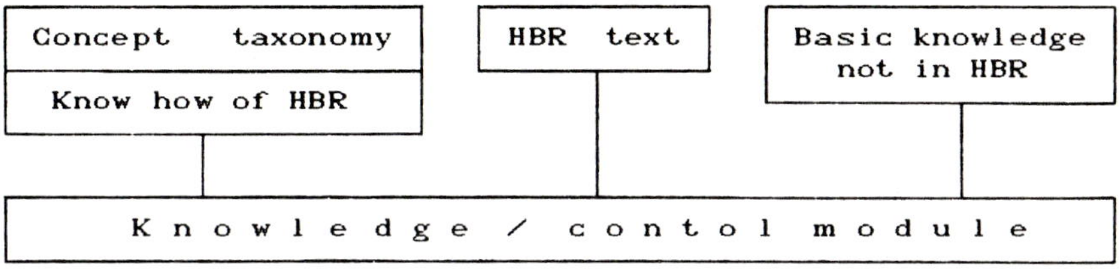

FIGURE 3
The structure of the knowledge base of the expert system processing the Hungarian Building Regulations subject to building authorization

4. THE KEYWORD SEARCHING SYSTEM OF THE HUNGARIAN BUILDING REGULATIONS

This program can be applied separately or as a supplementary function to the expert systems based on the knowledge of the Building Regulations to find all the occurences of any group of keywords specified in advance and to display the marked text parts. This program is like an intelligent subject index: complicated concepts can be found in the text quickly and efficiently as well as the informations refering to them. The user specifies his own concept to be searched for himself and the system finds not only the explicit occurences but also the implicit ones as well. (Implicit occurences of a certain concept are either those which are not contained explicitly in a certain textpart, but they refer to other parts of the text where that concept occures explicitly, or all the references to the paragraph titles.)

We are using keywords to define a concept. The Building Regulations contain nearly 20.000 words. This set of words involves only 5000 different words that means at most 2000 etymons that can potentially form keywords. The words of the Building Regulations can be classified as follows:

- Articles, conjunctives, words denoting grammatical relations etc. are not keywords;
- Nouns and verbs expressing actions or operations are keywords on their own;
- Adjectives occuring in the text can be used only with other keywords as a part of a compound concept.

The occurence of a specified concept is the minimum understandable part of the text where it occures explicitly or implicitly. This text consists of chapters, subchapters (we consider the titles to belong also to the text), paragraphs and subparagraphs. The minimum unit of the text is the subparagraph, so we refer to an occurence by the actual paragraph and subparagraph number, (the whole text consists of 175 paragraphs and 654 subparagraphs).

During the session a concept comprising of 16 keywords at most can be searched for, and the occurences are displayed or can optionally be printed. The implementation language is PASCAL.

ACKNOWLEDGEMENTS

The authors would like to express their special thanks and indebtedness to Mr. János Aszalós, Dr. Dezső Holnapy and Mr. Ferenc Csizmás, without whose invaluable help and advice, this work would not have come to fruition.

REFERENCES

[1] Aszalós J., 'Feasibility Study on an Expert System Utilizing the Knowledge of the Hungarian Building Regulations', (in Hungarian), (Építéstudományi Intézet, Budapest, 1986.)

[2] Böttger, H, Inferential Information Retrival over an Extended Semantic Network, Computers and Artificial Intelligence, 3 (1984), 115-126.

[3] Cross, R. G., Legal Knowledge, Proc. of the IEEE, 74 (1986), 1445-1454.

[4] Fameli, E., Artifical Intelligence and Expert Systems in the Law - Observations on Learning and Reasoning by Analogy, Proc. of the 7th Int. Workshop on ES & their Appl., Avignon, 1987., p. 1427-1443.

[5] Holnapy D., Rédey G. (eds.), 'The System Analysis and Knowledge Reperesentation Concept of the Expert System Utilizing the Knowledge of the Hungarian Building Regulations', (in Hungarian), (Építéstudományi Intézet, Budapest, 1987.)

[6] 'The Hungarian Building Regulations', (in Hungarian), Építésügyi Értesítő, 1986. május 7., p. 231-282.

[7] Stone, D.; Wilcox, D. A., Formulation of Building Regulations Using Interactive Logic Programs, Proc. of the 6th Int. Workshop on ES & their Appl., Avignon, 1986. p. 517-525.

[8] Waterman, D. A.; Paul, J.; Peterson, M., Expert Systems for Legal Decision Making, Expert Systems, 3 (1986), 212-226.

Network Information Processing Systems
K. Boyanov, R. Angelinov (Editors)
Elsevier Science Publishers B.V. (North-Holland)

REALISATION OF GKS WORKSTATION

I.K.GEORGIEV, R.D.ANDREEV and S.H.BLAGOEV

Central Institute for
Computer Technique
Boul.Lenin 7 km,
1113 Sofia, Bulgaria

A module structure of the GKS workstation following the International Graphics Standard GKS is suggested. The design concepts and implementation particularity are discussed. The proposed approach to realize GKS workstation is convinient to implement it in a network system.

1. INTRODUCTION

Tne International Graphics Standard GKS describes the conseptial model of a hypothetical graphics system and its funstions [9]. The model consist of two main parts: graphics kernel system and GKS workstations. The kernel is a common device independent part which interacts uniformly with the different applications on the one hand and the different workstations on the other. The GKS workstation is an abstraction which represents a logical unit consisting of zero or one display surface and zero or more input devices . The described concept reguires two different interfaces to exist in the graphics system: the GKS application interface defined in the GKS document and the workstation interface which is not explicitly defined in the standard (fig.1).

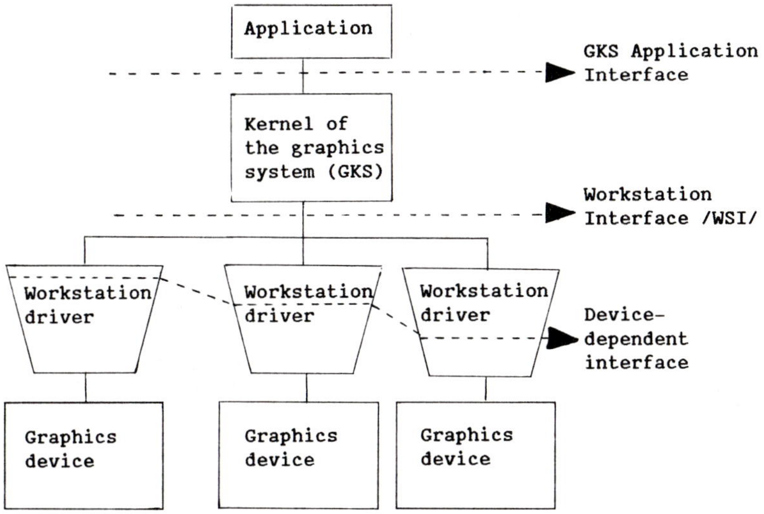

FIGURE 1

Although GKS graphics system model shown on fig.1 is suggested by the standard and its functionality is specified in detail, great freedom is left to its implementors. Architecture is central to understanding the purpose of a standard, to estimating the performance characteristics of an implementation based on such a standard. There is nothing in the architecture shown on fig.1 that reguires the application, the kernel of the graphics system and the workstation driver to be resident on the same host computer. Some of the graphics processing can be off-loaded from the host. The GKS application interface or the workstation interface can be the point at which responsibility is partitioned across systems [1]. In that way the complete graphics system or the workstation driver can reside on a computer separately of the application, as a node in a local area network [2].

2. THE GKS WORKSTATION INTERFACE

The workstation interface /WSI/ separates the device-independent and the device-dependent parts of GKS. As the workstation contains most of the GKS funstions, the WSI is a high level interface. It consist of device-independent functions some of which remain unfulfil by many devices. So these functions must be simulated by the workstation driver. The WSI is not explicitly described by the GKS document. Thus its detailed functional description is the task of the implementor.

The workstation interface designer must conform to the following conditions:

- WSI is designed for workstations of category IN, INOUT, MO, MI but not for category WISS;
- WSI supplies the full GKS functionality of level 2C;
- WSI allows the connection of highly intelligent devices to the GKS kernel and using the full set of GKS workstation capabilities within the graphics device hardware or firmware.

The workstation interface satisfying the above conditions can be defined on the basis of [5]. A lot of GKS funstions are reflected in the WSI without changes in the semantics or parameter lists. The workstation interface is presented with the following GKS funstion groups: control functions excluding OPEN GKS, CLOSE GKS, ACTIVATE WORKSTATION, DEACTIVATE WORKSTATION; all output funstions, output attributes, input funstions; segment functions excluding COPY, ASSOCIATE; workstation transformation adding CLIP RECTANGLE function. It is useful in many cases to include the functions ACTIVATE WORKSTATION and DEACTIVATE WORKSTATION when of workstation drivers are realized in a common software.

The definition of workstation interface allows the precise definition of GKS kernel and workstations driver functions. The GKS kernel functions are: converting GKS interface functions into workstation interface functions; error handling; storing information about the state of whole system; transforming the world coordinates into normalized; controling simultaneously different abstract workstations.

3. WORKSTATION DRIVER

So far the graphics system is decomposed into two levels in order to show its main parts: GKS application interface and workstation interface. GKS contains another, third level - a device dependent interface. It defines the capabilities of the graphics device, used in the workstation configuration and presented by its device driver. So the system is descrided as a sequence of layers each of which can be seen as a set of functions (routines, services) implemented by the functions of lower layers. This approach conceals a great number of processes on the graphical information taking place in the workstation driver. So it is suggested to use module decomposition in designing workstation driver. This allows a comprehensible and flexible workstation driver description whose separate parts developed independently.

The workstation driver is a hierarchy of connected modules. Each one of them receives commands and data from the higher level module in the output process and records of realized events from the lower level module in the input process. When decomposing the workstation driver we assume it is of category INOUT and it is a part of a GKS graphics system satisfying GKS level 2C. It is assumed that we have a "dumb" graphics device.

3.1. Functions of the workstation driver

To define the structure of a workstation driver its functions must be first defined. They can be divided in two groups: functions of output process and functions of input process. The former are following:

- workstation dependent storage maintenance and control;
- inclusion of new output functions in WDSS;
- coordinate transformations: segment transformations and workstation transformation;
- clipping: clip against clip rectangle and clip against workstation window;
- attribute representation functions. This is a set of algorithms generating different line types, line widths, characters and markers, hatching and filling of the of interior of an area with patterns and solid, realization of TEXT accordingly TEXT FONT and PRECISION;
- rasterization algorithms for lines, characters, closed areas, ets.

The functions of the latter group are:

- simulation of logical input devices;
- echo realization;
- realization of different modes of logical input devices.

3.2. General structural model of workstation driver

The workstation driver is roughly divided into two parts: device-independent and device-dependent. The connection between them is realized by device dependent interface specified of device several modules. Each one of them combines functions with the same purpose. Fig. 2 shows the general structure of the workstation driver.

The module **Control** executes following functions: interpretation of the workstation interface functions; synchronization between the input and the output processes; management of the workstation data base; realization of the function DEFERRAL STATE; control of the output primitive processing; clipping control; ESCAPE. Depending on the workstation category and the GKS level some functions of the module **Control** drop out.

The module **Segment transformation** includes rotation, scale and translation. It is connected with WDSS whose realization is not obligatory for GKS level 0.

The module **Clipping** clips different primitives: lines, polygons, text's, markers. The clip can be realized against workstation window or against the intersection of the workstation window and the clip rectangle.

The module **Workstation transformation** presents output primitives and geometrical attributes in a device coordinate system /DC/.

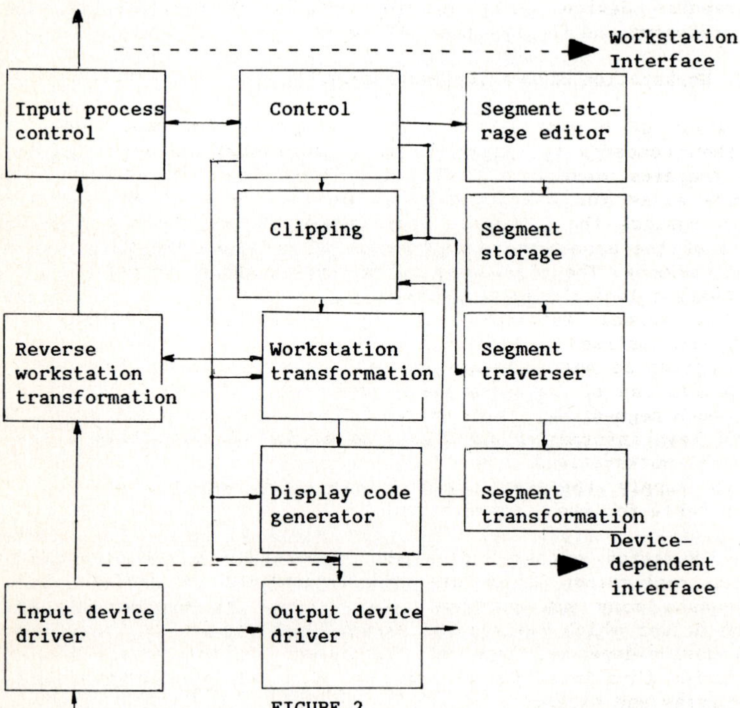

FIGURE 2

The module **Display code generator** includes attributes functions, supports display files if it is needed and includes the submodule **Vector-raster converter** in case of "dumb" raster devices. The submodule **Vector-raster converter** performs rasterization of the graphics primitives, such as line, text, marker, fill area, etc. The vector to raster conversion of the graphics information is performed by slides. Slide limits coinside with the size of the frame buffer, defined in the output device driver. Another task of this module is to present all the graphics information by the functions of the device-dependent interface.

The module **Output device driver** connects graphical device with the operation system and can maintain transformed display file or frame buffer.

The module **Input device driver** must provide connection with the operation system, data and signals coming from interactive devices. It may often be in connection with the output device driver and provides some sort of echo at this level.

The module **Input process control** maintains a logical input device model, provides simulation of logical input device and is in connection with the **Control** module for echo realization.

The described workstation driver structure is not constant. Parts of some modules or whole modules may drop out according to the capabilities of the graphics device, used in the workstation configuraton, the workstaton category and the realized GKS level.

3.3. Workstation driver implementation

The realization of a workstation driver brings up two questions. The first of them concerns the implementation of several GKS workstations, including graphics devices of the same type. It's clear that the programs are alike for all workstation drivers. This allows a common software to realize the different workstation drivers. So the computer is relieved of the unnecessary maintenance of the same programs several times in the memory. The realization of several workstation drivers with common software solves the following problems:

- the kernel functions ACTIVATE WORKSTATION and DEACTIVATE WORKSTATION are realized in the **Control** module;
- to organize one data base for all workstations and to minimize the ineffective use of the memory. In that way it is ensured a single storage of each segment desplayed on several workstations simultaneously;
- to keep information for the echo device of each logical input devices in all workstations;
- to supply the workstation state list and the workstation description table for every workstation.

The second guestion concerns the fast generation of a workstation driver. The realization of a new GKS workstation, including "dumb" device requests many new programs. We can use an already realized workstation driver which was created for a "dumb" device if there exist a constant device-dependent interface for "dumb" devices. In the case of a raster device this interface can consist of three types of functions: control, display and escape.

The control functions are the following:

- CLEAR. Clears the frame buffer with the background colour and/or the display surface:

- TERMINATE. Finishes the dialogue with the output device;
- INITIALIZE. Initializes the output device driver and returns the size of the display surface (Xmin,Ymin,Xmax,Ymax) and the size of the frame buffer;
- COPY. Copies the current slide raster form from the frame buffer in the output device driver to the display surface.

The display function is SET_PIXEL. It passes the coordinates of a pixel from the current slide and its colour /intensity/.

The escape function ESCAPE adresses specific abilities of the output device, such as dots per inch, black-white or coloured picture, inverse image, etc..

The same constant device dependent interface can be designed for a nonintelligent vector device, where display functions can be LINE, MARKER, TEXT, etc..

4. GKS WORKSTATION AND LOCAL AREA NETWORK

The workstation concept is the main tool building a destributed graphics system which may be spread over a network [3,6,8]. The workstation interface is used to embed a communication system in GKS. Based on the functional specification of the workstation interface two protocols are defined according to open system interconnection reference model: the workstation interface application layer protocol and the workstation interface presentation layer protocol.

To implement the communication, three software modules are added to the workstation driver (fig.3):

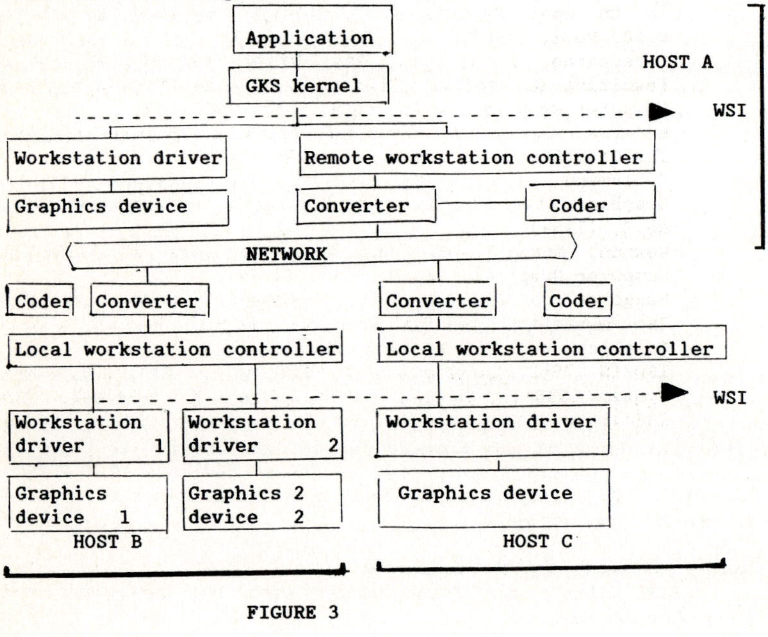

FIGURE 3

1. The workstation controller consist of remote workstation controller /RWC/ which is attached to the kernel and local workstation controller /LWC/ which maintains the workstation driver. RWC communicates with LWC via the abstract syntax WSI. The workstation controller establishes, maintains and release the connection and transports the graphical information addressed to the workstation of the remote host.
2. The converter builds the transmission elements from the WSI functions. It uses the coder to do the actual codes.
3. The coder is responsible for coding and decoding the data elements of the workstation interface, based on the selected coding.

5. CONCLUSION

The module structure of the workstation driver allows independence of the design and the implementation of every component of it. The use of a common software for the realization of several workstation drivers increases the speed and efficiency of the GKS workstation. Besides, the proposed approach to realize a workstation driver is convenient to implement it in a network system.

REFERENCES

[1.] Bono, P.R., **A Survey of Graphics Standards and their Role in Information Interchange**, Computer, v.18, No.10, (Oct. 1985).

[2.] Cambell, R.H., and Rubitz W.J. **The Professional Workstation Research Project**, IEEE Computer Graphics & Applications, v.6, No5, (May 1986).

[3.] Egloff, P., **Graphics and Communication: Computer Graphics in an Open Systems Environment**, Computers & Graphics, v.10, No.2, (1986).

[4.] Encarnacao, J. et all, **The Workstation of GKS and the Resulting Conceptual Differences to the GSPC Core System**, Computer Graphics, v.14, No.3, (Jul. 1980).

[5.] Enderle, G. et all **Computer Graphics Programming. GKS - The Graphics Standard**, Springer-Verlag, Berlin, (1983).

[6.] Kuhlamann, H.W., and Alheit, B.W. **Communicating via Graphics Standards Interfaces**, Computers & Graphics, v.10, No.2, (1986).

[7.] Newman, Sproull, W., and R., **Principles of Interactive Computer Graphics**, McGraw Hill, (1979).

[8.] Waggoner C.N. et all, **Nova*GKS: A Distributed Implementation of the Graphical Kernel System**, Computer Graphics, v.18, No.3, (Jul. 1984).

[9.] ISO/IS 7942 Information Processing - Graphical Kernel System (GKS), Functional Description, ISO, Geneva, (Sept. 1984).

Network Information Processing Systems
K. Boyanov, R. Angelinov (Editors)
Elsevier Science Publishers B.V. (North-Holland)

DESIGN OF NETWORK-BASED INFORMATION SYSTEMS — A CASE STUDY

Dipak Khakhar
Department of Information and Computer Science
University of Lund
Sölvegatan 14 A
S-223 62 Lund, SWEDEN

Abstract

Complexity of Network-Based Information Systems (N-BIS) is a consequence of integration of Information Systems and Data Communication with organization structure and strategy. This paper examines design of a N-BIS in a large organization and gives guidelines for design of a N-BIS.

1. Introduction

In recent years there has been a dramatic fall in the cost of hardware processors and memory, combined with similar cost reductions and technological advances in the communications field. Users have recognized the advantages of network-based information systems (N-BIS) by interconnecting what were independent computer systems to permit interaction, cooperation and sharing of facilities. The feasibility of developing N-BIS opens the door to new and more demanding applications. It is therefore not surprising that the field of N-BIS has gained in popularity over the past ten years especially as such systems can offer many potential advantages, such as reduced incremental cost, better reliability, extensibility, better response and performance.

Although the potential advantages of N-BIS have been recognized at the corporate level not many senior managers have known how to play an active role in the development of the systems. They have delegated the problems to technical units that have until recently been isolated from the wider organization and that have often lacked credibility with business units. Common mistakes corporate manager make when they recognize the importance of N-BIS are to look for simple concepts or to get involved in the complex details of technical planning. Neither extreme works. It can be hard to find a midpoint between these extremes. It is essential to begin at a level of abstraction high enough to highlight the key business criteria and technical design issues. It is vital to carry the analysis down to the point where the practical and tough details that dominate data communications implementation and operations are recognized and addressed.

Design of a N-BIS includes a number of aspects such as applications opportunities, policy choices, availibilities of technology, choice of vendors and architecture, regulations, quality of services, capability, flexibility, field support, backup, operation and control. This paper addresses some of these aspects with respect to a N-BIS project realized at a nationwide cold-storage company.

2. Frigoscandia AB

Frigoscandia AB is a large concern with subsidaries in Denmark, England and USA; and joint-venture companies in Brazil and Venezuela. The main business of Frigoscandia consists of manufacturing and installation of cold storage plants. The company also has a number of their own cold storage plants where different food manufacturing companies and farmers can store their goods. The concern has about 2500 employees and annual turnover of about 3000 billions SEK. Major part of all IP-activities of Frigoscandia is carried out at Infonova Systems AB, earlier IP-department of Frigoscandia.

For about 15 years ago the concern decided to adapt to a decentralised organization philosophy. This applied also to the information system development. In reality the organization philosophy meant that the subsidaries of the concern both in Sweden and abroad developed their business according to different ideas and prospects. As long as the works of the different units were isolated the information systems were also isolated. However, after some time it was desired by the subsidaries to use central processing power for some of their information systems, for example accounting. During the period of decentralization, the different subsidaries were operating as independent companies. Some of these subsidaries had also developed their EDP-systems, in some cases integrated with their customer's EDP-systems.

2.1 IS-strategy at Frigoscandia AB

The management of Frigoscandia took active part in supporting different subsidaries in their information processing requirements. Today the concern is in the process of developing integrated information system based on distributed philosophy. In order to achieve the goals specified by the Frigoscandia group the concern has defined an IS-strategy.

Some of the aspects specified in the IS-strategy are as follows:

- EDP-systems must reflect the structure of the organization.

- Information gathered and registered for a specific application must be accessable to the other application systems.

- In order to coordinate the concern's different information systems successfully, the data processing and communication equipments and softwares in the concern must be coordinated.

- Education of the top and middle management personnel and as well as of other employees in information processing must be of the highest priority.

- As the awareness of the possibilities with information technology increases in the organization, information systems for the unstructured information such as office information systems should also be developed.

3. Design of N-BIS for Cold Stores

Design of N-BIS for cold stores presented here deals with the aspects of assessing communication requirements, design of communication network and selecting a suitable vendor and equipments. The process consisted of a number of phases. The first phase was to evaluate the existing EDP-environment and assess the information processing requirements. The next phase in the project was to design a conceptual communication network and define the communication requirements. The communication requirements along with the expected communication environment were then sent to a number of vendors. Offers from the different vendors were evaluated and a solution that met the N-BIS requirements best was proposed and selected.

3.1 EDP-Environment

Prior to the design of the N-BIS the EDP-related environment for a cold store can be characterized by the following dominating factors:

- The organization was essentially centralized and only the administrative routines regarding cold store operations were conducted locally.

- Order handling for the entire bulk operations and major break-up operations were served by a terminal network based on a central computer in Helsingborg.

- Frigoscandia's customers were allowed (in fact encouraged) to utilize the network by installing terminals at their own premises and use them for order entering, stock record checking, in some cases stock bookkeeping of their own stores, and other extensions. At the beginning of the N-BIS project there were seven customers connected to the network enabling them instantaneously to control their activities and obtaining accurate stock balancies at any of the different cold stores. This facility has been used as a marketing argument in discussons with customers.

- Infonova AB's total communication network at the beginning of the project served about 280 display terminals and 50 terminal printers at 65 different locations around Sweden. Frigoscandia's part of this total network for the cold stores routines consisted of 60 display terminals and 16 terminal printers at 10 different locations.

- Cold store related load on the computer was around 25% of the total on-line load.

- Basic routines were mostly old and batch-oriented.

- The cold store applications had been integrated with a centralized transport information system. This was becoming increasingly important.

3.2 Functions Needed at the Cold Stores

The cold stores needed computer support in a number of areas regarding the operation of the store. A list covering the major functions are as follows:

- Order handling bulk/break-up.

- Pallet localization, that is where to put/find a certain pallet.

- Customer integration, that is connection of various customer EDP-equipments to the Frigoscandia's system.

- Connection of microcomputer based equipments used by receiving routines etc.

- Connection of weighing machines.

- Control of equipments involving automatic cranes and automatic break-up.

- Collection of various data required by the central systems such as transport information system and accounting information system.

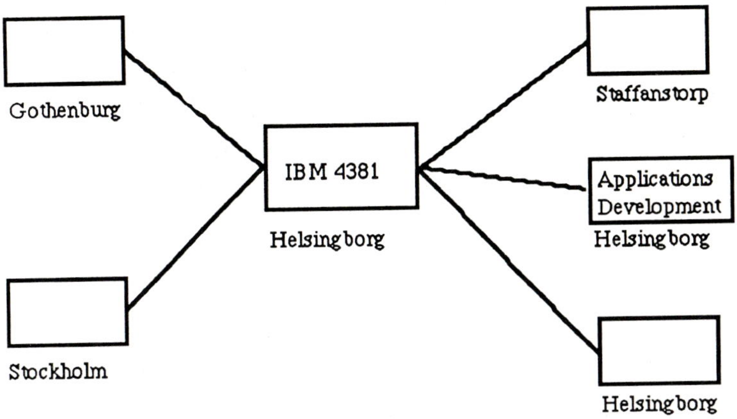

Figure 1. Distributed configuration — connections from the central node in Helsingborg to the local computers located at different cold stores in Sweden.

- Printing centrally produced listings.
- Integration of despatch and traffic office routines.
- Connectability to the electronic mail system.

3.3 Conceptual Design and Communications Requirements

Based on functional requirements of the cold stores a logical network is designed. Figure 1 shows the possible configuration viewed from the central processing node. Figure 2 shows a local processing node at a cold store. The communication requirements between different processing nodes are as follows:

- Four local computers serves 9 cold stores. Protocols used for information exchange between nodes are SNA/SDLC, X.25 (X.21 bis, LAPB) and PAD (X.3, X.28, X.29).
- All computers in the network should be able to establish connection and communicate in real-time with any other computer in the network.
- All local computers should be able to "operated" either by the central computer or by the computer used for the development of the applications.

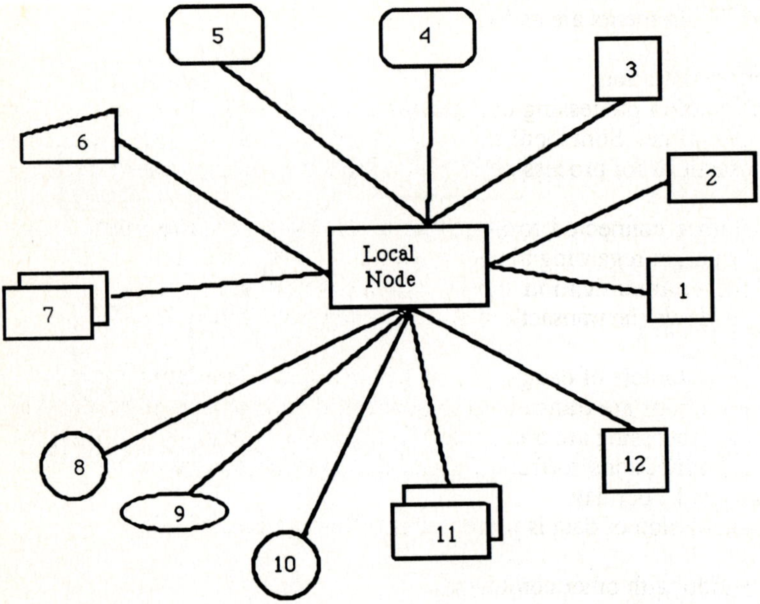

1. Central node, IBM 4381 — SDLC
2. RJE-terminals
3. Customers computer — online applications
4. Remote terminals at the customers premises for online processing
5. Local terminals connected to the local processing unit
6. Portable registration equipment, Micronic 445 — BSCC
7. Printers
8. Automatic weighing machines
9. PDP 11/xx with operative system RSX11M for automatic crane control
10. Bar Code registration — code-39, EAN-8, EAN-13, ITF-14
11. Bar Code printing — Printonix MVP
12. IBM PC — 2780/3780

Figure 2. Distributed configuration — local node at a cold store.

- From the central node it should be possible to print lists on a printer connected to a local node.

- PC should be able communicate with a local node in an interactive environment. Furthermore software for selecting information from databases located at a local node, e.g. lotus, should be available.

- A cold store has two catagories of customers. For customer of catagory 1, the IP-requirements are as follows:

- Online registration.
  - Information processing capabilities at central node through a local node in real-time. Some online transactions at a local node can generate transactions for processing at the local node.

- A customer connected to a cold store should be able to make access to information regarding his goods stored at other cold stores.
  - If the communication between a local and the central node should break-down the transactions should be logged at the local node.

- For the customers of catagory 2, the following facilities are required:
  - Transactions are transmitted to the central node in a batch-mode. Results of the processing are transmitted to the customer also in a batch-mode.
  - RJE connections to/from the central node from a customer can be as many as 12 per day.
  - Transmission of data is permitted at different times of a day.

- Connection with other computers.
  - PDP/11xx computer for crane administration located at the cold store in Stockholm.
  - Texas Instrument TI-990 located at a customer premises.
  - IBM-4381 located at a customer premises.

- It should be possible to develop and maintain application systems at a local node either through the central node or from a dedicated computer for applications development.

3.4 Selection of Vendor and Equipments

Selection of a most appropriate vendor and choice of equipments is an important phase of the project. If too many vendors are asked to submit offers it can take a long time to evaluate these. Before approaching any vendor two things were done. The first was to prepare a list of aspects (Table 1) and questions that must be answered by the vendors. There were about 80 questions prepared covering vendor's organization, experience, service, hardware, software, communications strategy and so on. These questions were based on Frigoscandia's overall IS-strategy and requirements of the N-BIS for the cold stores.

Based on the questions and knowledge about different vendors in the market a short list of three vendors was made. The list included IBM, Digital Equipment and Hewlett Packard. Prior to the evaluation of the offers submitted by the

1.	Description of the vendor	2.5	Standard applications/systems
1.1	Organization	2.5.1	Word processing
1.1.1	The Worldwide	2.5.2	Electronic Mail
1.1.2	In Sweden	2.5.3	Spread sheet
1.1.3	In Helsingborg, Malmö, Gothenburg and Stockholm	2.5.4	Graphics
		2.5.5	Order/stock administration
1.1.4	Competence in system software/ Communication	2.6	Other systems offered by the vendor but not specified above
1.1.5	Development plans		
1.2	Experience	3	Computer system
1.2.1	Similar N-BIS configuration	3.1	Central processing unit
1.2.2	Communications environment	3.1.1	Minimum configuration
1.2.3	Stock/order applications	3.1.2	Extensions/modulation
		3.1.3	Communication to IBM PC
1.3	References	3.1.4	Hardware backup (replacement)
1.3.1	Installations Worldwide	3.1.5	Environment, power, space
1.3.2	Installations in Sweden		
1.3.3	Istallations of distributed systems	3.2	Periphery equipments
1.3.4	Installations for stock/order applications	3.2.1	Disks
		3.2.2	Magnetic tapes
		3.2.3	Printers
1.4	Technical service	3.2.4	Terminals
1.4.1	Service organization in Sweden		
1.4.2	Services in Helsingborg, Malmö, Gothenburg and Stockholm	3.3	Capacity
		3.3.1	Accessability (up-time) guarantee
1.4.3	Service contract/ guarantee	3.3.2	Response and access times
1.5	Training and Education	4	Communications
1.5.1	Organization in Sweden	4.1	Communication software
1.5.2	For application development	4.1.1	Description of functions
1.5.3	For operation of equipments	4.1.2	Transparency
1.5.4	For EDP-managers	4.1.3	Local Area Network
		4.1.4	Communication protocols
1.6	Assistance	4.1.5	Extern communications
1.6.1	Support given at installation time	4.1.6	Security functions
1.6.2	Documentations		
1.6.3	System maintenance	4.2	Communication hardware
		4.2.1	Communication equipments/ protocol converter
2.	Software		
2.1	Operative systems	4.2.2	Local Area Network
2.1.1	Detailed description of functions		
		5	Prices
2.2	Database systems	5.1	Configuration
2.2.1	Detailed description of functions	5.2	Technical and development support
		5.3	Training and Education
2.3	Applications development tools	5.4	Other expenses
2.3.1	Detailed specification of functions		
		6	Supplying terms
2.4	Applications development tools for end-users	7	Arguments for why your solution should be accepted
2.4.1	4th generation language		
2.4.2	Query language		
2.4.3	Report generator		
2.4.4	File handling facilities		

Table 1. Aspects that vendors had to specify for the design of N-BIS for cold stores.

vendors the project group had weighted the importance of different aspects in the questionnaire. The answers from the vendors were graded from 1 to 5 depending on how well they met the N-BIS requirements. These grades were then multiplied by corresponding weight functions. By this procedure a vendor who best met the information processing requirements of the cold storage would get the highest rating. However, the rating was not the only ground for selecting a vendor. The final selection was a subjective evaluation based on suitability of the suggested solution. This was necessary because some specific requirements must be met by a vendor.

4. Experience Gained From The N-BIS Design Project

Network-Based information systems (N-BIS) are mixture of centralized, decentralized, distributed and interorganizational systems. Transition to N-BIS requires carefully chosen IS-strategy at corporate level of an organization. It is crucial to understand the service level requirements of the organization's business functions. This is often difficult information to pin down, but N-BIS plan consisting both network plans and IS-development plan, must be driven by the goals of the business.

A N-BIS project is complex. A project group for N-BIS must involve participation from senior management, technical personnel and the end users. The cold storage N-BIS project included people from all these decipline. This was found to be very important since all had different operational objectives for the system and they had to be merged together. A N-BIS design project should include at least the following stages:

Identification of application opportunities. This phase identifies the main priorities for applying the technology based on the coorporate strategy. Decisions focus on how to choose a profit maximized information flow in an organization and between organizations. The decision includes factors like; how can we for our purposes use IT, how are investments to be paid off, how to maintain information channels, how to link current applications to each other. It also includes new applications and how these can be supported by a new communication infrastructure. These are decisions that are both business and technically oriented (There is a growing body of articles and books focusing on these problems, opportunities, and obstacles, see for example Keen (1988), Cash & Konsynski (1985), McFarlan (1984), Clemons & McFarlan (1986)).

Specification of design variables. This phase evaluates at least following four major factors:

1. *Capacity*. What services can the system provide and what volumes can it handle?

2. *Flexibility*. Can the system handle today's requirements cost-efficiently and be easily modified to meet tomorrow's? How the system is related to the other systems and can it be modified without affecting other systems?

3. *Quality of service*. How reliable is it?

4. *Pricing and costing*. What is the unit of cost from the user's perspective and what are the dynamics of cost over ranges of time and volumes?

It is the balance between these factors with which the designers have to deal. The cost of adding extra flexibility, for instance, adopting a concept that may have substantial overhead. For some system, reliability may be vital; for others it may be less critical than low cost of use.

Conceptual/Logical design, which is design of a specific communication network in general terms (not product specific). In this case existing terminals, computers, nets etc are given. The design includes how to link existing equipment with new ones such that the requirements are fulfilled. Problems at this level include how to choose suitable clusters, switching functions, network functions, conversions due to different protocols etc. The output of this phase is a conceptual model of the network used for the N-BIS.

Selection of vendors and equipments. An organization may choose from a number of suppliers and make its selection on the basis cost and ability to meet particular technical specifications. But there are many vendors to choose from. Similarly, there is still substantial uncertainty about standards and even more about the practicality of particular products and approaches. International standards help make products compatible so they can communicate with each other. Designers of N-BIS often disagree with each other regarding capability of particular product or solution. If the organization has a policy regarding the selection of vendors or technology, it helps to develop a coherent information processing environment. The following list identifies the major policy issues that an organization must address:

- The degree and pace of change management is willing to accept.
- Vendor policy.
- Architecture policy and the range of services to be accommodated by it.

- Planning horizon, including funding and cost recovery.
- The level of risk, technical and financial, that is acceptable.
- Security and degree of privacy.

Physical design, i.e. implementing the conceptual model of the data communication network. To this area belong problems like choosing specific equipment like cables, multiplexers, modems, switches, etc. It also comprises the problem of how to optimize the system economically.

Operation and control. This phase include the process of:

- Setting service level objectives that will meet the business needs.
- Monitoring service levels.
- Restoring service in the case of a failure.
- Fault isolation and resolution.
- Ensuring security of information by controlling access.

5. Acknowledgement

I would like to extend my thanks to Göran Hagberg, managing director of Infonova Systems AB and Hans Tuvesson, senior information strategy manager of Frigoscandia AB for their support in making the writing of this paper possible.

References

Bakos J Y & Treacy M E: Information Technology and Corporate Strategy: A Research Perspective, MIS Quarterly, June 1986.

Barrett S & Konsynski B R: Inter-Organization Information Sharing Systems, MIS Quarterly, Special Issue, 1982.

Cash J I & Konsynski B R: IS Redraws Competitive Boundaries, Harvard Business Review, March-April, 1985, pp 134-142.

Cash J I, McFarlan F W & McKenney: Corporate Information Systems Management, Second Edition, Irwin, Homewood, Ill, 1988.

Eveland J D & Bikson T K: Evolving Electronic Communication Networks: An Empirical Assessment, Office: Technology and People, Vol. 3, 1987.

Farwell B M & Farwell D C: Telecommutig and Organizational Change, Computer Networks, Vol. 8, 1984.

Hunfnagel E M: Information Systems Planning: Lessons From Strategic Planning, Information & Management, Vol 12, 1987.

Keen, P G W: Competing in Time: Using Telecommunications for Competitive Advantage, Revised edition, Ballinger, Cambridge, MA, 1988.

King J L: Centralized versus Decentralized Computing: Organizational Considerations and Management Options, Computing Surveys, Vol. 15, No. 4, December 1983.

Lorin H, Ball L D & Eloy G: Interconnect Technology as a Management Challange, MIS Quarterly, December 1987.

Luhukay J: A Development Strategy for Network-Based Information Systems, Information Network and Data Communication, II (ed. Khakhar, D, & Iversen, V B), North-Holland, 1988.

Malone T W, Yates J & Benjamin R I: Electronic Markets and Electronic Hierarchies, Communications of the ACM, Vol. 30, No. 6, June 1987.

Mantelman L: AI Carves Inroads: Network Design, Testing, and Management, Data Communications, July, 1986.

McFarlan W F: Information Technology Changes the Way You Compete, Harvard Business Review, May-June, 1984, pp 98-103.

Srinivasan A & Kaiser K M: Relationships between Selected Organizational Factors and Systems Development, Communications of the ACM, Vol. 30, No. 6, June 1987.

AUTHOR INDEX